Seaforth WORLD NAVAL REVIEW

2019

Seaforth

WORLD NAVAL REVIEW

2019

Editor
CONRAD WATERS

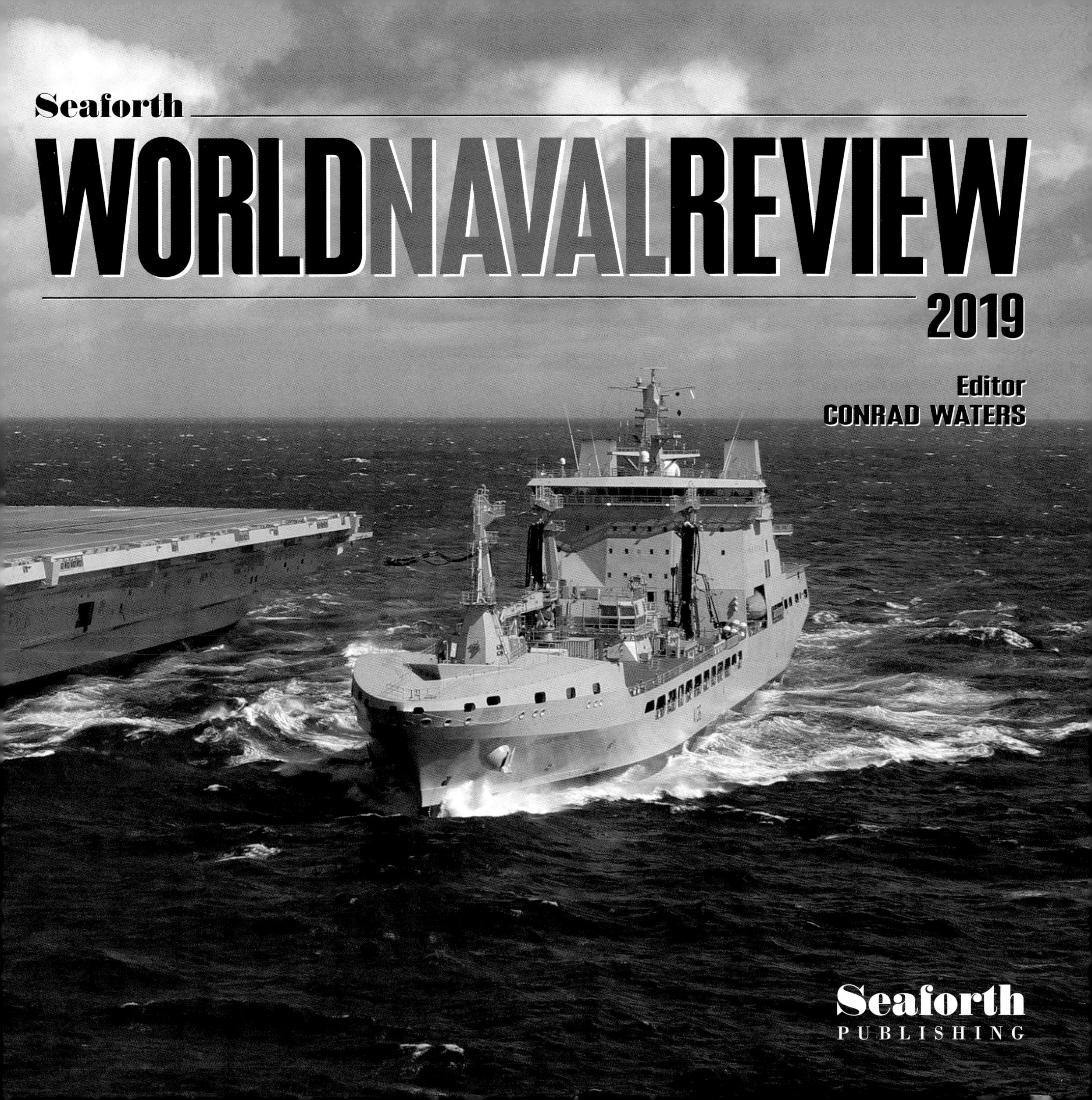

Seaforth
PUBLISHING

Frontispiece: The new British aircraft carrier *Queen Elizabeth* pictured during replenishment at sea (RAS) trials in June 2018. She became the largest warship ever to serve in the Royal Navy when she was commissioned in December 2017. The US Navy also took delivery of its own largest-ever warship, the carrier *Gerald R. Ford* (CVN-78), in the course of 2017. *(Crown Copyright 2018)*

Copyright © Seaforth Publishing 2018
Plans © John Jordan 2018

First published in Great Britain in 2018 by
Seaforth Publishing
An imprint of Pen & Sword Books Ltd
47 Church Street, Barnsley
S Yorkshire S70 2AS

www.seaforthpublishing.com
Email info@seaforthpublishing.com

British Library Cataloguing in Publication Data
A CIP data record for this book is available from the British Library

ISBN 978-1-5267-4585-9 (Hardback)

ISBN 978-1-5267-4587-3 (Kindle)

ISBN 978-1-5267-4586-6 (ePub)

Pen & Sword Books Limited incorporates the imprints of Atlas, Archaeology, Aviation, Discovery, Family History, Fiction, History, Maritime, Military, Military Classics, Politics, Select, Transport, True Crime, Air World, Frontline Publishing, Leo Cooper, Remember When, Seaforth Publishing, The Praetorian Press, Wharncliffe Local History, Wharncliffe Transport, Wharncliffe True Crime and White Owl.

Typeset and designed by Stephen Dent
Printed in China by 1010 Printing International Ltd.

CONTENTS

Note on Tables: Tables are provided to give a broad indication of fleet sizes and other key information but should be regarded only as a general guide. For example, many published sources differ significantly on the principal particulars of ships, whilst even governmental information can be subject to contradiction. In general terms, the data contained in these tables is based on official information updated as of June 2018, supplemented by reference to a wide range of secondary and corporate sources, such as shipbuilder websites.

1 OVERVIEW

INTRODUCTION

'**M**en grow tired of sleep, love, singing and dancing sooner than of war' lamented Menelaus, mythological King of Sparta in Homer's epic poem *The Iliad*.[1] Menelaus' words are an apposite opening to this tenth annual edition of *Seaforth World Naval Review*, given the renewal of Cold War-like tensions that have slowly emerged over the past decade. Whether it be island-building in the South China Sea; the destruction of a civilian airliner by a sophisticated surface-to-air missile over Ukraine; or the use of a chemical nerve agent to target a former spy in a British city, the new era of international peace seemingly heralded by the fall of the Berlin Wall seems little more than a distant memory.

Of course, the quarter-century that followed the Soviet Union's collapse was anything but peaceful. New security challenges, increasingly driven by new forms of religiously-motivated terrorism, emerged in the aftermath of the bipolar stand-off between NATO and the Warsaw Pact.[2] However, recent developments suggest the re-emergence of a much more fundamental challenge to the liberal rules-based global order – the international system based on the rule of law, a respect for nations' territorial sovereignty and the protection of human rights – established by the United States, the United Kingdom and their allies in the aftermath of the Second World War. A particular concern for the traditional 'Western' powers must be the steady emergence of a Russian-Chinese axis. Indeed, some commentators believe this relationship is developing into a full-blown partnership.[3]

An added complication is the increasingly fractured nature of the Western alliance. This is, perhaps, most evident in the current US Trump administration's approach to international relations. Whilst not the radical departure from past policies some had feared, the new US *National Security Strategy* (NSS) published in December 2017 was notable for focusing more on competition than collaboration and for placing less emphasis than previously on values such as democracy and human rights. Moreover, many commentators believe that there is a credibility gap between the more traditional, internationalist elements of the NSS and what the president himself believes.[4]

Many of these concerns are reflected in President Trump's own actions. For example, his warm praise for North Korean despot Kim Jong Un following apparently successful initial talks in June 2018 aimed at ending the dictator's nuclear weapons programme may well have been aimed at ensuring the resolution of a dangerous stand-off that has eluded previous American administrations. However, it still sits uneasily with the North Korean regime's human rights abuses and disrespect for international law. There is also an interesting contrast with his criticism of Canadian premier Justin Trudeau as 'very dishonest and weak' made against the backdrop of an escalating trade dispute just days earlier. Certainly, strained relationships between the leader of the United States and that of neighbouring Canada – one of the foremost

Table 1.0.1: COUNTRIES WITH HIGH NATIONAL DEFENCE EXPENDITURES 2008-17

RANK 2017 (2008)		COUNTRY	TOTAL US$ BN 2017[1]	SHARE OF GDP 2017	TOTAL US$ BN 2008[1]	SHARE OF GDP 2008	REAL CHANGE 2008–2017[2]
1	(1)	United States	610	3.1%	621	4.2%	-14%
2	(2)	China	[228]	[1.9%]	[86.4]	[1.9%]	110%
3	(9)	Saudi Arabia	[69.4]	[10.0%]	38.2	7.4%	34%
4	(5)	Russia	66.3	4.3%	[56.2]	[3.3%]	36%
5	(10)	India	63.9	2.5%	33.0	2.6%	45%
6	(3)	France	57.8	2.3%	66.0	2.3%	5%
7	(4)	UK	47.2	1.8%	65.6	2.3%	-15%
8	(7)	Japan	45.4	0.9%	46.4	0.9%	4%
9	(6)	Germany	44.3	1.2%	48.1	1.3%	9%
10	(11)	South Korea	39.2	2.6%	26.1	2.6%	29%
-	(-)	**World Total**	**1,739**	**2.2%**	**1,498**	**2.4%**	**10%**

Information from the Stockholm International Peace Research Institute (SIPRI) – https://www.sipri.org/databases/milex
The SIPRI Military Expenditure Database contains data on countries over the period 1949-2017.

Notes
1 US$ totals for 2017 and 2008 are based on then current (i.e. non-inflation adjusted) prices and exchange rates for the years in question. Exchange rate movements, in particular, can therefore result in significant movements in the US$ figures and explain apparent discrepancies in the table.
2 The 'real' change figure is based on constant (2016-based) US$ figures.
3 Figures in brackets are SIPRI estimates.

An American patrol launch escorts the Royal Canadian Navy submarine *Victoria* into Pearl Harbor at the time of the RIMPAC 2012 exercises. Whilst relations between the two countries' navies remain close, public spats between their leaders point to growing tensions within the Western alliance at a time when its common values are under threat. *(US Navy)*

supporters of the values on which the rules-based world order is founded – are indicative of a wider philosophical divide between NATO countries that does not bode well for the alliance's future cohesion

DEFENCE BUDGETS AND PLANS

The ramp-up of global tensions is inevitably having an impact on defence budgets and associated levels of naval spending. This is particularly evident amongst those European countries that took the lead in cutting military programmes as part of a post-Cold War 'peace dividend'. A good example is provided by the Netherlands. Its March 2018 *Defence White Paper* will ramp up planned defence spending from its current base of c. €8.8bn to a longer term level of c. €10.2bn. Much of the increase is being invested in new equipment.[5] Naval spending is a prime beneficiary, accounting for half of the additional €12.7bn that will be allocated to the modernisation programme over the next fifteen years. However, it is still noteworthy that the new financial settlement is essentially only sufficient to end the previous decline in naval strength rather than reverse it, being sufficient to do little more than replace existing kit. The sole major addition to the fleet will be a new combat support ship. Ultimately Dutch defence spending is still expected to level out at c. 1.25 percent of national output (GDP), around the level achieved at the start of the current decade. This is significantly below the NATO target of 2 percent and even further behind the global average of 2.2 percent. The picture in many other NATO countries is similar – defence

spending will rise, but only by enough to replace existing, much-depleted capabilities rather than fund any significant expansion.

The Dutch experience is also reflective of a wider trend, long commented upon by *World Naval Review*, which is seeing military – and naval power – shift eastwards away from Europe to the emergent Asian economies. This is illustrated by the data in

Table 1.0.1, which is based on information from the independent and widely-respected Stockholm International Peace Research Institute (SIPRI). This summarises spending by those countries with the largest military budgets over the past ten years from 2008 to 2017.

Whilst there has only been one change in the top ten spending nations – South Korea has replaced Italy – there is a clear pattern of Asian countries increasing their defence expenditure at rates greater than the global average compared with the opposite in Europe. One explanation is provided by long-standing regional rivalries in Asia; largely unaffected by the Cold War's end. However, it would be incorrect to view the figures as being indicative of a significant rise in Asian militarism. As the table demonstrates, the major Asian nations – even much-maligned China – are spending a broadly similar level of their national wealth on their armed forces as they were ten years ago. The simple explanation is that the emergent Asian countries have been far more economically successful than their European counterparts and have translated this success into relatively greater levels of military spending and influence. Moreover, as much of their new wealth is dependent on seaborne trade, spending on maritime security has been a relatively high priority.

The new Royal Fleet Auxiliary replenishment tanker *Tidesurge* enters Falmouth in March 2018 at the end of her delivery voyage from South Korea. The Asian nations have used their superior economic performance to expand their military strength and influence; one consequence has been much greater levels of success in securing exports of naval shipping around the globe. *(Crown Copyright 2018)*

Another interesting feature of the table for *World Naval Review*'s largely Anglo-American readership will undoubtedly be the fact that the United States and United Kingdom have the dubious distinction of suffering the only 'real terms' falls in defence spending amongst the world's leading military powers over the past decade. Indeed, data from IHS Markit – covering the slightly different period from 2007 to 2017 – suggests that the growth in Asia's share of global defence spending from eighteen percent to twenty-six percent of the world total over this period – has been much more at the expense of the United States than Europe.[6] As always, statistics can be misleading; data trends are heavily influenced by the exceptional cost of the heavy commitment to international stabilisation missions, particularly in Afghanistan, ten years ago. Nevertheless, the austerity measures adopted by both countries to bring government spending under control have had a marked impact on military readiness. This is possibly one underlying contributory factor to the high-profile collisions and associated loss of life suffered by US Navy in the course of 2017.

Fortunately future prospects under the current Trump administration look brighter for both the United States Armed Forces in general and the US Navy in particular. Great power competition rather than terrorism is now the major focus for America's national security, an emphasis that gives far greater prominence to the navy's 'high end' capabilities.[7] In addition, with budget controls at least temporarily relaxed, spending is set to rise significantly. The position for the United Kingdom is more uncertain; much will be revealed when a mid-term defence review – the Modernising Defence Programme – reports in the summer of 2018.

Before leaving discussion of the financial backdrop to current naval trends, two additional developments warrant mention. The first is the gradual slowing of China's economy from around ten percent p.a. at the start of the decade to under seven percent currently. According to International Monetary Fund (IMF) forecasts the rate of growth will decline further; to a little over five percent by 2023. Whilst still healthy by any measure, the trend suggests – absent other changes – the rapid growth in China's navy that has been the key feature of the last decade may also slow.

The other is the impact of economic sanctions and lower commodity prices on Russia's military ambitions, as evidenced by the recently approved State Armaments Programme (GPV) for 2018–2027. Notably, the new programme is more limited in scope than its predecessor, GPV 2020, and places less emphasis on naval forces. In particular, planned development of a new generation of 'blue water' surface vessels will probably be delayed in favour of continued prioritisation of the submarine fleet and investment in smaller frigates and corvettes. Whilst it would be unwise to underestimate the largely asymmetric potency of this planned force structure, any return to the direct challenge

TABLE 1.0.2: MAJOR FLEET STRENGTHS 2009–2018[1]

| REGION | THE AMERICAS | | | | EUROPE & RUSSIA | | | | | | | | | | ASIA | | | | | | | | IND. OCEAN | |
| COUNTRY | USA | | BRAZIL | | UK | | FRANCE | | ITALY | | SPAIN | | RUSSIA | | CHINA | | JAPAN | | KOREA(S) | | AUSTRALIA | | INDIA | |
	2009	2018	2009	2018	2009	2018	2009	2018	2009	2018	2009	2018	2009	2018	2009	2018	2009	2018	2009	2018	2009	2018	2009	2018
Carriers & Amphibious																								
CV/CVN	11	11	1	-	-	1	1	1	1	1	-	-	1	1	-	1	-	-	-	-	-	-	-	1
CVS/CVH	-	-	-	-	3	-	1	-	1	1	1	-	-	-	-	-	1	4	-	-	-	-	1	-
LHA/LHD/LPH	10	9	-	1	1	-	2	3	-	-	-	1	-	-	-	-	-	-	1	1	-	2	-	-
LPD/LSD	21	23	2	1	6	5	2	-	3	3	2	2	1	-	1	4	3	3	-	-	-	1	1	1
Submarines																								
SSBN	14	14	-	-	4	4	3	4	-	-	-	-	16	11	3	6	-	-	-	-	-	-	-	1
SSN/SSGN	57	54	-	-	8	7	6	6	-	-	-	-	20	25	5	9	-	-	-	-	-	-	-	1
SSK	-	-	5	5	-	-	-	-	6	8	4	3	20	20	55	50	16	18	11	16	6	6	16	14
Surface Combatants																								
BB/BC	-	-	-	-	-	-	-	-	-	-	-	-	2	2	-	-	-	-	-	-	-	-	-	-
CG/DDG/FFG	107	90	9	8	24	19	18	17	16	18	10	11	35	30	45	70	43	37	19	25	12	11	20	24
DD/FGS/FS	1	13	5	3	-	-	15	15	8	2	-	-	55	40	30	40	8	6	28	14	-	-	8	11
FAC[2]	-	-	-	-	-	-	-	-	-	-	-	-	50	35	65	75	6	6	1	18	-	-	12	8
Other (Selected)																								
MCMV	14	11	6	4	16	13	16	14	12	10	6	6	45	40	20	25	29	25	9	9	6	6	10	1
AO/AOR/AFS	31	29	1	1	9	8	4	3	3	3	1	2	20	20	5	12	5	5	3	3	2	2	2	4

Notes

1 Numbers are based on official sources, where available, supplemented by news reports, published intelligence data and other 'open sources' as appropriate. Given significant variations in available data, numbers should be regarded as indicative, particularly with respect to Russia, China and minor warship categories. There is also a degree of subjectivity with respect to warship classifications given varying national classifications and this can also lead to inconsistency.

2 FAC numbers relate to ships fitted with or for surface-to-surface missiles.

posted to NATO's navies by the later Cold War Soviet fleet has been – at the least – postponed. It seems unlikely that *World Naval Review* will be featuring assessments of vessels such as the mooted Project 23000 'Shtorm' aircraft carriers or Project 23560 'Lider' class destroyers during its second decade of publication.[8]

FLEET REVIEWS

The current state of the world's leading navies is summarised in Table 1.0.2. This also provides comparative figures for 2009, *World Naval Review's* first year or publication. The table inevitably provides only a snapshot. Moreover, there is a considerable lag between economic and political factors and current force levels. Nevertheless, the data is suggestive of a number of important trends that will remain relevant over the next decade. These are set out in further detail below:

- **US Naval Dominance:** In spite of the recent period of financial austerity impacting the American military, the US Navy remains the world's most powerful maritime force by a very considerable margin. China's People's Liberation Army Navy (PLAN) has undoubtedly seen rapid growth but it remains very much in the US Navy's shadow. This conclusion is reinforced when the US Navy's predominance in larger, more sophisticated vessels such as aircraft carriers and attack submarines – as well as its technological leadership in systems and weapons – is taken into account. This leadership is unlikely to be overturned in the near future.

- **European Resilience:** Although the table generally reflects the relative growth of the Asian navies that have already been discussed, forecasts of a collapse of European naval power remain premature. As for the US Navy, this is particularly the case with respect to 'blue water' power projection assets such as carriers, amphibious warfare vessels and replenishment support shipping. Notably, fleets such as the British Royal Navy and France's *Marine Nationale* will enter the second decade of the millennium with balanced fleets that provide an expeditionary capability equal or superior to that fielded by the PLAN. Whilst this position is being swiftly eroded, the significant strategic potential provided by these navies should not be overlooked.

- **'High End' Prioritisation:** Whilst not always

The Russian frigate *Yaroslav Mudry* pictured transiting the English Channel in April 2018. Built to a Cold War-era design, she was commissioned after a protracted building period in June 2009. Russia has regained its status as a major player on the world stage over the past decade, although many see its actions as being far from benign. Resulting sanctions have impacted its economy, causing previous naval expansion plans to be scaled back. With investment focused on submarines and smaller surface vessels, 'blue water' missions continue to be performed largely by Cold War designs. *(Crown Copyright 2018)*

readily apparent from the bare numbers, there is a continued preference for investment in smaller numbers of sophisticated, high-end warships as opposed to be more numerous fleets of less potent ships. This partly reflects the greater emphasis being placed on 'blue water' operations by emerging navies but is also probably indicative of a broader preference for quality over quantity at a time when personnel costs are an important consideration. However, with major surface combatants now costing in excess of US$1bn per unit this trend may be starting to run its course. The British Royal Navy's proposed Type 31e light frigate may be one potential straw in the wind in this regard.

- **'Flat Top' Fixations:** The huge costs associated with aircraft carrier construction and operation remain a massive potential obstacle to membership of the 'carrier club'. The last decade has seen China achieve this long-coveted status after considerable effort, whilst the United Kingdom is on the point of regaining admission after a period of suspension. Against this, both Brazil and Spain have found full membership beyond their means. However, both have acquired amphibious-type helicopter carriers that provide something of a substitute aviation capability, a route that is proving popular with other fleets. Short Take Off and Vertical Landing (STOVL) aircraft – notably the F-35B 'Lightning II variant – offer the prospect of fast jet operation from these ships. Spain already operates Harrier jets off its amphibious assault ship *Juan Carlos I* and Turkey is actively seeking this capability for the similar ship it currently has under construction. Meanwhile, Japan has also studied the possibility of integrating the F-35B into its own *Izumo* (DDH-183) class helicopter-carrying destroyers.[9]

■ **The Impact of Robotics:** One category of vessel that has seen a significant decline is the stand-alone mine countermeasures vessel, which has all but disappeared from a number of fleets. This is possibly partly indicative of a dangerous lack of attention to this low profile but vital capability but also reflects the progress made in using the new generation of robotic vehicles to provide a substitute capacity. It seems the development of autonomous warfare will have a much wider impact in the decade ahead.

Some of these themes are explored in more detail in the following chapters.

Turning initially to the chapters on significant fleets, Theodore Hughes-Riley's opening review assesses the Royal Canadian Navy's current structure and objectives. He focuses on the very heavy costs of renewing its high-end 'blue water' capabilities after a prolonged period of under-investment. This has essentially resulted in key elements of the fleet wearing out after being retained in service far longer than originally expected. A recent, 2017, defence review has been largely supportive of fleet renewal, whilst an earlier National Shipbuilding Strategy aims to combine this with the rebirth of the Canadian maritime sector. However, implementation is proving unexpectedly expensive given the seeming 'gold-plating' being applied to many of the ships being acquired.

Moving south to Latin America, Guy Toremans uses his prolonged acquaintance with the Peruvian Navy to provide a detailed review of a fleet which needs to combine open-ocean operations in the Pacific with responsibilities across a vast network of rivers in the Amazonian basin. In similar fashion to Canada, Peru's navy has been starved of funding since a major programme of investment in the 1970s. However, its rather less ambitious modernisation plans are realising rather more tangible results, including new classes of functional amphibious transport ships and coastal patrol vessels built with South Korean assistance. Interestingly, the navy also plays an important role in the government's plans for social development. It operates a series of riverine supply craft providing services such as healthcare, basic banking services and legal advice to communities that have not previously had access to such facilities.

The concluding review on the Republic of Singapore Navy – the subject of the latest of Mritunjoy Mazumdar's series on Asian fleets – is

The Italian *Lerici* class minehunter *Rimini* seen operating with its Romanian counterpart *Alexandru Axente* in May 2015. The development of robotic underwater vehicles has meant that traditional mine countermeasures vessels are generally less in demand, although the *Lerici* type is still gaining export success. *(Crown Copyright 2015)*

indicative of the huge strides being made by regional navies in recent years. Supported by high levels of funding and a strong indigenous industrial base, the small city state has developed one of the world's most progressive and technologically-advanced fleets to protect its vital maritime interests. Much of its approach – including an integrated maritime security network and the development of optimally-manned and autonomous vessels in the face of

human resource constraints – is likely to be of relevance to many navies over the next decade.

SIGNIFICANT SHIPS

The theme of technological advance is also a strong influence on this year's chapters on significant ships. These have purposely been limited to focus on the two new aircraft carriers, *Gerald R. Ford* (CVN-78) and *Queen Elizabeth*, the largest warships ever to be

The Peruvian Navy's new amphibious transport dock *Pisco* pictured at the time of her commissioning ceremony on 6 June 2018. A derivative of the Indonesian *Makassar* class, she was built by Peruvian builders SIMA with South Korean technical assistance. *(Guy Toremans)*

delivered to their respective navies. Both ships have been designed and built over a roughly similar timescale and share a number of common design influences. These include a desire to maximise aircraft sortie generation rates in the interests of operational effectiveness; a strong emphasis on survivability; and the use of technology to reduce manning requirements. However, the approach adopted to the two classes was somewhat different.

As explained by Scott Truver, *Ford* was originally envisaged as the second of a proposed series of three evolutionary ships intended to steadily transition the US Navy carrier force from the 1970s-era *Nimitz* (CVN-68) design to a new standard based on 21st-century technology. Whilst retaining the basic *Nimitz* class hull, the end result of this process would be a new baseline carrier standard with enhanced propulsion, aircraft launch and aircraft recovery systems, as well as significant improvements in areas such as flight-deck layout, electrical distribution, sensors and survivability. The incremental approach foundered in the era of Secretary of Defense Donald H Rumsfeld's transformational approach to military procurement, resulting in *Ford* introducing most of the improvements originally intended to be spread over three ships.[10] The result has been a huge design and construction challenge that *Ford's* builders – Huntington Ingalls Industries – have done well to manage in spite of cost and schedule overruns.

In contrast to *Ford*, the *Queen Elizabeth* was always likely to be a 'clean sheet' design given the lack of recent British experience in large aircraft carrier construction. This is evidenced by a number of innovative features in her layout, not least the distinctive twin island structure. This places navigational and air traffic control functions in optimal positions, reduces interference between key sensors and introduces a degree of redundancy in an aid to survivability. The ship can also be manned by far fewer crew than *Ford* in spite of being around two-thirds her size and has cost around a third as much to build. Against this, she lacks the flexibility and endurance provided by *Ford's* nuclear propulsion plant and her smaller air group's sustainable sortie generation rate is a little under half that of the US Navy ship. Another interesting difference between the two programmes has been the distributed build strategy adopted by the British ships, which has spread the industrial and technological benefits of the programme across a number of yards. This development of industrial skills has also spurred a British National Shipbuilding

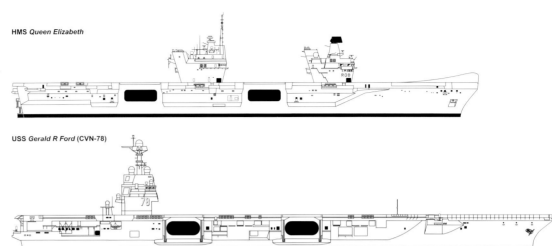

HMS *Queen Elizabeth*

USS *Gerald R Ford* (CVN-78)

© John Jordan 2017

These views of *Queen Elizabeth* and *Gerald R. Ford* (CVN-78) make for an interesting visual comparison of the two new ships. Whilst *Ford* is a much-modified development of the original *Nimitz* class hull, *Queen Elizabeth* is a 'clean sheet' design incorporating a number of innovative features, most obviously the twin island layout. The latter's ski-jump also marks her out as a STOVL carrier, albeit her adaptable design meant that she had to be adjustable to the CATOBAR configuration used by *Ford*. In any event, all carriers are driven by the same basic parameters, including the need to keep deck-edge lifts a certain height above the waterline to avoid water ingress and/or damage in heavy seas and the requirement for sufficient hangar depth to house a wide range of aircraft. These factors are reflected in the similar height of the flight deck above the waterline in both ships. Stability considerations are also important, notably the need to avoid excessive rolling motions whilst maintaining overall stability. In this regard, it is interesting to note the draught and beam of the two ships are also broadly similar. *Ford's* greater length is primarily a function of her higher aircraft capacity, c. 12m of additional ship length being required for each pair of F-35 equivalent aircraft requiring hangar stowage.

Table 1.0.3: *GERALD R. FORD* (CVN-78) AND *QUEEN ELIZABETH* COMPARISON

CLASS	*GERALD R. FORD* (CVN-78)	*QUEEN ELIZABETH*
Builder:	Huntington Ingalls Industries Newport News Shipbuilding yard	Aircraft Carrier Alliance Rosyth Dockyard[1]
Country:	United States of America	United Kingdom
First of Class Keel Laid:	14 November 2009	15 December 2008[2]
First of Class Commissioned:	22 July 2017	7 December 2017
Number in Class:	1+2[3]	1+1
Displacement:	c. 100,000 tons	c. 65,000 tons
Overall Dimensions:	333m x 78m x 12m	284m x 73m x 11m
Waterline Dimensions:	317m x 41m	263m x 39m
Propulsion:	Nuclear, 30+ knots, through four shafts	IEP, 25+ knots through two shafts
Aircraft:	Typical air group of 75 fast jets and helicopters	Air group if up to 40 fast jets and helicopter
Sortie Generation Rate:	160 sustained/270 surge	72 sustained/108 surge

Notes
1 The carrier was assembled at Rosyth from blocks constructed around the United Kingdom.
2 Refers to cutting of first steel. Construction formally commenced on 7 July 2009.
3 Additional ships are planned.

The F-35's development has been an enduring theme of the World Naval Review and the aircraft is now starting to enter service in the United States and United Kingdom, as well as in several other countries. This image shows the first Royal Air Force F-35B variants to be based in the United Kingdom arriving at RAF Marham at the end of their delivery flight on 6 June 2018. *(Crown Copyright 2018)*

The Royal Australian Navy's *Adelaide* – based on Spain's *Juan Carlos I* design – on exercises off Timor in September 2017. The growth of the Asian navies is an enduring theme over *World Naval Review*'s first decade. *(Royal Australian Navy)*

Strategy which may start from a more solid base than its Canadian counterpart.[11]

TECHNOLOGICAL DEVELOPMENTS

The air groups embarked in both *Gerald R. Ford* and *Queen Elizabeth* will ultimately come to rely heavily on variants of the Lightning II F-35 Joint Strike Fighter. The various ups and downs of this advanced and stealthy aircraft that, however, is costly to acquire and has suffered from the compromises inherent in being designed to operate in different configurations have been extensively covered in previous editions of *World Naval Review*. David Hobbs' latest annual review of naval aviation is therefore noteworthy for reporting on the F-35B STOVL variant's first operational deployment onboard the amphibious assault ship *Wasp* (LHD-1). Moreover, initial operational capability is expected to be achieved by the F-35C carrier variant before the year's end. Another notable achievement is the forthcoming attainment of an 'early' operational capability by the MQ-4C unmanned ocean surveillance aircraft, surely an indication of one likely direction of travel for naval aviation over the next decade.

Meanwhile, Norman Friedman's technological review assesses the technology and challenges of naval communication. He examines how the technology of communication developed in the post-Second World War era, as well some of the questions and vulnerabilities this raised. Notably, the best way of fusing real-time tactical data with broader intelligence information remains an ongoing question which has not yet been fully resolved.

We conclude with a short overview by Richard Scott looking how autonomous technology already commonly in use for certain underwater and aerial activities is now being applied to surface vessels. Focusing on separate programmes underway in the United States and the United Kingdom, he explores the hurdles that need to be overcome to make the concept a reality. The prospect of future networks of autonomous vessels being employed as cost-effective force multipliers in combination with traditional manned warships could have a significant impact on naval warfare in the years ahead.

SUMMARY

In concluding this introduction to *World Naval Review*'s tenth edition, it seems appropriate to look back to the opening remarks contained in the series' first edition, signed off on 30 June 2009. Some observations – the growth of the Asian fleets and the continued numerical and technological superiority of the US Navy – appear as applicable now as they did then. Even the contrasting fortunes of the Chinese and Indian naval shipbuilding sectors – particularly the latter's struggle to acquire the infrastructure necessary to build modern, indigenous designs – are a recurring theme. What has been a surprise has been the extent of the return to great power rivalry: first between China, the United States and its allies in Asia; more recently between Russia and its Cold War opponents in NATO and elsewhere. This is likely to have a profound impact on both fleet structures and warship design, particularly a renewed emphasis on 'hot' warfighting capabilities as opposed to lower intensity stabilisation.

From the editor's personal perspective, the most memorable event over *World Naval Review*'s first ten editions has been standing on the shoreline watching the new aircraft carrier *Queen Elizabeth* depart from Rosyth on her maiden voyage on 26 June 2017. The carrier's construction had just commenced when *World Naval Review* was first conceived. Along, doubtless, with more than a few others, the editor doubted whether she would ever be completed as an age of austerity dawned. A modern-day technological and industrial triumph, she is symbolic of the engineering skills that many thought had been lost from the home of the Industrial Revolution. The editor is pleased to conclude the introduction to the tenth *World Naval Review* with a rare moment of unashamedly patriotic flag waving to mark this momentous event.

ACKNOWLEDGEMENTS

Seaforth World Navy Review's continued success has been due to a collaborative effort marked by the ongoing support of publishing editor Robert Gardiner and the consistently first-class layouts produced by the series' designer, Steve Dent. Other enduring features have been the drawings of John Jordan and the contributions of a strong group of authors. Particular thanks go to Norman Friedman, David Hobbs, Mritunjoy Mazumdar and Scott Truver, all of whom wrote for the first edition, for their enduring input. Another important factor has been the book's ability to source illustrations from a wide range of photographers. This edition includes the images of Gordon Arthur, 'Baycrest', Derek Fox, Bruno Huriet, Michael Leek, Marc Piché, Arjun Sarup, Tetsuya Kakitani, Ian Thompson and Devrim Yaylali, many of whom have been longstanding contributors. From industry, the help of Babcock's Graeme Mair, Naval Group's Klara Nadaradjane, Navantia's Esther Benito Lope and Rolls-Royce's Craig Taylor in sourcing photographs and information has gone far beyond normal expectations. Finally, I acknowledge with gratitude the ongoing help of my wife Susan for undertaking the not-inconsiderable task of ensuring my draft text is fit for submission.

Comments and criticisms from readers are always appreciated; please direct them for my attention to: info@seaforthpublishing.com

Conrad Waters, Editor
30 June 2018

Notes

1. This widely-used statement is something of a misquotation, Homer's actual poem being along the lines of 'Man may be sated by anything; sleep, love, sweet song or dance; and all are better than war; but it is of war that these Trojans never get their fill.' Moreover, many academics believe that Homer represents a literary tradition rather than a single poet.

2. For a full review of naval developments in the post-Cold War era see the editor's *Navies in the 21st Century* (Barnsley: Seaforth Publishing, 2016).

3. An interesting essay heralding the demise of the post-Second World War order is provided by Richard N Haass in 'Liberal world order, RIP' posted to the Australian Strategic Policy Institute's blog *The Strategist* on 24 March 2018 available at: aspistrategist.org.au/liberal-world-order-rip/. The strengthening Sino-Russia alignment is assessed by Stephen Blank in 'Whither the Russia-Chinese Alliance?', *European Security & Defence* – 4/2018 (Bonn: Mittler Report Verlag GmbH, 2018), pp.22–5.

4. *The National Security Strategy of the United States of America* (Washington DC: The White House, 2017) can be found at: whitehouse.gov/wp-content/uploads/2017/12/NSS-Final-12-18-2017-0905.pdf. A valuable critique of its many contradictions is contained in Max Boot's 'Trump Security Strategy a Study in Contrasts' posted to the Council on Foreign Relations website on 18 December 2017 at: cfr.org/expert-brief/trump-security-strategy-study-contrasts

5. The *2018 Defence White Paper: Investing in our people, capabilities and visibility* (The Hague: Ministry of Defence, 2018) can be found at: english.defensie.nl/downloads/policy-notes/2018/03/26/defence-white-paper

6. See Craig Caffrey's 'Briefing: The Jane's defence spending review – Optimistic Outlook' in *Jane's Defence Weekly* – 28 February 2018 (Couldson: IHS Jane's, 2018), pp.26–30.

7. This focus was confirmed in the new *National Defense Strategy* announced in January 2018. The full report is classified but a summary is available at: defense.gov/Portals/1/Documents/pubs/2018-National-Defense-Strategy-Summary.pdf

8. The new Russian State Armaments Programme is a ten-year document that is updated every five years. The current programme was expected to be implemented with effect from the start of 2016 and run to 2025. However, the sharp decline in Russia's economy from around 2013 onwards caused the plan to be delayed by two years, resulting in the current GPV 2027. Good assessments of the programme's main elements are contained in Richard Connolly's and Mathieu Boulègue's *Russia's New State Armaments Programme: Implications for the Russian Armed Forces and Military Capabilities to 2027* (London: The Royal Institute of International Affairs, 2018) available at: reader.chathamhouse.org/russia-s-new-state-armament-programme-implications-russian-armed-forces-and-military# and in Julian Cooper's *The Russian State Armaments Programme 2018-27* (Rome: NATO Defense College, 2018) at: ndc.nato.int/news/news.php?icode=1167. The two reports differ slightly in their expectations for Russian construction of blue water surface combatants, with NATO's report suggesting a prototype carrier and destroyer may be laid down towards the end of GPV 2027.

9. See Kosuke Takahashi's 'Japanese study considers F-35B for carrier operations' in *Jane's Defence Weekly* – 9 May 2018 (Couldson: IHS Jane's, 2018), p.16. The *Jane's* report indicates that the *Izumo* class's flight deck, hangar and hangars have already been designed with F-35B operation in mind.

10. Donald H. Rumsfeld was US Secretary of Defense in the Ford administration between 1975 and 1977, returning to the role under President George W Bush between 2001 and 2006. One of his main objectives during his second tenure was to restructure the US military to make it more suitable for the twenty-first century but the implementation of his transformational modernisation programmes left much to be desired.

11. The National Shipbuilding Strategy is discussed in more detail in Chapter 2.4.

2.1 REGIONAL REVIEW

NORTH AND SOUTH AMERICA

Author: Conrad Waters

INTRODUCTION

Naval developments in the Americas are being spurred on by US rearmament in the face of the re-emergence of great power rivalry and the Trump Administration's focus on achieving a national competitive advantage evident in the new US *National Security Strategy* (NSS). America's military focus over recent years has been dominated by the assessment that Russia, China, Iran, North Korea and international terrorism pose the five main threats to US interests. The revised *National Defense Strategy* (NDS) – announced in January 2018 following publication of the NSS – maintains this assessment. However, the NDS is notable for prioritising long-term strategic competition from the 'revisionist' powers of China and Russia over 'rogue regimes' and non-state actors as the central challenge to US security. The strategy indicates that increased and sustained investment is required to build a more lethal force capable of countering this competition.[1]

Recent developments suggest there may be the broad-based political will to pay for this investment. Notably, the Bipartisan Budget Act of February 2018 temporarily eased the financial caps placed on the US Department of Defense (DOD) since the 2011 Budget Control Act. This, in turn, allowed approval of DOD appropriations somewhat in excess of US$650bn for FY2018. The total included US$65bn for Overseas Contingency Operations (OCO), notionally earmarked to pay for the one-off costs of the long 'war against terror'. The agreed amount was significantly higher than both the US$606bn approved for FY2017 and the US$639bn first requested by the Trump Administration for FY2018. Moreover, the Presidential Budget Request for FY2019 seeks a further rise in funding to US$686bn, of which US$69bn is earmarked for OCO. Longer term plans see spending exceeding US$700bn by FY2020, a record high in nominal terms. However, this will be dependent on an extended relaxation of Budget Control Act terms, as the current agreement expires in FY2019.[2]

US Navy construction has been one of the primary beneficiaries of this increased largesse. Approved FY2018 appropriations saw the shipbuilding budget grow by US$3.4bn over the initial US$20.4bn proposed. This will allow orders to be increased from nine to fourteen new ships. Acquisition of naval aircraft was also expanded. The Department of the Navy's FY2019 budget – amounting to US$194.1bn or some twenty-eight percent of the DoD total – requests US$21.9bn for a further ten vessels as part of a series of initiatives intended to increase force levels to the 355 frontline ships targeted in the 2016 Force Structure Assessment.

The new Department of the Navy budget continues to place a high priority on equipment maintenance to improve operational readiness, an area disproportionately impacted by the constraints of the Budget Control Act. In the words of current Defense Secretary Jim Mattis, 'As hard as the last 16 years have been on our military, no enemy in the field has done more to harm the readiness of the US military than the combined impact of the Budget Control Act's defense spending cuts.' Although things are now improving, it seems the navy remains under pressure to meet too many demands with too few worked-up ships. Indeed, navy leaders suggest it will be the early 2020s before overall readiness returns to an acceptable level.

The practical implications of this environment were brought home between June and August 2017 in two separate incidents. These saw the Seventh Fleet destroyers *Fitzgerald* (DDG-62) and *John S. McCain* (DDG-56) suffer a total of seventeen fatalities in collisions with merchant vessels. The immediate causes of both incidents appear to have been a failure to follow proper procedures and poor decision-making by the destroyer crews. However, the incidents revealed more systemic problems with respect to training and operating proficiency traceable to attempts to meet heavy operational requirements with an overstretched fleet. The immediate aftermath saw several senior officers relieved of their commands, most notably the Seventh Fleet's commander, Vice Admiral Joseph Aucoin. He was the first US Navy fleet commander to be dismissed since the Second World War. A major shake-up of training and deployment schedules has also been implemented. Nevertheless, the underlying problems facing the US Navy's surface fleet – notably a lack of emphasis on basic navigation skills and a fundamental mismatch between operational requirements and available resources – are unlikely to be resolved by making a few sacrificial officers carry the can for wider institutional failings.[3]

The US Navy's training processes and operating efficiency have been called into question by two fatal collisions between Seventh Fleet destroyers and merchant ships. This photo shows *John S McCain* (DDG-56) departing Subic Bay in the Philippines onboard the heavy lift vessel MV *Treasure* en route for repair in Yokohama in November 2017. She had collided with the Liberian-flagged *Alnic MC* in the Singapore Strait on 21 August 2017. Ten crew members lost their lives in this incident. *(US Navy)*

Table 2.1.1: FLEET STRENGTHS IN THE AMERICAS – LARGER NAVIES (MID 2018)

COUNTRY	ARGENTINA	BRAZIL	CANADA	CHILE	COLOMBIA	ECUADOR	PERU	USA
Aircraft Carrier (CVN/CV)	–	–	–	–	–	–	–	11
Strategic Missile Submarine (SSBN)	–	–	–	–	–	–	–	14
Attack Submarine (SSN/SSGN)	–	–	–	–	–	–	–	54
Patrol Submarine (SSK)	2	5	4	4	4	2	6	–
Fleet Escort (CG/DDG/FFG)	4	8	12	8	4	2	7	90
Patrol Escort/Corvette (FFG/FSG/FS)	9	3	–	–	1	6	2	13
Missile Armed Attack Craft (PGG/PTG)	2	–	–	3	–	3	6	–
Mine Countermeasures Vessel (MCMV)	–	4	12	–	–	–	–	11
Major Amphibious Units (LHD/LPD/LPH/LSD)	–	2	–	1	–	–	1	32

MAJOR NORTH AMERICAN NAVIES – CANADA

A full review of the developments impacting the Royal Canadian Navy is contained in Chapter 2.1A.

MAJOR NORTH AMERICAN NAVIES – UNITED STATES

The US Navy's fleet size under its current 'ship battle forces' definition amounted to 284 vessels as of mid-2018. This compared favourably with the 276-ship total recorded a year ago and is broadly similar to the level a decade earlier. However, it falls considerably short of the increased 355 requirement set out in the 2016 Force Structure Assessment (FSA). Closing the gap will be a costly and potentially time-consuming exercise that the navy wants to carry out in a measured and balanced fashion in line with an overall vision known as the Navy the Nation Needs (NNN). This is based on the six pillars of (i) readiness, (ii) capability, (iii) capacity, (iv) manning, (v) networks, and (vi) operating concepts. Whilst the NNN vision acknowledges that expanding the fleet to 355 ships is important, it seems an unstated aim is to avoid a fixation on increasing numbers at the expense of other capabilities.

The last few months has, however, seen greater clarity emerge as to how the navy intends to reach the 355-ship target. It appears that its approach will contain several elements, notably:

- Increasing planned acquisition rates in the navy's long-term shipbuilding plan to a level that allows the fleet to grow at a steady, sustainable rate. It is acknowledged that this option, on its own, would not allow the targeted 355-ship fleet to be achieved within the next thirty years. The short-term impact of this approach is shown in Table 2.1.2.
- Increase planned acquisition above the sustained rate by a process of aggressive growth governed by the extent financial resources and industrial capacity permit. Dependent on the number of additional ships acquired, this might allow a 355-ship navy to be achieved by the latter half of the 2030s.
- Extend the service lives of selected ships to achieve a quicker but relatively short-lived increase in available ship numbers.
- Extend the planned service lives of entire ship classes to provide a more sustained and longer lasting boost to the fleet.

Table 2.1.2: US NAVY BATTLE-FORCE DEVELOPMENT (FY2017 TO FY2023)

SHIP TYPE	FSA 2014	FSA 2016	ACTUAL 2017	ACTUAL 2018	PLAN 2019	PLAN 2020	PLAN 2021	PLAN 2022	PLAN 2023
Aircraft Carrier (CVN)	11	12	11	11	11	11	11	12	12
Strategic Submarine (SSBN)	12	12	14	14	14	14	14	14	14
Attack Submarine (SSGN/SSN)	48	66	55	54	56	57	56	56	55
Fleet Escort: (CG/DDG)	88	104	87	90	92	95	98	99	101
Patrol Escort: (FF/LCS/MCMV)	52	52	20	24	31	34	37	35	39
Amphibious Vessel (LHA/LHD/LPD/LSD)	34	38	31	32	33	33	34	34	35
Other – Logistics & Support Ships	63	71	58	59	62	64	64	68	70
TOTAL	308	355	276	284	299	308	314	318	326

Note

Actual numbers are drawn from the Naval Vessels Register for the year in question. Forward data is derived from the *Report to Congress on the Annual Long-Range Plan for Construction of Naval Vessels for Fiscal Year 2019*, published in February 2018. The next few years show positive momentum in fleet numbers but this tails off, with fleet numbers dropping back to 313 by 2028. At this point the fleet will be back to eleven aircraft carriers and there will be only forty-two attack submarines in the fleet.

The *Ohio* class strategic missile submarine *Maryland* (SSBN-738) pictured departing the Royal Navy submarine base at Faslane on 20 March 2018. The need to replace these submarines whilst simultaneously maintaining numbers of nuclear-powered attack submarines is one of the main challenges currently facing US Navy planners. *(Michael Leek)*

The FY2019 Presidential Budget Request reflected the first three elements of this approach. As illustrated by Table 2.1.3, the request provides for ten ships in the FY2019 programme and a total of fifty-four vessels across the five years of the Future Years Defense Program (FYDP). This equates to eleven more ships than previously planned – four to meet the requirements of sustainable growth and a further seven to achieve a more aggressive growth profile. The budget also allocated funds for mid-life extensions of six *Ticonderoga* (CG-47) class cruisers, four *Avenger* (MCM-1) class mine countermeasures vessels and one *Los Angeles* (SSN-688) class attack submarine. Nuclear attack submarine numbers are under particular short-term pressure and a further four *Los Angeles* class submarines may also receive life extensions. Subsequently, in April 2018, it was announced that the service lives of all *Arleigh Burke* (DDG-51) class destroyers would be extended to forty-five years – an increase of five or ten years dependent on flight (design batch) – to ensure 355 ships would be in the fleet by the mid-2030s.[4]

For the present, current US Navy fleet strength is summarised in Table 2.1.4. The table reflects recent trends, with the surface fleet benefitting from resumed construction of *Burke* class destroyers and, particularly, a steady flow of new Littoral Combat Ships. The major area remaining under numerical pressure is the force of nuclear-powered attack submarines. This reflects the withdrawal of Cold War-era *Los Angeles* class boats at a faster rate than the replacement *Virginia* (SSN-774) class can be delivered. More detailed comments under specific warship categories are provided below.

Aircraft Carriers: The commissioning of the new aircraft carrier *Gerald R. Ford* (CVN-78) in July 2017 brought the US Navy carrier fleet back to the eleven-strong Congressionally-mandated level. Her arrival has been followed by a post-delivery shakedown period of extensive tests and trials that have thrown up the usual crop of defects expected during this process. Post-shakedown rectification work should be completed by mid-2019. However, the need to perform shock trials – a process the navy had tried to postpone – means that it will be the early 2020s before she is able to deploy.

Meanwhile, structural work on sister-ship *John F. Kennedy* (CVN-79) was reported as being seventy-five percent complete as of the end of April 2018. Work has also started on the third member of the

The *Avenger* class mine countermeasures ship *Sentry* (MCM-3) pictured in the course of exercises in the Arabian Gulf in August 2017. The lives of some of these ships are being extended under latest US Navy plans, possibly because of the protracted development of the modular mine warfare packages intended to equip the Littoral Combat Ships. *(US Navy)*

class, *Enterprise* (CVN-80), following a formal steel cutting ceremony held at Huntington Ingalls Industries' (HII's) Newport News Shipbuilding facility on 21 August 2017. A formal contract for the ship's full construction has yet to be awarded. This is probably because of ongoing consideration of a possible two-ship purchase that would also include CVN-81.[5] Maintaining an eleven-strong carrier force in the longer term – let alone the twelve-strong fleet required by the 2016 FSA and backed by

Table 2.1.3: USN FY2019 FIVE YEAR SHIPBUILDING PLAN (FY2019–FY2023)

SHIP TYPE	FY2018 REQUEST	FY2018 FUNDED	FY2019 REQUEST	FY2020 PLAN	FY2021 PLAN	FY2022 PLAN	FY2023 PLAN	FY2019-23 TOTAL FYDP[1]
Aircraft Carrier (CVN-78)	1	1	-	-	-	-	1	1 (1)
Strategic Submarine (SSBN-826)	-	-	-	-	1	-	-	1 (1)
Attack Submarine (SSN-774)	2	2	2	2	2	2	2	10 (10)
Destroyer (DDG-51)	2	2	3	2	3	3	3	14 (10)
Future Frigate (FFG(X))	-	-	-	1	1	2	2	6 (6)
Littoral Combat Ship (LCS-1/2)	2	3	1	-	-	-	-	1 (1)
Amphibious Ship (LPD-17 F II)	-	1	-	1	-	1	1	3 (3)
Expeditionary Fast Transport (T-EPF)	-	1	-	-	-	-	-	-
Expeditionary Sea Base (T-ESB-3)	-	1	1	1	-	-	-	2 (-)
Replenishment Oiler (T-AO-205)	1	1	2	1	2	1	2	8 (5)
Fleet Tug (T-ATS(X))	1	1	1	2	1	1	1	6 (5)
Surveillance Ship (T-AGOS/(X))[2]	-	1	-	-	-	1	1	2 (1)
Total	9	14	10	10	10	11	13	54 (43)

Notes
1 Figure in brackets relates to the total of number of ships planned for the same FY2019–FY2023 period at the time of last year's FY2018 budget submission.
2 Table relates to Ship Battle Forces – however T-AGOS surveillance ships are not usually included within this definition.

Table 2.1.4: UNITED STATES NAVY: PRINCIPAL UNITS AS AT MID 2018

TYPE	CLASS	NUMBER	TONNAGE	DIMENSIONS	PROPULSION	CREW	DATE
Aircraft Carriers							
Aircraft Carrier – CVN	FORD (CVN-78)	1	100,000 tons+	333m x 41/78m x 12m	Nuclear, 30+ knots	4,600	2017
Aircraft Carrier – CVN	NIMITZ (CVN-68)	10	101,000 tons	333m x 41/78m x 12m	Nuclear, 30+ knots	5,200	1975
Principal Surface Escorts							
Cruiser – CG	TICONDEROGA (CG-47)	22	9,900 tons	173m x 17m x 7m	COGAG, 30+ knots	365	1983
Destroyer – DDG	ZUMWALT (DDG-1000)	2	15,800 tons	186m x 25m x 8m	IEP, 30+ knots	175	2016
Destroyer – DDG	ARLEIGH BURKE (DDG-51) – Flight II-A	38	9,400 tons	155m x 20m x 7m	COGAG, 30 knots[1]	320	2000
Destroyer – DDG	ARLEIGH BURKE (DDG-51) – Flights I/II	28	8,900 tons	154m x 20m x 7m	COGAG, 30+ knots	305	1991
Littoral Combat Ship – FS	FREEDOM (LCS-1)	5	3,500 tons	115m x 17m x 4m	CODAG, 45+ knots	‹50[2]	2008
Littoral Combat Ship – FS	INDEPENDENCE (LCS-2)	8	3,000 tons	127m x 32m x 5m	CODAG, 45+ knots	‹50[2]	2010
Submarines							
Submarine – SSBN	OHIO (SSBN-726)	14	18,800 tons	171m x 13m x 12m	Nuclear, 20+ knots	155	1981
Submarine – SSGN	OHIO (SSGN-726)	4	18,800 tons	171m x 13m x 12m	Nuclear, 20+ knots	160	1981
Submarine – SSN	VIRGINIA (SSN-774)	15	8,000 tons	115m x 10m x 9m	Nuclear, 25+ knots	135	2004
Submarine – SSN	SEAWOLF (SSN-21)	3[3]	9,000 tons	108m x 12m x 11m	Nuclear, 25+ knots	140	1997
Submarine – SSN	LOS ANGELES (SSN-688)	32	7,000 tons	110m x 10m x 9m	Nuclear, 25+ knots	145	1976
Major Amphibious Units							
Amph. Assault Ship – LHD	AMERICA (LHA-6)	1	45,000 tons	257m x 32/42m x 9m	COGAG, 20+ knots	1,050	2014
Amph Assault Ship – LHD	WASP (LHD-1)	8[4]	41,000 tons	253m x 32/42m x 9m	Steam, 20+ knots	1,100	1989
Landing Platform Dock – LPD	SAN ANTONIO (LPD-17)	11	25,000 tons	209m x 32m x 7m	Diesel, 22+ knots	360	2005
Landing Ship Dock – LSD	WHIDBEY ISLAND (LSD-41)	12[5]	16,000 tons	186m x 26m x 6m	Diesel, 20 knots	420	1985

Thomas Hudner (DG-116) is the latest DDG-51 type destroyer to be delivered to the US Navy. She is the first of the so-called Flight IIA 'technology insertion' ships that are seen as a bridge to the enhanced capabilities offered by the improved DDG-51 Flight III variant equipped with the new AN/SPY-6 radar. *(General Dynamics Bath Iron Works)*

Notes:

1 Plans to fit some ships with hybrid electric drive now limited to DDG-103.

2 Plus mission-related crew.

3 Third of class, SSN-23 is longer and heavier.

4 LHD-8 has many differences.

5 Includes four LSD-49 HARPERS FERRY variants.

President Trump – is one of the major force structure challenges currently facing the US Navy. Current plans envisage reducing the 'centers' or gaps between future carrier construction from the late 2020s to help tackle the problem. However, more will need to be done to achieve a complete solution.

Surface Combatants: The restarted DDG-51 programme – first announced in 2009 – is now producing tangible results. *John Finn* (DDG-113), the first of the new batch of Flight II A vessels, was commissioned on 15 July 2017. She was quickly followed by *Rafael Peralta* (DDG-115) at the end of the month. Subsequent deliveries have included *Ralph Johnson* (DG-114) – commissioned on 24 March 2018 – and *Thomas Hudner* (DDG-116). The latter is the first of the so-called Flight IIA 'tech-

The Littoral Combat Ship *Little Rock* (LCS-9) performing a high-speed run on Lake Michigan during acceptance trials in August 2017. Commissioned in December 2017, she was then stranded in the St Lawrence Seaway due to ice. After wintering in Montreal, she departed for the more favourable climatic conditions of Mayport, Florida at the end of March 2018. *(Lockheed Martin)*

nology insertion' ships that are seen as something of a bridge to the enhanced capabilities offered by the design's improved Flight III variant. Construction of the Flight III design, which incorporates the new AN/SPY-6 AMDR air and missile-defence radar and an upgraded power generation and distribution architecture, got underway on 7 May 2018 with the start of fabrication on *Jack H. Lucas* (DDG-125) at HII's Ingalls Shipbuilding yard in Mississippi. Current plans envisage her being delivered in 2023, followed by the Bath Iron Works' *Louis H. Wilson Jr.* (DDG-126) in 2024.

For the time being, Bath Iron Works still has a considerable backlog of Flight IIA destroyer construction to complete. This is partly due to delays with the assembly of *Zumwalt* (DDG-1000) class destroyers allocated to the yard. The second ship in the class, *Michael Monsoor* (DDG-1001), was delivered in April 2018. However, final fitting out has still to be completed, with commissioning not

scheduled until January 2019. Work is already well-advanced on *Lyndon B. Johnson* (DDG-1002), the third and final member of a class that was once expected to run to as many as thirty-two ships. However, it appears that the substantial research and development effort that accompanied *Zumwalt*-class construction might not be entirely wasted. Key design elements such as their integrated electric propulsion system and stealth characteristics are likely to be used in the next generation surface combatant being developed to replace the *Ticonderoga* class cruisers. Meanwhile, the decision to terminate the precision-guided Long Range Land Attack Projectile (LRAP) intended to form the core of the class's key fire support capability has been followed by a decision to refocus the ships towards a surface-strike role.[6]

Turning to the lower end of the surface combatant force mix, serial production of Littoral Combat Ships is translating into a rapidly-growing

fleet of these smaller vessels. At present, construction of the Austal USA-built *Independence* (LCS-2) variant is running somewhat ahead of the Lockheed Martin *Freedom* (LCS-1) type built by Fincantieri's Wisconsin-based Marinette Marine subsidiary. The former company has delivered three Littoral Combat Ships – *Omaha* (LCS-12), *Manchester* (LCS-14) and *Tulsa* (LCS-16) – in the course of the past twelve months. By contrast, production delays attributed to a lack of skilled labour and faults with propulsion system gears supplied by a German subcontractor mean that Martin Marinette has only completed *Little Rock* (LCS-9) over the same period.[7] Recent thinking has envisaged a total of thirty-two orders for the type prior to transition to the planned FFG(X) frigate from FY2020. However, Congress's decision to add a third ship to the pair requested in FY2018 meant that this total will be exceeded. The projected single FY2019 ship will be the thirty-third member of the class and – given continued Congressional appetite for further ships – it seems the final number will be higher.

Attention is, however, increasingly turning to the FFG(X) programme that was launched in the course of 2017. This envisages the acquisition of twenty frigates to supplement the (then) planned total of thirty-two Littoral Combat Ships, thereby meeting the 2016 FSA's requirement for fifty-two small surface combatants. The first FFG(X) order is planned for FY2020, a timescale that has effectively prevented development of an entirely 'clean sheet' design. Instead, five companies were awarded contracts in February 2018 to evolve existing 'parent designs' – ship designs that have already been constructed and operated at sea – to meet the FFG(X) requirement. The five selected companies are:

- **Austal USA** – offering an upgraded version of their *Independence* (LCS-2) design.
- **Lockheed Martin** – similarly proposing a frigate-type version of the *Freedom* (LCS-1) class.
- **General Dynamics Bath Iron Works** – putting forward a proposal based on the Spanish Navy's Aegis-equipped F-100 *Álvaro de Bazán* class frigate in conjunction with Navantia.
- **Fincantieri** – promoting a design based on the Italian Navy's FREMM variant.
- **Huntington Ingalls Industries** – possibly considering a proposal based on its 'Legend' class National Security Cutter but also rumoured to be

The US Navy's new FFG(X) programme may be met by the evolution of one of the existing LCS designs; this image shows Austal USA's FFG(X) concept. The design has a clear similarity to the existing *Independence* (LCS-2) type but is equipped with VLS technology. *(Austal USA)*

The 'Freedom-Variant Frigate' is Lockheed Martin's proposed evolution of its LCS-1 design for the FFG(X) programme. Other shortlisted designs are based on existing European frigates. *(Lockheed Martin)*

developing a variant of Denmark's *Iver Huitfeldt* design.

Completion of these conceptual designs will be followed by a further competition in the course of 2019 to select a final proposal for detailed design and construction. An interesting detail of the process is the fact the final design competition will not be restricted to the companies awarded conceptual design work. This opens up the possibility than an unexpected winner could emerge. Cost of series-built ships is expected to be as much as US$950m. This is significantly more than the c. US$570m of a Littoral Combat Ship but only around half the US$1.8bn price of a DDG-51 type destroyer.[8]

One factor behind the higher cost of the new frigates over that of the previous Littoral Combat Ships is the fact that the comparison ignores the expense of the LCS modular mission packages associated with the latter type. All Littoral Combat Ships carry a basic armament that will soon be boosted by integration of an over-the-horizon surface-strike capability following a deal announced on 31 May 2018 to equip them with the Norwegian Naval Strike Missile. However, they remain heavily reliant on installation of additional modular systems to undertake their assigned missions. These comprise separate surface warfare, anti-submarine warfare and mine countermeasures packages that have undergone somewhat protracted development. The full surface warfare mission package is expected to gain initial operating capability from the end of 2018. It will be followed by the anti-submarine mission package a year or so later. However, many elements of the mine countermeasures package have been considerably delayed and the integrated system will only be available from 2021 at best. This may explain the decision to extend the lives of some of the legacy *Avenger* class mine countermeasures vessels that has previously been mentioned. It is also noteworthy that no operational deployments of Littoral Combat Ships are scheduled during 2018. This will allow maintenance backlogs to be dealt with whilst facilitating the transition to the revised crewing and operating model for the type announced in September 2016.[9]

Amphibious and Support Shipping: The current focus of US Navy amphibious ship procurement is the transition in production from the current *San Antonio* (LPD-17) class amphibious transport docks to the LX(R) programme destined to replace the *Whidbey Island* (LSD-41) and *Harper's Ferry* (LSD-49) dock landing ships. The new ships are to be a modified variant of the LPD-17 type and, in April 2018, it was determined that the LX(R) programme would be re-designated LPD-17 Flight II in view of the similarities between the two classes. It was also decided that the first Flight II ship would be LPD-30, an additional amphibious transport dock inserted into the FY2018 shipbuilding programme by Congress. This should ultimately balance the class between thirteen ships of each Flight.

To date, eleven LPD-17 class vessels have entered service with the commissioning of *Portland* (LPD-27) in December 2017. Work commenced on *Fort Lauderdale* (LPD-28), one of two transitional ships paving the way for the Flight II configuration, on 13 October 2017. The final Flight I ship, *Richard M. McCool Jnr.* (LPD-29) has also been ordered. Fabrication should commence before the end of 2018.

The US Navy also continues to acquire new second-line amphibious ships derived from mercantile designs to supplement its more expensive amphibious assault ships and amphibious transport docks. Nine of thirteen planned Expeditionary Fast Transports – the former Joint High Speed Vessels – are now in service with the Military Sealift Command (MSC) following delivery of *City of Bismarck* (T-EPF-9) by Austal USA in December 2017. The much larger Expeditionary Transfer Dock (ESD) and Expeditionary Mobile Base (ESB) concepts – the former Mobile Landing Platforms and Afloat Forward Staging Bases – are also proving successful. The second ESB variant – *Hershel "Woody" Williams* (T-ESB-4) was delivered to the MSC in February 2018. The keel of the third – *Miguel Keith* (T-ESB-5) was laid by General Dynamics NASSCO a few days earlier on 30 January. At least two more are planned. Meanwhile, the first Expeditionary Mobile Base, *Lewis B. Puller* (T-ESB-3) deployed to the Persian Gulf in July 2017 to replace the veteran interim Afloat Forward Staging Base *Ponce* (AFSB(I)-15).[10] Her possible use in active military operations resulted in her being commissioned as a naval warship on 17 August 2017 after arrival at Bahrain. This was reported to have been the first time a US Navy ship had been commissioned outside of the United States.

NASSCO is also tasked with constructing the new *John Lewis* (T-AO-205) class replenishment oilers that are eventually slated to replace the existing *Henry J. Kaiser* (T-AO-187) class vessels in the MSC. Many of the latter ships fail to meet current environmental standards by virtue of being single-hulled and the replacement programme is being pursued with a degree of urgency. NASSCO has already been awarded a block-buy contract for the first six ships of a twenty-ship class but the FYDP for 2019 to 2023 suggests the rate of procurement may be accelerated. This could reflect a recognition that the more distributed fleet implied by recent US Navy operating concepts will increase the demand on logistical support assets.

Submarines: Maintaining the effectiveness of its submarine forces is, perhaps, the most pressing challenge currently facing the US Navy in terms of force-structure considerations. The hiatus in submarine construction after the end of the Cold War means that it is proving difficult to build sufficient numbers of *Virginia* class attack submarines to

Portland (LPD-27), the latest *San Antonio* amphibious transport dock to be delivered, pictured in the course of sea trials. A Flight II variant of the design will replace the *Whidbey Island* and *Harper's Ferry* class dock landing ships. *(Huntington Ingalls Industries)*

The second Expeditionary Mobile Base – *Hershel "Woody" Williams* (T-ESB-4) – being floated out of General Dynamics' NASSCO yard in August 2017. These new amphibious auxiliaries are proving a successful addition to the front-line amphibious fleet and more are being ordered. *(General Dynamics NASSCO)*

A computer-generated representation of the US Navy's new *Columbia* class strategic missile submarines. Twelve of these boats will enter production from FY2021 onwards to replace fourteen existing *Ohio* class submarines as part of the underwater element of the United States' triad of strategic nuclear weapon delivery systems. *(US Naval Sea Systems Command)*

compensate for the large numbers of Cold War era *Los Angeles* class submarines that are reaching the end of their service lives. The challenge is exacerbated by the need also to replace the *Ohio* (SSBN-726) class strategic missile submarines that form a key part of the United States' nuclear deterrent. Managing the financial and industrial consequences of these coinciding programmes is no easy task.

The replacement for the legacy *Ohio* class boats will be the new *Columbia* (SSBN-826) class strategic submarines, previously referred to as the SSBN(X). Twelve of these submarines will replace the fourteen members of the *Ohio* class that retain their strategic missile-carrying role.[11] Elements of the programme – notably a common missile compartment – are being developed in conjunction with the British Royal Navy's project for new *Dreadnought* class submarines, which will carry out a similar strategic role. The lead *Columbia* class boat will not be officially ordered until the FY2021 construction programme. However, a significant amount of work is already underway to meet a tight schedule that will see the class's first operational deployment in 2031. Reports suggest that the programme is currently progressing on schedule, doubtless aided by a significant degree of component commonality with the *Virginia* class attack submarines. The *Columbia* design does, however, incorporate a new integrated electrical propulsion system conceptually similar to that used in French nuclear-powered submarines and there have been problems with a pre-production prototype of the electric motor that this will use. Another major challenge is controlling costs in a programme that is estimated to involve procurement expenditure in excess of US$100bn for the submarines alone.

Meanwhile, construction of the *Virginia* class is starting to recover from a hiccup in a strong record that has seen many boats completed early and under cost. *Washington* (SSN-787) – the fourteenth in the class – was delivered around three months late from Newport News Shipbuilding in May 2017. The next Newport News boat – *Indiana* (SSN-789) – is also running several months late. However, *Colorado* (SSN-788) was only a few weeks behind schedule

when handed over by General Dynamics' Electric Boat facility in September 2017 and subsequent boats from both yards are expected to be on time. Looking to the future, the FY2019 programme is likely to see the first order for a class member equipped with the Virginia Payload Module (VPM), an additional 84ft long mid-body hull extension. This incorporates four large-diameter vertical launch tubes capable of holding a total of twenty-eight additional Tomahawk cruise missile-sized weapons, increasing total weapons-carrying capacity to c. sixty-five torpedoes and missiles. All subsequent boats will be built to this design. Current plans envisage construction transitioning to a new SSN(X) design in FY2034 once forty-eight members of the *Virginia* class have been ordered. However, it seems current efforts to accelerate production will result in total numbers, the transition date, or both being adjusted.

The key factor in the development of future submarine numbers will be the extent to which industrial infrastructure can be expanded to support future construction. Current orders are shared between the Electric Boat and Newport News ship-

The latest *Virginia* class nuclear-powered attack submarine *Indiana* (SSN-789) pictured in the course of initial sea trials in Chesapeake Bay in May 2018. The submarine's builders – HII's Newport News Shipbuilding – will be responsible for assembling a greater proportion of the class as part of plans to allow GD Electric Boat to focus on construction of the new *Columbia* class strategic missile submarines. *(Huntington Ingalls Industries)*

yards in an arrangement under which each yard undertakes construction of certain parts for all the navy's submarines but shares fabrication of the reactor compartments and final assembly to preserve key skills. The arrangement supported the relatively low rate of orders of just one submarine p.a. achieved in the first decade of the millennium and was retained when production expanded to a sustained rate of two *Virginia* class submarines from FY2011.

The imminent start of *Columbia* class construction and the pressure on overall submarine numbers has resulted in plans to increase capacity to allow three submarines (viz. one *Columbia* and two *Virginia*s) to be ordered in some years. The new programme will also involve a re-allocation of work that will see all *Columbia* class assembly focused on Electric Boat in return for a greater proportion of *Virginia* class completion being undertaken at Newport News. Consideration is also being given to ordering a third *Virginia* class boat in those years when strategic submarines are not being procured. Significant investment is being made by the shipyards to support the expansion in work. However, a much broader supply chain will be involved in delivering the programmes. There has to be some question as to the extent that they will be able to step up to the demands being made of them.

Operational Highlights: The operational context presentation accompanying the US Navy's FY2019 Presidential Budget Request suggested an average of 100 of the navy's c. 280 battle force ships were deployed.[12] The deployed figure is the same as provided last year but the overall fleet is slightly larger. By FY2023, it is anticipated the deployed total will increase to an average of 131 from an average ship count of 326, suggesting an even higher operational tempo than currently. This may be optimistic given the backlog of maintenance and other readiness issues that still need to be overcome, particularly the training deficiencies laid bare by the destroyer collisions described in the introduction.

Shipbuilding and Support Infrastructure

The challenges posed by the US Navy's expanding requirements for submarine construction are indicative of the wider problems created by the rundown in American shipbuilding and support infrastructure that has occurred since the end of the Cold War. This issue was considered in the long-range plan for naval construction issued at the start of the FY2019 budget request.[1] In line with many other countries, increased emphasis is being placed on creating a more stable warship procurement plan to support a sustainable naval sector.

The historical 'boom and bust' profile of US naval shipbuilding is shown in the diagram. This depicts the decline in shipyards with a significant involvement in military-related new construction over a sixty-year period overlaid against the number of battle-force ships. Over the past half century, fourteen naval construction yards have closed and three have left the defence industry compared with just one that has opened. This leaves just seven yards controlled by four industrial groups left in the sector, viz.

Austal
Austal USA, Mobile AL

Fincantieri
Fincantieri Marinette Marine, Marinette WI

General Dynamics
GD Bath Iron Works, Bath MA
GD Electric Boat, Groton CT
GD NASSCO, San Diego CA

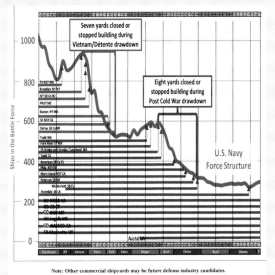

Note: Other commercial shipyards may be future defense industry candidates.

New Construction Shipyards: Industrial Base Reductions

Huntington Ingalls Industries
HII Ingalls Shipbuilding, Pascagoula MS
HII Newport News Shipbuilding, Newport News VA

The navy considers that the remaining industrial base for warship construction represents 'significantly less capacity' than that available to competitor nations.

The problem has been exacerbated by an equivalent decline in the infrastructure available for maintenance. This includes the four main publicly-owned naval shipyards – at Norfolk, Pearl Harbor, Portsmouth and Puget Sound – that have been starved of investment over many years and where a backlog of maintenance has steadily accumulated. If anything, the impact of the Budget Control Act has been to prioritise shipbuilding over readiness, meaning maintenance has suffered disproportionately.

Part of the solution is to encourage private sector investment in additional capacity through procurement plans that avoid the emergence of new boom-and-bust cycles. This is having some success, as evidenced by substantial investment being made by both General Dynamics and HII to support the expanded submarine construction objective. There remains, however, something of a conflict between the imperative of stability and the desire to achieve a relatively swift uplift in fleet size. It also seems that additional private sector involvement in maintenance is being sought, which might extend to providing government funds for the modernisation of privately-owned facilities. Meanwhile, as much as US$21bn is being earmarked for a 'public shipyard optimization plan' that will involve a major overhaul of the four navy-operated shipyards.[2]

Notes
1. *Report to Congress on the Annual Long-Range Plan for Construction of Naval Vessels for Fiscal Year 2019*, op. cit.
2. See Megan Eckstein's 'Navy Plans to Spend $21B Over 20 Years to Optimize, Modernize Public Shipyards' posted to the *USNI News* site on 17 April 2018 at: news.usni.org/2018/04/17/navy-plans-spend-21b-20-years-optimize-modernize-public-shipyards

Globally, the navy's focus of operations remains the Pacific, where the majority of forward-deployed ships are based. Two of the perceived major threats to US interests – viz. China and North Korea – are based in the region and the US Navy is central to the response to both. The potential thawing of North Korean-US relations following the summit between Kim Jong Un and Donald Trump may reduce the immediate importance of the ballistic missile defence role played by the Seventh Fleet's Aegis-equipped cruisers and destroyers. However, deterring Chinese maritime expansionism is likely to remain a high priority. This has included ongoing freedom of navigation operations (FONOPs) in sea areas subject to what the United States considers 'excessive maritime claims', as well as bilateral and multi-national exercises.[13] These included a rare three carrier strike group exercise involving *Nimitz* (CVN-68), *Theodore Roosevelt* (CVN-71) and *Ronald Reagan* (CVN-76) in the Western Pacific in November 2017; the first such deployment in the region since Exercise Valiant Shield 2007 off Guam.

Vladimir Putin's Russia ranks alongside China as the most significant threat to American security, a challenge reflected by an announcement in May 2018 that the US Second Fleet would be re-established to counter increasing Russian naval activity in the North Atlantic and Arctic. The new command will be stood-up in July 2018. It will have a particularly important role in training and certifying US Navy east coast-based ships in similar fashion to that already performed by the Third Fleet on the west coast.[14]

In spite of the higher priority allocated to other threats, the Middle East remains the navy's main theatre of actual combat operations. The US Marine Corps (USMC) is inevitably at the centre of these missions. For example, USMC's Special Purpose Marine Air-Ground Task Force Crisis Response Force in US Central Command (SP-MAGTF-CR-CC) reportedly had personnel operating simultaneously in as many as twenty-four locations in ten countries during the past year. The MAGTFs – another is based in Spain in support of Africa Command – have been particularly useful in covering gaps when Marine Expeditionary Units based on sea-going Amphibious Ready Groups have been absent from the area. The availability of the ESB *Lewis B. Puller* in theatre has provided additional flexibility in this regard.[15]

The most intensive combat mission in the past year has been the missile strikes on Syrian chemical weapons facilities on 14 April 2018 in response to allegations of continued use of these munitions by the Assad regime on rebel areas. The strikes – carried out in association with France and the United Kingdom – included the launch of sixty-six Tomahawk cruise missiles from three surface vessels and the *Virginia* class submarine *John Warner* (SSN-785). This was the first time a *Virginia* class boat had fired missiles in combat. The operation also saw the inaugural use of the new French *Missile de Croisière Naval* (MdCN), reportedly from the FREMM-type

The US Navy destroyer *Higgins* (DDG-76) indulges in a spot of flag waving alongside the aircraft carrier *Theodore Roosevelt* (CVN-71) in March 2018. The destroyer was one of several units involved in strikes against Syrian chemical weapons facilities the following month, firing twenty-three Tomahawk cruise missiles. *(US Navy)*

frigate *Languedoc*. The attack additionally involved units of the Royal and US Air Force, as well as the *Armée de l'Air Française*.

US Coast Guard: The last year has seen the US Coast Guard continue to make progress with a major fleet replacement programme that is intended to see a total of ninety-one new vessels replace ninety legacy cutters and patrol craft that form the vast bulk of its sea-going fleet.[16] The overall programme is summarised in Table 2.1.5 with key elements described in further detail below:

■ **National Security Cutters:** Representing the 'high end' of the US Coast Guard's patrol vessel fleet, the original aim was to purchase eight 'Legend' or *Bertholf* (WMSL-750) class ships to replace the twelve veteran *Hamilton* (WHEC-715) class high endurance cutters. There was initially some doubt as to whether this total would be achieved. However, Congressional action has actually extended planned procurement, authorising acquisition of the tenth and eleventh members of the class in the FY2018 Homeland Security appropriations. Six of the 4,500-ton vessels have been delivered to date. The eighth – *Midgett* (WMSL-757) – was launched by HII's Ingalls' facility in November 2017. Average cost is c. US$580m per ship.

■ **Offshore Patrol Cutters:** The newest class of cutter in the USCG's construction programme, the 'Heritage' or *Argus* (WMSM-915) will be c. 3,500-ton vessels based on the 'Vard 7-110' patrol

vessel concept. They will replace two existing classes of medium endurance cutters. A contract for up to nine of what should eventually be a 25-strong class was awarded to Eastern Shipbuilding of Panama City, Florida in 2016. Much of the detailed design work has been sub-contracted to the UK's Babcock International, which has experience of building Vard designs for the Royal and

A computer-generated image of the US Coast Guard's new 'Heritage' class offshore patrol cutter *Argus* (WMSM-915), which is based on the Vard 7-110' patrol vessel concept and will be built by Eastern Shipbuilding Group. Much of the detailed design work has been sub-contracted to the UK's Babcock International, which has experience of building Vard designs for the Royal and Irish navies. *(Babcock International)*

Irish Navies. The first ship was funded in the FY2018 appropriations. Construction should begin later this year for completion around 2021. Subsequent vessels are likely to follow at annual intervals. Estimated average procurement cost is likely to be US$390m per ship.

■ **Fast Response Cutters:** The smallest of the cutter fleet, fifty-eight 'Sentinel' or *Bernard C. Webber* (WPC-1101) class vessels will replace existing 'Island' class patrol boats. They are being built by Louisiana's Bollinger Shipyards to a Damen Stan patrol 4708 design. Twenty-seven have been commissioned to date and deliveries are continuing at a rate of around five p.a. A total of fifty of the type had been funded as of FY2018. A request for a further four for FY2019 will bring the programme close to its conclusion. Average procurement cost approaches US$60m per cutter.

Progress is also being made with an ambitious polar icebreaker programme. This envisages acquisition of three heavy icebreakers and three medium icebreakers to replace just two existing operational ships. A request for proposals for the detailed design and construction of the first heavy

Table 2.1.5: UNITED STARES COAST GUARD CUTTER PROGRAMMES

TYPE	NATIONAL SECURITY CUTTER (WMSL)	OFFSHORE PATROL CUTTER (WMSM)	FAST RESPONSE CUTTER (WPC)
Class	'Legend' (*Bertholf*)	'Heritage' (*Argus*)	'Sentinel' (*Bernard C. Webber*)
Displacement	4,500 tons	3,500 tons	350 tons
Dimensions	127m x 17m x 7m	110m x 16m x 5m	47m x 8m x 3m
First of Class Delivered	2008	[2021]	2012
Programme of Record	8	25	58
Funded	11[1]	1	50
Completed	6	0	27
Legacy Ships Replaced	12 (high endurance cutters)	29 (medium endurance cutters)	49 (patrol boats)

Note

1 More ships have been funded than included in the original programme.

Table 2.1.6: BRAZILIAN NAVY: PRINCIPAL UNITS AS AT MID 2018

TYPE	CLASS	NUMBER	TONNAGE	DIMENSIONS	PROPULSION	CREW	DATE
Principal Surface Escorts							
Frigate – FFG	GREENHALGH (Batch I Type 22)	2	4,700 tons	131m x 15m x 4m	COGOG, 30 knots	270	1979
Frigate – FFG	NITERÓI	6	3,700 tons	129m x 14m x 4m	CODOG, 30 knots	220	1976
Corvette – FSG	BARROSO	1	2,400 tons	103m x 11m x 4m	CODOG, 30 knots	145	2008
Corvette – FSG	INHAÚMA	2	2,100 tons	96m x 11m x 4m	CODOG, 27 knots	120	1989
Submarines							
Submarine – SSK	TIKUNA (Type 209 – modified)	1	1,600 tons	62m x 6m x 6m	Diesel-electric, 22 knots	40	2005
Submarine – SSK	TUPI (Type 209)	4	1,500 tons	61m x 6m x 6m	Diesel-electric, 22+ knots	30	1989
Major Amphibious Units							
Helicopter Carrier – LPH	ATLÂNTICO (OCEAN)	1	22,500 tons	203m x 35m x 7m	Diesel, 18 knots	490	1998
Landing Ship Dock – LSD	BAHIA (FOUDRE)	1	12,000 tons	168m x 24m x 5m	Diesel, 20 knots	160	1998

icebreaker was requested in March 2018. It is hoped to commence construction within the next year for delivery by 2023. The ambitious schedule is being driven by the questionable condition of the existing *Polar Star* (WAGB-10), which is already more than a decade beyond its original 30-year service life.

OTHER NORTH AND CENTRAL AMERICAN NAVIES

Immediately to the south of the United States, **Mexico** has long directed its navy towards constabulary missions in the absence of any significant external threat. Recent construction has focused on the indigenously-designed and built *Oaxaca* class offshore patrol vessels and the smaller *Tenochtitlan* class inshore patrol vessels. The latter are also assembled locally to a licensed Damen Stan Patrol 4207 design. These ships have been supplemented by large numbers of fast interception craft, mainly of the Polaris I and Polaris II types derived from the Swedish CB-90. The last year has seen further deliveries under this construction programme. *Hidalgo* – second of an improved batch of *Oaxaca* class vessels built by the ASTIMAR 20 yard at Salina Cruz – was commissioned on 24 November 2017. She joined *Bonampak* and *Chichén Itzá* – the ninth and tenth members of the *Tenochtitlan* class – delivered by ASTIMAR 1 at Tampico between July and November. Two further improved members of the *Oaxaca* class are currently under construction. However, orders for additional *Tenochtitlan* class units – past reports suggest twenty are ultimately envisaged – may need to await confirmation of the next naval replacement programme. This is due to take effect from 2019.[17]

The most significant development in the past twelve months has, however, been the commencement of construction of a new *Patrullera Oceánica de Largo Alcance* (POLA). This is based on the Damen 'Sigma' 10514 light frigate design already built for the Indonesian Navy. As for the Indonesian vessels, fabrication of constituent modules will be carried out both in the Netherlands and locally. Commencement of work was marked by a formal keel-laying ceremony at Vlissingen in August 2017. It is anticipated that launch will take place in Mexico in the second half of 2018 prior to entry into operational service during 2020. Various reports suggest a total class of four and six ships are eventually planned, probably superseding further *Oaxaca* class construction. Although nominally a patrol vessel, the 2,600-ton ship will be far more powerfully armed than the previous OPVs. Specified weapons fit is reported to include Harpoon surface-to-surface and RAM surface-to-air missiles. These are supplemented by anti-submarine torpedo launchers, an embarked helicopter and a 57mm gun. The ship should therefore be seen more as the start of a replacement programme for Mexico's elderly former US Navy frigates than a continuation of the previous line of offshore patrol vessels.

Elsewhere in Central America, Damen's domination of the local market for patrol and logistic support vessels was further evidenced by the commissioning of the Stan Lander 5612 multipurpose support ship *Presidente Manuel Amador Guerreco* by **Panama**'s National Naval-Air Service. The new ship replaces a cancelled order for Colombia's similar BAL-C type and will support anti-narcotics and other constabulary operations along Panama's Pacific coastline.

The Dutch Damen group continues to use its network of shipyards and licenced-construction arrangements to gain a wide range of contracts in the Americas. This shows the new LCT-like logistic support vessel *Presidente Manuel Amador Guerreco* delivered to Panama's Naval-Air Service from the group's Vietnamese yard in May 2018. *(Presidency of Panama)*

MAJOR SOUTH AMERICAN NAVIES – BRAZIL

The *Marinha do Brasil* continues to experience decidedly mixed fortunes in the aftermath of the financial and political crisis in the middle of the decade. This saw a severe economic recession and the ultimate imprisonment of former premier Lula de Silva. The Brazilian economy is now showing some signs of recovery and defence spending benefitted from an easing of government financial controls in 2017. However, the political environment remains uncertain pending presidential elections towards the end of 2018. A truck drivers' strike over high fuel prices in May 2018 that paralysed the country was bought off by subsidies funded by cuts to other government spending. One programme to suffer was the plan to build four *Tamandaré* class corvettes. It will lose a fifth of the budget previously allocated to commence the programme in 2018. It is not yet clear how this will impact a bidding process to select an overseas company to assist local construction of the design. Nine consortia have responded to the request, with a preferred partner due to be selected before the year's end.[18]

The *Tamandaré* class programme is being given added urgency by the run-down nature of Brazil's surface fleet. As evidenced by Table 2.1.6, this has been reduced to just eleven frigates and corvettes in recent years. Many of these are not fully operational. The core of the surface fleet remains the six 1970s-era *Niterói* class frigates, which have all benefitted from significant modernisation. However, further planned combat system upgrades will now only be performed on three of the six, probably due to financial restrictions.[19] Surveys are being carried out on the class and the more recent corvette *Barroso* to establish if a fifteen year life extension is possible.

It has, however, not all been bad news over the past year. Notably, sufficient funds have been found to acquire the former Royal Navy amphibious helicopter carrier *Ocean*. She was formally handed over on 29 June 2018 following a short refit at Devonport. Whilst not a like-for-like replacement for the retired aircraft carrier *São Paulo*, the new *Atlântico* provides a large platform for helicopter operations and complements the amphibious capabilities provided by the amphibious transport dock *Bahia*. Meanwhile, the Naval Aviation Arm has been benefitting from deliveries of new locally built H225M Super Cougar helicopters. A total of sixteen are being acquired in UH-15 utility, UH-15A

The Brazilian Navy frigate *Liberal* pictured in company with the amphibious transport dock *Bahia* in June 2017. Brazil's amphibious forces are being bolstered by opportunistic purchases but the fragile state of its elderly frigates and corvettes is a cause for concern. *(Brazilian Navy)*

The Brazilian Navy's helicopter carrier *Atlântico* - the former Royal Navy *Ocean* - was handed over at a formal ceremony on 29 June 2018. *(Brazilian Navy)*

combat search and rescue, and UH-15B sea control configurations. The navy's existing Super Lynx helicopters are also being upgraded. Along with the surplus Seahawks acquired from the US Navy and a number of older utility types, there are therefore plenty of rotary assets to form the newly-acquired ship's air group.

The huge PROSUB project initially launched in 2009 also continues to move ahead. Physical integration of the various hull sections of *Riachuelo*, the lead 'Scorpène' type submarine being built with the assistance of France's Naval Group at Itgauaí, was completed in February 2018. Current plans envisage her being launched in December. This is in line with a revised schedule that anticipates entry into service during 2020. Work continues on three further boats, as well as longer term plans to construct a nuclear-powered attack submarine. However, it seems unlikely to be before the 2030s that this long-planned ambition will be achieved.

OTHER SOUTH AMERICAN NAVIES

The improving fortunes of Brazil's submarine fleet stands in marked contrast to that of neighbouring **Argentina**. Its small submarine force suffered a major setback in November 2017 when its TR-1700 class submarine *San Juan* was lost without trace with forty-four crew members onboard. The loss of life was the highest in such an incident since the loss of Russia's *Kursk* in 2000. The disaster seems to have followed a previous fire caused by water leakage that disabled a proportion of the submarine's batteries. The elderly submarine had been subject to a protracted mid-life modernisation between 2008 and 2013 but there had been subsequent reports of defects.[20]

The response to the disaster revealed the low serviceability of other Argentine military assets. Many of the country's maritime patrol aircraft and major surface vessels were unable to join a search operation that benefitted from significant international assistance. A significant backlash has seen the dismissal of several senior Argentine naval officers, including the navy's commander Admiral Marcelo Srur.

The Argentine Navy had been making some progress in the face of protracted financial constraints at the time of *San Juan*'s loss. Notably, completion of long delayed repairs to the icebreaker *Almirante Irízar* had been followed by successful sea trials, making her available to resume Antarctic operations for the first time in over a decade. Agreement had also been reached to procure a

The Brazilian Navy's PROSUB submarine construction project has made considerable progress over the past year, with physical integration of the various hull sections of the lead boat *Riachuelo* completed in February 2018 prior to anticipated launch around the end of the year. These photographs include an unusual bird's-eye view of the submarine's forward part being transported by road to the final assembly hall, where it was joined to the remaining sections. (*Brazilian Navy/Naval Group*)

handful of retired *Marine Nationale* Super Étendard to reconstitute a limited strike capability; a deal that has subsequently been funded. However, possibly the most significant development relates to plans to acquire France's *L'Adroit* and three similar new-build 'Gowind' OPV90 type ships to fulfil long-standing plans for new constabulary vessels. A contract was reportedly close to signature as June 2018 drew to a close.

More broadly, however, a recent deterioration in Argentina's financial stability will probably mean the uptick in defence spending is short-lived. This – and the distraction arising from ongoing investigations into *San Juan*'s loss – will likely further delay other long-pending acquisition plans. A similar situation exists, on a much smaller scale in neighbouring **Uruguay**. Here lack of funding has effectively put a plan to acquire new offshore patrol vessels on ice.

Chile's relatively modern and efficient navy is currently focused on the modernisation of its three Type 23 frigates. The programme of weapons and sensor upgrades commenced in March 2018 with the start of work on *Almirante Cochrane* (the former Royal Navy *Norfolk*) at local shipbuilder ASMAR's yard in Talcahuano. Each upgrade package is expected to take around eighteen months to complete. Reports suggest that Chile would like to acquire at least one additional Type 23 when the remaining ships start to be retired from the Royal Navy around 2023. This would replace the sole Type 22 frigate *Almirante Williams* (previously HMS *Sheffield*).

The remainder of the eight-strong 'National Squadron' comprises two 'L' and two 'M' class frigates acquired from the Netherlands. Upgrading the obsolescent anti-air capability provided by the latter's SM-1 missiles is a pressing requirement. Although a major modernisation programme is not ruled out, the fact that support for the ships' elderly Olympus and Tyne gas turbines will end during the course of the 2020s is a major complication. Accordingly, other options are being considered. Construction of new ships in Chile by ASMAR with foreign assistance is probably the preferred way forward.

Meanwhile ASMAR delivered its fourth Fassmer OPV-80 type patrol vessel, *Cabo Odger*, on 10 August 2017. Two additional units of a more heavily-armed 90m variant are planned. However, a more immediate project is construction of a new icebreaker of the 'Vard 9-203' type, under a contract

The Chilean Navy's latest offshore patrol vessel, *Cabot Odger*, pictured during her launch from ASMAR's Talcahuano yard in August 2016. She was subsequently commissioned on 10 August 2017. *(ASMAR)*

signed in November 2017. Construction will start in 2018 to replace the existing elderly *Almirante Óscar Viel* in the early 2020s.

A full update on the other major South American naval power, **Peru,** is provided in Chapter 2.1B.

Elsewhere in Latin America, **Colombia** is similar to Chile in developing a strong local shipbuilding capability through state-owned COTECMAR. This company has also arranged a licence to construct the Fassmer OPV-80 design. *Victoria*, the third of six planned ships, was delivered in September 2017.[21] As for Chile, the design has been subject to incremental improvements as the programme has progressed. Accordingly, the last pair are also likely to be a larger, more heavily-armed variant. Another successful programme has been that for the LCT-like BAL-C logistic support ship. Five of these had been completed as of mid-2018. An additional vessel ordered by Honduras is due for delivery by the end of the year. Looking to the future. COTECMAR is also likely to be involved in a programme to replace the existing quartet of *Almirante Padilla* class frigates, which is expected to be launched by the end

of the decade. There has also been interest in Peru's new *Pisco* and it is possible that a programme of mutual construction might be arranged given previous Peruvian evaluation of the BAL-C design.

The situation is far less positive in **Venezuela**. Here continued political and economic chaos are reflected in limited operational availability of many vessels, including both of the navy's two submarines. Replacement boats have been promised – possibly of Chinese or Russian origin – but no tangible details have been forthcoming. One notable development has been the commencement of sea trials for the fourth Navantia-designed BVL type patrol vessel, *Comandante Eterno Hugo Chávez*. She commenced sea trials from builder DIANCA on 20 April 2018, some seven years after the last of her three Spanish-built sisters. Once delivered, she will be a numerical replacement for the larger 'Avante 2200' class oceanic patrol vessel *Warao*, one of a quartet ordered from Navantia at the same time. She was heavily damaged in a grounding incident off Brazil in 2012 just a year after delivery. A decision has now been taken to abandon planned repairs.

Notes

1. Online references for the December 2017 *The National Security Strategy of the United States of America* and the published summary of the January 2018 *National Defense Strategy* are provided in Chapter 1.

2. Trying to understand the US defence budgetary process is not for the faint-hearted. Overall 'discretionary' spending – typically that not specifically earmarked for various healthcare and social programmes – is currently controlled by the 2011 Budget Control Act. This is intended to reduce the large US government financial deficit by placing strict caps on both military and non-military spending, a process often known as sequestration. In practice, however, Congress has found the extent of these restrictions unpalatable and the caps have been temporarily eased on a number of occasions. Moreover, OCO funding is outside of the Budget Control Act spending caps and many critics believe it has been used as a device to circumvent spending restrictions. It is also worth noting that the funding amounts appropriated to defence spending fall under a number of budget headings and are sometimes supplemented by separate appropriations to cover discrete items. For example, specific appropriations were made outside of the main process in FY2018 for repairs to the damaged destroyers *Fitzgerald* and *McCain* (see below). This means that amounts quoted in different reports are often calculated on different bases and therefore fail to reconcile with each other.

3. The US Navy's conclusions on the causes of the *Fitzgerald* and *McCain* collisions are detailed in two reports by David B Larter posted to the *Defense News* site: 'Navy crews at fault in fatal collisions, investigations find' on 1 November 2017 at: defensenews.com/breaking-news/2017/11/01/navy-crews-at-fault-in-fatal-collisions-investigations-find/ and 'Navy finds deep-rooted failures lead to fatal collisions' on 2 November at: defensenews.com/breaking-news/2017/11/02/navy-finds-deep-rooted-failures-led-to-fatal-collisions/. A number of judicial and non-judicial punishments have been imposed on some of the destroyers' personnel held accountable for the collisions; in additional *Fitzgerald*'s commander and a more junior officer are to be subject to court martial proceedings that some commentators believe may have been impacted by prejudicial statements made by navy leadership on the tragic events.

4. For further detail of current shipbuilding plans see the *Report to Congress on the Annual Long-Range Plan for Construction of Naval Vessels for Fiscal Year 2019* (Washington DC: Office of the Chief of Naval Operations, 2018). Excellent analysis on the current state of these plans and the issues surrounding them can be found in Ronald O' Rourke's *Navy Force Structure and Shipbuilding Plans: Background and Issues for Congress RL32665* (Washington DC: Congressional Research Service, 2018). Like many of Mr O'Rourke's other periodically updated reports, this has been posted as a public service on the Federation of American Scientist's website at: fas.org/sgp/crs/weapons/

5. More details on this approach are contained contained in Chapter 3.1.

6. The potential use of technologies developed for the *Zumwalt* class to be used in the US Navy's next major surface combatant was discussed by Sam LaGrone in 'CNO: Lessons from Zumwalt-class Key to Next Surface Combatant' posted to the *USNI News* site on 25 April 2018 at: news.usni.org/2018/04/25/cno-lessons-zumwalt-class-key-next-surface-combatant. The same site carried an article by Megan Eckstein on 4 December 2017 focusing on the class's new surface strike role under the title 'New Requirements for DDG-1000 Focus on Surface Strike. This is available at: news.usni.org/2017/12/04/navy-refocus-ddg-1000-surface-strike

7. See Anthony Capaccio's 'Lockheed's Littoral Ships Running 11 Months Late, U.S. Navy Says' posted to the *Bloomberg* website on 12 December 2017 at: bloomberg.com/news/articles/2017-12-12/lockheed-s-littoral-ships-running-11-months-late-u-s-navy-says

8. The comparative costs were quoted by Ronald O' Rourke in the 6 April 2018 update of his *Navy Frigate (FFG[X]) Program: Background and Issues for Congress R44792* (Washington DC: Congressional Research Service, 2018), p.5. His Navy Littoral Combat Ship (LCS) Program: Background and Issues for Congress RL33741 (Washington DC: Congressional Research Service, 2018) also provides significant amounts of background information on small combatant procurement.

9. Further background on LCS and Frigate procurement is found in the editor's 'US Navy Littoral Combat Ship & Frigate Programmes', *European Security & Defense* – 2/2018 (Bonn: Mittler Report Verlag GmbH, 2018), pp.65–8.

10. *Ponce* – formerly LPD-15 – was an *Austin* (LPD-4) class amphibious transport dock that first entered service in July 1971. She was decommissioned on 14 October 2017 following her return to her homeport of Norfolk, Virginia.

11. An additional four *Ohio* class boats have been converted to guided missile submarine (SSGN) configuration armed with Tomahawk cruise missiles.

12. See *Department of the Navy FY2019 President's Budget* (Washington DC: Department of the Navy, 2018) at: secnav.navy.mil/fmc/fmb/Documents/19pres/DON_Press_Brief.pdf

13. The US Navy's FONOPs are not limited to China. Citing the Annual Freedom of Navigation Report: Fiscal Year 2017 (Washington DC: Department of the Navy, 2017), Ankit Panda reported in The Diplomat that Cambodia, India, Indonesia, Malaysia, Maldives, the Philippines, Sri Lanka, Taiwan, and Vietnam were other Asian countries targeted for FONOPs from October 2016.

14. For further detail see David B Larter and Mark D Faram's 'The US Navy's new command puts Russia in the crosshair's', *Defense News* – 4 May 2018 at: defensenews.com/naval/2018/05/04/the-us-navys-new-command-puts-russia-in-the-crosshairs/

15. The extent of the snappily-named SP-MAGTF-CR-CC's operations was reported by Megan Eckstein on 11 June 2018 in the *USNI News* article 'Crisis Response Marines in Middle East Focused on Operations in Syria, Afghanistan' currently available at: news.usni.org/2018/06/11/crisis-response-marines-middle-east-focused-operations-syria-afghanistan

16. An excellent overview of the USCG's cutter replacement programmes is provided by another of Ronald O' Rourke's regularly updated reports, *Coast Guard Cutter Procurement: Background and Issues for Congress R42567* (Washington DC: Congressional Research Service, 2018).

17. Good sources on naval developments in the Spanish-speaking American countries remain the Spanish language *infodefensa.com* and *defensa.com* websites.

18. This section has benefitted from the ongoing coverage of the Brazilian Navy in the Portuguese-language Poder Naval website at: naval.com.br/blog/

19. See Victor Barriera's 'Brazil to upgrade fewer frigates' - *Jane's Defence Weekly* – 14 February 2018 (Coulsdon: IHS Jane's, 2018), p.12.

20. A review of the disaster and the response by Argentina's armed forces was provided by Josè Higuera in 'Hopes lost of finding Argentine submarine crew alive' – *Jane's Defence Weekly* – 29 November 2017 (Coulsdon: IHS Jane's, 2017), p.12. The damage to the submarine's batteries was referred to in several contemporary reports.

21. The ship was originally to be named *Santander* and was launched as such on 1 December 2016. However, that day also marked the first day of peace in Columbia after the ending of the FARC insurgency and the ship's name was changed in commemoration.

2.1A Fleet Review

Author:
**Theodore
Hughes-Riley**

ROYAL CANADIAN NAVY

Recent Developments and Current Status

The early history of Canada as a nation is intrinsically linked to colonial expansion into North America by European powers. In 1867 various British colonies in North America entered into a self-governing federation within the British Empire, forming the Dominion of Canada. Steadily increasing autonomy culminated in effective independence through the Statute of Westminster in 1931. However, complete transfer of residual powers was not completed until the Canada Act of 1982.

Canada is the second largest country in the world (at almost 10,000,000km²) and has the world's longest coastline (202,080km) flanking the Atlantic, Pacific and Arctic oceans.

Canada is a wealthy nation with the tenth highest

The Royal Canadian Navy *Halifax* class frigate *Montréal* pictured in the vicinity of Greenland's capital, Nuuk, in August 2017. Canada's coastline is bordered by three oceans – the Atlantic, Pacific and Arctic – and the RCN has to operate in each. The increasing importance of the Arctic is having a particularly marked influence on RCN operations and procurement. *(Royal Canadian Navy)*

The RCN 'River' class *Lasalle* pictured on anti-submarine operations in the North Atlantic in 1945. She was built at the Davie shipyard in Québec during 1943-44. A massive programme of domestic naval construction propelled the RCN to becoming one of the world's largest navies at the end of the Second World War. It also resulted in a focus on anti-submarine operations that has endured to this day. *(Crown Copyright 1945)*

The RCN's last aircraft carrier – the *Majestic* class *Bonaventure* – pictured in 1962. The Cold War focus on anti-submarine operations off Canada's extended Atlantic coastline meant that it proved impossible to maintain general-purpose naval forces. *Bonaventure* became focused on anti-submarine operations before being retired in 1970. *(Editor's Collection)*

gross domestic product (GDP) globally, earning it membership to both the G7 and G20. The nation has considerable natural resources including timber, gold and uranium, which contribute heavily to the nation's economy. They include significant petroleum and natural gas reserves, making Canada the fourth largest exporter of both of those resources. As a result Canada's economy is driven heavily by international trade; in 2016 around a third of the nation's GDP was generated from the export of goods and services. While many of these exports – around seventy-five percent – were to the United States, Canada also has other close trading partners that do not share a land border. These include the United Kingdom and China. It is estimated that the role that maritime shipping plays in Canada's international trade adds about US$30bn to the economy (~2 percent GDP).

Canada holds memberships in a number of major international organisations including NATO, the UN, the Group of Ten and the Asia-Pacific Economic Cooperation. The country is a global power with interests across the world. As a result, Canada's defence decisions are in part informed by a desire to maintain global stability. By maintaining the freedom of the seas, Canada supports its trading interests and – hence – its economy.

HISTORICAL BACKGROUND

The Naval Service of Canada was formed as a consequence of the Naval Service Act of 1910 and was renamed the Royal Canadian Navy (RCN) in 1911.[1] The RCN entered the First World War with two cruisers gifted by the British and a little over 300 personnel but had grown significantly by the end of the four-year conflict in which a total of around 9,500 served in its ranks. Whilst post-war economies inevitably made their mark – dissolution was even considered at times – the navy entered the Second World War with a fleet of eleven combat vessels and somewhat under 2,000 men. Subsequently, a sustained programme of local shipbuilding, as well as transfers of vessels from the United States and United Kingdom, saw the RCN become one of largest navies in the world, peaking at over 400 fighting ships. Equally importantly, the RCN was highly active during the conflict, taking a particularly prominent role in fighting the U-boat menace in the North Atlantic. The experience it gained in anti-submarine warfare (ASW) had a considerable impact on the service's subsequent direction that has endured to this day.

Post-war Canadian defence policy inevitably turned its attention towards the Soviet Union. The country became a founding member of NATO in 1949, and formed NORAD with the United States in 1958.[2] The latter reflected an increasing emphasis on North American defence in the nuclear era that was also seen in a joint RCN-Royal Canadian Air Force (RCAF) Concept of Maritime Operations agreed in 1957. This shifted the RCN's focus towards the western North Atlantic, including the prevention of Soviet submarine operations in littoral waters such as the Labrador Sea. Key technological developments during this period included the introduction of a very capable series of destroyer escorts (frigates) commencing with the *St Laurent* class of 1955–7 and the pioneering deployment of large helicopters on frigate-sized vessels. A more negative result of the ongoing importance of the RCN's anti-submarine forces to meet self-defence and NATO requirements was a realisation that there were insufficient resources to retain more general-purpose maritime equipment. This led to the loss of some key capabilities. It was reflected, for example, by the transformation of the aircraft carrier *Bonaventure* into an anti-submarine vessel and, subsequently, an end to the RCN's foray into carrier aviation with her decommissioning in 1970. This period also saw a major change in the structure of the RCN, with the unification of the RCN, Canadian Army and RCAF into the single Canadian Forces in 1968. Canadian Forces Maritime Command (MARCOM) took over most of RCN's responsibilities, with the ultimate exception of its aviation assets. The title Royal Canadian Navy was not reinstated until 2011.

MARCOM essentially continued the former RCN's primary anti-submarine, North Atlantic emphasis built around an escort force of largely ASW-orientated destroyers and frigates, as well as three submarines. In large part, these forces were intended to operate in coordination with other NATO forces that could provide capabilities – such as area air defence – Canada lacked. Changes in NATO maritime strategy in the mid-1980s saw a shift towards a concept based on self-supporting national task groups. Canada initially agreed to provide three of these units. This resulted in a reconstruction of the four most modern *Iroquois* class destroyers, changing their primary warfighting function from ASW to anti-air warfare so that they could provide air-defence to their assigned task group. The vessels also received upgrades to their command and

The now decommissioned RCN *Iroquois* class destroyer *Athabaskan* refuelling from the Spanish replenishment vessel *Cantabria* in October 2015. Delays to procurement programmes have meant that the RCN has lost the critical air defence and command facilities provided by its destroyers and been forced to temporarily 'gap' its fleet replenishment capacity because the relevant ships reached the end of their lives before construction of replacements began. *(Royal Canadian Navy)*

control facilities to enable them to act as the groups' flagships. Subsequent plans to acquire an expensive fleet of nuclear-powered attack submarines were ultimately cancelled in 1989 due to domestic and US opposition as the Cold War drew to a close.

The end of the Cold War saw the navy's focus move towards more distant, expeditionary operations. Notably, a Canadian task group was deployed in support of the US-led Operation 'Desert Storm' in 1990, the first of a series of numerous international deployments to support international stability in the post-Cold War environment. The change in the navy's expected tasks led to revised equipment requirements. In the mid-2000s, a programme was launched to obtain a strategic sealift and amphibious capability – an ambition still to come to fruition.[3]

A notable development during this time was the launch of the Canada First Defence Strategy in 2008. Setting out key missions of the Canadian Forces in the post-Cold War era, it placed increased emphasis on enforcing Canada's sovereignty over its Arctic regions. A key result of this approach has been the purchase of the *Harry DeWolf* class Artic offshore patrol vessels and the establishment of the Nanisivik Naval Facility in the Arctic Circle, both previously announced in 2007. The new naval facility is due to be completed by the end of 2018. The strategy also affirmed plans to construct fifteen ships to replace the navy's existing frigate and destroyer classes and

up to three replenishment ships. The subsequent 2010 National Shipbuilding Procurement Strategy (now the National Shipbuilding Strategy or NSS) laid out plans to ensure all these ships would be built domestically as part of plans to bolster indigenous shipbuilding capabilities.

A key feature of many of these procurement programmes has been a lack of adequate funding to undertake renewal of an aging fleet in a timely fashion. For example, the new surface combatants will include replacements for the *Iroquois* class destroyers and their much-needed command and control and area air defence capabilities. However, much of this capacity has been 'gapped' with the decommissioning of the last of the *Iroquois* class, *Athabaskan*, in 2017. The RCN's ability to operate globally was further hindered by the decommissioning of the *Protecteur* class replenishment oilers before construction of their replacements had even begun, in part due to hull corrosion in one of the vessels and fire damage to the other.[4]

MARITIME DEFENCE PRIORITIES

The release of the most recent defence policy – *Strong, Secure, Engaged* – in June 2017 provides a clear overview of Canada's current defence priorities.[5] The policy discusses the core missions of the armed forces: the defence of (i) Canada and of (ii) the broader North American region from attack, as well as (iii) a contribution to operations supporting global stability. The policy highlights how these goals will be accomplished, emphasising some of the key alliances that Canada is a member of. These include the bilateral partnership with the United States of America, including NORAD; NATO; and the so-called 'Five Eyes' intelligence-sharing partnership with Australia, New Zealand, the United Kingdom and the United States. Importantly, additional funding will be provided to support these priorities: spending will rise from C\$18.9bn (c. US\$14.5bn) in 2016/17 to C\$32.7bn (c. US\$ 25bn) in 2026/27 and reach 1.4 percent of GDP by 2025.

Within the new policy's mission framework, a key defensive priority for the RCN is the protection of Canada's extensive exclusive economic zone (EEZ). This covers c. 5,600,000km^2 of water, one of the world's largest. The EEZ includes areas in the Arctic and the defence policy discusses increasing the presence of the Canadian Forces in this region. The Canadian Government's concern is likely a result of changes in the global climate that have resulted in a reduction in sea ice increasing the number of open sea-lanes through the region, as well as its significant natural resources. Canada plans to work closely with partners such as the United States, Norway and

Denmark to ensure effective surveillance; a task in which the new patrol ships will play a key role.

The policy also lays out a clear aspiration to maintain a blue water fleet. This is to be capable of generating two naval task groups each comprising up to four surface combatants, a joint support ship, and – when warranted – a submarine. These groups are identified as units that could make a meaningful contribution to international operations. Beyond combat operations, and protection of the EEZ, the policy also discusses that the RCN may be required to provide humanitarian assistance, as well as conduct defence diplomacy.

Canadian defence policy has taken a multilateral approach for a number of years, and the policy acknowledges that Canada is unlikely to act independently. Instead, it focusses on conducting operations with its allies and partners. Canada remains fully committed to NATO and makes regular contributions to the alliance. For example, the RCN has been a key participant in Operation 'Reassurance' – Canada's contribution to NATO deterrence activities against recent Russian assertiveness – including overlapping deployments as part of both of the NATO Standing Maritime Groups. Canada also has strong bilateral defence ties with many NATO

members, principally the United States, United Kingdom and France. This is in part due to historical ties as well as shared values and interests. Their close proximity and the high level of integration between their economies further strengthens Canada's defence ties with the United States. This close relationship with the United States has seen Canadian vessels deployed as an integrated component of US Navy carrier groups.

The RCN also regularly engages with a broader range of international partners, and conducts a variety of deployments globally. This includes its contributions to the Combined Maritime Forces in support of maritime security off the Horn of Africa. The RCN is also involved in supporting US-led operations to stop organised crime in the Caribbean and East Pacific, with warships regularly deployed to these regions to support the US Coast Guard.

Further insight into how the RCN is to achieve the ambitions set by the new defence policy framework was provided with the release of a *Royal Canadian Strategic Plan 2017-2022* at the end of 2017.[6] The latest in a series of strategic documents, the plan stresses the importance of the ongoing programme of fleet renewal that the additional funding provided in the defence review will help support. Other areas of focus include much greater emphasis on the use of digital technology to enhance organisational efficiency and improve personnel conditions. The latter forms part of broader efforts to provide better social and career support to serving sailors and their families.

PERSONNEL AND ORGANISATION

The RCN is an environmental command of the unified Canadian Armed Forces (CAF), focusing on the naval forces of Canada.[7] As such the head of the RCN is directly subordinate to the Chief of Defence Staff (CDS). While the title of the head of the RCN has changed many times over the years, it is currently the Commander of the Royal Canadian Navy (CRCN) and Chief of Naval Staff. The CRCN is based at the National Defence Headquarters in Ottawa along with the CDS and the other so-called 'environmental' commanders.

The RCN currently consists of approximately 8,300 regular personnel, 4,600 reserves, and 3,700 civilians in supporting roles.[8] Within the RCN there are three major commands: Maritime Forces Atlantic (MARLANT), Maritime Forces Pacific (MARPAC), and the Naval Reserve.

The RCN *Victoria* class patrol submarine *Chicoutimi* (the former RN *Upholder*) seen docking at the US Navy facility at Yokosuka in Japan in October 2017. The RCN's current plans envisage an ability to operate 'blue water' orientated task groups comprising frigates and a replenishment vessel on both Atlantic and Pacific coasts, supported by one of the *Victoria* class submarines as appropriate. *(US Navy)*

MARLANT: This command is responsible for the fleet training and readiness in the Atlantic Ocean. The Commander of Maritime Forces Atlantic (COMMARLANT) is also double-hatted as commander of Joint Task Force Atlantic (COMMJTFA), one of six regionally-based joint task forces responsible for operations in Canada that report to Joint Operations Command. COMMARLANT is assisted by the Commander of Canadian Fleet Atlantic, who is responsible for the readiness of ships within the command. The Commander of Canadian Fleet Atlantic can also act as Canadian Task Group Commander for deployed vessels.

MARLANT is headquartered at CFB (Canadian Forces Base) Halifax, in Nova Scotia. Focused on HM Canadian Dockyard Halifax, it includes Fleet Maintenance Facility (FMF) Cape Scott and the 'stone frigate' *Trinity* at Stadacona. The latter is responsible for maintaining MARLANT communications with the aid of two remotely-operated radio stations. Other facilities include the Shearwater Heliport at which most of RCAF's 12 Wing is stationed. This includes 423 Maritime Helicopter Squadron (which provides ship flights for the Atlantic Fleet) and 406 Maritime Operational Training Squadron (which is responsible for training all maritime helicopter air crew). MARLANT also has responsibility for Canadian Forces Station St. John's, Newfoundland.

Canadian Fleet Atlantic currently includes: seven *Halifax* class frigates, six *Kingston* class coastal defence vessels, two *Victoria* class submarines and the interim replenishment vessel *Asterix*.

MARPAC: The duties of MARPAC are to maintain fleet readiness and conduct training for vessels stationed in the Pacific Ocean, and it is similar in structure to its counterpart on the Atlantic coast. Its commander is both Commander of Maritime Forces Pacific (COMMARPAC) as well as commander of the Joint Task Force Pacific (COMMJTFP). His deputy is the Commander Canadian Fleet Pacific, who is tasked with ensuring the readiness of the ships in the fleet.

MARPAC is situated near Victoria, British Columbia at CFB Esquimalt. The base includes FMF Cape Breton, which provides maintenance services to the ships stationed there. Aviation support to the fleet is provided by the RCAF 12 Wing's 443 Maritime Helicopter Squadron, which is based at the nearby Patricia Bay. Canadian Fleet Pacific currently

The *Halifax* class frigate *Calgary* operating alongside the US Navy carrier *John C. Stennis* (CVN-74) in the course of the RIMPAC 2016 exercises in August 2016. Canadian defence policy emphasises a multilateral approach to security and links with its larger southern neighbour are particularly strong. *(US Navy)*

includes: five *Halifax* class frigates, six *Kingston* class coastal defence vessels, two *Victoria* class submarines, and the sail training vessel *Oriole*. CFB Esquimalt is also home to the *Orca* class patrol craft.

Naval Reserve: The Naval Reserve is headquartered in Québec City and comprises twenty-four Naval Reserve Divisions located across Canada. It provides the bulk of the personnel for the *Kingston* class coastal defence vessels, which carry out surveillance and patrol activities throughout the Canadian littoral. The Naval Reserve also has an important emergency support role.

The growing importance of the Arctic and the imminent opening of the Nanisivik Naval Facility on Baffin Island is unlikely to have a significant impact on this overall organisational structure, particularly as the scope of the Arctic facility has been reduced to providing support only during the short summer season. It appears current plans envisage the new *Harry DeWolf* class vessels being based at Halifax and Esquimalt, largely using Nanisivik as a refuelling stop.

Although there is a large Canadian Coast Guard (CCG) – comprising over 100 vessels and more than

20 helicopters – operating as an agency of Fisheries and Oceans Canada, this has neither naval nor law enforcement responsibilities. It can – and does – however operate in support of the CAF and other agencies on occasion.

MARITIME AVIATION

All aviation assets in the Canadian Forces come under the control of the RCAF. It operates two wings that support naval activities: 12 Wing provides maritime helicopters, and 14 Wing is responsible for maritime patrol.

In total 12 Wing now operates fewer than twenty Sikorsky CH-124 Sea King helicopters, with these currently being replaced by a total of twenty-eight CH-148 Cyclone helicopters. Eleven CH-128s had been delivered to an interim standard as of mid-2017 and are used for training. Deliveries of CH-128s to a more complete, Block 2 standard, are expected to allow initial operational capability to be achieved before the end of 2018.

The RCAF's maritime patrol capability is provided by the Lockheed CP-140 Aurora (a variant of the P-3 Orion) of which the RCAF operate fourteen aircraft (and a single trainer variant). Three

Table 2.1A.1: ROYAL CANADIAN NAVY – PRINCIPAL UNITS AS AT MID-2018

TYPE	CLASS	NO.	YEAR[1]	TONNAGE	DIMENSIONS	PROPULSION	PRINCIPAL ARMAMENT
Submarines (4)							
Submarine (SSK)	VICTORIA (UPHOLDER)	4	1990	2,500 tons	70m x 8m x 6m	DE; 20+ knots	6 x 533mm torpedo tubes for Mk 48 Mod 7 torpedoes
Class: *Victoria* (SSK-876), *Windsor* (SSK-877), *Corner Brook* (SSK-878), *Chicoutimi* (SSK-879)							
Fleet Escorts (12)							
Frigate (FFH)	HALIFAX	12	1992	4,800 tons	134m x 6m x 5m	CODOG; 29 knots	16 Mk 48 VLS cells, 8 x Harpoon SSM, 1 x 57mm, 1 x Phalanx CIWS, MGs, 4 x TT, 1 x helicopter
Class: *Halifax* (FFH-330), *Vancouver* (FFH-331), *Ville de Québec* (FFH-332), *Toronto* (FFH-333), *Regina* (FFH-334), *Calgary* (FFH-335), *Montréal* (FFH-336), *Fredericton* (FFH-337), *Winnipeg* (FFH-338), *Charlottetown* (FFH-339), *St John's* (FFH-340), *Ottawa* (FFH-341)							
Patrol Vessels (20+5)[2]							
Patrol Vessel (CDV/MM)	KINGSTON	12	1996	970 tons	55m x 11m x 3m	DE; 15 knots	1 x 40mm gun, MGs
Class: *Kingston* (MM-700), *Glace Bay* (MM-701), *Nanaimo* (MM-702), *Edmonton* (MM-703), *Shawinigan* (MM-704), *Whitehorse* (MM-705), *Yellowknife* (MM706), *Goose Bay* (MM-707), *Moncton* (MM-708), *Saskatoon* (MM-709), *Brandon* (MM-710), *Summerside* (MM-711)							
Patrol Vessel (PCT)	ORCA	8	2006	210 tons	33m x 8m x 2m	Diesel; 20 knots	Not normally armed
Class: *Orca* (PCT-55), *Raven* (PCT-56), *Caribou* (PCT-57), *Renard* (PCT-58), *Wolf* (PCT-59), *Grizzly* (PCT-60), *Cougar* (PCT-61), *Moose* (PCT-62)							
Patrol Vessel (AOPV)	HARRY DEWOLF	(5/6)[2]	(2018)	6,500 tons	104m x 19m x 4m	DE; 17 knots	1 x 25mm gun, MGs, 1 x helicopter
Class: *Harry DeWolf* (AOPV-430), *Margaret Brooke* (AOPV-431), *Max Bernays* (AOPV-432), *William Hall* (AOPV-433), *Frédérick Rolette* (AOPV-434) plus 1 option							
Replenishment Vessels (1)							
Interim AOR (MV)	ASTERIX	1	2018	26,000 tons	183m x 25m x 7m	Diesel; 22 knots	MGs, 2 x helicopters. Provision for CIWS
Class: *Asterix*							

Other ships include the sail training vessel *Oriole* and various tugs and other harbour craft.

Notes :

1 Date relates to the date the first ship of the class entered naval service. For the *Victoria* class, this corresponds to initial British Royal Navy service.

2 Second number refers to ships of the type/class currently under construction or ordered.

The RCN's interim auxiliary oiler replenishment ship MV *Asterix* pictured docking in Halifax Harbour for the first time on 27 December 2017. There is currently only one fleet oiler in the RCN's line-up due to delays in ordering replacement vessels. *(Royal Canadian Navy)*

squadrons are based at CFB Greenwood, Nova Scotia, on the Atlantic coast including the training squadron and the development squadron. A fourth squadron is based on the Pacific coast at CFB Comox, British Columbia.

FLEET COMPOSITION

The current composition of the RCN is shown in Table 2.1A.1, with major units discussed below.

Halifax **Class Frigates:** The *Halifax* class frigate is the RCN's workhorse and sole major surface combatant. A product of the Cold War, the design of the class was born out of the 1970s Canadian Patrol Frigate Programme that sought to replace twenty aging ASW destroyer escorts of the *St. Laurent, Restigouche, Mackenzie* and *Annapolis* classes with new ships. The *Halifax* class's equipment – including hull-mounted and towed-array sonar, capacity for a heavy helicopter and provision of ASW torpedo tubes – also lent itself to anti-submarine warfare. However, the design was always intended to have general-purpose capabilities, with armament also comprising a 57mm gun, Harpoon surface-to-surface and Sea Sparrow surface-to-air missiles and a Phalanx CIWS. The frigates were ordered in two batches of six, in 1983 and 1987. A third batch was not taken up in favour of the unrealised nuclear submarine project of the late 1980s, referenced previously. The twelve *Halifax* class were constructed at two Canadian shipyards: Saint John Shipbuilding (nine vessels) and MIL Davie Shipbuilding (three vessels). The first ship, *Halifax*, was commissioned in June 1992, with the twelfth and final vessel, *Ottawa*, entering service in September 1996.

The vessels have also seen a number of notable overseas deployments including a sustained presence in the Persian Gulf region in support of US operations in Afghanistan from 2001 to 2003, the Standing NATO Maritime Groups, and counter piracy operations in the Indian Ocean.

Now twenty-six years on from first commissioning, the 4,800-ton vessels have received a series of upgrades over their life. The most significant has been the *Halifax* Class Modernisation/Frigate Life Extension (HCM/FELIX) programme launched in 2007. This C$4.3bn (c. US$3.3bn) project has involved a large midlife modernisation. It has included installation of an enhanced combat management system by Lockheed Martin Canada; a Thales SMART-S Mk 2 3-D radar; Saab's CEROS

The Sikorsky CH-148 Cyclone helicopter is scheduled to commence operational duties with the RCN before the end of 2018 after a protracted and difficult design and construction phase. This shows an early helicopter delivered to test and training configuration undergoing trials with the new replenishment oiler *Asterix* in January 2018. *(Royal Canadian Navy)*

The *Halifax* class frigate *Toronto* pictured in heavy Atlantic seas in January 2018. The twelve *Halifax* class frigates are now Canada's only major surface combatants and form the core of the fleet. They have recently undergone an extensive HCM/FELIX modernisation programme to allow them to serve late into the 2030s. *(Canadian Armed Forces)*

200 fire-control director; and various enhancements to electronic countermeasures and communications. All in all, the class's ability to deal with modern threats such as sea-skimming anti-ship missiles, particularly in the littoral, has been much enhanced.[9] Other improvements – notably the fitting of a new integrated platform management system – should assist reliable service until the ships start to decommission. The final upgrade was completed on schedule and to cost towards the end of 2016.

The *Halifax* class are due to be phased out as the new Canadian Surface Combatants enter service from the mid-2020s. The final vessel of the new class is expected in the late 2030s, meaning that the last *Halifax* class frigate will be decommissioned nearly fifty years after the first ship entered service.

Victoria Class Submarines: The *Victoria* class submarines began their service lives as the *Upholder* class of the British Royal Navy (RN), ultimately serving as a replacement for the *Oberon* class in both the RN and RCN. The first of class was initially commissioned by the RN in June 1990 after prob-lematic sea trials. The submarines only had a very short service within the RN and were soon laid up due to cutbacks after the end of the Cold War.

With their plans to acquire a nuclear-powered submarine fleet abandoned, the RCN looked to the acquisition of new conventional submarines. Acquisition of the *Upholder* class was identified as a preferred option in the Canadian National Defence White Paper of 1994; however, a deal was not struck with the UK until 1998. Canada paid C$896m (c. US$620m) – including simulators, training and infrastructure – for the four boats.[10]

The submarines had a troubled entry into Canadian service after at least four years being laid up. Most notably, during its delivery voyage from HMNB Clyde in Scotland in October 2004, *Chicoutimi* (the former *Upholder*) took on seawater which led to a fire in which nine members of the crew were injured, one of whom later died. It took a long time to bring the submarines into effective and reliable service, although a Victoria Class in Service Support Contract (VISSC) awarded to Babcock's Canadian subsidiary has now achieved an acceptable level of operational availability.

The *Victoria* class are referred to as Long Range Patrol Submarines in Canadian service. *Windsor* was the first of the class to commence operations beginning in June 2005. The final vessel of the class, *Chicoutimi*, entered into operational service in 2015; its commissioning being severely delayed due to both the fire damage and other defects in the vessel. The RCN identify submarines' roles as including supporting Special Operation Forces, surveillance of Canada's coasts, and even constabulary duties such as counter narcotics. The submarines have also been involved in exercises with NATO partners, in particular the United States.

As built the c. 2,500-ton vessels were armed with six 533mm (21in) torpedo tubes for British-designed heavy torpedoes. However, the boats have now received changes to the fire-control system under a 'Canadisation' programme to allow the US Mk 48 heavyweight torpedo to be used.[11] Eighteen of these torpedoes are carried as the submarines' standard weapons compliment. Canadian modifications have also seen an upgrade to the submarines' already impressive sonar suite, including the addition of the Canadian Towed Array Sonar.

The Canadian government are currently exploring the possibility of a life extension programme for the submarine fleet, which have a predicted end-of-life in the mid-2020s. The programme would look at extending the submarines service into the 2030s.

Replenishment Ship *Asterix* (Project Resolve): In 2014 the *Protecteur* class auxiliary oilers were withdrawn from service, many years before their intended replacements were to be commissioned, leaving the RCN without an at-sea resupply capability. To fill this gap the RCN initially approached other navies for temporary support. A mutual logistic support arrangement with Chile in 2015 led to the deployment of *Almirante Montt* in support of the Canadian Pacific Fleet for forty days. A similar deal with the Spanish government saw the deployment of two replenishment oilers of the Spanish Navy (*Patiño* and *Cantabria*) in support of the Canadian Atlantic Fleet for around four months during 2016.

To support replenishment operations in the medium term, the Canadian Government approved the conversion of a civilian cargo ship into an auxiliary vessel under the auspice of Project Resolve in late 2015.[12] For this purpose the MV *Asterix*, an

The *Victoria* class submarine *Windsor* pictured in December 2017. These former Royal Navy *Upholder* class boats had a troubled entry into RCN service but are now starting to demonstrate their potential. *(Canadian Armed Forces)*

RESOLVE CLASS AOR

A graphic highlighting the key capabilities of the interim auxiliary oiler *Asterix,* which is operated for the RCN by Federal Fleet Services under Project Resolve. She was delivered at the end of 2017. The programme is intended to provide the RCN with a bridge to the delayed fleet replenishment capability that will be provided by the *Protecteur* class JSS-type joint support ships in the early 2020s. *(Federal Fleet Services)*

KEY SPECIFICATIONS

Length	182.5m
Beam	25.2m
Crew	150 persons
HADR complement	350 persons
Helicopters	2 x CH-148 Cyclone
Small craft	8 craft
Cranes	2
RAS masts	4 STREAM-type
F76 Marine Diesel	10,500 m3
F44 Aviation Fuel	1,300 m3

Resolve-Class Auxiliary Oiler Replenishment Ship
Displacement: 26,000 tonnes

Halifax-Class Canadian Patrol Frigate
Displacement: 4,700 tonnes

Harry Dewolf-Class Arctic / Offshore Patrol Ship
Displacement: 6,440 tonnes

HELICOPTER DECK AND TWO HANGARS
Designed for the Cyclone CH-148, capable fo accommodating up to Chinook-size

MULTIPLE OPERATIONS ROOMS, BRIEFING AND CONFERENCE FACILITIES
For operational command and control function

SMALL CRAFT WITH LAUNCH AND RECOVERY SYSTEMS
2 x Rigid Hulled Inflatables
2 x Fast Rescue Craft
2 x Lifeboats
2 x Landing Craft

MEDICAL AND HUMANITARIAN
Large medical facilities + emergency accommodation for up to 350 passengers

VEHICLE CAPABILITIES
Vehicle bay on tween-deck for light vehicles
Mexeflote-ready for ship-to-shore operations

UNMANNED AERIAL VEHICLES
Ready for installation of Unmanned Aerial Vehicles

LCVP
2 x LCVP (Landing Craft, Vehicle and Personnel) for transfer of personnel, stores and vehicles and humanitarian operations

INTEGRATED NAVIGATION, MACHINERY AND DAMAGE CONTROL SYSTEM
Fully integrated bridge from which to control and monitor navigation, machinery and damage control systems

REPLENISHMENT AT SEA
NATO STREAM-type liquid and solid replenishment for alongside replenishment on both sides of the ship simultaneously. Four Replenishment At Sea stations in order to be fully compliant with NATO requirements (ATP-16).

SHORE CONNECTIONS
Capability to provide power and desalinated water to shore for humanitarian operations.

CONTAINERISED STORAGE AREA
A protected, environment-controlled area for the storage of containerised stores, supplies and ammunition serviced by cargo elevators for packing / unpacking while at sea

EXTRA PROPULSION SYSTEM
A retractable thruster for extra redundancy, improved maneuvering and dynamic station keeping offshore

18,200-ton container ship that was completed in 2010, was acquired by Federal Fleet Services for conversion by sister company Chantier Davie of Québec. The C$700m (c. US$540m) contract included both the supply and operation of the ship over a five-year period, with the option of further lease extensions. The aim is to bridge the gap until the new *Protecteur* class are expected to become operational.

Asterix was accepted into Canadian service in March 2018. Now displacing around 26,000 tons, the ship is fitted with four replenishment at sea (RAS) stations and can carry 10,500m³ of marine diesel and 1,300m³ of aviation fuel. She is also able to transport solid stores, ammunition and light vehi-

cles. Although unarmed, the vessel has significant capabilities for conducting humanitarian operations. This includes a large Role 2/3 hospital facility for up to 30 patients and sufficient accommodation for 200 additional persons (e.g. refugees or disaster relief personnel) over the 150 berths provided for the ship's crew. The ship is equipped with hanger facilities and landing spots to accommodate two CH-148 or Chinook helicopters and can deploy an array of small watercraft, including two LCVPs.

***Harry DeWolf* Class Arctic Offshore Patrol Vessels:**
Named after a former Chief of Naval Staff, the *Harry DeWolf* class Arctic Offshore Patrol Ships (AOPSs) are being procured to protect Canada's

Arctic waters. Five ships have been ordered from Irving Shipbuilding's Halifax Shipyard under a C$3.5bn (c. US$ 2.7bn) programme, with first steel cut in late 2015.[13]

The ships will displace c. 6,500 tons and be assigned a Polar Class 5 classification, allowing them to perform limited all-year icebreaking duties in medium, first-year ice. Their main armament is limited to a single BAE Systems Mk 38 25mm cannon, although offensive capabilities are supplemented by the inclusion of a hanger able to house a CH-148 helicopter. Other features include a vehicle bay, and small multi-role boats. The ships also have a 20-ton crane for loading of shipping containers and other equipment.

National Défense
Defence nationale

ROYAL CANADIAN
NAVY

FACT SHEET

HARRY DEWOLF-CLASS ARCTIC/OFFSHORE PATROL SHIP

The Arctic/Offshore Patrol Ship (AOPS) project will deliver six ice-capable ships, designated as the Harry DeWolf Class, after Canadian wartime naval hero Vice-Admiral Harry DeWolf. The AOPS will be capable of:

- armed sea-borne surveillance of Canada's waters, including the Arctic
- providing government situational awareness of activities and events in these regions
- cooperating with other partners in the Canadian Armed Forces and other government departments to assert and enforce Canadian sovereignty, when and where necessary.

Construction of the first AOPS will begin in September 2015, with HMCS *Harry DeWolf* scheduled for delivery in 2018.

AOPS SPECIFICATIONS:

Length:	103 metres
Beam:	19 metres
Complement:	65

Halifax-class Canadian Patrol Frigate
Displacement: 4,770 tonnes

Harry DeWolf-class Arctic/Offshore Patrol Ship
Displacement: 6,440 tonnes

Kingston-class Maritime Coastal Defence Vessel
Displacement: 970 tonnes

To scale

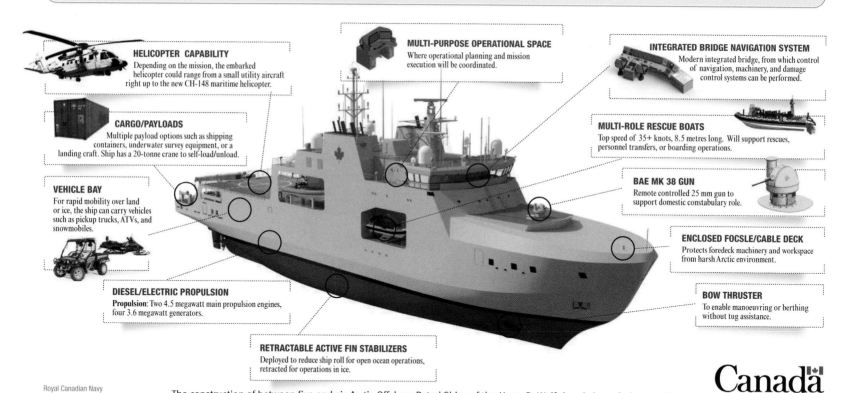

HELICOPTER CAPABILITY
Depending on the mission, the embarked helicopter could range from a small utility aircraft right up to the new CH-148 maritime helicopter.

MULTI-PURPOSE OPERATIONAL SPACE
Where operational planning and mission execution will be coordinated.

INTEGRATED BRIDGE NAVIGATION SYSTEM
Modern integrated bridge, from which control of navigation, machinery, and damage control systems can be performed.

CARGO/PAYLOADS
Multiple payload options such as shipping containers, underwater survey equipment, or a landing craft. Ship has a 20-tonne crane to self-load/unload.

MULTI-ROLE RESCUE BOATS
Top speed of 35+ knots, 8.5 metres long. Will support rescues, personnel transfers, or boarding operations.

VEHICLE BAY
For rapid mobility over land or ice, the ship can carry vehicles such as pickup trucks, ATVs, and snowmobiles.

BAE MK 38 GUN
Remote controlled 25 mm gun to support domestic constabulary role.

ENCLOSED FOCSLE/CABLE DECK
Protects foredeck machinery and workspace from harsh Arctic environment.

DIESEL/ELECTRIC PROPULSION
Propulsion: Two 4.5 megawatt main propulsion engines, four 3.6 megawatt generators.

BOW THRUSTER
To enable manoeuvring or berthing without tug assistance.

RETRACTABLE ACTIVE FIN STABILIZERS
Deployed to reduce ship roll for open ocean operations, retracted for operations in ice.

Royal Canadian Navy
Public Affairs – January 2015
www.forces.gc.ca

Canadä

The construction of between five and six Arctic Offshore Patrol Ships of the *Harry DeWolf* class is intended to provide the CAF with a much more effective ability to police Canada's Arctic waters. The ships will be lightly armed but able to operate a range of equipment, including vehicles, small boats and a helicopter. *(Canadian Armed Forces)*

Delivery of *Harry DeWolf* is expected before the end of 2018, with all the class scheduled for delivery by 2022. Service life is estimated at twenty-five years.

Small Surface Units: The RCN operates a number of smaller surface vessels and auxiliaries to fulfil a number of secondary tasks, such as coastal patrol and training. The most numerous are the twelve 970-ton *Kingston* class maritime coastal defence vessels, multi-role ships that were originally intended to provide a limited minesweeping capability. Advances in mine warfare since the first ship commissioned in 1996 have made this ability largely obsolete but they can conduct route survey functions and could well be suitable for deploying the new generation of autonomous mine countermeasures systems that are now entering service. Up to three 20ft (6m) ISO containers with mission-specific payloads can be shipped. At present, their primary role is to patrol the Canadian coastline and sovereign waters and they are equipped with one 40mm Bofors cannon and two 12.7mm machine guns for this task. Primarily crewed by Naval

The *Kingston* class coastal defence vessels were initially purchased to provide a modest minesweeping capability but are now focused on littoral patrol and training tasks. Their main armament is a 40mm Bofors gun which is not always shipped. These pictures shoe *Kingston* in July 2016 and *Yellowknife* in August of the previous year. *(Marc Piché)*

Reservists, the class also has an important training role. Replacement of the class is mentioned neither in the NSS nor the later 2017 defence policy paper and must therefore be regarded as a matter of conjecture.

The RCN operate another class of patrol vessels, the 210-ton *Orca* class, which are largely used as training tenders. The eight ships entered service from 2006 to 2008 and provide the at-sea portion of naval officer training, as well as experience at sea for non-commissioned officers and for the Royal Canadian Sea Cadets. While not normally armed, the vessels can be fitted with a 12.7mm machine gun. Indeed, three were temporarily armed in this way to provide port security for the 2010 Winter Olympics.

Also acting in the training role is *Oriole*, which is the RCN's sail training ship. Receiving its commission in 1952, *Oriole* is currently the oldest commissioned vessel in the navy.

Finally, in common with most other navies, the RCN operates a variety of auxiliary support ships and harbour craft, including torpedo and sound-ranging vessels, diving tenders, fireboats and tugs.

FUTURE PROCUREMENT STRATEGY

The RCN is currently in the process of undertaking a major fleet renewal that will run into the 2040s. The planned series of procurements is in part driven by the ageing surface fleet and also by the desire for Canada to rebuild a sovereign naval ship-building capacity, as outlined in the NSS. First announced in June 2010, the strategy covered what was then estimated at over C$35bn (c. US$27bn) of future construction projects for the RCN and CCG. Its overriding aim was to establish a stable and sustainable maritime industry by channelling construction of larger vessels – those displacing over 1,000 tons – through two pre-selected yards. In October 2011 Irving Shipbuilding was selected to produce the combat vessels outlined in the strategy, with Seaspan Marine Corp of Vancouver tasked with building the non-combat vessels. Construction of smaller vessels was to be awarded through competitive tender to other Canadian yards. No reference was made to submarine construction in the NSS. This possibly reflected the expected longevity of the existing boats, as well as the challenges associated with undertaking construction of any eventual *Victoria* class replacement in a domestic yard.

The package of work awarded to Irving relating to future combatants is by far the more valuable of the two, being calculated at c. C$25bn when the selection was announced. At that stage it was expected to cover six *Harry de Wolff* class AOPSs and fifteen Canadian Surface Combatants. The non-combatant budget, roughly C$8 billion, included the two new vessels of the *Protecteur* class, and fifteen vessels of various types for the CCG. It has subsequently become apparent that the overall budget for the NSS was significantly under-estimated, with spending of between C$56bn and C$60bn now likely for the fifteen surface combatants alone.

Details of the two RCN projects on which construction is not yet underway are as follows:

Canadian Surface Combatant: By far the largest single component of the NSS, the Canadian Surface Combatant (previously known as the Single Class Surface Combatant) project will be responsible for procuring fifteen vessels to replace the now-retired *Iroquois* class destroyers and the *Halifax* class frigates. Like many Canadian naval projects, the programme has had a prolonged gestation period and increased considerably in cost.

In June 2016 it was announced that an off-the-shelf design would be purchased to reduce potential project risk and delay, albeit adapted for Canadian-specific systems. A significant number of international firms were invited to submit proposals, although it appears that only three designs were submitted when the process closed towards the end of 2017, viz.

■ **The British Type 26 Global Combat ship:** Submitted by Canada's Combat Ship Team led by Lockheed Martin Canada and including the Type 26's designer BAE Systems.
■ **The Dutch LCF *De Zeven Provinciën* class air-**

defence frigate: Submitted by Alion Canada as part of a team that includes the Dutch-based Damen shipbuilding group.

■ **The Spanish F-105 variant of the *Álvaro de Bazán* class air-defence frigate:** Submitted by Spanish shipbuilder Navantia as part of a consortium including Saab Australia and a number of Canadian companies.

A fourth, opportunistic proposal of the Franco-Italian FREMM design submitted outside the formal competition was rejected for non-compliance with the selection process in spite of claims it might cost only around half the expected programme cost.

Of the three designs known to be under consideration only the Type 26 offers a true replacement of the anti-submarine warfare capabilities offered by the *Halifax* class. The other two proposals are based on anti-air warfare designs that lack the focus on acoustic stealth built into the ASW-orientated Type 26's hull. However, the maturity of the designs will also be an important consideration for the Canadian Government and here the 'paper' Type 26 suffers

against the proven nature of its two competitors. It should also be noted a modified variant of the Spanish F-105 was a strong if ultimately unsuccessful contender for Australia's similar ASW-optimised future frigate programme. A decision on which ship to choose should be made before the end of 2018.

***Protecteur* Class Joint Support Ships:** The *Protecteur* class JSS joint support ships are intended to replace the retired auxiliary replenishment oilers of the same name. The project was initially announced in 2004. It was to see the acquisition of three vessels capable of performing the refuelling and resupply tasks of the preceding class as well as providing sealift and some amphibious support. The first ship was due to enter into service by 2012. Lack of money forced these plans to be recast and, by the time the NSS was announced in 2010, the requirement had dropped to two ships (with an option for a third) focused on the replenishment role. Two designs – the German Type 702 *Berlin* class and Spain's *Cantabria* – were shortlisted for the revised requirement, with the German proposal being

selected in June 2013. Assembly is expected to commence in the summer of 2018 following an announcement by the Canadian Government and Seaspan in May. However, previous delivery schedules of 2021 and 2022 look ambitious in the face of ongoing delays.[14]

The new *Protecteur* class ships have distinct advantages over the vessels that they replace, including a double hull that allows them to freely operate in international waters. Assuming similar characteristics to their German predecessors, they should be able to carry around 10,000 tons of liquid stores and 600 tons of other cargo. Loading and off-loading of containerised cargo will be facilitated by two 24-ton capacity cranes and there will probably be two beam RAS positions. The class will be equipped with command facilities and a hangar for two CH-148 helicopters, whilst a containerised medical centre based on the German modular MERZ concept is also likely to be provided. Some reports suggest the vessels will also have an 'ice-edge' capability so that they can access the Nanisivik Naval Facility in the summer months.

The most significant planned RCN procurement programme is that for the Canadian Surface Combatant, which involves the delivery of fifteen ships from the mid-2020s onwards. A 'Canadianised' variant of the British Type 26 Global Combat Ship is regarded as a key contender for the project. *(BAE Systems)*

The Canadian Surface Combatant has also drawn interest from Dutch and Spanish naval shipbuilders; the latter are offering a variant of the F-105 frigate *Cristóbal Colón* that formed the last, somewhat improved member of the *Álvaro de Bazán class*. The Spanish ship is pictured alongside *Montréal* in October 2017. The growth in the size of frigates from the 1990s-era Canadian frigate is noteworthy. *(Royal Canadian Navy)*

CONCLUSION

Until very recently the RCN was a well-equipped naval force capable of multi-region power projection. Slow progress in renewing the aging fleet – requiring decommissioning of key vessels such as the *Iroquois* class destroyers and *Protecteur* class oilers without immediate replacement – has taken its toll, severely limiting the RCN's ability to project power globally. Whilst much of the remaining fleet has – or will be – upgraded to extend its useful life, the fact that current plans suggest the *Halifax* class will remain in service into its fifth decade highlight the extent of the problem. The renewed focus on the Arctic is an added complication that will demand further resources.

The additional funding promised by the recent defence policy statement – *Strong, Secure, Engaged* – supported by the NSS offers the hope that replacement vessels will now be forthcoming. The success of the NSS procurement strategy will be essential if the fleet is to be retained at its current strength, let alone restore lost capabilities. The programme is too early in its life to draw definitive conclusions. However, the price of rebuilding a domestic naval shipbuilding sector does look expensive. Much still needs to be done if the RCN is to achieve its ambition of re-establishing a blue water navy with global reach.

The *Halifax* class frigate *Vancouver* pictured on 10 April 2018. The RCN has suffered badly from procurement delays and the *Halifax* class will be in its fifth decade of service by the time a replacement programme is completed. *(Royal Canadian Navy)*

Notes

1. A much more detailed historical review of the Royal Canadian Navy can be found in the Canadian Government's online history *The Naval Service of Canada 1910-2010* at: canada.ca/en/navy/services/history/naval-service-1910-2010.html. Commander Tony German's *The Sea is at Our Gates* (Toronto: McClelland & Stewart Inc., 1990) is another valuable resource.

2. NORAD – originally the North America Air Defense Command, now the North American Aerospace Defense Command – was established in 1957 as a joint US/Canadian structure to provide an integrated early warning and air defence organisation for the protection of North America from, in effect, Soviet attack.

3. Canada did lease the MV *Wloclawek* for four years between 2007 and 2011 to provide some measure of sealift capability, but reports indicate that it was underutilised during that time. This may have influenced the focus on replenishment adopted in the current JSS joint support ship programme.

4. The replenishment-at-sea deficiency has been partly remedied by the conversion of the commercial vessel MV *Asterix* to provide an interim refuelling capability.

5. See *Strong, Secure, Engaged: Canada's Defence Policy* (Ottawa: Department of National Defence, 2017) at: dgpaapp.forces.gc.ca/en/canada-defence-policy/docs/canada-defence-policy-report.pdf

6. See *Royal Canadian Navy Strategic Plan 2017-2022* (Ottawa: Department of National Defence, 2017) at: navy-marine.forces.gc.ca/assets/NAVY_Internet/docs/en/analysis/rcn_strategicplan_2017-2022_en-s.pdf

7. The Canadian military has been referred to as both the Canadian Forces and the Canadian Armed Forces since unification. The latter term currently has prominence.

8. Source Royal Canadian Navy website – www.navy-marine.forces.gc.ca/en/about/index.page – updated as of January 2016.

9. Evolved Sea Sparrow and Phalanx upgrades have also been completed under separate programmes.

10. The C$896m procurement cost was set out in a CAF background briefing to the submarine acquisition published in June 2008. Various figures have been quoted with respect to the overall submarine programme cost, which will have been much higher once the expense of bringing the boats into a fully operational state is taken into account.

11. The RCN was unwilling to acquire British torpedoes as it already held the US Mk 48 in its inventory. However, this necessitated modifications to fire-control and discharge systems to use the American weapon. Further expenditure was required to bring the stock of Mk 48 Mod 4 torpedoes to the latest Mod 7 standard.

12. Conversion of a second vessel was also proposed, but this option has been rejected by the Canadian Government.

13. The contract includes provision for a sixth ship if it can be constructed within the agreed budget.

14. The two ships were originally to be named *Queenston* and *Châteauguay* but these were changed to *Protecteur* and *Preserver* in September 2017 to commemorate the vessels they replaced. Some reports suggest the original RCN requirement was for four JSS type ships.

2.1B Fleet Review

Author: **Guy Toremans**

THE PERUVIAN NAVY

Making Great Strides

The Peruvian Navy's newly-modernised *Lupo* class frigate *Bolognesi* pictured on 8 October 2015 at ceremonies commemorating the 194th anniversary of the navy's establishment. The navy has benefitted from significant investment programmes recently but much needs to be done to complete the modernisation process. *(Peruvian Ministry of Defence)*

Peru has one of the oldest naval forces of South America's 'Big Four' navies: Argentina, Brazil, Chile and Peru. The Peruvian Navy – the *Mariña de Guerra del Perú* (MGP) – was founded on 8 October 1821 by General José de San Martín with the hoisting of the national ensign onboard the schooner *Sacramento*. On this date the MGP also commemorates the Battle of Angamos (1879) in which its greatest naval hero, Admiral Miguel Grau Seminario, was killed onboard the ironclad BAP *Huáscar*.[1]

The Peruvian Navy operates over an immense maritime area. Peru has a coastline of some 2,900km along the Pacific Ocean and its Exclusive Economic Zone (EEZ) covers c. 900,000km^2. Moreover, search and rescue responsibilities extend deep into the Pacific, with Peru having responsibility for navigation and meteorological warnings over the vast NAVAREA XVI. Additional burdens are placed by the need to police the waters of a vast Amazonian region that covers nearly 785,000km^2 (sixty-one percent of Peru's land mass), as well as 4,995km^2 of the 8,300km^2 landlocked Lake Titicaca. Traditional naval roles are largely defined by national economic interests, the most critical being the export and import trade (eighty percent of which moves by ship) and the country's fishing industry. However, heightened levels of organised crime – particularly the use of the maritime domain for smuggling illegal drugs and other illicit traffic – have considerably increased the service's commitments.

This broad span of multifaceted maritime interests means that the MGP requires a wide spectrum of capabilities; an asset designed for operating in one particular environment may not be so well-suited to operating in another. In order to meet its responsibilities, a major programme of fleet recapitalisation commenced in December 2012 with a keel-laying ceremony for the sail training vessel *Unión* at the Peruvian state-run shipyard, *Servicios Industriales de la Marinha* (SIMA), in Callao. As of mid-2018, some twenty new vessels of various types and sizes had been inducted into the fleet under a programme initiated with the support of former President Ollanta Humala and continued by subsequent administrations. However, overall Peruvian defence expenditure has dropped from a post-Millennial peak of c. US$3.3bn equivalent in 2015 and this could well have a future impact.[2] It is understood that the MGP has received in the region of between twenty and twenty-five percent of total defence spending in recent years.

ORGANISATION

Headed by the Commander General, since 26 December 2016 Admiral Gonzalo Nicolás Ríos Polastri, the MGP is organised into three major functional commands:

- **The Pacific Command**: Headquartered in Callao and comprising the Surface Force, the Submarine Force, Naval Aviation and Naval Infantry, as well as the Special Operations Force.
- **The Amazon Command**: Based in Iquitos, responsible for policing the region's extensive inland rivers.
- **The Coast Guard Command**: Also headquartered in Callao, responsible for constabulary, pollution control and search and rescue operations.

There are also five geographically-based naval zones, which are consistent with similar zones established by the Peruvian Army and Air Force. Three – the 1st Naval Zone (based in Piura), 2nd Naval Zone (Callao) and 3rd Naval Zone (Arequipa) – are under the Pacific Command; two – the 4th Naval Zone (based at Pucallpa) and the 5th (Iquitos) – fall under the Amazon Command's jurisdiction. The Coast Guard Command operates in all five zones.

The major naval base is located in Callao and includes most of the navy's training installations. Smaller bases are situated at Chimbote, Mollendo, Paita and Iquitos; and there are naval stations at El Estrecho, Pichari and Pucallpa, with a further station in Puno on Lake Titicaca. The Naval Academy - the *Escuela Naval del Perú* – is located in La Punta near Callao.

Total numbers of naval personnel – including

The Peruvian Navy's Pacific Command is responsible for the fleet's seagoing warships and submarines. This July 2017 picture shows the frigate *Mariátegui*, one of the Command's major units. Commissioned in 1986, she was one of the first modern frigates to be built in a Peruvian shipyard. *(Guy Toremans)*

In addition to having responsibilities for the security of Peru's Pacific coastline, the Peruvian Navy also maintains a substantial presence across the inland rivers of the country's Amazonian basin. This picture shows naval personnel operating a River Runner fast assault craft. *(Guy Toremans)*

civilians and those assigned to the coast guard – are believed to be approaching 30,000, of which commissioned officers account for c. 2,100. Female personnel amount to around fifteen percent of the total. The budget for personnel training has increased substantially in recent years and increasing the proficiency of both officers and ratings is an important area of focus. There are plans to increase the numbers of both the coast guard and naval infantry over the next decade.

THE PACIFIC COMMAND: SURFACE FLEET

Current MGP force levels are summarised in Table 2.1B.1. As of mid-2018, the surface fleet was made up of thirteen major combatants and additional amphibious vessels, auxiliaries and smaller vessels.

Surface Combatants: The navy's front-line force of surface combatants comprises three *Carvajal* class and four *Aguirre* class frigates. They are all based on the Italian *Lupo* design. The *Carvajal* class units were inducted into the fleet between 1979 and 1987. *Villavisencio*, built in Italy, was commissioned in June 1979 and the two other units were built at SIMA. *Montero* (now *Almirante Grau*) became the navy's first modern frigate to be constructed by SIMA. Laid down in October 1978 and launched on 8 October 1982, the frigate joined the fleet on 25 July 1984. She was followed by *Mariátegui*, delivered in 1987.[3] The MGP subsequently took delivery of the four *Aguirre* class – originally Italian Navy *Lupos* acquired second-hand – between 2004 and 2006. They are named *Aguirre, Bolognesi, Palacios* and *Quiñones*.

The MGP has been undertaking a modernisation programme for its frigate force pending the acquisition of new warships. This is being implemented to two different standards. The most extensive involves installation of the indigenously-developed Varayoc combat management system (CMS) and MAGE QHAWAX Mk1 ESM suite in place of existing systems. The old RAN-10S (SPS-774) radar is replaced by a Kronos 3D multi-purpose array. Other upgrades include retrofitting Exocet MM40 surface-

Table 2.1B.1: PERUVIAN NAVY – PRINCIPAL UNITS AS AT MID-2018

TYPE	CLASS	NO.	YEAR[1]	TONNAGE	DIMENSIONS	PROPULSION	PRINCIPAL ARMAMENT[2]
1. PACIFIC COMMAND							
Submarines (6)							
Submarine (SSK)	**ISLAY** (T 209/1100)	2	1974	1,300 tons	56m x 6m x 6m	DE, 21+ knots	8 x 533mm torpedo tubes, 14 torpedoes
Class: *Islay* (SS-35), *Arica* (SS-36).							
Submarine (SSK)	**ANGAMOS** (T 209/1200)	4	1980	1,300 tons	56m x 6m x 6m	DE, 21+ knots	8 x 533mm torpedo tubes, 14 torpedoes
Class: *Angamos* (SS-31), *Antofagasta* (SS-32), *Pisagua* (SS-33), *Chipana* (SS34).							
Fleet Escorts (7)							
Frigate (FFG)	**AGUIRRE** (LUPO)	4	1977	2,600 tons	114m x 11m x 4m	CODOG, 34 knots	8 x SAM, 8 x SSM, 1 x 127mm gun, 2 x twin 40mm, 6 x TT, 1 x helicopter
Class: *Aguirre* (FM-55)[3], *Palacios* (FM-56), *Bolognesi* (FM-57),[3] *Quiñones* (FM-58).							
Frigate (FFG)	**CARVAJAL** (LUPO)	3	1979	2,600 tons	114m x 11m x 4m	CODOG, 34 knots	8 x SAM, 8 x SSM, 1 x 127mm gun, 2 x twin 40mm, 6 x TT, 1 x helicopter
Class: *Villavisencio* (FM-52), *Almirante Grau* (FM-53), *Mariátegui* (FM-54)							
Corvettes/Fast Attack Craft (6)							
Missile Corvettes (FAC)	**VELARDE** (PR-72P)	6	1980	570 tons	64m x 8m x 3m	Diesel, 37 knots	4 x SSM, 1 x 76mm gun, 1 x twin 40mm
Class: *Velarde* (CM-21), *Santillana* (CM-22), *De Los Heros* (CM-23), *Herrera* (CM-24), *Larrea* (CM-25), *Sánchez Carrión* (CM-26)							
Amphibious Ships (3+1)							
Amp. Transport Dock (LSD)	**PISCO**	1+1	2018	11,400 tons	122m x 22m x 5m	Diesel, 16 knots	2 x 30mm, MGs, 1 x helicopter
Class: *Pisco* (AMP-156). A further member of the class, *Paita* (AMP-157) is under construction.							
Tank Landing Ship (LST)	**TERREBONNE PARISH**	2	1953	5,800 tons	117m x 17m x 5m	Diesel, 15 knots	5 x 40mm guns
Class: *Callao* (DT-143), *Eten* (DT-144)							
Fleet Auxiliaries (1)							
Replenishment Oiler (AOR)	**AMSTERDAM**	1	1995	17,000 tons	166m x 22m x 8m	Diesel, 21 knots	2 x 30mm CIWS, MGs
Class: *Tacna* (ARL-158)							

There are also two *Bayóvar* class tankers and three small harbour tankers in the replenishment fleet.

Other Pacific Command assets include the oceanographic research vessel *Carrasco* (BOP-171) and a number of smaller research and survey ships. There also two sail training ships – including the new *Unión* – and around eight tugs, including the new diving support and salvage tug *Morales* (RAS-180). These are supplemented by three floating docks and a number of other harbour and auxiliary craft.

to-surface missiles and Rheinmetall Multi Ammunition Softkill Systems (MASS), as well as upgrades to the main 127mm gun and its fire-control system. As of mid-2018, *Aguirre* and *Bolognesi* had completed this modernisation package and returned to operational service. *Palacios* and *Quinones* are also due to receive the upgrade. Modernisation of the remaining ships will be less extensive and will probably only encompass *Mariátegui* and *Montero*. The latter was renamed *Almirante Grau* and became fleet flagship on 26 September following the decommissioning of the former cruiser of the same name after sixty-four years of service under two flags.[4]

Further details of the eventual frigate replacement programme were revealed by Admiral Gonzalo Nicolás Ríos Polastri at the end of 2017. Six new vessels will be procured over the 2021–5 timeframe. Two of these will be built abroad and the remaining four by SIMA in Callao. The baseline requirements for these new units call for platforms in the 3,500/5,000-ton range with state-of-the-art, yet proven, sensor and weapon systems that must be compatible with the navy's indigenously-developed Varayoc CMS. The ships should be capable of embarking a range of mission-specific modules and a medium-sized helicopter in addition to armament comprising surface-to-surface and surface-to-air missiles, anti-submarine torpedo tubes and a medium-calibre gun.

The other major surface combatants are the six 625-ton *Velarde*-class (French PR-72P type) missile corvettes. They were built at the SFCN Villeneuve la Garenne Shipyard in France.[5] Completed between 1980 and 1981, these units are equipped with four MM38 Exocet missiles, an 76mm/62 OTO Melara compact gun, a twin 40mm/70 Breda and two 12.7mm machine guns. Three – *Santillana*, *Herrera* and *Sánchez Carrión* – were re-engined in 2000. However, plans to upgrade the other three appear to have been abandoned.

Amphibious Vessels: One of the most important projects in the MGP's modernisation roadmap is the procurement of an amphibious capability centred on

TYPE	CLASS	NO.	YEAR[1]	TONNAGE	DIMENSIONS	PROPULSION	PRINCIPAL ARMAMENT[2]
2. AMAZON COMMAND							
River Gunboats (6)							
Gunboat (PGR)	LORETO	2	1935	300 tons	44m x 7m x 1m	Diesel, 12 knots	2 x 76mm guns, 4 x 40mm guns, MGs
Class: *Loreto* (CF-12), *Amazonas* (CF-11)							
Gunboat (PGR)	MARAÑON	2	1951	370 tons	47m x 10m x 1m	Diesel, 12 knots	2 x 76mm guns, 3 x 40mm guns, MGs
Class: *Marañon* (CF-13), *Ucayali* (CF-14)							
Gunboat (PGR)	CLAVERO	2	2012	350 tons	48m x 11m x 1m	Diesel, 17 knots	Light weapons (armament of 2 ships varies)
Class: *Clavero* (CF-15), *Castilla* (CF-16)							
Hovercraft (7)							
Hovercraft	Griffon 200TD	7	2009	7 tons	12m x 6m x 0m	Diesel, 35 knots	1 x MG
Class: UIF-101 to UIF-107							

Other Amazon Command vessels include four riverine hospital ships and the initial *Río Napa* class river supply craft. There are large numbers of smaller riverine patrol craft, many operated by the Coast Guard

TYPE	CLASS	NO.	YEAR[1]	TONNAGE	DIMENSIONS	PROPULSION	PRINCIPAL ARMAMENT[2]
3. COAST GUARD							
Offshore Patrol Vessels (2)							
Offshore PV (OPV)	CARVAJAL (LUPO)	1	1979	2,400 tons	114m x 11m x 4m	CODOG, 34 knots	1 x 127mm gun, 2 x twin 40mm, 1 x helicopter
Class: *Guardamarina San Martin* (PO-201)							
Offshore PV (OPV)	PO HANG	1	1984	1,200 tons	88m x 10m x 3m	CODOG, 32 knots	1 x 76mm gun, 2 x twin 30mm guns
Class: *Ferre* (PM-211)							
Coastal Patrol Vessels (10 +2)							
Coastal Patrol Vessel (CPV)	RÍO PATIVILCA	4+2	2016	470 tons	55m x 9m x 2m	Diesel, 22 knots	1 x 30mm gun, 2 x MGs
Class: *Río Pativilca* (PM-204), *Río Cañete* (PM-205), *Río Piura* (PM-206), *Río Quilca* (PM-207).							

The *Río Pativilca* class are likely to replace the five remaining *Río Nepeña* class coastal patrol vessels and the sole PGM-71 class patrol vessel *Río Chira*.
There are numerous small inshore and riverine patrol vessels of various classes, all of less than 20 tons displacement.

Notes
1 Date relates to the date the first ship of the class entered naval service, not necessarily with the MGP.
2 Second number refers to ships of the type/class currently under construction or ordered.
3 Modernised with upgraded radar and electronics

two multi-purpose LPD-type amphibious transport docks (*buques multipropósitos*). Peru is located in an area of the world prone to natural disasters and often restricted by limited transportation infrastructure. As such, the navy's ability to provide sealift for timely and effective assistance and relief has been recognised as being of strategic importance. The new ships are based on the Indonesian Navy's *Makassar* design but incorporate several Peruvian specific features. On 6 June 2018, the MGP took delivery of the first member of the class – *Pisco*. Her keel was laid by SIMA on 12 July 2013 and she was launched on 25 April 2017. At 122m in length and displacing 11,400 tons at full load, she is amongst the navy's largest ships.

Powered by a twin-shaft diesel plant, *Pisco* has a maximum speed of c. 16 knots and an impressive endurance at economical speed of 14,000 nautical miles. She is equipped with a strengthened vehicle deck and access ramps to allow the embarkation of vehicles weighing up to 40 tons. These could, for example, include the LAV II amphibious armoured vehicles recently acquired by the Naval Infantry. Other options include artillery, tanks or heavy trucks. The c. 1,000m² flight deck can operate all types of helicopters in service with Peru's armed forces, with landing spots for two medium-sized

rotorcraft. There is also a hangar capable of supporting one medium-sized helicopter. A stern well-dock can accommodate two 23m LCU-type utility landing craft and up to four smaller personnel landing craft or rigid inflatable boats (RHIBs) can be carried on davits. There is sufficient accommodation to house an embarked force of c. 450 troops in addition to the basic crew. Option loads could include disaster relief supplies and/or a modular hospital. She is, however, only lightly armed.

In October 2017, former Peruvian President Pedro Pablo Kuczynski confirmed the construction of the second member of the class, *Paita*. Her keel was laid on 14 December 2017 and she is expected to join the fleet in 2020

Prior to *Pisco*'s delivery, amphibious forces were limited to a pair of 1950s-vintage former US Navy *Terrebonne Parish* (LST-1156) tank landing ships. They are the survivors of four units transferred in the mid-1980s. It would seem likely these will be retired on completion of the new ships. The MGP is, however, interested in the Colombian *Buque de Apoyo Logístico y Cabotaje* (BAL-C) type logistic support landing craft. Delegations have apparently visited the COTECMAR yard in Cartagena on two occasions since the end of 2017 to inspect the design. These 575-ton ships are some 49m long and

can embark up to 210 tons of cargo or ten TEU containers. If the plan proceeds, it seems likely an initial pair of vessels would be built by COTECMAR and two more by SIMA.

Replenishment Ships: For the present, the fleet's logistic support component is focused on the 17,000-ton fast combat support ship *Tacna*. She is the former HNLMS *Amsterdam*, acquired from the Royal Netherlands Navy in July 2014 and delivered on 4 December of that year. *Tacna* is to receive the indigenous Varayoc CMS, a Mage QHAWAX ESM suite and four EO-equipped remotely controlled guns. Other support units comprise two former Russian oil tankers – *Bayóvar* and *Zorritos* – purchased in December 2006 and re-commissioned into the MGP in 2007; and the three 1,400-ton harbour tankers acquired from the US Navy between 1975 and 1985.

Other Vessels: In addition to the vessels already described, the MGP also operates a number of other research vessels, training ships tugs and other auxiliaries. Of these, two major recent acquisitions warrant special mention.

One is *Carrasco*, one of the most advanced polar oceanographic research vessels afloat. Ordered from Spanish shipyard Construcciones Navales P Freire in Vigo in 2014, the vessel was ordered to support Peru's research activities in Antarctica. The ship undertook her maiden deployment to the Peruvian Machu Picchu Research Station on King George Island in December 2017. She returned home in March 2018. Displacing c. 5,000 tons, she is equipped with research laboratories and a number of submersible vehicles and can accommodate up to sixty scientists in addition to her fifty-strong crew. She has a Polar Class 7 classification, permitting summer and autumn operation in first-year ice.

A very different type of vessel and symbolic of Peru's maritime heritage is the four-masted barque *Unión*. Built by SIMA with the assistance of Spain's CYPSA and Navantia, she was commissioned on 27 January 2016. With a length of c. 115m, and displacing c. 3,500 tons, she is the largest sail training ship in Latin America. Since her commissioning, *Unión* has already deployed on three training cruises: a three-month maiden deployment to the Caribbean in 2016, a seven-month deployment to the United States and Europe in 2017 and the four-month Velas LatinoAmerica in 2018.

One of the most important projects set out in the Peruvian Navy's current modernisation plans is the procurement of two indigenously-built multi-purpose amphibious landing dock ships based on the Indonesian Navy's *Makassar* class. Seen here on sea trials, the first of class, *Pisco*, was delivered in June 2018. (*Peruvian Navy*)

THE PACIFIC COMMAND: SUBMARINES

The Peruvian Navy is a pioneer of submarine operations in Latin America. The history of the submarine service can be traced back to 1879 when the engineer Juan Carlos Federico Blume Othon built the submarine *Toro*. The outbreak of the War of the Pacific (1879–84) saw the *Toro* used operationally in an attempted attack on Chilean warships.[6] Though the targets moved out of range the submersible was a technological success, achieving a speed of 4 knots at a depth of some 3m. After this false start, the establishment of a permanent submarine force got under way in August 1911 with the acquisition of two French Laubeuf-type submarines, named *Ferre* and *Palacios*.

Today the submarine force is made up of two *Islay* class (Type 209/1100) boats – *Islay* and *Arica* – ordered from HDW in 1969 and commissioned between 1974 and 1975; and four *Angamos* class (Type 209/1200) submarines ordered in 1976 and 1977. These latter boats – *Angamos, Antofagasta, Pisagua* and *Chipana* – joined the fleet between 1980 and 1983. Their fins and masts were extended compared with the first pair better to cope with the wave size in the Pacific. Primary tasks include sea control, protection of the sea lines of communication (SLOC), support for Special Forces operations, and participation in multinational exercises. Intelligence collection and reconnaissance – often to counter drug running and other illicit operations – has also become increasingly important.

Despite their age the submarines are in good condition. In 2017, a complex midlife update of the four *Angamos* class boats commenced at SIMA with the technical support of Germany's ThyssenKrupp Marine Systems (TKMS). The update includes overhaul of the submarines' MTU diesel engines and replacement of their batteries. There will also be upgrades to their combat, communications and fire-control systems, the last-mentioned reportedly to allow use of the AEG SUT 264 heavyweight torpedo and surface-to-surface missiles. Sensor upgrades will include installation of a Hensoldt SERO 250 optronic mast, whilst an

A symbol of Peru's maritime tradition is the four-masted barque *Unión*, built by the Peruvian state-run shipyard SIMA in cooperation with Spanish companies Cypsa and Navantia. With a length of 113.75m and displacing 3,500 tons she is the largest sail training ship in Latin America. *(Guy Toremans)*

Based on the ST 344 Skipsteknisk design, the newly-completed *Carrasco* is similar to the UK Natural Environment Research Council's (NERC's) research vessel *Discovery*. Both ships were built by the Freire yard in Spain. Delivered in 2017, she is intended for service in the Antarctic and is one of the most advanced oceanographic research vessels afloat. *(Peruvian Navy)*

The *Angamos* class (Type 209/1200) submarine *Antofagasta* pictured in September 2014. The four boats in the class are currently commencing a major mid-life modernization programme. *(Guy Toremans)*

Sea King helicopters are operated in anti-submarine, anti-surface and utility search and rescue operations by the Pacific Command's Naval Air Squadron 22. It is believed that around six of these veteran aircraft remain in service – five are seen here. *(Peruvian Ministry of Defence)*

Elbit Timnex II ESM suite has also been specified. The first submarine to enter the programme, *Chipana*, was placed on SIMA's new syncrolift on 11 December 2017 prior to having her hull parted for work to begin. She is expected to rejoin the fleet in 2021. The three other boats should have been upgraded by the middle of the decade. The aim is to keep the quartet operational for another decade pending replacement by new boats. The older pair – modernised under an earlier programme – seem likely to be retired once their upgraded sisters rejoin the fleet.

THE PACIFIC COMMAND: NAVAL AVIATION

The Naval Aviation Force (*Faenza de Aviación Naval*) is stationed at Jorge Chavez International Airport, Callao, and has a training base in San Juan de Marcona. Among the tasks performed by its current assets are maritime patrol and interdiction operations; search and rescue; joint operations with the Naval Infantry and other personnel and cargo transportation missions. Its helicopters are also capable of wartime anti-surface and anti-submarine operations. There are currently over thirty front-line fixed wing and rotary aircraft – supported by a number of training assets – operated by the following squadrons:[7]

- **Naval Air Squadron 11:** The main maritime surveillance squadron, this comprises four Fokker 60 and two Fokker 50 aircraft, as well as five Beechcraft King Air B200s. The squadron also undertakes aeromedical evacuation and transportation roles.
- **Naval Air Squadron 21:** An anti-submarine and anti-surface warfare helicopter squadron, it operates five SH-2G Super Seasprite helicopters acquired from the Royal New Zealand Air Force. They received radar, sonar and communications upgrades before entering MGP service. There are also five Agusta-Bell AB212 anti-submarine and three Bell 206B helicopters, the latter largely used for night vision training.
- **Naval Air Squadron 22:** Equipped with two Sikorsky SH-3D and four Sikorsky UH-3H Sea King helicopters for, respectively, anti-submarine and anti-surface and general utility roles.
- **Naval Air Squadron 23:** A logistical support and general utility helicopter unit equipped with three Agusta-Bell AB412 helicopters.

- **Naval Air Squadron 32:** The main transportation squadron, equipped with two Antonov AN-32B transport aircraft and two Mi-8T helicopters. The latter are reportedly due to be replaced by upgraded Mi-17Sh P variants. Viking Air DHC-6-400 Twin Otter amphibious transport aircraft are also being acquired, possibly from a larger Peruvian Air Force order.
- **Naval Air Squadron 33:** The training squadron for helicopter pilots, equipped with six Enstrom F28F light helicopters.
- **Naval Air Squadron 3:** The equivalent basic and intermediate training squadron for fixed-wing pilots, based at San Juan de Marcona. Equipped with Beechcraft T-34C Mentor aircraft.

Three Fokker 27s are also believed to remain in service, largely assigned to Coast Guard Command duties.

Mi-8T transport helicopters are operated by Naval Air Squadron 32. They are mainly deployed to the VRAEM region to assist the deployment of troops in this troubled area, which is a centre for cocaine production. *(Guy Toremans)*

THE PACIFIC COMMAND: NAVAL INFANTRY AND SPECIAL FORCES

The Naval Infantry (*Infanteria de Marina*) numbers around 5,000 personnel. It has its headquarters and main training areas located in Ancón. There is also a Riverine Training Centre in Nanay, near to Iquitos.

The main Naval Infantry Brigade is based at Ancón. It comprises three infantry battalions (First Marine Battalion, BIM-1, Second Marine Battalion, BIM-2 and Third Marine Battalion, BIM-3) as well as supporting commando, amphibious vehicle, engineers and artillery units. A new logistics unit is currently being created. There are also two specialist jungle battalions assigned to the Amazon Command – the First Jungle Marines Battalion (BIMA-1) in Iquitos, the Second Jungle Marines Battalion (BIMA-2) in Pucallpa. It appears that the main battalions are often used to supply detachments to the smaller naval bases and stations, as well as a naval infantry component in the Valley of the Apurimac, Ene and Mantaro rivers (VRAEM).

Since 1982 Peru's marines have been deployed on counterinsurgency duties in the Ayacucho and Huancavelica departments. In recent years, they have also participated in peacekeeping operations in Cyprus, Haiti and the Central African Republic and their officers have acted as military observers and mission staff members for other UN deployments. Perhaps their best-known and most successful operation was the liberation of the seventy-two hostages from the residence of the Japanese Ambassador in Lima on 22 April 1997 (*Operación Chavín de Huantar*).

Tracing their origins to an Underwater Demolition School first established in 1969, the MGP's Special Forces – the *Fuerza de Operacionales Especiales* or FOE – provide Peru with the capability to perform high-risk and specialised tasks outside the normal capabilities of the armed forces. These include covert operations, counter-terrorism activities and the protection of national infrastructure and VIPs. A Salvage and Rescue Group (*Grupo de Salvamento*) is also embodied within the FOE and is capable of performing a wide range of diving and salvage tasks. Current FOE personnel numbers are understood to be in the region of 700 but an increase to around 1,000 has been authorised by the Ministry of Defence.

THE AMAZON COMMAND

The MGP's presence across the Amazon Basin dates back to 1864 when a Maritime Military Department was established in Loreto Region. The rationale for this seemingly unusual inland naval role was driven by the fact that the only access to this dense rainforest was by means of its extensive network of over 14,000km of navigable rivers. These connect the Peruvian heartland with the Atlantic Ocean via Brazil and form the basis of significant land borders with both Colombia and Brazil. Discoveries of significant natural resources in the region resulted in a significant growth in economic activity and maritime traffic along the Amazon. Unfortunately this has also driven illicit activity. All this calls for a continued, intensive MGP presence.

The current Amazon Operations Command is based in Iquitos. This is some 1,046km north-east of Lima and encompasses two of the five naval zones and a number of bases and smaller command posts. Operation focus is inevitably on the rivers and is driven by the need to combat drug and other illegal trafficking, as well as illicit gold mining and logging activities. There is a particular focus on the VRAEM region, which is home to considerable cocaine growing and production activities.

The command's most significant riverine assets are six large river gunboats of the *Loreto*, *Marañon* and *Clavero* classes. The two first-mentioned classes were delivered in pairs from the United States and United Kingdom in, respectively, 1935 and 1951. The last is a new indigenous design constructed by SIMA in Iquitos. The lead ship, *Clavero*, was commissioned in April 2010 but was severely

The second *Clavero* class river gunboat, *Castilla*, joined the fleet on 10 March 2016. She features some improvements over the first-of-class, such as a new SACAF III Remote Weapon Station for a 12.7mm machine gun. She is seen here undergoing trials in December 2015. *(Guy Toremans)*

The 1935-built river gunboat *Loreto* pictured inboard of the 1951-built *Ucayali* at the Peruvian river naval base at Iquitos. Although the age of gunboat diplomacy is largely regarded as belonging to a long-past era, such vessels still have value in policing the inaccessible and sometimes lawless area of the Amazon jungle. *(Guy Toremans)*

damaged by fire on her first deployment. She returned to service after repairs in 2012. Her sister, *Castilla*, commissioned in 2016, and incorporated some improvements. Displacing around 350 tons with a length of c. 47.5m, these shallow-draught vessels have ballistic-resistant hybrid protection and portholes in their aluminium superstructures that double as rifle slots. Armament varies between the two vessels but is focused on light-calibre weapons supported by embarked fast interception craft. Future plans envisage the procurement of two helicopter-capable patrol vessels. These will be based on a Colombian COTECMAR design under an agreement signed with Colombia and Brazil. The gunboats are supported by numerous smaller riverine craft, largely operated by the coast guard.

The gunboats and smaller craft are supplemented by small floating platforms – the so-called River Bases of Operation – that can be deployed anywhere on the rivers and used as mobile bases. They offer refuelling, repairs, accommodation and galley facilities for the riverine patrol boats. These bases extend the MGP's reach into the more difficult and distant areas of the Amazonian river network.

Other important assets include seven Griffon Hoverwork V2000TD hovercraft equipped with a 7.62mm machine gun that can achieve 35 knots in fully-laden condition. Based at Pichari in the VRAEM region, they provide a rapid and flexible response to illegal activities and counter-terrorism operations in the area's inaccessible and harsh terrain. The command also operates an Amazon Naval Air Squadron, which appears to use many of the aircraft previously listed in Naval Air Squadron 22's inventory.

The Peruvian Navy plays a prominent role in the government's plans for the region's socio-economic development by providing assistance and support to many of the Amazon's more remote communities. Notably, four river hospital ships – *Morona*, *Corrientes*, *Curaray* and *Pastaza* – were constructed between 1976 and 1983 to provide medical services to the riverine population. More recently, the navy has started taking delivery of a planned twelve *Rio Napa* class river supply craft. They are referred to locally as *Plataforma Itinerante de Accón Social con Sostenibilidad* (PIASS). These platforms are intended to bring a range of social support such as healthcare, basic banking services, legal advice and registration for civil services to citizens who have previously struggled to access such basic rights.[8] The lead ship was commissioned in May 2013. Four others had been delivered as of 2017, with the keel of the sixth – *Río Yaravi* – laid at SIMA Iquitos on 31 March 2018. The ultimate plan is to base two units in the Río Putumayo basin; two on the Arabela and Curaray rivers in the Río Napo basin; two in the Río Ucayali basin; one each on the Río Yavari, the Río Marañón, the Río Tigre, and the Río Morona, one on Lake Titicaca and the twelfth in reserve or in maintenance. These unique vessels have drawn attention from a number of other Latin American countries struggling to provide social services to their remote riverine territories.

THE COAST GUARD COMMAND

Peru's Coast Guard Command is an integral part of the MGP. Headquartered alongside the Pacific Command in Callao, it is responsible for nineteen harbourmaster type 'captaincies' and over forty harbour posts across its five districts. It operates numerous patrol vessels and craft from offshore patrol ship size downwards.[9] Of these ships, only the two offshore patrol ships and c. ten coastal patrol vessels displace more than 100 tons. Just as for the wider navy, the coast guard has responsibility for both inland waters and the open sea. The latter is sub-divided into coastal (out to 50km), maritime (50km–150km) and oceanic (over 150km) zones. Within these areas, the coast guard has responsibility for a broad range of policing and security activities. These include EEZ surveillance, search and rescue operations, coordination and control of maritime and riverine traffic, protection of the maritime environment, and – in conjunction with other elements of the armed forces – action against terrorism and organised crime. There are particular concerns that the largely land-based war against illegal drug trafficking will increasingly expand into the maritime domain.

The coast guard has benefitted from a substantial investment programme in recent years. this has seen the arrival of several new vessels. Prominent amongst these have been two ships suitable for blue water operations – the lead *Carvajal* class frigate – now renamed *Guardamarina San Martin* – transferred in 2013 and the former South Korean *Po Hang* class corvette *Ferre* (the former *Kyung Ju*), which arrived at Callao in July 2016. Discussions for transfer of a second *Po Hang* class corvette are also well advanced. Both ships have been refitted and modernised for their new role, swapping warfighting equipment

The lead *Río Napa* class PIASS platform is the first of twelve planned river logistics craft designed to strengthen the state's provision of social and economic services such as medical care and basic banking facilities to remote riverine communities. *(Peruvian Ministry of Defence)*

A picture of the Peruvian Coast Guard's new offshore patrol vessel *Ferre* arriving at her new homeport of Callao on 15 July 2016. A former South Korean Navy *Po Hang* type corvette, she may be joined by a second vessel as part of an ongoing process of fleet renewal. *(Peruvian Ministry of Defence)*

The launch of the new amphibious landing dock *Pisco* in the presence of the then Peruvian Premier Pedro Pablo Kuczynski at SIMA's Callao yard on 25 April 2017. Callao is state-owned SIMA's main shipyard and it is currently benefitting from a major programme of modernisation. *(Peruvian Ministry of Defence)*

The parting of the *Angamos* class (Type 209/1200) submarine *Chipana* on 15 May 2018 at the start of her planned mid-life upgrade at SIMA Callao. The yard has been upgraded with the installation of a new syncrolift and submarine hangar to help support the four-boat modernisation programme. *(Peruvian Ministry of Defence)*

such as missile systems for equipment such as fast interception craft more suitable for the maritime policing role.

The coastal patrol vessel force is also benefitting from new arrivals. A series of new-build vessels based on the 500-ton South Korean *Tae Geuk* has been ordered from SIMA at Chimbote. Known as the *Río Pativilca* or PGCP-50 class, four ships have been delivered to date. Orders for two more were confirmed in early 2018 and at least two more are planned. They are likely to replace the five ageing *Río Nepeña* class units, which were first delivered in the 1980s. Meanwhile, a prototype fast riverine patrol vessel owing much to the Swedish CMB-90 design – *Río Itaya* – was commissioned in 2013. It seems there are plans to build at least three more of this type.

The Coast Guard Command's maritime assets are supported by a network of coastal surveillance radar and communications stations. The SIM-TRAC (*Sistema de Información y Monitoreo del Tráfico Acuático*) maritime traffic information and monitoring centre at Callao was inaugurated at the end of 2012. The system allows the visualisation of vessels navigating in national waters in real-time by using satellites, coastal radar, and other data acquisition systems.

SERVICIO INDUSTRIAL DE LA MARINA (SIMA)

Tracing its origins to the creation of a State Naval Factory in 1845, the Peruvian state-run shipyard SIMA is one of the country's leading industrial companies. It specialises in the construction of naval, merchant and fishing vessels up to 50,000 deadweight tons.[10] It is also involved in vessel repair, fabrication of steel structures and the development of electronic systems. SIMA operates three shipyards: one in Callao, one in Chimbote – Peru's main fishing port, some 440km from Lima – and a third one on the Nanay River, a tributary of the Amazon, in Iquitos. Callao is also home to SIMA Electronica, a subsidiary that has developed, amongst other systems, the Peruvian Navy's Varayoc combat system.

SIMA has been expanding and modernising its infrastructure at the main hub of Callao in recent years in line with the facility's role as the cornerstone of the navy's modernisation programme. Current facilities include two slipways, a 195m dry dock and three floating dock facilities as well as several specialised workshops. An important enhancement recently completed has been the installation of a new 100m syncrolift and submarine 'hangar' to support the Type 209 modernisation programme. A further phase of the modernisation programme is likely to see the construction of a larger dry dock and two additional slipways.

CONCLUSION

It is readily apparent from this brief overview that the MGP is a key instrument in protecting Peru's security and economic interests, often far from the open sea. It is also an important instrument of the nation's foreign policy. The growing importance of the Pacific as a focal-point of global trade and commerce is of particular relevance and the MGP has expanded its ties with counterparts of the Asia-Pacific region. For example, the navy is an active participant in the Western Pacific Naval Symposium (WPNS), has an officer permanently assigned to the Republic of Singapore Navy's Maritime Information Fusion Centre and has appointed naval attachés to Peru's embassies in Australia, Singapore and South Korea. The navy has been an active participant in international exercises such as RIMPAC, UNITAS and PANAMAX. Its participation in the submarine-focused SIFOREX and SUBDIEX has been particularly valuable in fostering links with the US Navy. Inland, the MGP regularly interacts with Colombia on the Río Putumayo and Río Amazonas, and with the Brazilian Navy on the Río Yavari. The tri-lateral exercise BRACOLPER involves all three countries.

From a matériel perspective, the MGP faces the pressing need to recapitalise a fleet that was largely acquired before the Latin American debt crisis of the 1980s brought significant investment to a halt. The first phase of fleet rejuvenation – focused largely on amphibious and constabulary capabilities – is now drawing to a successful conclusion. The MGP hopes to follow this progress with the procurement of, first, new surface combatants to replace its elderly Italian designs and, then, replacement submarines. Current modernisation and mid-life upgrade programmes are intended to hold the line until these new vessels arrive. The big question is whether sufficient funds will be made available to pay for replacement units given a limited defence budget and a seeming lack of significant external threats at a nation state level. Given this backdrop, it seems that priority might be given to further expansion of tailored law enforcement intervention capabilities at a regional level, often in collaboration with other government agencies and neighbouring international partners. This will, however, inevitably give rise to its own challenges and demands.

To conclude with the words of Admiral Polastri, 'As complexity and uncertainty continue to increase, things are not going to get easier. Notwithstanding the fact that we already made significant investments in modernising the fleet, our requirements are still considerable.'[11]

Notes

1. BAP is an abbreviation for *Buque Armada Peruana*.

2. Data from the Stockholm International Peace Research Institute's military expenditure database accessible at: sipri.org/databases/milex. Proposed Peruvian defence spending for 2018 is reported as being in the order of US$3.1bn in cash terms of which approximately US$0.8bn is allocated to the navy.

3. The lead ship *Carvajal*, built in Italy 1979, was transferred to the Coast Guard in November 2013 and renamed *Guardamarina San Martin*. See further under 'The Coast Guard Command' section.

4. The Peruvian Navy's flagship is traditionally named after the famous Peruvian Admiral Miguel Grau Seminario (1834–79), hero of the naval Battle of Angamos. Until 26 September 2017, this was the world's last all-gun-armed cruiser, the former Royal Netherlands Navy *De Ruyter*. Laid down in the Netherlands in September 1939, the cruiser's completion was delayed by the German occupation of the Netherlands during the Second World War. She was eventually commissioned in November 1953 and subsequently transferred to Peru in 1973. In March 1985, she underwent a 2½ year major modernisation in the Netherlands, returning to Peru on 22 January 1988. Between 1993 and 1996 further upgrades were carried out by SIMA in Callao, encompassing the fitting of eight OTOMAT Mk2 surface-to-surface missile launchers and two OTO Melara Twin 40L70 DARDO compact gun mountings. The last-mentioned replaced four single 40mm/70 Bofors

guns. On 11 October 2010. *Almirante Grau* conducted her last live-fire exercise at sea. The Peruvian Navy placed the cruiser in reserve in 2014. However, they still used her as a flagship and an alongside command platform, as well as for pier-side training and for important ceremonial functions. The cruiser's fate remains uncertain.

5. The hulls of three – *Velarde*, *De Los Heros* and *Larrea* – were subcontracted to the then Lorient Naval Yard.

6. The War of the Pacific (1879–84) was fought between Chile and an alliance of Bolivia and Peru over competing territorial claims in the area of the barren but resource-rich Atacama Desert. Given the nature of the terrain, sea control was a decisive factor in the war. The small Peruvian Navy – under the inspirational leadership of Admiral Miguel Grau Seminario – held its own against the larger Chilean Navy during the early months of the conflict. However, Grau was killed and his flagship *Huáscar* captured by a larger Chilean Navy force at the Battle of Angamos in October 1879. Thereafter, Chile advanced steadily into Peruvian territory through a series of amphibious landings, capturing the capital Lima in January 1881. The war ended with the Treaty of Ancón between Chile and Peru in 1883 and a truce between Chile and Bolivia the following year. Both allied countries ceded significant amounts of territory to Chile, including Bolivia's only access to the sea.

7. The list of Naval Air Squadrons is derived from the MGP's website. There are some differences between sources on the current number of operational aircraft so numbers

should be regarded as being only indicative. However, figures quoted have been checked with the MGP. Whilst Naval Aviation is listed as being subordinate to the Pacific Command, it seems that a number of aircraft are assigned to the other two commands on a semi-permanent basis.

8. An interesting presentation on the role of the PIASS concept was provided by Ana Isabel Fiafilio Rodriguez in a workshop at the CIMS3 conference on Intelligent Towns (*Ciudades Inteligentes*) held in Buenos Aires in late 2016 relating to social action in the Amazon. Spanish speaking readers can access a copy at: cims3.dc.uba.ar/CIMS3/PosterFiafilio.pdf

9. Noteworthy amongst these captaincies is the lake captaincy for Lake Titicaca, focused on the naval base and shipyard at Puno. Some 3,840m above sea level, this is probably the highest naval facility in the world. In addition to patrol craft, naval vessels include the fifth PIASS supply vessel *Lago Titicaca I*. The ship was built at SIMA-Callao and then broken up in modules and transported by truck up the Andes Mountains, where she was commissioned on 16 October 2017.

10. SIMA's extensive and informative website can be found at: sima.com.pe/

11. Interview with the author, 2017.

12. The Peruvian Navy's website at marina.mil.pe contains a wealth of information.

Author:
Conrad Waters

2.2 REGIONAL REVIEW

ASIA AND THE PACIFIC

INTRODUCTION

At 06.45 on Sunday 13 May 2018, China's first indigenously-built aircraft carrier – an as-yet unnamed ship based on Russia's *Kuznetsov* and known as the Type 001A – edged away from China Shipbuilding Industry Corporation's Dalian yard to commence sea trials. The event marked another step in the rise of China's People's Liberation Army Navy (PLAN) from a 'near seas' coastal defence force towards a balanced fleet encompassing 'blue water' oceanic forces capable of projecting Chinese influence globally. Supported by China's dramatic economic growth, the PLAN has evolved into a force to be reckoned with and a focal point for debate on the nature of China's international ambitions. For the concerned observer, the PLAN is 'China's point of the spear in its quest for global hegemony'.[1]

Any detailed analysis of the true motives behind China's significant investment in naval power are beyond this book's scope. Many would argue that the PLAN's rise is a natural consequence of China's peaceful emergence as a global trading powerhouse with a legitimate interest in the security of its maritime trade routes. Sinophobes point to China's aggressive assertion of maritime claims across its near seas and the strategic significance of more distant investments associated with the 'Belt and Road Initiative'.[2] An added cause for concern is the recent successful culmination of Chinese Premier Xi Jinping's efforts to be effectively declared president for life. This was achieved by removal of the previous constitutional provision limiting his term in office. Some see his reinforced authority as heralding a further round of bullying and intimidation aimed at achieving an authoritarian agenda of territorial gains at home and commercial dominance abroad as part of the oft repeated mantra of the 'rejuvenation of the Chinese nation'.

Those – including, seemingly, the US Trump administration – viewing China as a strategic competitor have had plenty to exercise their minds over the past year. From a technological perspective, the imminent arrival of the Type 001A carrier has been accompanied by growing evidence of an intention to build a follow-on nuclear-powered aircraft carrier. When completed, this would more closely rival its US Navy counterparts in size and capacity. Meanwhile, the PLAN's existing capabilities were displayed at a review performed in President Xi Jinping's presence on 12 April 2018. The event included forty-eight vessels, including the carrier *Liaoning* and both nuclear-powered strategic and attack submarines. It was the largest ever event of its kind that the PLAN has ever held.

The PLAN's activities at home have been complemented by developments abroad. Notably, an expansion of the country's first-ever overseas base at Djibouti opened in 2016 has recently seen construction of berthing facilities capable of supporting a considerable naval flotilla.[3] A foretaste of potential tensions to come has been provided by formal US complaints that lasers at the base have been used to target American military aircraft using neighbouring facilities. There are ongoing reports that Djibouti will serve as a model for other overseas installations. The port of Gwadar in Pakistan is frequently mentioned in this regard.

One measure of American ire at Chinese actions – particularly with respect to militarisation of the South China Sea – has been a decision to 'disinvite' the PLAN from the biennial RIMPAC exercises off Hawaii in 2018. This can be seen as one of a series of US responses on many levels to its strategic competitor, the most obvious of which is a growing trade war. This has made it more expensive for China to export many products to the United States and, significantly, may see additional restrictions placed on Chinese access to US technology. There are growing concerns that China is seeking to leap frog the United States' current leadership in military technologies, although the latest moves seem to be as much about retaining economic as military advantage.[4]

One area where the last year has seen apparent progress in ratcheting down Asian tensions is the agreement reached between the North Korean and American administrations aimed at ensuring denuclearisation of the Korean peninsula. However, the deal's precise nature remains vague and there is scepticism as to whether it will produce tangible results. Notably, neighbouring Japan is sticking with plans to acquire the Aegis Ashore ballistic missile defence system. These were approved at the end of 2017 during heightened unease over North Korea's nuclear and missile programmes. Past experience of failed diplomacy suggest such caution is appropriate.

The PLAN Type 054A frigates *Yangzhou* and *Huanggang* pictured on deployment in September 2017. The fact this photograph was taken in the English Channel rather than, e.g. the South China Sea, provides some indication of the PLAN's expanding global reach. *(Crown Copyright 2017)*

Table 2.2.1: FLEET STRENGTHS IN ASIA AND THE PACIFIC – LARGER NAVIES (MID 2018)

COUNTRY	AUSTRALIA	CHINA	INDONESIA	JAPAN	S KOREA	SINGAPORE	TAIWAN	THAILAND
Aircraft Carrier (CV)	–	1	–	–	–	–	–	–
Support/Helicopter Carrier (CVS/CVH)	–	–	–	4	–	–	–	1
Strategic Missile Submarine (SSBN)	–	6	–	–	–	–	–	–
Attack Submarine (SSN)	–	9	–	–	–	–	–	–
Patrol Submarine (SSK/SS)	6	50	4	18	16	4	4	–
Fleet Escort (DDG/FFG)	11	70	8	37	25	6	26	7
Patrol Escort/Corvette (FFG/FSG/FS)	–	40	24	6	14	9	1	11
Missile Armed Attack Craft (PGG/PTG)	–	75	21	6	18	–	c.30	6
Mine Countermeasures Vessel (MCMV)	6	25	11	25	9	4	10	6
Major Amphibious Units (LHD/LPD/LSD)	3	4	5	3	1	4	1	1

Notes: Chinese numbers approximate; Some additional Indonesian patrol gunboats are able to ship missiles; South Korean fleet escorts include thirteen deployed in littoral warfare roles; Taiwan's submarines are reported to have limited operational availability.

MAJOR REGIONAL POWERS – AUSTRALIA

Table 2.2.2 summarises Royal Australian Navy (RAN) fleet composition as at mid-2018. The major development over the past year has been the arrival of the first *Hobart* class air warfare destroyer. Based on the Spanish F-100 *Álvaro de Bazán* design, she is one of three ships ordered from the AWD Alliance in 2007 under Project SEA 4000. She was delivered in June 2017 but not commissioned until 23 September. The second member of the class, *Brisbane*, started her sea trials in November 2017 and will commission before the end of 2018. The final ship, *Sydney*, was launched on 19 May 2018. Her delivery in 2019 will mark a turnaround for a programme that was previously marked by delays and cost overruns but which has remained largely on schedule and budget since a major restructuring.[5]

The arrival of the *Hobart* class is being counter-balanced by the ongoing rundown of the remaining *Adelaide* class (FFG-7) frigate fleet. *Darwin* was decommissioned in a ceremony held at Sydney in December 2017, leaving just the more recent *Melbourne* and *Newcastle* in service. Although there was some interest from Poland in acquiring the pair to replace its own older FFG-7 type vessels, it seems likely they will join their sisters at the scrap yard or as artificial reefs.

The next major programme of surface-combatant construction is for nine anti-submarine Future Frigates under Project SEA 5000. These will replace the eight existing *Anzac* class vessels. A closely-fought competition to select the winning design was resolved on 28 June 2018. It was announced that a

The RAN AWD *Brisbane* pictured during preliminary sea trials in November 2017. She is due to be delivered in the middle of 2018. *(Royal Australian Navy)*

Table 2.2.2: ROYAL AUSTRALIAN NAVY: PRINCIPAL UNITS AS AT MID 2018

TYPE	CLASS	NUMBER	TONNAGE	DIMENSIONS	PROPULSION	CREW	DATE
Principal Surface Escorts							
Frigate – FFG	**HOBART** (F-100)	1	6,300 tons	147m x 19m x 5m	CODOG, 28 knots	200	2017
Frigate – FFG	**ANZAC**	8	3,600 tons	118m x 15m x 4m	CODOG, 28 knots	175	1996
Frigate – FFG	**ADELAIDE** (FFG-7)	2	4,200 tons	138m x 14m x 5m	COGAG, 30 knots	210	1980
Submarines							
Submarine – SSK	**COLLINS**	6	3,400 tons	78m x 8m x 7m	Diesel-electric, 20 knots	45	1996
Major Amphibious Units							
Amph Assault Ship – LHD	**CANBERRA** (JUAN CARLOS I)	2	27,100 tons	231m x 32m x 7m	IEP, 21 knots	290	2014
Landing Ship Dock – LSD	**CHOULES** (LARGS BAY)	1	16,200 tons	176m x 26m x 6m	Diesel-electric, 18 knots	160	2006

proposal from BAE Systems based on the Type 26 Global Combat Ship had been selected over Fincantieri's FREMM and an evolution of Navantia's F-100 for a project that will eventually cost an estimated AU$35bn (c. US$26bn). The new *Hunter* class ships will be assembled at Osborne Naval Shipyard in Adelaide, Southern Australia by ASC Shipbuilding, which will become a BAE Systems' subsidiary for the contract's duration. A number of important decisions had previously been made with respect to the class's equipment, notably the selection of the Aegis combat-management system used in the F-100 class for the new ships. This will interface with Australia's indigenous CEAFAR radar system rather than the AN/SPY-1 arrays more commonly associated with Aegis.

Australia's other current surface warship programme is for twelve offshore patrol ships to replace the smaller *Armidale* class patrol vessels. In November 2017, a proposal based on the Lürssen OPV 80 already used by Brunei was selected over offers from Damen and Fassmer. Perth-based Austal – Australia's current patrol vessel producer – had

A graphic of the Australian variant of BAE Systems' Global Combat Ship, which was selected to meet Australia's Future Frigate requirement at the end of June 2018. The ships will be known as the *Hunter* class in Australian service. *(BAE Systems)*

Project SEA 1180 Phase 1

Project SEA 1180 Phase 1 is intended to replace the thirteen existing *Armidale* class patrol boats with twelve new offshore patrol vessels. Following a competitive evaluation process, proposals from Damen and Fassmer were rejected in favour of a design based on Lürssen's OPV 80 already delivered to the Royal Brunei Navy. Construction of the first two vessels will commence at the Osbourne Naval Shipyard in Adelaide in the last quarter of 2018. However, the remaining ships will be built by Australian Maritime Shipbuilding and Export Group (AMSEG) – a joint venture between Lürssen and Civmec – at a facility in Henderson, a suburb of Perth in Western Australia. The switch is ostensibly to free up capacity in Adelaide to build the new Future Frigates but also has a lot to do with the economic and political advantages of spreading work around Australia's states.

The new ships are reported to displace c. 1,750 tons with a length of 80m, a beam of 13m and a draught of 4m. The steel-hulled vessels will have a speed in excess of 20 knots and a range of over 4,000 nautical miles on diesel propulsion. A Saab Australia 9LV combat management system similar

The Royal Brunei Navy's OPV 80 type patrol vessel *Darulaman* pictured in November 2014. The RAN's new OPVs are based on this design. *(US Navy)*

to that used in other, non-Aegis equipped Australian warships will control an armament comprising a 40mm gun and two 12.7mm machine guns. The ships will also embark three fast

interceptor RHIBS and have a platform for a medium-sized helicopter such as the MH-60R already in Australian service. Accommodation will be provided for up to sixty personnel.

partnered Fassmer in the bidding process and political pressure was brought to bear to give the company a role in the project. However, it proved impossible to broker a satisfactory deal and the bulk of the contract will be performed at a neighbouring facility in Western Australia by a joint venture between Lürssen and Civmec. It appears that attempts are being made to secure Austal a role in the frigate programme by way of compensation.[6]

Meanwhile, Austal is currently working on a series of 'Guardian' class patrol vessels that are being donated by the Australian government to a number of small Pacific nations. The project now extends to a total of twenty-one vessels following award of a contract for two additional units for Timor-Leste. The first of the class was launched in May 2018 prior to delivery to Papua New Guinea before the year's end.

Elsewhere, construction continues in Spain on two new replenishment ships ordered from Navantia under Project SEA 1654 Phase 3. First steel for the second unit was cut in April 2018 in line with a schedule that should see both enter full operational service in the early years of the next decade. In November 2017, it was announced that the ships

will be named *Supply* and *Stalwart*, commemorating previous Australian auxiliaries.

The propulsion problems with another of the RAN's Navantia designs – the *Canberra* class amphibious assault ships derived from Spain's *Juan Carlos I* – have now been fixed and both new vessels have been extremely active. Notably, *Adelaide* has led two joint task groups – Indo-Pacific Endeavour (IPE) 2017 and 2018 – designed to build partnerships and enhance military interoperability with key allies in the region. Both operations are in line with the self-contained task group concept previously envisaged under the 2015 *Plan Pelorus*. They mark a departure from the previous operational practice of deploying single ships at distance. IPE 2017 was billed as Australia's biggest coordinated task group deployment since the early 1980s, when the former carrier *Melbourne* was still in service. It appears that the deployments are scheduled to be annual events and will be further strengthened as the new *Hobart* class achieve full operational capability.

The other pieces in the jigsaw for the RAN's future fleet are the 'Shortfin Barracuda' submarines designed by France's Naval Group (formerly DNCS) that are being acquired under the SEA

1000 programme. These will replace the current six-strong flotilla of *Collins* class boats and ultimately expand the underwater fleet to twelve submarines. Construction will not commence until the early 2020s, when detailed design work currently underway will be complete. In the meantime, the existing *Collins* class are being upgraded with modern cylindrical arrays based on British Sonar 2076 technology designed by Thales UK and flank sonars based on the company's French-developed technology.[7] The enhancements form part of a wider package of modernisation and sustainment efforts intended to bridge the gap until the new submarines arrive.

MAJOR REGIONAL POWERS – CHINA

As noted in this chapter's introduction, the PLAN has continued to develop its technological and operational capabilities over the last year. Although most press attention has inevitably focused on the first indigenous carrier, fleet modernisation has continued across a wide range of warship types. Table 2.2.3 provides an overview of current fleet composition. This is supplemented by the following remarks on major warship categories.[8]

Aircraft Carriers and Amphibious Ships: The new Type 001A aircraft carrier's initial sea trials in May 2018 focused largely on propulsion and other mechanical equipment. They lasted a comparatively short five days. The timing of the ship's first voyage – only just over a year after launch – suggests that outfitting might not yet be fully complete. As such it would be reasonable to expect a more protracted series of subsequent trials as the ship moves to full completion, suggesting final delivery may still be some time away. The Type 001A is broadly similar to the existing Soviet-origin *Liaoning*. However, open source reports consistently suggest the follow-on Type 002 project will be a catapult assisted take off but arrested recovery (CATOBAR) design, possibly equipped with electro-magnetic catapults and using nuclear propulsion. As of yet, there is no tangible evidence to support this speculation.

The mooted Type 075 amphibious assault ship has also yet to make a tangible appearance. However, the fifth Type 071 amphibious transport dock – reportedly named *Longhushan* – is now close to completion. A sixth and possibly final member of the class was launched from Shanghai's Hudong-Zhonghua yard on 20 January 2018. Additional

The PLAN's fourth Type 053C destroyer *Zhengzhou* pictured at the time of the ASEAN International Fleet Review in November 2017. Although only commissioned at the end of 2013, it is indicative of the rapid pace of China's naval development that two improved classes of destroyer have subsequently entered production. *(Arjun Sarup)*

Type 726 'Yuji' class hovercraft – similar to the US Navy's LCACs – are also being acquired to operate from these ships.

Surface Combatants: Recent PLAN surface-combatant construction has focused on three separate lines of development. These have encompassed large oceanic destroyers of the Type 052 series; intermediate-sized frigates of the Type 054 series; and coastal corvettes of the Type 056 series. The last twelve months have seen something of an emphasis on larger destroyers. This may reflect a future switch to carrier and amphibious task group operations on the US Navy model.

The most numerous destroyer design is currently the Type 052D 'Luyang III' class. These are derived from the six destroyers of the previous Type 052C 'Luyang II' class and are built by the Changxingdao-Jiangnan Shipyard in Shanghai and by Dalian Shipbuilding. Nine had been delivered as of mid-2018 and a further eight are fitting out. However, attention is increasingly being focused on the new Type 055 'Renhai' class, much larger 10,000-ton vessels broadly equivalent in size to South Korea's Aegis-equipped KDX-III class. These are built by the same yards responsible for the Type 052D destroyers. Each facility currently has three of the class under construction and two of these have already been launched at Shanghai. Published details on the new ships remain sparse but current reports suggest equipment includes around 112 vertical launch cells and a dual-band radar arrangement similar to that found on *Gerald R. Ford* (CVN-78). Much other equipment is seemingly carried over from the Type 052D design.[9] A disparate collection of older destroyers of the Type 051 and earlier Type 052 series classes currently remain in service, increasingly in secondary roles.

Construction of the intermediate Type 054A 'Jiangkai II' class frigates for the PLAN now appears to be drawing to a close after an extended production run. Twenty-seven of the class were in service as of mid-2018 and a further three have been launched. Future PLAN requirements are likely to be met by a much-discussed Type 054B or Type 57 frigate. This will benefit from technological developments in the twenty or so years since the original Type 054 series was first conceived, most likely including some form of electrical propulsion. However, production of the design may continue for a while yet to meet export demand. Pakistan has recently ordered four of the type and it has been rumoured that Bangladesh is also interested in the design. The PLAN itself continues to operate mean-

Table 2.2.3: PEOPLE'S LIBERATION ARMY NAVY: PRINCIPAL UNITS AS AT MID 2018

TYPE	CLASS	NUMBER	TONNAGE	DIMENSIONS	PROPULSION	CREW	DATE
Aircraft Carriers							
Aircraft Carrier – CV	Project 1143.5/6 **LIAONING** (Kuznetsov)	1	60,000 tons	306m x 35/73m x 10m	Steam, 32 knots	Unknown	2012
Principal Surface Escorts							
Destroyer – DDG	Type 052D **KUNMING** ('Luyang III')	9	7,500 tons	156m x 17m x 6m	CODOG, 28 knots	280	2014
Destroyer – DDG	Type 051C **SHENYANG** ('Luzhou')	2	7,100 tons	155m x 17m x 6m	Steam, 29 knots	Unknown	2006
Destroyer – DDG	Type 052C **LANZHOU** ('Luyang II')	6	7,000 tons	154m x 17m x 6m	CODOG, 28 knots	280	2004
Destroyer – DDG	Type 052B **GUANGZHOU** ('Luyang I')	2	6,500 tons	154m x 17m x 6m	CODOG, 29 knots	280	2004
Destroyer – DDG	Project 956E/EM **HANGZHOU** (Sovremenny)	4	8,000 tons	156m x 17m x 6m	Steam, 32 knots	300	1999
Destroyer – DDG	Type 051B **SHENZHEN** ('Luhai')	1	6,000 tons	154m x 16m x 6m	Steam, 31 knots	250	1998
Destroyer – DDG	Type 052 **HARBIN** ('Luhu')	2	4,800 tons	143m x 15m x 5m	CODOG, 31 knots	260	1994
Plus c. 5 additional obsolescent destroyers of Type 051 **JINAN** ('Luda') class							
Frigate – FFG	Type 054A **XUZHOU** ('Jiangkai II')	27	4,100 tons	132m x 15m x 5m	CODAD, 28 knots	190	2008
Frigate – FFG	Type 054 **MA'ANSHAN** ('Jiangkai I')	2	4,000 tons	132m x 15m x 5m	CODAD, 28 knots	190	2005
Frigate – FFG	Type 053 H3 **LIANYUNGANG** ('Jiangwei II')	10	2,500 tons	112m x 12m x 5m	CODAD, 27 knots	170	1992
Frigate – FSG	Type 056/056A **BENGBU** ('Jiangdao')	40+	1,500 tons	89m x 12m x 4m	CODAD, 28 knots	60	2013
Plus c.10 additional obsolescent frigates of Type 053 H1/H1G/H2 **TAIZHOU** ('Jianghu II–V') classes							
Submarines							
Submarine – SSBN	Type 094 ('Jin')	c.4+	9,000 tons	133m x 11m x 8m	Nuclear, 20+ knots	Unknown	2008
Submarine – SSBN	Type 092 ('Xia')	1	6,500 tons	120m x 10m x 8m	Nuclear, 22 knots	140	1987
Submarine – SSN	Type 093/093G ('Shang')	c.6	6,000 tons	107m x 11m x 8m	Nuclear, 30 knots	100	2006
Submarine – SSN	Type 091 ('Han')	3	5,500 tons	106m x 10m x 7m	Nuclear, 25 knots	75	1974
Submarine – SSK	Type 039A/039B (Type 041 'Yuan')	12+	2,500 tons	75m x 8m x 5m	AIP, 20+ knots	Unknown	2006
Submarine – SSK	Type 039/039G ('Song')	13	2,300 tons	75m x 8m x 5m	Diesel-electric, 22 knots	60	1999
Submarine – SSK	Project 877 EKM/636 ('Kilo')	12	3,000 tons	73m x 10m x 7m	Diesel-electric, 20 knots	55	1995
Plus c.15 obsolescent patrol submarines of the Type 035 ('Ming' class). A Type 032 'Qing' trials submarine has also been commissioned.							
Major Amphibious Units							
Landing Platform Dock	Type 071 **KULUN SHAN** ('Yuzhao')	4	18,000 tons	210m x 27m x 7m	CODAD, 20 knots	Unknown	2007

ingful numbers of older Type 053 series frigates, although many have now been decommissioned, transferred to the coast guard or sold to overseas fleets.

Meanwhile, there seems to be no let-up in commissioning the smaller Type 056/Type 056A series of littoral corvettes. Over forty of these diminutive vessels are in service across China's three fleets and production is believed to continue across the four yards involved in the programme.

Submarines: The development of the PLAN's underwater forces is difficult to assess given ongoing lack of transparency with respect to force structure and capabilities. There are, however, some indications that a rapid modernisation of the force in the early years of the millennium has slowed. This is probably to allow experience with the current designs to be incorporated into a new generation of improved boats. Recent assessments of existing Chinese submarines suggests they remain noisier than Soviet boats developed towards the end of the Cold War and therefore vulnerable to the stealthier designs employed by many neighbouring navies.[10] It may also be the case that there are constraints on training capacity and other support infrastructure that hinder the more rapid expansion in capabilities seen in the surface fleet.

The most comprehensive recent open source assessment of the PLAN's submarine force was published by the IISS in October 2017.[11] This indicated that four Type 094 'Jin' class strategic submarines and six Type 093/Type 093A 'Shang/Shang II' nuclear-powered attack submarines were in service, supported – perhaps – by three remaining first-generation Type 091 'Han' class boats. The analysis suggests that there will be no additions to this force structure until new submarine designs enter service in early 2020s. Most other assessments tend to agree with this analysis. However, there is some doubt over the status of the older Type 092 'Xia' class strategic submarine and whether a fifth Type '094' boat may have been completed.

Turning to diesel-powered submarines, ISS confirms previous assessments that each of the PLAN's three fleets operate two eight-strong submarine flotillas. This results in a requirement for forty-eight operational boats. Their analysis suggests there are twelve modern 'Kilo', twelve Type 039 'Song' and thirteen Type 039A/B 'Yuan' class submarines to

The ninth Japanese *Soryu* class submarine *Seiryu* (SS-509) pictured at her commissioning ceremony on 12 March 2018. The JMSDF is slowly expanding submarine numbers towards a targeted total of twenty-two boats. *(JMSDF)*

support this requirement. Obsolete Type 035 'Ming' class submarines make up the balance. Additional 'Ming' class hulls and the original Type 039 prototype are probably not fully operational. Renewed construction of 'Yuan' class submarines suggest that the majority of the remaining 'Mings' will have been replaced over the next few years but overall submarine numbers are not expected to rise. The assessment is probably more realistic than alternative US Department of Defense and Office of Naval Intelligence analysis that suggests a rather larger submarine fleet.

MAJOR REGIONAL POWERS – JAPAN

The coming twelve months will see Japan update its National Defense Program Guidelines and the associated Mid-Term Defense Program acquisition plan. Previous guidelines have heralded an intention to create a naval force structure based on fifty-four (previously forty-seven) major surface combatants and twenty-two (previously sixteen) submarines. These will be supported by sixty-five maritime patrol aircraft and eighty sea control helicopters. As demonstrated by Table 2.2.4 highlighting the Japan Maritime Self Defence Force's (JMSDF's) principal ships as of mid-2018, this build-up has been labo-

rious. There are currently forty-seven surface combatants – including four helicopter-carrying destroyers – and eighteen submarines in front-line service. Both categories have increased by a count of one year-on-year as new vessels commissioning have not replaced existing units.

The main development for the surface fleet over the past year has been the arrival of the lead *Asahi* (DD-119) class destroyer. She commissioned on 7 March 2018. A derivative of the previous *Akizuki* (DD-115) class, the new ship was intended to be cheaper to construct and place a greater emphasis on anti-submarine warfare than her local area air defence-focused predecessors.[12] A key design feature is an innovative combined gas and electric and gas (COGLAG) propulsion system. This encompasses two GE LM2500 series gas turbines and two 2.5MW electric motors. A second ship – *Shiranui* (DD-120) – was launched on 12 October 2017 for delivery in 2019. However, in spite of the emphasis on economy, the new ships have not been markedly cheaper than the previous class. Accordingly, future construction will shift to a smaller 130m '30DD' medium surface combatant displacing around 3,900 tons in standard condition. This smaller design has a number of similarities with neighbouring South

Table 2.2.4: JAPAN MARITIME SELF-DEFENCE FORCE: PRINCIPAL UNITS AS AT MID 2018

TYPE	CLASS	NUMBER	TONNAGE	DIMENSIONS	PROPULSION	CREW	DATE
Support and Helicopter Carriers							
Helicopter Carrier – DDH	IZUMO (DDH-183)	2	27,000 tons	248m x 38m x 7m	COGAG, 30 knots	470	2015
Helicopter Carrier – DDH	HYUGA (DDH-181)	2	19,000 tons	197m x 33m x 7m	COGAG, 30 knots	340	2009
Principal Surface Escorts							
Destroyer – DDG	ATAGO (DDG-177)	2	10,000 tons	165m x 21m x 6m	COGAG, 30 knots	300	2007
Destroyer – DDG	KONGOU (DDG-173)	4	9,500 tons	161m x 21m x 6m	COGAG, 30 knots	300	1993
Destroyer – DDG	HATAKAZE (DDG-171)	2	6,300 tons	150m x 16m x 5m	COGAG, 30 knots	260	1986
Destroyer – DDG	ASAHI (DD-119)	1	6,800 tons	151m x 18m x 5m	COGLAG, 30 knots	230	2017
Destroyer – DD	AKIZUKI (DD-115)	4	6,800 tons	151m x 18m x 5m	COGAG, 30 Knots	200	2012
Destroyer – DDG	TAKANAMI (DD-110)	5	6,300 tons	151m x 17m x 5m	COGAG, 30 knots	175	2003
Destroyer – DDG	MURASAME (DD-101)	9	6,200 tons	151m x 17m x 5m	COGAG, 30 knots	165	1996
Destroyer – DDG	ASAGIRI (DD-151)	8	4,900 tons	137m x 15m x 5m	COGAG, 30 knots	220	1988
Destroyer – DDG	HATSUYUKI (DD-122)	2 (3)	3,800 tons	130m x 14m x 4m	COGOG, 30 knots	200	1982
Frigate – FFG	ABUKUMA (DE-229)	6	2,500 tons	109m x 13m x 4m	CODOG, 27 knots	120	1989
Submarines							
Submarine – SSK	SORYU (SS-501)	9	4,200 tons	84m x 9m x 8m	AIP, 20 knots+	65	2009
Submarine – SSK	OYASHIO (SS-590)	9 (2)	4,000 tons	82m x 9m x 8m	Diesel-electric, 20 knots+	70	1998
Major Amphibious Units							
Landing Platform Dock – LPD	OSUMI (LST-4001)	3	14,000 tons	178m x 26m x 6m	Diesel, 22 knots	135	1998

Note: Figures in brackets refer to trials or training ships.

Korea's *Incheon* class, including CODLAG propulsion focused on a single Rolls-Royce MT30 gas turbine. The aim is to make achievement of the 54-strong surface fleet more affordable and this is supported by cost comparisons. Two DD-30 vessels were included in Japan's 2018 defence budget at a total cost of Yen 922bn (c. US$850m) plus non-recurring costs of Yen 133bn (US$120m). This compares with Yen 701bn (c. US$635m) and non-recurring costs of Yen 58bn (US$50m) in FY2014 for a single *Asahi*.

The submarine flotilla saw the commissioning of the ninth *Soryu* class submarine, *Seiryu* (SS-509), on 12 March 2018. Three further submarines of the class are under construction but production transferred to a new 3,000-ton type with effect from the 2017 budget. The 2018 programme saw an order for a second boat of this type, which will be delivered in 2023. Whilst externally similar to the existing class, the new type incorporates a number of detailed improvements. This reportedly includes replacement of the Stirling type air-independent propulsion (AIP) system with high-capacity lithium-ion batteries. Meanwhile, 2018 also saw the arrival of a new submarine rescue ship with the delivery of *Chiyoda* (ASR-404) on 20 March. The first vessel of

The Japanese helicopter-carrying destroyer *Izumo* (DDH-183) and the *Takanami* class destroyer *Sazanami* (DD-113) practicing replenishment operations from an unidentified *Henry J. Kaiser* class replenishment oiler. Studies have been undertaken to identify the modifications required to operate F-35B Lightning II strike fighters from the *Izumo* class in what would be a major change in Japanese defence policy. *(JMSDF)*

the type to be commissioned since 2000, she replaced an older vessel of the same name.

Looking forward, the forthcoming defence review will make important decisions with respect to a challenging security situation driven by Chinese expansionism and North Korean instability. Japanese Premier Shinzo Abe has previously proved willing to challenge the practical application of the strict constitutional limitations on the Japanese military and has indicated the updated guidelines will not merely be a linear development of what has gone before.[13] The recent study of the practicalities of embarking F-35B strike fighters on the *Izumo* class 'destroyers' could be indicative of one area where the defensive tenets of Japan's existing policy may be relaxed. It seems likely there will also be continued prioritisation of defences against ballistic missile attack. This will build on the December 2017 decision to acquire two Aegis Ashore systems to defend the Japanese mainland from missile attack, as well as the reported installation of cooperative engagement capability in a pair of additional Aegis-equipped destroyers currently under construction.

MAJOR REGIONAL POWERS – SOUTH KOREA

The Republic of Korea Navy continues to make headway with a balanced naval modernisation programme. This aims to develop the fleet's oceanic 'blue water' capabilities whilst providing a powerful deterrent to the very real threat of asymmetric incursions into its littoral waters by its unpredictable northern neighbour. The picture of South Korea's major naval combatants revealed by Table 2.2.5 is

The Republic of Korea Navy's Type 209/1200 *Chang Bogo* class submarine *Park Wi* pictured arriving at Pearl Harbor in advance of the RIMPAC 2018 exercises in June 2018. Although Korea has just delivered submarines to the same basic design for Indonesia, its own boats are likely to be replaced by a new KSS-III *Chang Bogo III* class in the 2020s. *(US Navy)*

partly influenced by the emphasis placed on strengthening littoral warfare capabilities after the destruction of the corvette *Cheonan* by a North Korean submarine in 2010. However, recent investment decisions suggest something of a return to the

previous emphasis in the 1999 *Navy Vision 2020* document. This set out a 'strategic mobile' concept of independent high seas operations by independent task groups.[14]

South Korea's submarine command serves both

Table 2.2.5: REPUBLIC OF KOREA NAVY: PRINCIPAL UNITS AS AT MID 2018

TYPE	CLASS	NUMBER	TONNAGE	DIMENSIONS	PROPULSION	CREW	DATE
Principal Surface Escorts							
Destroyer – DDG	KDX-III SEJONGDAEWANG-HAM	3	10,000 tons	166m x 21m x 6m	COGAG, 30 knots	300	2008
Destroyer – DDG	KDX-II CHUNGMUGONG YI SUN-SHIN	6	5,500 tons	150m x 17m x 5m	CODOG, 30 knots	200	2003
Destroyer – DDG	KDX-I GWANGGAETO-DAEWANG	3	3,900 tons	135m x 14m x 4m	CODOG, 30 knots	170	1998
Frigate – FFG	FFX INCHEON	6	3,000 tons	114m x 14m x 4m	CODOG, 30 knots	140	2013
Frigate – FFG	ULSAN	6	2,300 tons	102m x 12m x 4m	CODOG, 35 knots	150	1981
Corvette – FSG	POHANG	14	1,200 tons	88m x 10m x 3m	CODOG, 32 knots	95	1984
Submarines							
Submarine – SSK	KSS-2 SON WON-IL (Type 214)	7	1,800 tons	65m x 6m x 6m	AIP, 20+ knots	30	2007
Submarine – SSK	KSS-1 CHANG BOGO (Type 209)	9	1,300 tons	56m x 6m x 6m	Diesel-electric, 22 knots	35	1993
Major Amphibious Units							
Amph Assault Ship – LHD	LPX DOKDO	1	18,900 tons	200m x 32m x 7m	Diesel, 22 knots	425	2007

littoral and 'blue water' functions. An important stage in the command's expansion was marked on 7 September 2017 with the launch of the country's ninth and final Type 214 submarine, *Sin Dol-Seok*, by Hyundai Heavy Industries (HHI). The boats have been licence-built in accordance with an agreement with Germany's ThyssenKrupp Marine Systems under the KS-II programme. Seven are currently in service following the commissioning of *Hong Beom-do* in January 2018. Construction is now transitioning to the indigenous KS-III design, which will start to enter service in the early 2020s. Known as the 'Chang Bogo III' class, they will probably replace the original *Chang Bogo* class Type 209 submarines acquired under the KS-I programme from 1993 onwards on a one-for-one basis. This suggests an objective of maintaining an eighteen-strong submarine fleet. The navy also has longer term ambitions of operating nuclear-powered submarines. The French 'Barracuda' type was reportedly identified as a possible reference design in a feasibility study concluded in early 2018.

Recent surface-ship construction has been dominated by littoral requirements. This is seeing progressive retirement of the 1980s era *Ulsan* and *Pohang* classes and their replacement by far more capable frigates and fast attack craft. The frigates are being acquired in three batches under the FFX programme. All six FFX Batch 1 *Incheon* class frigates were in service by late 2016 and the first of eight planned FFX Batch 2 *Daegu* ships commissioned on 6 March 2018. These are supplemented by eighteen PKX-A 'Gumdoksuri' missile-armed fast attack craft. The final member of the class, *Jeon Byeongik*, entered service some three years after the seventeenth ship in January 2018 after suffering serious damage in a storm whilst under construction. A series of smaller PKX-B patrol vessels is also planned. A prototype was delivered in October 2017.

Perhaps the most significant development impacting the surface fleet over the past year was the launch of the second *Dokdo* class amphibious assault ship *Marado* on 14 May 2018. The ship incorporates a number of enhancements resulting from practical experience operating the first member of the class. These include specification of an Israeli ELM-2248 (MF-STAR) multi-function radar in place of *Dokdo*'s distinctive Thales SMART-L. This is supplemented by an indigenous SPS-550K three-dimensional air- and surface-surveillance radar from

The Indonesian 'Sigma' 10514 class light frigate *Raden Eddy Martadinata* pictured refuelling from a US navy auxiliary in May 2018. She has been joined by a sister ship, *I Gusti Ngurah Rai*, as the Indonesian Navy starts to bring some standardisation to its force of major surface combatants. *(US Navy)*

LIG Nex1. Other changes include a different defensive armament and a revised flight deck layout to allow simultaneous operation of two V-22 Osprey tilt-rotors. Although clearly having a potential littoral role, it seems attention is shifting back to using *Dokdo* and *Marado* as command ships for oceanic task groups. This perspective was reinforced by Defence Minister Song Young-moo's remarks at the ship's commissioning ceremony, where he declared, 'In order to preserve our maritime sovereignty at sea and play a role as a member of the international community, we have to move farther toward greater oceans. I'm convinced that the *Marado* will bring honour to the Republic of Korea by contributing to north-east Asian and global maritime security.'[15] Other new units involved in this role will be the second batch of three, KDX-III destroyers currently being designed by HHI. Scheduled for delivery from 2023 onwards, they will also introduce a ballistic missile defence capability to the fleet.

OTHER REGIONAL FLEETS

Indonesia: A major step forward was achieved in implementing Indonesia's Minimal Essential Force modernisation programme in August 2017 with the delivery of the new Type 209/1400 submarine *Nagapasa* from South Korea's Daewoo Shipbuilding & Marine Engineering (DSME). She was the first submarine to join the navy since the two existing Type 209/1300 *Cakra* class boats were commissioned at the start of the 1980s. She was subsequently joined by a sister, *Ardadedali*, in April 2018. A third boat, *Alugoro*, is being assembled by PT PAL in Surabaya for delivery in 2021. A further trio of submarines is required to meet a revised force requirement of eight boats (previously twelve) by 2024. Whilst it might seem sensible to standardise on the existing type, reports suggest various alternatives are being considered.

The reduction in planned submarine numbers is probably a reflection of the need to prioritise modernisation of the navy's front-line combatant force. The Dutch 'Sigma' 10514 light frigate design has been selected to meet this requirement. The second of an initial pair assembled by PT Pal from blocks built in both Indonesia and the Netherlands was delivered in October 2017. Named *I Gusti Ngurah Rai*, she subsequently commissioned on 10 January 2018. More are required to replace the six existing modified *Leander* class *Van Speijk* type frigates but further orders have yet to be announced. In the meantime, four smaller 'Sigma' '9113' corvettes bring a useful degree of homogeneity to a surface fleet that also includes a number of other corvette-sized vessels of various origins.

The need to undertake constabulary, logistical support and humanitarian operations across Indonesia's vast archipelago mean that demand for basic patrol and amphibious vessels remains high. Current projects include an additional *Makassar* class amphibious transport dock to supplement the four members of the class already in service. The new ship was formally laid down on 28 August 2017. She should be launched before the end of 2018. Work is also underway on a series of 120m *Teluk Bintuni* class tank landing ships at PT DRU in Banten as part of plans to replace an assortment of obsolete vessels with a more standardised design. Meanwhile, production continues at various yards on additional PC-40 type patrol vessels. A more lightly-armed variant of the eight KCR-40 *Clurit* class missile-armed fast attack craft, they appear to be scheduled for extended production.

Malaysia: The Royal Malaysian Navy remains focused implementing its '15 to 5' Transformation Plan. This is intended to improve effectiveness whilst reducing costs by rationalising existing warship types.[16] The most significant element of this plan that is currently underway is the construction of six Naval Group 'Gowind' type littoral combat ships. The first of these 3,000-ton frigate-like vessels, named *Maharaja Lela*, was launched from Boustead Naval Shipyard in August 2017. She is expected to be completed by 2019. Another two ships of the class are under construction and the others are expected to follow at roughly annual intervals. Up to twelve ships may ultimately be acquired.

Other warship types in the '15 to 5' plan include up to twelve additional MEKO 100 type *Kedah* class corvettes to supplement the six already in service and a series of eighteen smaller littoral mission ships destined for coastal patrol. Boustead are reportedly finalising plans for the second *Kedah* class batch. The pending arrival of the larger littoral combat ships to fulfil front-line duties mean these will have more of a constabulary focus. According capabilities will be scaled down to meet a cost cap of around US$125m per ship.[17] Boustead will also have a role in the construction of later littoral mission ships, which are being developed in association with China Shipbuilding and Offshore International. Constriction of an initial batch of four ships reportedly based on Bangladesh's *Durjoy* is being split between China and Malaysia. However, it seems future batches will be based on an indigenous-development of the concept that will be longer and offer a helicopter-operating potential.

The two other elements of the Transformation Plan are focused on the acquisition of additional 'Scorpène' type submarines and a new class of multi-role support vessel. The latter will probably be similar in function to an amphibious transport dock. Realisation of both these programmes seems to be somewhat further into the future than those for the other warship types.

New Zealand: The Royal New Zealand Navy (RNZN) has commenced the mid-life modernisation of the two *Anzac* class frigates that form the core of its combat capabilities. *Te Kaha* arrived at Seaspan's Victoria Shipyards in April 2018 to undertake a programme of work contracted to Lockheed Martin Canada. It emerged in late 2017 that the planned modernisation programme – including installation of new combat systems, radar and the Sea Ceptor missile system – is running over US$100m over budget. Balancing spending reductions have seen plans for a new littoral support vessel significantly downgraded by New Zealand's government to encompass a non-military specification.

The RNZN has also suffered from two reductions to its small fleet over the past year. The decommissioning of the fleet oiler *Endeavour* in December 2017 was followed by that of the diving support vessel *Manawamui* on 23 February 2018. *Endeavour*

The RNZN fleet oiler *Endeavour* pictured refuelling the RAN frigate *Ballarat* in May 2017. The withdrawal of the New Zealand ship at the end of 2017 means that the RNZN will need to rely on the RAN for logistical support until the new *Aotearoa* arrives. *(Royal Australian Navy)*

will be replaced in 2020 by the far more capable replenishment vessel *Aotearoa* ordered from HHI and on which fabrication work started in January 2018. However, the commercial replacement for *Manawamui* has yet to be selected. News is also pending on the way forward for the third, ice-strengthened offshore patrol vessel heralded by the New Zealand *Defence White Paper 2016.*

North Korea: Although the run-up to the June 2018 Singapore summit between the North Korean and US leaders saw something of an easing of tensions on the Korean peninsula, the latter part of 2017 was marked by considerable progress with the North's nuclear weapons and missile programmes. This included the apparently successful testing of a hydrogen bomb with a yield of up to 300 kilotons in September 2017. This was followed by the launch of a Hwasong-12 intercontinental ballistic missile with the potential of targeting the continental United States in November of the same year. There has, however, been only limited tangible news with respect to North Korea's strategic submarine programme that forms a key part of its wider nuclear ambitions. This is believed to encompass one or more 'Sinpo' class submarines. Late 2017 reports suggest that an improved variant of the original boat – termed 'Sinpo-C' – is in the early stages of construction.[18] The future direction of this programme will doubtless be influenced by whether or not a lasting denuclearisation deal can be struck. Meanwhile, North Korea continues to undertake limited modernisation of existing Cold War-era seagoing submarines and frigates, whilst focusing largely on the asymmetric littoral capabilities of its numerous smaller submarines and fast attack craft.

The Philippines: The future direction of the Philippine Navy under the Duterte regime has become a little clearer with the June 2018 announcement that c. US$5.6bn would be allocated to the second stage of its Revised Armed Forces of the Philippines Modernization Program. Commonly referred to as the 'second horizon' programme, this covers the period from 2018–22. There had been considerable speculation that the current government would slow the Philippine military's shift away from internal security towards territorial defence. However, a number of 'big ticket' items appear to remain in the plan. For the navy, the most significant development is the likely acceleration of plans

The RNZN diving tender *Manawanui* leading the RAN minehunter *Huon* out of the Port of Honiara on 1 October 2016. *Manawanui* was decommissioned on 23 February 2018, before her replacement had been ordered. *(Royal Australian Navy)*

to acquire a submarine capability. This project was previously expected to be launched in the 'third horizon' 2023–7 but will now be started in the life of the current plan. The total amount of hardware on the military's 'wish list' does, however, far exceed the promised funding. As such, it is far from clear which equipment will meet the final cut.

In the meantime, the most significant current project is the acquisition of two modified *Incheon/Daegu* series frigates from South Korea's HHI under a contract signed in October 2016. Unlike their Korean counterparts, they will have a diesel-only propulsion system. However, they will introduce modern naval capabilities such as surface-to-air and long-range surface-to-surface missiles into the Philippine fleet. Work on the lead ship commenced in May 2018 and delivery is expected before the end of 2020. Another pair may be ordered within the duration of the 'second horizon' programme. However, the deal has become clouded by allegations of irregularities relating to selection of the combat management system specified for the vessels. Navy chief Vice Admiral Ronald Joseph

Mercado was dismissed for 'insubordination' in December 2017 after opposing the politically-preferred choice for this equipment.

The new ships will make a welcome addition to three *Gregorio de Pilar* 'frigates' – former *Hamilton* class high endurance cutters transferred from the United States Coast Guard – that form the core of the current surface fleet. The rest of the front-line surface fleet remains focused on a motley collection of largely Second World War-era vessels. However, some progress is being made with their long overdue retirement. Notably, the *Cannon* class destroyer escort *Rajah Humabon* – the former US Navy *Atherton* (DE-169) – was decommissioned on 15 March 2018 after nearly seventy-five years of service. Appropriately, she appears destined for further life as a naval museum.

Singapore: A full review of the Republic of Singapore Navy is contained in Chapter 2.2A.

Taiwan: Whilst Taiwan's Republic of China Navy announced ambitious plans for a twenty-year

The Royal Thai Navy coastal patrol boat *T225* is one of large numbers of similar vessels in the navy's service that are steadily being supplemented by new locally-built vessels. She is pictured here at the International Fleet Review Thailand hosted to the mark the fiftieth anniversary of ASEAN in November 2017. *(Arjun Sarup)*

Vietnam's new 1166.1E 'Gepard' class light frigate *Tran Hung Dao* pictured transiting the Bosphorus onboard the heavy lift vessel *Rolldock Star* 16 September 2017. She is an anti-submarine variant of two previous 'Gepard' type frigates delivered to Vietnam by Russia's inland Zelenodolsk yard. *(Devrim Yaylali)*

programme of force modernisation in 2014, tangible progress remains modest. The most important element is probably the plan to commission a flotilla of eight locally-built submarines to fulfil a long-standing requirement to upgrade the island's obsolescent submarine force. Design work on the new submarines is expected to conclude around 2020 to allow delivery of the new force to commence around the end of the decade. The United States has agreed to permit the sale of submarine technologies to Taiwan to fill gaps in locally available technology but delivery of the programme still appears challenging.

Pending delivery of the new submarines, the Republic of China Navy's large fleet of fast attack craft probably pose the primary deterrent to any incursion by the PLAN. In May 2018 it was announced that construction of the larger *Tuo Chiang* (*Two River*) catamaran missile corvette design would be accelerated to bolster this force. Three anti-aircraft variants of the initial prototype were originally due to be completed by 2025 but they will now be joined by five anti-surface warship orientated vessels within the same timescale. A subsequent batch of three ships will complete the class in the 2030s.[19] The navy will hope that construction progresses more smoothly than plans for domestic construction of a derivative of Italy's *Lerici* class minehunters, which has reportedly been shelved due to local shipyard Ching Fu Shipbuilding's failure to make progress with the contract. It is understood that the lead ship is currently in build by Intermarine in Italy. It is possible the yard may take a greater role in completing the other five ships planned.

Thailand: The Royal Thai Navy enjoyed a brief moment in the spotlight in November 2017 when it hosted an international fleet review in Pattaya Bay to mark the 50th anniversary of the Association of South East Asian Nations (ASEAN) regional inter-governmental organisation. The event, which also encompassed the inaugural ASEAN Multilateral Naval Exercise (AMNEX) was attended by around twenty-five vessels from eighteen international navies, supplemented by some fifteen Thai ships. Although providing a valuable showcase for ASEAN unity, it is questionable whether the event will markedly strengthen regional naval collaboration given differing national approaches to the challenges facing the region.

Meanwhile, the Royal Thai Navy is waiting the

results of previous procurement decisions that should result in the arrival of the first of a potentially extended class of Korean-designed frigates and the re-establishment of a submarine flotilla. The new DWH300H type frigate – reportedly based on the KDX-1 series of destroyers but bearing a strong resemblance to the *Daegu* class – is scheduled to be delivered from DSME in the second half of 2018. However, the first of a planned flotilla of three submarines will take longer to arrive. Meanwhile construction continues locally on a number of second line patrol vessels ranging from the 'River' class OPV *Trang* to smaller 58m, 36m and 21m types.

Vietnam: Completion of deliveries of Russian Project 636 'Kilo' class submarines for the Vietnam People's Navy has been followed by commencement of work on a new submarine rescue vessel to support the six strong-flotilla. The MSSARS (multi-purpose submarine search-and-rescue ship) 9316 is being built by the state-owned Z189 ship-yard to a Damen design. It is similar to two previous ships – MV *Besant* and MV *Stoker* – built in Vietnam to support the Royal Australian Navy and is also capable of survey work and oceano-graphic research. Delivery is expected before the end of 2020.

Meanwhile, reinforcement of the surface flotilla has seen the arrival of another two Russian Project 1166.1E 'Gepard' class light frigates to supplement the existing pair. *Tran Hung Dao* and *Quang Trung* were built at the inland Zelenodolsk yard that completed the earlier ships. They were delivered to Vietnam by heavy lift ship, travelling via the Black Sea and the Bosphorus. Arriving in Vietnam in October 2017 and January 2018, they both commissioned at the Cam Rahn Bay base on 6 February 2018. They are anti-submarine variants of the initial ships and are expected to be joined by two further sisters ordered in 2014.

Notes

1. The observation was made by retired US Navy Pacific Fleet intelligence officer Captain James Fanell in remarks to the US House of Representative's Permanent Select Committee on Intelligence Hearing on China's Worldwide Military Expansion in May 2018. Fanell was previously removed from his post in 2014 for 'off message' comments on Chinese bellicosity. An excellent assessment of his testimony is provided by Bonnie Girard in 'Time to Counter China and Rebuild the US Navy?' posted to *The Diplomat* on 23 May 2018 at: thediplomat.com/2018/05/time-to-counter-china-and-rebuild-the-us-navy/. The full text of Captain Fanell's testimony can currently be found at: docs.house.gov/meetings/IG/IG00/20180517/108298/H HRG-115-IG00-Wstate-FanellJ-20180517.pdf

2. The 'Belt and Road Initiative', previously referred to as 'One Belt One Road', refers to Chinese efforts to recreate the historic Silk Road connecting Asia with Europe and Africa by a series of investments aimed at fostering land and maritime communication. Whilst promoted as a means of achieving mutually beneficial prosperity, critics see it more in the context of fostering China's strategic military interests. For example, a cynical but informative analysis of the real reasons for China's substantial expenditure on port infrastructure was provided by Devin Thorne & Ben Spevack in *Harbored Ambitions: How China's Port Investments Are Strategically Reshaping the Indo-Pacific* (Washington DC: C4ADS, 2018).

3. See Jeremy Binnie's 'China begins construction of pier at Djibouti military base', *Jane's Defence Weekly* – 30 May 2018 (Coulsdon: IHS Jane's, 2018), p.19.

4. A good review of some of the areas of Chinese technological endeavour is provided by Gabriel Dominguez's 'China seeking to surpass US in military technologies, says Canadian report', *Jane's Defence Weekly* – 6 June 2018 (Coulsdon: IHS Jane's, 2018), p.6.

5. A very comprehensive overview of the overall AWD

programme was provided by Julian Kerr in: 'Briefing Australia's AWD programme: Even Keel', *Jane's Defence Weekly* – 13 September 2017 (Coulsdon: IHS Jane's, 2017), pp.24–30.

6. See Andrew Greene's article entitled '$35 billion warship announcement delayed as Cabinet grapples with final project details' carried by *ABC News* on 23 June 2018 at: abc.net.au/news/2018-06-24/navy-warship-announcement-delayed/9902708.

7. See Pierre Tran's 'Australian subs to get sonar boost' posted to the *Defense News* site on 19 June 2018 at: defensenews.com/global/asia-pacific/2018/06/19/australian-subs-to-get-sonar-boost/

8. The *China Defense Blog* at: china-defense.blogspot.co.uk/ remains a useful source of updates on PLAN developments.

9. A more detailed assessment of the Type 055 in comparison with similar ships in the Asian region is provided by Andrew Tate's 'Assessing the capabilities of China's Type 055 destroyer', *Jane's Defence Weekly* – 12 July 2017 (Coulsdon: IHS Jane's, 2017), pp.22–3.

10. Relative assessments on Chinese submarine detectability are included in Ronald O'Rourke's *China Naval Modernization: Implications for U.S. Navy Capabilities – Background and Issues for Congress* RL33153 (Washington DC: Congressional Research Service, 2018).

11. See Henry Boyd and Tom Waldwyn, 'China's submarine force: an overview' posted to IISS's *Military Balance Blog* on 4 October 2017 at: iiss.org/blogs/military-balance/2017/10/china-submarine-force

12. The *Akizuki* class was described by Tomohiko Tada in '*Akizuki* Class Destroyers', *Seaforth World Naval Review*

2017 (Barnsley: Seaforth Publishing, 2016) pp.104–19.

13. An interesting assessment of the issues facing Japan's forthcoming defence review was undertaken by Yuki Tatsumi in 'Japan's Defense Policy Decisions in 2018', *The Diplomat* – 3 January 2018, currently available at: /thediplomat.com/2018/01/japans-defense-policy-decisions-in-2018/

14. A detailed review of the 'Republic of Korea Navy' was undertaken by Mrityunjoy Mazumdar in last year's *Seaforth World Naval Review 2018* (Barnsley: Seaforth Publishing, 2017) pp.44–55.

15. Defence Minister Young-moo's speech was reported by Jeff Jeong in 'South Korea changes mission for its newly launched assault ship', carried on the *Defense News* site on 21 May 2018 at: defensenews.com/global/asia-pacific/2018/05/21/south-korea-changes-mission-for-its-newly-launched-assault-ship/

16. The details of the Royal Malaysian Navy's modernisation programme have been reported in previous issues of *Seaforth World Naval Review*

17. See Jon Grevatt's 'Boustead lines up second batch of NGPVs, *Jane's Defence Weekly* – 25 April 2018 (Coulsdon: IHS Jane's, 2018), p.8.

18. An evaluation of the new submarine – based largely on satellite imagery – was contained in Joseph S. Bermudez Jr.'s 'North Korea's Submarine Ballistic Missile Program Moves Ahead: Indications of Shipbuilding and Missile Ejection Testing' posted to the *38 North* site on 16 November 2017. *38 North* is a project of The Henry L. Stimson Center, a Washington DC based think tank.

19. See Lo Tien-pin, Lu Yi-hsuan & Jake Chung, 'Ministry accelerates warship program', *Tapei Times* – 15 May 2018 (Tapei: The Liberty Times Group, 2018).

Author:
Mrityunjoy Mazumdar

2.2A Fleet Review

REPUBLIC OF SINGAPORE NAVY
To Defend and Deter

Singapore – the Lion City – is South East Asia's principal commercial hub. The island city-state, situated in the Straits of Malacca and Singapore (SOMS), is dependent upon an unimpeded flow of maritime commerce for its economic well-being. It is the world's busiest trans-shipment port and an estimated 1,500 commercial ships ply its waters daily. As such, freedom of navigation in the sea lanes that pass through the SOMS and their approaches is a necessity for Singapore's economic survival.

Given this backdrop, ensuring these sea lanes remain free of threats is, perhaps, the key *raison d'?tre* for Singapore's navy – the Republic of Singapore Navy (RSN). Other important missions include the defence of Singapore against maritime threats, support for international naval cooperation in furtherance of a rules-based international order at sea; and participation in a range of humanitarian and similar military operations other than war. These duties have led to peace support operations further afield, notably as part of the Combined Maritime Forces in the Gulf of Aden and off the Horn of Africa. The RSN has been striving to establish a full-spectrum of naval capabilities to meet these responsibilities, now extending increasingly into the cyber domain.

The RSN has certainly evolved into one of the most efficient, sophisticated and trend-setting navies anywhere since Singapore – a former British colony with a predominantly ethnic Chinse population – separated from Malaysia in August 1965. In May 2017 – the RSN's Golden Jubilee – Singapore's Prime Minister Lee Hsien Loong fittingly described the service as having become a '… full-fledged third generation navy …': a network-centric fighting force including submarines, frigates and maritime

The RSN frigate *Supreme* leads the smaller missile-armed corvette *Valiant* during exercises with the US Navy in April 2018. Singapore has developed one of the most sophisticated and efficient navies anywhere since the force was first founded a little over fifty years ago. *(US Navy)*

patrol aircraft, operating unmanned vehicles and aircraft and with operational experience in waters far beyond Singapore.

This path has not been without its share of challenges. Notably, the influx of former South Vietnamese 'boat people' from the mid-1970s onwards severely tested the mettle of a young navy which faced many operational and doctrinal problems. This experience 'bore valuable lessons' for the service, according to analyst Dr Collin Swee Lean Koh of the Rajaratnam School of International Studies (RSIS).[1] Most importantly, it was only until a clear strategic mission could be articulated – the need to protect the country's trade routes and deter potential aggressors at distance from its shores – that the navy's fortunes began a clear upward trajectory.

THE REPUBLIC OF SINGAPORE NAVY'S EVOLUTION

Following Singapore's secession from Malaysia in 1965, the Singapore Division of the Royal Malaysian Naval Volunteer Force – whose antecedents harked back to the local colonial naval forces raised by the British Royal Navy – was reconstituted as the Singapore Naval Volunteer Force (SNVF) in January 1966. Subsequently, on 5 May 1967, the embryonic naval service raised its new naval ensign for the first time. This date is now celebrated as marking the RSN's official foundation. Various name changes followed over the next few years as Singapore's armed services steadily developed. The title Republic of Singapore Navy was finally adopted on 1 April 1975 when the navy became one of three separate services within the Singapore Armed Forces.[2]

The new navy started life in 1966 with just two small, seaworthy hulls and an alongside base and training ship. As of 1967, its ranks comprised just 89 mobilised personnel and 278 volunteers. Early efforts focused on building trained personnel numbers – helped by the arrival of national service conscripts from 1968 onwards – and the establishment of shore-based infrastructure. Steps were also taken to develop an effective fleet, a process given additional impetus by the United Kingdom's 1968 announcement that it planned to withdraw its substantial military presence on the island over the next few years. Early acquisitions included an order for six *Independence* class gun-armed fast patrol craft from the UK – four built locally – in 1968. This was followed by a contract with Germany's

Singapore was effectively forced to create a navy from scratch after it decided to separate from Malaysia in 1965. Early acquisitions included six Vosper-designed *Independence* class patrol vessels. This image shows the lead ship, which was built in the United Kingdom, being loaded onto the cargo ship *Neptune Zircon* on 20 October 1970 before beginning the long voyage to the Far East. Most vessels of the class were built locally in Singapore. *(Editor's Collection)*

Lürssen for six *Sea Wolf* class missile-armed fast attack craft in 1970. Second-hand tank landing craft and minesweepers were also acquired from the United States.

Whilst these steps undoubtedly provided Singapore with a credible naval service, the influx of 'boat people' from 1975 onwards briefly referenced above exposed significant operational and doctrinal weaknesses. These included inadequate command and control (C2), poor platform availability, difficulties in operating high-speed strike craft on extended low-speed patrol and rescue operations for which they were fundamentally unsuited, and generally overstretched resources. Short-term effects included a drop in warfighting proficiency and morale, as well as more fundamental questions within Singapore's Ministry of Defence as to the navy's overall utility. However, longer term lessons – particularly the fundamental importance of

networked C2 systems and the ability to sustain operations at distance – were to have profound beneficial effects.

These lessons started to be incorporated into the second-generation navy of the 1980s and 1990s. These decades were pivotal in seeing the RSN develop from a coastal defence force to a more balanced, three-dimensional navy characterised by the arrival of larger, more capable vessels. Notably, six larger *Victory* class missile corvettes with anti-air and anti-submarine warfare equipment and greater endurance were built to Lürssen's MGB-62 design. These supplemented twelve slightly smaller *Fearless* class patrol vessels. Another important acquisition was for state-of-the-art minehunters based on the Swedish *Landsort* class. A number of existing ships received major modernisations. In the air, long-range maritime patrol capabilities received a major boost with the delivery of Fokker F-50 Enforcer

The 1980s and 1990s saw the RSN develop into a second-generation navy characterised by the arrival of larger, more capable ships such as the *Fearless* class patrol vessels. Twenty years on, these are now starting to be replaced by the new innovative *Independence* class design. This is *Dauntless* in 2013. (*Royal Australian Navy*)

aircraft to the Republic of Singapore Air Force's (RSAF's) 121 Squadron. They replaced old, shorter-ranged Shorts Skyvan aircraft in this role

The navy also began establishing the foundation for future submarine operations, sending a small group of personnel for submarine familiarisation training in Germany. This ultimately saw the acquisition of four used *Sjöormen* class submarines from Sweden between 1995 and 1997. Largely acquired for training purposes, the first of the renamed *Challenger* class arrived in Singapore in 2000. By the start of the new millennium, all the key components of the RSN's third-generation force structure were starting to come together.

The last two decades have essentially built on and expanded the foundations laid by this earlier groundwork. Major inductions have included the four locally-designed and built *Endurance* class

amphibious transport docks and six stealthy *Formidable* class frigates. The latter are of French Naval Group provenance but five of the six were built locally by ST Marine. Their construction was

accompanied by the purchase of Sikorsky S-70B Seahawk helicopters. These are operated by the RSAF's 123 Squadron. The three-dimensional force construct has been completed by the arrival of a pair of AIP-modified *Västergötland* class submarines from Sweden. Known as the *Archer* class in the RSN, they are another reflection of the navy's ongoing focus on expanding longer-range force projection capabilities. This will be further enhanced by deliveries of new-build Type 218SG boats from Germany's ThyssenKrupp Marine Systems in the early 2020s. Another notable development that is indicative of future trends has been the acquisition of unmanned vehicles such as the Israeli-built 'Protector'.

With most of these acquisitions now complete, recent attention has been turning to the fourth-generation force structure likely to be in place in 2030 and beyond. As well as taking into account an evolving maritime security environment – particularly with respect to non-state based threats – a major consideration is demographically-driven. Notably, falling birth rates in Singapore mean that the human resource pool available to man the armed services is likely to shrink by over twenty percent by 2030. Consequences have been the emphasis placed on greater levels of automation; the replacement of role specific vessels with fewer but more capable multi-mission platforms; and ever-expanding use of unmanned systems. This is being accompanied by greater use of technology –

Falling birth rates mean that the RSN is looking to technology to counter a shrinking human resource pool. This includes increasing use of a range of unmanned surface vehicles for surveillance tasks – initially Israeli 'Protectors' but increasingly indigenous types such as the 'Venus' series. (*Gordon Arthur, King Arthur's Writes*)

The frigate *Steadfast* seen shortly after delivery in 2008. Singapore's strong economy has allowed it to seek a qualitative advantage over neighbouring armed forces. *(Tetsuya Kakitani)*

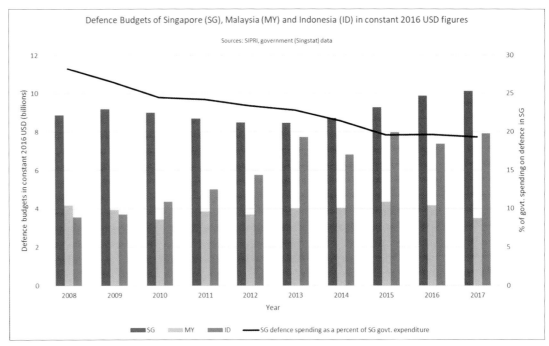

Diagram 2.2A.1: Republic of Singapore Defence Spending

including data analytics and artificial intelligence – for threat detection and identification.

Indicative of the current approach are the eight new *Independence* class littoral mission vessels. The first was commissioned on the service's fiftieth anniversary in May 2017. Operated by a minimal core crew but capable of accommodating modular mission payloads and accompanying specialised personnel, they are replacing the old *Fearless* class as they start to enter their decommissioning cycle. They could act as substitute minehunters as well. Another pointer to the future has been the deployment of Scan Eagle unmanned aerial vehicles on *Victory* class corvettes and the operational evaluation of several types of locally-developed 'Venus' series unmanned surface vehicles in force protection, maritime security and mine warfare roles.

SINGAPORE'S MARITIME SECURITY ENVIRONMENT

Defence Resources: Maintenance of national security has been a consistently high priority for Singapore's government. Indeed, at first glance, Singapore's armed forces and associated levels of defence spending appear to be disproportionate to the country's size and the potential threats it faces given peaceful relations with neighbours. For example, defence expenditure at the start of the current decade was at least equal to the combined budgets of neighbouring Indonesia and Malaysia, as demonstrated by Diagram 2.2A.1

Very high levels of defence spending – as much as five percent of GDP historically – have suffered a relative decline in recent years. This partly reflects mounting political pressure for increased social spending. As such, the defence budget has now fallen to under twenty percent of total government expenditure and is somewhat lower than Indonesia and Malaysia combined. Nevertheless, defence spending remains robust by most measures. Looking forward, future plans are based on spending growth of about four percent year-on-year, sufficient to keep pace with inflation.[3]

National Defence Strategy: Reasons for the focus on defence have much to do with Singapore's lack of geostrategic depth – both territorially and in the maritime dimension – as well as the vulnerabilities inherent in its trade-based economy.[4] Other factors have included historical fears of invasion by its larger, predominantly Muslim neighbours and, more recently, the emergence of non-state centric threats. Equally, Singapore's relatively strong economy has meant that it has been realistic to seek a qualitative advantage in comparison with the armed forces deployed by its neighbours and to adopt a forward defence posture. Very simply, its defence strategy seeks to deal a severe blow to potential adversaries by identifying and striking at appropriate targets from afar before any of its own territory is breached.

In maintaining this proactive, forward defence strategy, the Singapore Armed Forces (SAF) as a whole are focused on the extensive use of technology and the development of network-centric operations to gain a winning advantage through compressed reaction times. 'The SAF look to use an extensive C4ISR network for real-time early warning, rapid dissemination and synthesis of information and then translation of this data into deterrence or direct action' in the words of Dr Koh. This approach applies as much to non-state based threats as those posed by potentially hostile powers. One practical demonstration of this philosophy is the establishment of the Singapore Maritime Crisis Centre in 2011.[5] This was intended to facilitate a 'whole of government' approach response to maritime security threats by combining the resources of several government agencies to detect and deter threats as early and as far away from Singapore as possible.

Maritime Security: Threats and Responses: While Singapore's threat matrix has several elements, a consistent primary concern has been the need to ensure persistent maritime security. Incidences of piracy in the SOMS have registered an uptick recently. Other challenges include illegal immigration and illicit activities such as the smuggling of weapons and drugs, as well as human trafficking. However, it is possibly the threat of seaborne infiltration by terrorists and other acts of seaborne terrorism from non-state actors that have come into sharpest focus in recent times. Singapore has been named as an Islamic State target. The danger of the spill-over of Islamic extremism in neighbouring countries – or even from within – are real concerns for Singapore's security agencies.

By contrast, current threats from state-centric actors are negligible, with past territorial disputes with Indonesia and Malaysia now largely resolved.

China's assertive actions in the South China Sea are, however, one potential source of future instability. Although Singapore is not a claimant with respect to the sea's various disputes, it is a firm advocate of freedom of navigation. The well-publicised basing of US Navy warships in Singapore has certainly been a cause of friction with China, even if the country has been a major American logistics hub for several decades.

According to a 2012 RSN presentation, the maritime security response to these threats has six pillars, viz.

- Situational and domain awareness.
- Flexible and calibrated capabilities.
- Presence and deterrence.
- Speed and responsiveness.
- Sustainability.
- Engagement and cooperation.

These pillars are very much in line with the broader national defence strategy and the focus on early warning of potential threats and the ability to

respond quickly, flexibly and at distance. In the maritime domain, this means having a credible ability to defend Singapore's sea lines of communication as far out as 1,000 nautical miles from Singapore.

International Collaboration: The sixth pillar referenced above reflects the fact that Singapore is mindful of regional sensitivities and the need to avoid upsetting bilateral and multinational ties – 'It is careful not to be seen as acting unilaterally, opting instead for a consolidated approach towards threat mitigation/neutralisation' according to Dr Koh. There is particularly extensive regional collaboration between Indonesia, Malaysia, Singapore and Thailand. This includes inter-agency cooperation, intelligence and information sharing, and coordinated actions such as the sea and air components of the Malacca Straits Patrol.[6] Singapore also has important links with international partners such as the United States and India, both of whom have put in place logistical support arrangements on the island. The Five Power Defence Arrangements (FPDA) with Australia, Malaysia, New Zealand and the United Kingdom – first agreed in 1971 – also retain significance. Other important bilateral relationships include those with Israel and Japan, whilst Germany, France and Sweden have all been major suppliers of defence equipment. Efforts are also being stepped up for 'mutually beneficial interactions' with China in spite of the potential tensions previously referenced.

Warfighting Strategy: For all its sophistication and capabilities, the RSN remains a peacetime navy that has never seen armed conflict. Whilst it has demonstrated its ability to mobilise at short notice and performed well in support of humanitarian missions, actual warfighting conditions could pose challenges despite a good reputation earned on exercises. It is notionally capable of fending off all but the most serious threats in a warfighting scenario. However, hampered by its geostrategic constraints, it could eventually suffer from an exponential decline in capability under a prolonged conflict scenario.

While there has been no recent White Paper on the subject, analysts point to some obvious choices. Clearly, in an actual conflict, one ready way to mitigate the lack of institutional warfighting experience would be to call on friendly navies – either regionally or as part of an international coalition. 'It is for this reason that the RSN has built and continues to

The *Formidable* class frigate *Stalwart* pictured operating with the now-decommissioned Royal New Zealand Navy fleet oiler *Endeavour* in May 2017. Fostering international collaboration forms a key part of Singapore's security strategy. *(Royal Australian Navy)*

build warfighting interoperability with friendly partners such as India, Thailand and the United States, and even as part of FPDA. Going alone may be too risky for the RSN, though if it does become necessary for the navy to fight on its own, it will still do its utmost best' explains Dr Koh.

RSN TODAY: STRUCTURE AND INFRASTRUCTURE

Definitive information on RSN personnel strength is difficult to come by. However, as of 2018, it is believed serving numbers approach 5,000 regulars, supplemented by smaller cadres of national service personnel at various stages of readiness. There are also significant numbers of reservists, perhaps a further 5,000 of whom would be ready for operational deployment. Over ninety percent of regular personnel are male.

The RSN's organisational structure is set out in Diagram 2.2A.2. The Chief of the Navy, a two-star admiral – currently Rear Admiral Lew Chuen Hong – commands the service from naval headquarters at Changi Naval Base. He reports directly to the Chief of the Defence Force and is assisted by a naval staff led by the Chief of Staff, Naval Staff, currently Rear Admiral (one-star) Timothy Lo Khee Shik. The Chief of Staff, Naval Staff directly oversees the Naval Staff Inspectorate and Navy Medical Service, as well as coordinating the functions of the other main staff officers. A notable feature of the RSN leadership is their relative youth – typically in their early forties – compared with many other navies' considerably older top brass. Many RSN leaders assume significant positions in government or industry after the end of their naval careers.

The Chief of the Navy is responsible for (i) six departments with largely planning, intelligence and research-focused functions and for (ii) five formations with operational roles. These formations include the Fleet – responsible for all operations beyond the Singapore Straits – and the Maritime Security Task Force, which is tasked with the surveillance and security of Singapore's territorial waters. The Fleet – split into the First Flotilla, Third Flotilla and a stand-alone Submarine Squadron – is the home of the navy's major warfighting vessels. It is also responsible for two Base Defense Squadrons that provide security for the naval bases and has 'dotted line' responsibility for the RSAF's maritime aviation-focused squadrons. The Maritime Security Task Force is responsible for the squadrons that

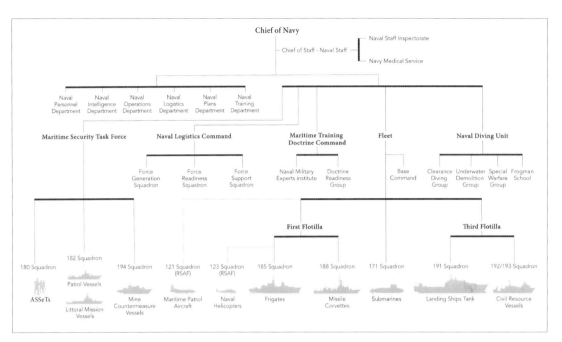

Diagram 2.2A.2: Republic of Singapore Navy Organisational Structure

The Maritime Security Task Force is tasked with policing Singapore's territorial waters in collaboration with other government agencies as part of a broader National Maritime Security System. This picture shows the *Fearless* class patrol vessel *Daring* on a security training exercise with a Singapore Police Coast Guard vessel. *(Republic of Singapore Navy)*

Table 2.2A.3: REPUBLIC OF SINGAPORE NAVY – PRINCIPAL UNITS AS AT MID-2018

TYPE	CLASS	NO.	YEAR[1]	TONNAGE	DIMENSIONS	PROPULSION	PRINCIPAL ARMAMENT
Submarines (4+4))[2]							
Submarine (SSK)	**CHALLENGER** (SJÖÖRMEN)	2	1968	1,200 tons	51m x 6m x 6m	DE, 20 knots	4 x 533mm torpedo tubes, 2 x 400mm torpedo tubes
Class: *Conqueror; Chieftain*							
Submarine (SSK)	**ARCHER** (VÄSTERGÖTLAND)	2	1987	1,600 tons	61m x 6m c 6m	DE +AIP, 20 knots	6 x 533mm torpedo tubes
Class: *Archer, Swordsman*							
A further four Type 218SG AIP-equipped submarines are under construction by ThyssenKrupp Marine Systems							
Frigates and Corvettes (15+5)							
Frigate (FFG)	**FORMIDABLE**	6	2007	3,300 tons	114m x 16m x 5m	Diesel, 27 knots	32 Sylver VLS cells, 8 x Harpoon SSM, 1 x 76mm gun, 2 x 25mm guns, MGs, 6 x 324mm torpedoes. 1 x hel.
Class: *Formidable* (68), *Intrepid* (69), *Steadfast* (70), *Tenacious* (71), *Stalwart* (72), *Supreme* (73)							
Corvette (FSG)	**VICTORY** (MGB-62)	6	1990	600 tons	62m x 9m x 3m	Diesel, 37 knots	16 Barak VLS cells, 8 x Harpoon SSM, 1 x 76mm gun, MGs, 1 x UAV
Class: *Victory* (88), *Valour* (89), *Vigilance* (90), *Valiant* (91), *Vigour* (92), *Vengeance* (93)							
Littoral Mission Vessel (LMV)	**INDEPENDENCE**	3+5	2017	1,300 tons	80m x 12m x 3m	Diesel, 27+ knots	12 MICA VLS cells, 1 x 76mm gun, 1 x 25mm gun, MGs, helicopter deck
Class: *Independence* (15), *Sovereignty* (16), *Unity* (17), *Justice* (18), *Indomitable* (19), *Fortitude* (20), *Dauntless* (21), *Fearless* (22)							
Patrol Vessels (7)							
Patrol Vessel (PV)	**FEARLESS**	7	1996	500 tons	55m x 9m x 3m	Diesel, 20+ knots	1 x 76mm gun, 1 x 25mm gun, MGS, 6 x 324mm torpedo tubes[3]
Class: *Fearless* (94), *Brave* (95), *Gallant* (97), *Daring* (98), *Dauntless* (99), *Resilience* (82), *Freedom* (86)							
Mine Countermeasures Vessels (4)							
Minehunter (MCMV)	**BEDOK** (LANDSORT)	4	1995	400 tons	48m x 10m x 2m	Diesel, 15 knots	1 x 40mm gun, MGs, mine rails
Class: *Bedok* (M105), *Kallang* (M106), *Katong* (M107), *Punggol* (M108)							
Amphibious Vessels (4)							
Amph. Transport Dock (LSD)	**ENDURANCE**	4	2000	8,500 tons	141m x 21m x 5m	Diesel, 15+ knots	1 x 76mm gun, 2 x 25mm guns or Mistral launchers, MGs, 2 x helicopters
Class: *Endurance* (207), *Resolution* (208), *Persistence* (209), *Endeavour* (210)							

Other vessels include the civilian resource vessel *Avatar* and the submarine rescue ship *Swift Rescue*. There are large numbers of landing craft and patrol craft, some of the latter being unmanned.

Notes

1 Date relates to the date the first ship of the class entered naval service. For the submarines, this corresponds to initial Swedish Navy service.

2 Second number refers to ships of the type/class currently under construction or ordered.

3 Armament differs from ship-to-ship. Some have a launcher for Mistral surface-to-air missiles in lieu of the 25mm gun. The torpedo tubes have been removed from many of the class.

incorporate the navy's smaller patrol and mine countermeasures vessels, as well as the Accompanying Sea Security Teams (ASSeTs). Other formations comprise a training and tactical development arm – the Maritime Training & Doctrine Command – a Naval Logistics Command and a Naval Diving Unit. The last-mentioned encompasses the Frogman School, Clearance Diving Group, Underwater Demolition Group and Special Warfare Group and shares a similar ethos and challenging selection and training regime to similar Special Forces units the world over. Depending on the operational needs, composite task forces, drawn from available units, are created as required.

There are currently two naval bases. The larger, Changi Naval Base, was opened in 2004. It encompasses 86 hectares, has 6.2km of berthing space and is large enough to accommodate visiting US Navy supercarriers. It houses many of the larger warships and submarines operated by the Fleet and is home to the main naval training base. It replaced the former Brani Naval Base, which was the navy's main facility for much of its early history but which was closed in 2000 due to lack of space for expansion. Opened in 1994, the smaller Tuas Naval Base covers around 28 hectares and is largely home to the smaller vessels operated by the Maritime Security Task Force. Both facilities incorporate significant amounts of automation to ease the logistical support burden.

CURRENT EQUIPMENT

RSN's current warships are summarised in Table 2.2A.3. As of mid-2018, its principal warfighting platforms comprise four submarines, six frigates and six missile corvettes. In addition, the eight new *Independence* littoral mission vessels are steadily replacing older patrol vessels to provide a total of twenty surface combatants by 2020. Other important warships include four mine countermeasures vessels and four amphibious transport docks. These ships are supplemented by numbers of assault and patrol craft, including growing numbers of unmanned surface vessels. There are also two leased 'civilian resource vessels' with distinctive red hulls and white superstructures. These are the helicopter-capable ro-ro ship MV *Avatar*, which is primarily used for training purposes, and the submarine rescue ship MV *Swift Rescue*. One notable omission from this list is an at-sea replenishment capability. This is provided by other friendly navies in case of need under bilateral logistic support agreements.

Submarines: The RSN's 171 Squadron commenced operations in Singapore's waters with the recommissioning of the former Swedish *Sjölejonet* as *Conqueror* in July 2000. She was followed by three more *Challenger* (ex-*Sjöormen*) class boats, as well as a fifth hull used as a source of spares.[7] The submarines underwent a major programme of refurbishment and tropicalisation prior to their departure for Singapore. However, most commentators regarded the acquisition largely as a temporary expedient intended to train the embryonic submarine force pending the arrival of more capable boats. This view was largely confirmed with an agreement to acquire two substantially more capable *Archer* class submarines – modified former *Västergötland* class boats retrofitted with air-independent propulsion – from Sweden in 2005. These were recommissioned in 2011 and 2013, allowing two of the *Challenger* class to be withdrawn in 2015. The precise capabilities of the refitted *Archer* class have been kept under wraps. However, they are likely to have minelaying and Special Forces-insertion capabilities.

Beyond their obvious deterrent potential, the submarine force has also been a useful tool for the RSN to use fostering engagement with other navies, often deploying for anti-submarine exercises in bilat-

The RSN has been steadily developing its underwater capabilities. *Swordsman*, pictured here soon after delivery in 2013, is one of two modernised Swedish *Västergötland* class boats retrofitted with air-independent propulsion. *(Ian Thompson)*

eral and multilateral settings. On an operational note, the RSN is very conscious of submarine operating safety and possesses a state-of-the-art submarine rescue capability. However, it remains concerned about the risk of underwater incidents in the very congested and shallow waters of the SOMS and has been one of the leaders driving a new underwater safety management framework – the Underwater Code for Unplanned Encounters at Sea (UCUES) – to minimise the risk of submarine accidents.[8]

Frigates: Ordered from France's DCNS (now Naval Group) in March 2000 and derived from the *La Fayette* class, the six *Formidable* class frigates were commissioned between 2007 and 2009. They will remain the mainstay of the RSN's combatant forces for the next decade or more. In contrast to the earlier *Marine Nationale* class, they have strong anti-air warfare potential based on the Herakles multifunction radar and Aster surface-to-air missiles.[9] The ships have received a series of incremental upgrades since first entering service, including a Thales STIR EO Mk2 fire-control system, Leonardo C310 anti-torpedo countermeasure launchers, 25mm Typhoon gun mounts in a stealthy configuration, and improved satellite communications links.

Missile Corvettes: The six Lürssen MGB-62 type

Victory class missile corvettes were commissioned between 1990 and 1991. One was built by Lürssen in Bremen and the rest locally by what is now ST Marine. Originally general-purpose vessels, they have recently been re-rolled to serve as littoral strike platforms, losing their anti-submarine capability in the process. By way of compensation, they have received a range of system and other upgrades in a mid-life update programme undertaken between 2009 and 2013. This has resulted in changes to the mast structure and the installation of a launcher for Scan Eagle unmanned aerial vehicles, thereby providing an over-the-horizon targeting capability. Sensors and electronic countermeasures have also been improved and the combat management system upgraded.

Littoral Mission Vessels: The RSN is excited about its new large multi-mission patrol vessel – the *Independence* class littoral mission vessel or LMV. Described as being smarter, faster, and sharper than the RSN's existing patrol vessel fleet, eight LMVs will replace eleven *Fearless* class patrol vessels and, potentially, the four *Bedok* class mine countermeasures vessels. Six of the eight vessels have been launched to date and the new ships started to commission in 2017. All will have entered service by 2020.

The LMV has been jointly designed by Saab

The lead littoral mission vessel *Independence* pictured at the International Fleet Review held to mark the fiftieth anniversary of ASEAN at Pattaya Bay, Thailand in November 2017. These modular, minimally-manned corvette type vessels are replacing the old *Fearless* class. *(Tetsuya Kakitani)*

An interesting photo of one of the RSN's stealthy, low-profile SM Type 2 Specialised Marine Craft taken in May 2017. They perform maritime security, base defence and force protection roles alongside the larger patrol vessels. *(Tetsuya Kakitani)*

Kockums AB – which supplies the ship's composite superstructure – and builders ST Marine. The highly-automated 1,250-ton LMV has a base crew of twenty-three personnel. These can be supplemented by up to about forty additional mission specialists as required. It has an integrated command centre at bridge level with co-located engineering, navigation, combat direction and command and control functions. The flexible command and control software makes extensive use of advanced sense-making and decision support systems to enhance situational awareness and accelerate decision making. The ships are fully networked internally and externally to other RSN ships.

The ships have a ' … highly configurable mission modular capability to perform a wide range of missions …' according to the head of the LMV project Lt Col C C Chew. For example, the ship can embark any number of combinations of modular kits from a list that includes Scan Eagle or rotary unmanned aerial vehicles, autonomous underwater vehicles, other mine warfare equipment, manned interception launches and/or humanitarian and disaster-relief equipment. Up to six containerised mission modules can be stowed onboard at any one time, including two in a mission bay equipped with standardised network interfaces. A stern launching and recovery system equipped with reconfigurable hydraulic wheels for ships' boats takes just two people two minutes to deploy a boat.

Weapons comprise a 76mm gun, a Typhoon gun mount, two Hitrole remotely-operated gun mounts equipped with machine guns, and a vertical launcher for MICA anti-air missiles. In addition to operating unmanned aircraft, the vessels can also act as staging platforms for medium-sized helicopters. The main radar is a Thales NS 100 air- and surface-surveillance array and there is a Sagem gunfire-control system. These are supplemented by ST Engineering's STELOP Compass D EO sensor package and an all-round camera surveillance system.

The eleven *Fearless* class patrol vessels are paying off after a relatively short twenty-year service life to make way for the LMVs. The old *Independence*, first of the class to be withdrawn, decommissioned in 2016. A further three followed in October 2017, leaving seven in service.[10]

Patrol Craft and Interceptors: A range of small craft are used by various units for duties including patrolling, high-speed interception, special operations and diving support. Amongst the most significant are the stealthy, low-profile Specialised Marine Craft (SMC). The RSN first revealed their existence in 2015. However, initial development work is believed to have started in the early years of the Millennium and a prototype probably existed by 2006. Two variants are known to exist. One is a 22m, 40-ton design fitted with a remotely-operated light machine gun. This may have served as a test bed for the larger 25m, 45-ton design with a stealthy Hitrole G remotely-controlled weapon system. The RSN has previously said eight SMCs were slated for entry into service by 2017. These craft are operated by a specialised craft group within the Maritime Security Task Force. Working alongside the patrol vessels and LMVs, they perform maritime security, base defence and force protection as one of the 'kinetic responses' in Singapore's layered maritime security architecture.

The RSN is also expanding its fleet of unmanned surface vehicles for patrol operations. Types in use include the Israeli built 'Protector' and the locally built 'Venus' 9m USV for force protection. A larger 16m Venus USV has been developed for coastal patrolling. It is eventually intended that coastal defence unmanned surface vehicles will take over routine patrolling of the Singapore Straits, freeing-up manned warships for longer-ranged or more complex missions.

A variety of Special Forces craft – including very slender vessels – are known to exist but details are sparse.

Mine Countermeasures Vessels: The four *Bedok* class minehunters were all commissioned in 1995. Based on Sweden's *Landsort* design, one was built by Kockums in Karlskrona and the others in Singapore. They were upgraded between 2009 and 2014 under a Thales-led programme that included a mine countermeasures command and control system, a TSM-2022 Mk III hull-mounted sonar and a DUBM-44 towed synthetic aperture sonar. Other equipment includes the Remus 100 autonomous underwater vehicle and ECA K-Ster expendable mine disposal vehicles. The integration of these systems has allowed the class to undertake area services much quickly – up to five times faster according to the RSN – and also permits more effective mine clearance.

The RSN has also been experimenting with Venus 16 USVs in mine countermeasures roles, matched with the DUBM-44 for detection and with K-Ster

The lead *Endurance* class amphibious transport dock pictured on exercises with the US Navy in August 2017. A compact and innovative design, the type has also been sold to the Royal Thai Navy. *(US Navy)*

for disposal. However, these are not yet considered sufficiently mature to replace the *Bedok* class and a mixed manned/unmanned solution seems the most likely way forward.

Amphibious Ships: The four locally designed and built *Endurance* class LPDs were commissioned between 2000 and 2001. Displacing around 8,500 tons in full load condition, they can embark two medium-sized helicopters – currently Super Pumas/Cougars – and have a dock well for 23m fast utility landing craft. Additional, smaller 13m fast equipment and personnel landing craft are carried on davits. The vessels have been heavily tasked supporting SAF requirements for sea transportation of personnel and matériel to distant overseas training ranges, as well as for stabilisation operations off the Horn of Africa and elsewhere. From 2013, they started to receive upgrades to, in the words of the RSN, '… better support operational requirements for maritime security and operations other than war'. These include combat management system updates to ensure commonality with the frigates and

corvettes, new sensors and datalinks and improved helicopter support equipment.

It is understood that there is a fairly large fleet of small landing craft, with at least ten fast utility landing craft and perhaps twenty fast equipment and personnel craft in operational service, with considerably more of the latter in storage. For anti-piracy deployments off the Horn of Africa, some of the 23m utility craft have been modified for the boarding and force protection roles, including installation of armoured panels and boarding ladders.

Support Ships: The RSN was the first regional navy to operate a state-of-the-art submarine rescue capability with the delivery of a submarine rescue ship and rescue submersible in 2009. Unusually, its submarine rescue assets were acquired under a twenty-year public private partnership with ST Marine in conjunction with James Fisher Defence. These comprise the ST Marine-built submarine rescue vessel MV *Swift Rescue* – an 85m ship equipped with a helicopter deck and housing a

The *Victory* class corvette *Valiant* seen in November 2017. A mid-life modernisation has seen the class re-rolled to serve as littoral strike platforms but their replacement is now being planned. *(Arjun Sarup)*

transfer under pressure chamber – and the James Fisher Defence-supplied deep submergence and rescue vehicle DSAR-6. It can operate down to depths of 500m and has sufficient space for seventeen rescuees.

The largest vessel operated by the RSN is the MV *Avatar* – a converted 173m long ro-ro merchant ship leased for many years as a 'civilian resource vessel'. Extensive modernisation has seen her equipped with a large flight deck with two landing spots and additional accommodation. She performs a wide variety of training roles and could also be used operationally as a transport or hospital ship, the latter with a containerised hospital facility.

The RSN also operates another leased training vessel – the 25m *STET Polaris* built by Sam Aluminium Engineering Pte Ltd. In use by the RSN since June 2010, it serves as a navigation and training vessel for RSN midshipmen. The vessel has a crew of four and can embark up to thirty trainees.

NAVAL AVIATION

With the exception of its Scan Eagle unmanned aerial vehicles, the RSN's naval aircraft are effectively joint assets piloted by the RSAF but crewed by naval mission system operators. Five Fokker F50 Enforcer Mk2 maritime patrol aircraft are operated by 121 Squadron from Changi Airbase, whilst eight S-70B Seahawk deployed for anti-submarine warfare and anti-surface warfare tasks aboard the frigates are operated by 123 Squadron based at Sembawang.

Other aircraft routinely deployed at sea are the Super Puma/Cougar medium-lift helicopters of 125 and 126 Squadrons, also based at Sembawang. These are slated for replacement by Airbus H225 Super Puma variant from 2020. The RSAF also operates a number of surveillance platforms with maritime applications. These include Gulfstream G-550 airborne early warning aircraft and Hermes and Heron unmanned aerial vehicles.

SHIPBUILDING AND SYSTEMS INFRASTRUCTURE

From the outset, the majority of the RSN's platforms have been built locally. At first, this typically involved the overseas construction of the lead ship of a class, followed by local assembly of the following units with licensed transfer of technology. However, there has

been a progressive move to largely indigenous solutions, albeit frequently with international collaboration. There are also now examples of successful export campaigns, including the sale of an *Endeavour*-type amphibious transport dock to Thailand and patrol vessels to Oman. Singapore's defence technology community – encompassing the Ministry of Defence, the Defence Science & Technology Agency (DSTA), DSO National Laboratories, the SAF itself and ST Engineering – employs the largest concentration of scientists and engineers in the country – almost one in every twelve!

From the early 1970s the RSN has emphasised a navy-wide systems engineering approach towards the integration of new capabilities. Over time, RSN acquisitions have become highly customised platforms with significant levels of input by Singapore's defence technology community to meet the RSN's specific operational requirements. Singapore's DSTA typically manages these programs, even when they are acquired from overseas. For example, combat systems integration on the *Formidable* class frigates was undertaken in-country by the DSTA, assisted by the wider defence industrial base in Singapore. There are, however, strong ties to similar defence and industrial partners in friendly states to develop new platforms and systems on a collaborative basis. Typically, the model adopted is a mutually beneficial one under which there is a balanced collaboration based on co-funding, and the exchange of information and technology.

FUTURE PROJECTS

The RSN is already working towards a planned 2030 force structure and several projects are already underway or in the pipeline. The most significant of these is probably that for four new Type 218SG AIP-equipped submarines ordered from Germany's ThyssenKrupp Marine Systems in pairs in 2013 and 2017. Deliveries are slated to take place from 2021 onwards. Details of the new boats are sketchy but they are commonly reported as being derived from the earlier Type 214 design but incorporating technology – such as the 'X' rudder configuration – derived from the Type 212A. The Atlas Elektronik-based combat management system will also incorporate significant input from ST Engineering's ST Electronics subsidiary.

Turning to the surface fleet, the RSN is conducting 'engineering studies' for an *Endeavour* class replacement dubbed the joint multi-mission ship (JMMS). These will have double the lift capacity of the existing vessels and have sufficient flexibility to support both stabilisation and humanitarian missions. A LHD-type helicopter carrier along the lines of concepts already displayed by ST Marine is one possible design option. A replacement is also required for the existing *Victory* class corvettes and a new class of multi-role combat vessels is envisaged to meet the requirement. They will act as manned motherships for robotic vehicles, providing greatly enhanced surveillance capabilities. Given the ongoing LMV and submarine projects – both of which are costly – both new projects are unlikely to pick up pace until fiscal pressures ease off.

There are also longer-term requirements for other new equipment, including a new maritime patrol aircraft. The Boeing P-8 would seem to be a strong contender but funding constraints and a desire to achieve commonality with existing types might result in a Gulfstream G550-based platform being chosen. Continued development work on unmanned and autonomous surface and underwater vehicles to conduct a broadening range of surveillance and mine countermeasures tasks is likely to be a persistent theme.

CONCLUSION

Despite its relatively small size, the RSN is a sophisticated, network-centric navy that is able to deploy a wide range of modern warfighting capabilities and which is steadily expanding its capacity for power projection. Strategically, a strong national awareness of the need to avoid upsetting regional sensitivities is reflected in the RSN's focus on collaboration and confidence-building measures, including regular exercises with regional and international navies. Influenced by Singapore's dependence on maritime trade for its economic prosperity, there is a strong emphasis on working to maintain good order at sea, both in the SOMS and more broadly.

Widely regarded as an efficient and effective navy, the RSN still faces some challenges. Manpower woes continue to be a problem; in fact, the RSN probably has more platforms than it can adequately man. Quite aside from the demographic issue of a dwindling human resource pool, the navy has its work cut out in terms of personnel retention. Whilst the current generation of conscripts are highly educated and tech savvy, few opt to stay in the military after their two-year stint. 'The persistent problem faced by the RSN is the need to maintain a critical mass of this human capital – by incentivising recruitment vis-à-vis other lucrative maritime sectors, and by ensuring retention of skilled personnel' says Dr Koh.

To mitigate this problem, the RSN is placing increasing reliance on automation. However, there are risks in using technology as the panacea. An appreciation of this is demonstrated by the decision to opt for a mix of manned and unmanned systems for the next generation mine countermeasures capability. Another important approach adopted by the RSN is fleet rationalisation through the use of mission-flexible platforms like the LMV. 'It is about exploiting modularity – plug and play capacity – to maximise capabilities within a limited set of platforms and manpower to perform a maximum spectrum of missions' notes Dr. Koh.

Going forward, the RSN has adopted the mantra of a 'sharper and smarter' navy, leveraging technology in the face of evolving threats such as seaborne terrorism and disruptive technologies whilst taking note of the strategic implications of a rising China. Other navies and observers alike will be watching developments with interest as the RSN evolves towards a fourth-generation fleet.

Notes

1. Named after Singapore's first foreign minister, the Rajaratnam School of International Studies (RSIS) is a leading graduate school and policy-oriented think tank first established in 1996. It is an autonomous entity within Singapore's Nanyang Technological University. The author wishes to thank Dr Koh for his invaluable input and helpful insights.

2. A more detailed account of the RSN's development can be found in Joshua Ho's 'The Republic of Singapore Navy: From Humble Beginnings to a Balanced Fleet' published in *The Northern Mariner/Le marin du nord* XXIV, Nos. 3 and 4 – July and October 2014 (Ottawa: Canadian Nautical Research Society, 2014) and currently available at: cnrs-scrn.org/northern_mariner/vol24/ tnm_24_34_124-134.pdf

3. This approach was confirmed in a speech to Parliament by defence minister Ng Eng Hen in March 2018. See 'Parliament: Defence spending to remain steady even as other countries spend more on wide-ranging security threats, says Ng Eng Hen', *The Straits Times* – 2 March 2018 (Singapore: Singapore Press Holdings, 2018).

4. Singapore's maritime zone comprises just 343km[2] of sea space.

5. The Singapore Maritime Crisis Centre is the cornerstone of Singapore's National Maritime Security System, which aims to provide a 24/7 monitoring capability, threat assessment and coordinated response to maritime threats. For further details of this remarkable system see the Singapore Ministry of Defence fact sheet, *Safeguarding Singapore's Maritime Security*, available by searching the web.

6. The Malacca Strait Patrols (MSP) is a regional initiative to counter maritime piracy and terrorism in the Straits of Malacca and Singapore. It was originally established by Malaysia, Singapore and Indonesia in 2004 and subsequently joined in 2008 by Thailand. MSP comprises the Malacca Strait Sea Patrol, the 'Eyes-in-the-Sky' air patrols, and the Intelligence Exchange Group. For further information see the Singapore Ministry of Defence fact sheet, *The Malacca Straits Patrol*, again available by searching the web.

7. Many sources suggest that only three of these boats were ever fully commissioned.

8. See Prashanth Parameswaran's 'Where is Singapore's New Naval Protocol?' posted to *The Diplomat* website on 24 May 2017, available at: thediplomat.com/2017/05/where-is-singapores-new-underwater-naval-protocol/

9. Sources differ as to whether or not the class is partly or wholly equipped with the Sylver A-50 vertical launch system (VLS) capable of launching the longer-range Aster 30 surface-to-air missile. The shallower A-43 VLS referenced as equipping the ships in some publications is only capable of accommodating the shorter-ranged Aster 15.

10. There were originally twelve members of the class. One, *Courageous*, was severely damaged in a collision on 3 January 2003 and subsequently prematurely withdrawn from service.

11. A wealth of information on the RSN's structure, operational units and ongoing developments can be found on the Singapore Defence Ministry (MINDEF) website at mindef.gov.sg/web/portal/mindef/home/. Two more permanent sources providing valuable overviews of the issues and challenges involved in naval modernisation in South East Asia for both the RSN and other regional navies are *Naval Modernisation in Southeast Asia - Problems and Prospects for Small and Medium Navies* edited by Geoffrey Till and Ristian Atriandi Supriyanto and the accompanying *Naval Modernisation in Southeast Asia*, Part Two. *Submarine Issues for Small and Medium Navies* edited by Geoffrey Till and Collin Swee Lean Koh, both (London: Palgrave Macmillan, 2017).

2.3 REGIONAL REVIEW

THE INDIAN OCEAN AND AFRICA

Author: Conrad Waters

INTRODUCTION

March 2018 brought the third anniversary of Yemen's civil war, described by the United Nation's Secretary General as the 'world's worst humanitarian crisis'.[1] The conflict's origins are complex in nature. However, it is often simplified as part of a wider struggle between Shia Islam-dominated Iran and the Sunni Muslims of Saudi Arabia for political and military domination in the Middle East. Other aspects of this struggle are reflected in Iranian support for President Bashar al-Assad's resurgent regime in Syria's own civil war and its ongoing efforts to strengthen its power base in Iraq. Adding to this complex, volatile situation is the long-standing enmity between Iran and Israel. In May 2018, the US Trump administration threw its weight decisively behind its Israeli and Saudi allies by withdrawing from the international deal – the Joint Comprehensive Plan of Action – agreed in 2015 to limit Iran's nuclear programme. President Trump's decision to tear up America's participation agreement in the face of International Atomic Energy Agency verification that Iran had been meeting its obligations has been a further cause of friction between the US and European countries, who remain committed to the deal.

The intervention of Saudi Arabia and its allies on the Gulf Cooperation Council and elsewhere against Houthi rebel forces in Yemen has been notable for a number of reasons. One has been the considerable difficulty the Saudi-led forces have experienced in defeating the rebels despite the rise in Saudi Arabia's c. US$70bn defence budget to amongst the top three globally. Another has been the considerable – if often little reported – maritime aspect to the campaign. Saudi coalition forces have resorted to a maritime blockade to prevent military and other supplies reaching rebel-held areas. They have also used naval vessels for logistical support and amphibious operations. In turn, coalition shipping been subject to a number of retaliatory attacks. The most notable of these was the destruction of the former US Navy-operated high speed vessel *Swift* – then under charter to the United Arab Emirates – by an anti-shipping missile in October 2016.

Although the Saudi-led coalition has been unforthcoming on the attacks on its warships and other shipping, it appears the challenge has been relatively significant. In May 2018, *Jane's Defence Weekly* reported that there had been more than ten attacks on naval and civilian vessels in the Red Sea and Gulf of Aden since the *Swift* incident.[2] This total included four engagements with coalition warships since June 2017. Subsequently, in June 2018, the Houthi repel group Ansar Allah claimed another strike on a vessel whilst repelling an amphibious landing undertaken as part of the coalition's attempts to capture the strategic port city of Al-Hudaydah.

Whilst publicly-available details of these maritime engagements are scant, they will doubtless provide food for thought for navies in and beyond the region. Lessons learned are likely to include the risks that remain inherent in operating off a hostile coast in the absence of operational anti-missile equipment supported by well-trained and alert crews. This lesson was previously demonstrated by the missile attack on the Israeli corvette *Hanit* off Lebanon in July 2006 but appears to need relearning. The use of unmanned maritime vehicles carrying improvised explosive devices has also revealed vulnerabilities, notably in the apparently unchallenged attack on the Saudi frigate *Al-Madinah* in January 2017. Equally, the rapid destruction of *Swift* suggests the seemingly successful adaptation of commercial designs for secondary military roles may not appear so attractive if the resulting vessels find themselves in a combat zone.

At a regional level, the Yemen experience might result in the acquisition of effective local naval forces being accorded greater priority than hitherto. Despite the region's turbulent nature, Middle Eastern countries have largely restricted naval investment to protecting their ports and coastal waters. Reliance has been placed on US and European allies for trade protection and broader maritime security. However, a revised approach is now becoming evident. Notably, Qatar confirmed a US$3.8bn order for surface combatants and an amphibious transport dock from Italy's Fincantieri in August 2017 whilst Egypt is already mid-way through a major naval expansion programme reportedly paid for with Saudi money. Saudi Arabia itself is also moving forward with delayed naval modernisation plans. Acquisition of multi-mission surface combatants based on the US Navy's LCS is being supplemented by purchases of new patrol vessels from Spain's Navantia.

The Royal Saudi Navy frigate *Makkah* pictured in company with the British Royal Navy's *Bulwark* in September 2014. The ongoing civil war in Yemen is giving many of the region's navies their first taste of combat, with mixed results. *(Crown Copyright 2015)*

Table 2.3.1: FLEET STRENGTHS IN THE INDIAN OCEAN, AFRICA AND THE MIDDLE EAST – LARGER NAVIES (MID 2018)

COUNTRY	ALGERIA	EGYPT	INDIA	IRAN	ISRAEL	PAKISTAN	SAUDI ARABIA	SOUTH AFRICA
Aircraft Carrier (CV)	–	–	1	–	–	–	–	–
Strategic Missile Submarine (SSBN)	-	-	1	-	-	-	-	-
Attack Submarine (SSN/SSGN)	–	–	1	–	–	–	–	–
Patrol Submarine (SSK/SS)	4	6	14	3	5	5	–	3
Fleet Escort (DDG/FFG)	2	8	24	–	–	9	7	4
Patrol Escort/Corvette (FFG/FSG/FS)	10	4	11	6	3	–	4	–
Missile Armed Attack Craft (PGG/PTG)	c.12	c.30	8	c.24	8	9	9	3
Mine Countermeasures Vessel (MCMV)	1	c.14	1	–	–	3	3	4
Major Amphibious (LPD)	1	2	1	–	–	–	–	–

Notes:

1 Algerian fast attack craft and Egyptian fast attack craft and mine-countermeasures numbers approximate.

2 Iranian fleet numbers exclude large numbers of indigenously-built midget and coastal submarines, as well as additional missile-armed craft operated by the Revolutionary Guard.

3 The South African attack craft and mine-countermeasures vessels serve in patrol vessel roles.

INDIA

The last year has seen the Indian Navy's expansionary ambitions continue to be held back by a poisonous cocktail of inadequate funding, industrial problems and operational mishaps. At first glance, the 2018–19 defence budget estimate of INR 279, 305 crore (c. US$41bn) – some seven percent above last year's total – shows solid growth. However, this has only been sufficient to stabilise the past trend of growth in revenue expenditure – particularly salaries – running ahead of the total. As such, capital expenditure – essentially equipment procurement – remains at around a third of overall expenditure, down from forty percent at the start of the decade. This trend is also reflected in the dominance of the manpower-heavy army's share of total spending: a massive fifty percent compared to just fifteen percent allocated to the Indian Navy. Whilst navy modernisation funding is expected to show a reasonable six percent growth year-on-year, this does not restore the previous year's decline. Moreover, the INR 19,927 (c. US$2.1bn) allocated remains insufficient to support any significant expansion.[3]

Inadequate funding is being exacerbated by ongoing procurement and industrial problems. Not without reason did former Indian Chief of Staff General V K Singh declare that Indian procurement was, 'a version of snakes and ladders, where there is no ladder, but only snakes'.[4] The most recent debacle has been the January 2018 termination of a US$5bn deal with South Korea's Kangnam Corporation for the licensed-built construction of minehunters after a failure to agree detailed terms, the second time the deal had been cancelled. The result will be the total withdrawal of India's mine countermeasures fleet before replacements arrive. Another problem is lack of industrial capacity to implement the current government's 'Made in India' policy. The aim was to alleviate this by allocating work to private yards. However, a number have experienced financial difficulties, placing construction of patrol vessels and auxiliaries in jeopardy.

Substantial investment in modernising India's publicly-owned shipyards has also been authorised to ease capacity constraints. However, even this approach has not been entirely successful. On 17 April 2018, a 250-ton capacity 'Goliath crane' installed at Kolkata's Garden Reach Shipbuilders and Engineers Ltd (GRSE) collapsed in what were claimed to be cyclonic conditions. The accident badly damaged infrastructure supporting construction of the three new Project 17A frigates the yard is scheduled to deliver from 2023. GRSE has claimed, somewhat improbably, that the accident will not delay completion of the programme. Speaking to *The Times of India*, their spokesperson added – apparently without irony – that 'somebody may have taken this opportunity to tarnish our image'.[5] The accident is just one of many to impact the navy in the last years, with recent incidents apparently resulting in both the strategic submarine *Arihant* and the attack submarine *Chakra* being sidelined following significant accidents.[6] Whilst the demanding nature of warship construction and operation inevitably result in accidents, the Indian Navy's track record of disasters is indicative of a more systematic malaise.

Current Indian fleet composition is outlined in Table 2.3.2. The major development in the past year has been the commissioning of the first Indian-built Project 75 'Scorpène' type submarine *Kalvari* on 14 December 2017, some six years behind schedule. However, the programme now appears to be back on track. The second boat, *Khanderi*, in the final stages of sea trials and the third, *Karanj*, was launched on 31 January 2018. A further three submarines are in various stages of construction. Whilst a welcome boost to the fleet, many of the existing 'Kilo' (*Sindhughosh*) and Type 209 (*Shishumar*) boats have now passed their thirtieth birthdays. Accordingly, more submarines are needed to maintain fleet numbers. Four companies – France's Naval Group, Germany's TKMS, Russia's Rubin Central Design Bureau and Sweden's Saab Kockums – have responded to a request for information to partner Indian industry in delivering six AIP-equipped submarines under Project 75(I). The Indian Navy also has plans to build a flotilla of six nuclear-powered attack submarines but it is hard to conceive of this being achieved in the foreseeable future. For the present, the priority is progressing construction of the *Arihant* strategic submarines. The plan is to follow the prototype with three further boats of an improved design. The first of these, named *Arighat*, was reportedly launched on 19 November 2017.

Turning to the surface fleet, there has been something of a pause in deliveries of major surface combatants pending delivery of the new Project 15B

The Indian Navy is starting to see delivery of its *Kalvari* ('Scorpène') class submarines after several years of delays. This image shows second of class *Khanderi* on sea trials in 2017. *(Naval Group)*

Table 2.3.2: INDIAN NAVY: PRINCIPAL UNITS AS AT MID 2018

TYPE	CLASS	NUMBER	TONNAGE	DIMENSIONS	PROPULSION	CREW	DATE
Aircraft Carriers							
Aircraft Carrier (CV)	Project 1143.4 **VIKRAMADITYA** (KIEV)	1	45,000 tons	283m x 31/60m x 10m	Steam, 30 knots	1,600	1987
Principal Surface Escorts							
Destroyer – DDG	Project 15A **KOLKATA**	3	7,400 tons	163m x 17m x 7m	COGAG, 30+knots	330	2014
Destroyer – DDG	Project 15 **DELHI**	3	6,700 tons	163m x 17m x 7m	COGAG, 32 knots	350	1997
Destroyer – DDG	Project 61 ME **RAJPUT** ('Kashin')	5	5,000 tons	147m x 16m x 5m	COGAG, 35 knots	320	1980
Frigate – FFG	Project 17 **SHIVALIK**	3	6,200 tons	143m x 17m x 5m	CODOG, 30 knots	265	2010
Frigate – FFG	Project 1135.6 **TALWAR**	6	4,000 tons	125m x 15m x 5m	COGAG, 30 knots	180	2003
Frigate – FFG	Project 16A **BRAHMAPUTRA**	3	4,000 tons	127m x 15m x 5m	Steam, 30 knots	350	2000
Frigate – FFG	Project 16 **GODAVARI**	1	3,850 tons	127m x 15m x 5m	Steam, 30 knots	315	1983
Corvette – FSG	Project 28 **KAMORTA**	3	3,400 tons	109m x 13m x 4m	Diesel, 25 knots	195	2014
Corvette – FSG	Project 25A **KORA**	4	1,400 tons	91m x 11m x 5m	Diesel, 25 knots	125	1998
Corvette – FSG	Project 25 **KHUKRI**	4	1,400 tons	91m x 11m x 5m	Diesel, 25 knots	110	1989
Submarines							
Submarine – SSBN	**ARIHANT**	1	7,500+ tons	112m x 11m x 10m	Nuclear, 25+ knots	100	2016
Submarine – SSN	Project 971 **CHAKRA** ('Akula II')	1	9,500+ tons	110m x 14m x 10m	Nuclear, 30+ knots	100	2012
Submarine – SSK	Project 75 **KALVARI** ('Scorpène)	1	1,800 tons	68m x 6m x 6m	Diesel-electric, 20 knots	45	2017
Submarine – SSK	Project 877 EKM **SINDHUGHOSH** ('Kilo')	9	3,000 tons	73m x 10m x 7m	Diesel-electric, 17 knots	55	1986
Submarine – SSK	**SHISHUMAR** (Type 209)	4	1,900 tons	64m x 7m x 6m	Diesel-electric, 22 knots	40	1986
Major Amphibious Units							
Landing Platform Dock – LPD	**JALASHWA** (AUSTIN)	1	17,000 tons	173m x 26/30m x 7m	Steam, 21 knots	405	1971

Visakhapatnam class destroyers and as-yet unnamed Project 17A frigates. These are planned to enter service from the 2020s onwards. As for the submarine fleet, there is a risk that fleet numbers will fall in consequence. A contract to acquire additional Project 1135.6 *Talwar* class frigates is therefore reportedly in the final stages of negotiation. This would see two additional units of the class completed by Russia's Yantar Shipyard at Kaliningrad and a second pair built under licence at Goa Shipyard in India. It is not entirely clear whether the Yantar-built ships will be the existing Russian *Admiral Grigorovich* class variants of the design laid up for want of Ukrainian turbines or entirely new vessels.

In the absence of major warship deliveries, the main recent arrival in the surface fleet has been the third Project 28 *Kamorta* class corvette *Kiltan*. Built by GRSE, she was commissioned on 16 October 2017. A fourth vessel, *Kavaratti*, is reportedly close to completion but the design appears not to have been completely satisfactory. Consequently, production of further ships is likely to be superseded by larger 'Next Generation Corvettes'. However, a more pressing requirement is the need to replace the navy's

Delays with surface combatant programmes has resulted in India seeking to increase its flotilla of Russian-built *Talwar* class frigates from six to ten. This image shows *Tarkash* on exercises with the British Royal Navy Type 23 frigate *Richmond* in May 2017 *(Crown Copyright 2017)*

coastal anti-surface and anti-submarine vessels of the *Veer* (Project 1241.1) and *Abhay* (Project 1241.2) classes. These are starting to be retired as they reach the end of their design lives, with *Nirbhik* and *Nirghat* the most recent to leave the fleet on 11 January 2018. A new class of shallow-water anti-submarine vessels has been authorised, with construction of sixteen vessels to be split equally between Cochin Shipyard and GRSE.

OTHER INDIAN OCEAN NAVIES

Bangladesh: 2018 has seen the Bangladesh Navy continue to make steady progress with its modernisation programme following a momentous 2017 that saw achievement of its targeted three-dimensional force structure with the delivery of two former PLAN Type 035G 'Ming' class submarines. China has also played a major role in more recent fleet enhancements, the most significant of which has been the commissioning of a second pair of *Durjoy* class patrol vessels on 8 November 2017. Unlike the two earlier Chinese vessels, *Durgam* and *Nishan* were assembled under licence at Khulna

Shipyard. The ships are equipped for coastal anti-submarine duties and previous reports suggest at least eight are planned.

2018 should also see delivery of a second pair of Type 13B coastal corvettes derived from the PLAN's Type 056 design. *Shongram* and *Prottasha* were both launched in the first half of 2018 from the Wuchang shipyard that completed the earlier ships. Published images suggest they will incorporate a number of detailed changes, including a new phased-array radar. As for the *Durjoy* class, it has been suggested that production may transition to Bangladesh under a licensed arrangement. However, a high priority seems to be the acquisition of larger frigates to supplement the early Type 053 series vessels previously acquired second hand from the PLAN. This could be followed by construction of new Type 054 series frigates in due course.

Myanmar: One influence on Bangladesh's fleet modernisation programme is the expansion of neighbouring Myanmar's naval capabilities. It has slowly developed a significant indigenous naval

construction capability and has been steadily evolving a series of new frigate and corvette designs. Fleet modernisation has been accompanied by attempts to build links with other regional fleets, most notably with the Indian Navy. In late March and early April 2018, the two fleets held the first ever joint naval exercise – IMNEX-18 – off India's east coast. The developing association between the two fleets has not been without controversy given human rights concerns over Myanmar's treatment of the minority Rohingya community. However, it is yet another indication of the priority India attaches to countering growing Chinese regional sway throughout the Indian Ocean region and has been reflected in a stepping up of similar exercises with other regional fleets.

Pakistan: India's main regional concern is the developing economic and military axis between China and Pakistan. Pakistan has been increasingly turning to China to upgrade its defence capabilities, not least in the naval sphere. In 2015 it agreed to modernise and expand its submarine flotilla with the acquisition of eight export-variants of China's Type 039A 'Yuan' class. Construction of the 'Hangor II' type is being split between China and Pakistan. Deliveries will commence in the 2022/2023 timescale and all eight will be in service by 2028. In the meantime, the three existing 'Agosta 90B' submarines are being modernised under a US$350m deal with Turkey's STM announced in 2016. Upgrades are focused on command systems and sensors, with work being performed at Karachi Shipyard & Engineering Works (KSEW) from internationally-sourced packages of equipment and systems. The first modernised submarine, *Khalid*, is expected to be delivered by 2020. She will be followed by *Saad* and – if an option is confirmed – *Hamza* at annual intervals.[7]

With modernisation of its submarine fleet now well in hand, Pakistan has also turned to China for the renewal of its surface fleet. Reports emerged in the second half of 2017 that Chinese frigates would be acquired to replace the fleet's remaining 1970s-era former British Royal Navy Type 21 frigates. Subsequently, in June 2018, it was confirmed that a total of four of the PLAN's Type 054A design had been ordered for delivery by 2021. The ships will join the four existing upgraded Type 053H3 *Zulfiqar* class vessels inducted between 2009 and 2013 to provide a relatively homogenous force of front-line surface combatants. Maintaining the

The Sri Lanka Navy is continuing its transition to a constabulary force with longer-range patrol vessels. This image shows the new 'advanced offshore patrol vessel' *Sayurala*, one of two new ships delivered by India's Goa Shipyard in the last twelve months. She subsequently undertook the Sri Lanka Navy's lengthiest deployment in over half a century to participate in the ASEAN 50th Anniversary Fleet Review, where this image was taken in November 2017. *(Arjun Sarup)*

theme of joint reliance on Chinese and Turkish suppliers, discussions are also reportedly close to completion on the acquisition of four 'Milgem' type corvettes, which would be focused on anti-submarine warfare in the littorals. If the deal goes ahead, two of the ships will be built in Turkey and two at KSEW.

The proposed 'Milgem' acquisition can be seen in the context of a likely anti-access/area denial (A2/AD) strategy that also encompasses the submarine flotilla and missile-armed fast attack craft. A variant of the Chinese Type 037II 'Houjian' has been selected for this role and delivery of the lead ship, *Azmat*, has been followed by licensed construc-

tion of additional vessels by KSEW. The shipyard delivered the third ship, *Himmat*, on 27 July 2017. Work is now well advanced on a fourth vessel and more are planned. The last year also saw KSEW complete construction of the STM-designed replenishment vessel, *Moawin*, which completed its first trials at the end of March 2018.

Looking forward, KSEW will be involved in yet another new construction project following an order for two Damen-designed OPV1900 patrol vessels in June 2017. The 90m, 1,900-ton vessels are equipped for helicopter operations and will carry an armament suitable for their constabulary mission. Construction of the lead vessel has been assigned to Damen's yard at Galati in Romania, where construction got underway in the first quarter of 2018. However, assembly of the second will transition to KSEW in a further move to enhance the yard's skills.

Sri Lanka: The Sri Lanka Navy's investment in improved long-range constabulary capabilities has seen the delivery of two new *Saryu* class offshore patrol vessels ordered from India's Goa Shipyard. The lead ship, *Sayurala*, was commissioned on 7 August 2017 and was followed by her sister *Sindurala* on 19 April 2018. The 2,200-ton vessels are the largest vessels to service in Sri Lanka's fleet. *Sayurala* participated in the November 2017 ASEAN fleet review soon after her delivery. This marked the longest deployment made by the navy for over fifty years.

AFRICAN NAVIES

Although **South Africa's** navy continues to be the only maritime force of significance south of the Sahara, it continues to suffer from the impact of weak economic performance and associated inadequate levels of defence funding. The 2018/19 budget showed a small decline over the previous year and remains wholly inadequate for the force structure outlined in the 2014 Defence Review. The consequences of lack of money are already being felt. In August 2017, it transpired that the acquisition of three offshore patrol vessels under the long-running Project Biro had been shelved, leaving only three smaller inshore vessels in the current plan. They were subsequently ordered from Damen Shipyards Cape Town in February 2018. The ships will be based on the company's Stan Patrol 6211 design and incorporate a Sea Axe hull. Although

Indian Ocean Island Navies

The remote Indian Ocean island groups have become a key focal point in India's efforts to counter growing Chinese regional influence. This is reflected in the development of an Indian-led network of coastal surveillance radars, controversial attempts to establish a naval base and airstrip in the Seychelles, and the ongoing promotion of Indian equipment for use by the various island nations' paramilitary forces. The Indian shipbuilding industry has been successful in supplying an increasing number of constabulary vessels as part of this approach. Typical of the new vessels are the Mauritius National Coast

Guard fast patrol ships *Victory* and *Valiant*, which were commissioned in December 2016 and August 2017. Part of a series of orders from India's Goa Shipyard that also included ten fast interceptors, the ships join the offshore patrol vessel Barracuda delivered by GRSE in 2014. The 300-ton, 50m *Victory* class vessels are based on the Indian Coast Guard's Sarojini Naidu class design and are intended for coastal constabulary missions. A diesel-powered waterjet propulsion system provides a maximum speed of 37 knots whilst armament includes a 30mm CRN-91 gun and heavy machine guns.

Many of the small Indian Ocean Island coast guards are upgrading their constabulary capabilities. India is providing significant financial and technical assistance, partly to counter growing Chinese regional influence and partly to boost Indian industry. This image shows the Mauritius National Coast Guard's fast patrol craft *Victory*, one of a pair of ships delivered by Goa Shipyard. *(Arjun Sarup)*

The Algerian Navy is slowly growing its ability to assemble increasingly complex ships. This image shows *Rais Hassan Barbiear*, the latest in a series of four *Djebel Chenoua* class corvettes built at ECRN Mers el Kébir. *(US Navy)*

The Egyptian Navy is in the middle of a major programme to update its naval capabilities. This is seeing new ships such as the lead 'Gowind 2500' class corvette *El Fateh* join the fleet, significantly enhancing effectiveness over an earlier generation of warships. *(Naval Group)*

doubtless a welcome addition to the navy's capabilities, there has been criticism over prioritisation of ships which are arguably too large for inshore patrol but unsuitable for longer range duties given local oceanic conditions.

Meanwhile, it seems that maintaining the operational capabilities of existing vessels is also a growing issue. Speaking at the inaugural South African Maritime Security Conference in Cape Town in May 2018, the navy's head, Vice Admiral Mosuwa Hlongwane, blamed inadequate provision for logistical support when the navy's sophisticated frigates and submarines were acquired during the 1990s for the problem.[8] Attempts to boost the number of hours the navy spends at sea appear to have been abandoned, partly due to limited availability of serviceable ships.

Elsewhere in Sub-Saharan Africa, there is an ongoing, if patchy, trend to improve maritime constabulary capabilities to secure valuable offshore resources and combat piracy. The International Chamber of Commerce's Commercial Crime Services arm reported a major surge in armed attacks against shipping off West Africa in the first quarter of 2018, with twenty-nine incidents – more than forty percent of the global total – occurring in this region.[9] The acquisition of new-build inshore and coastal patrol vessels has been one response, with French industry using its long association with the former French West African colonies to carve out a strong market niche in these and neighbouring

countries. Aluminium-build specialist OCEA appears to have been particularly successful. It has delivered a series of 24m, 32m and 35m patrol vessels to **Nigeria**, as well as the larger 59m *Fouladou* to **Senegal**. A 60m hydrographic survey vessel similar to ships completed for Indonesia is also under Nigerian order. Another interesting development in Senegal has been the establishment of a joint venture between Brittany-based Piriou and local company Ngom & Freres to provide shipbuilding, maintenance and repair services to the naval and fisheries sectors. Many African navies have previously suffered from poor support and serviceability; the import of international expertise may well prove an effective way of tackling this perennial problem.

Turning to North Africa, Algeria and Egypt have been the twin drivers of regional naval expansion in recent years. The impact of lower energy prices apparently slowed **Algeria's** previously ambitious procurement plans in the middle of the decade but recent reports suggest a willingness to commit to new programmes. The most advanced of these is a plan to undertake licensed-construction of the heavily-armed Project 22160 patrol vessel design by Russia's Zelenodolsk yard, six of which are currently under construction for the Russian Navy's Black Sea fleet. Algeria has previously completed a series of four *Djebel Chenoua* class corvettes at ECRN Mers el Kébir, the most recent delivered in August 2017 but local completion of the much larger Project

22160 ships would be a major undertaking.[10] Meanwhile, 2018 should see the fruits of earlier procurement funding with the arrival of two new Project 636.1 'Kilo' class submarines from Russia to supplement the four already in service. The fleet has already been reinforced by the commissioning of the new minehunter *El-Kasseh 1*, which was commissioned on 30 September 2017. A derivative of the Finnish *Katanpää* class, she is part of a larger order that could ultimately extend to three or four more vessels.

Egypt's impressive modernisation plans are also moving ahead with the arrival of further new major combatants. In total, Egypt has taken delivery of two amphibious assault ships, two submarines, a FREMM frigate, a 'Gowind' corvette and five missile-armed fast attack craft in the past few years, with at least two more submarines and three corvettes to follow. This has been supported by significant investment in upgraded infrastructure.[11] Major deliveries over the past year include the second new Type 209/1400 submarine, *S42*, which was handed over by ThyssenKrupp Marine Systems (TKMS) at Kiel on 8 August 2017. Two further submarines of the class are currently under construction. Another new arrival was the first Naval Group 'Gowind 2500' type corvette *El Fateh*, which was delivered at Lorient the following month. Three additional units are under construction at Alexandria. However, some reports suggest the rate of progress is slower than initially anticipated. This may result in further construction in France to fill the gap. The remarkable rate of expansion – which many believe has been assisted with Saudi Arabian funding – goes far beyond that needed for defence of the Suez Canal and other territorial maritime interests. It is therefore probably best viewed in the context of an intention to create a regional naval interventionist capability to support broader Arab interests throughout the Middle East.

MIDDLE EASTERN NAVIES

The theme of increased naval investment is also apparent elsewhere in the broader Middle Eastern region. A particularly notable development has been long-awaited progress with **Saudi Arabia's** naval modernisation plans for its Eastern Fleet based at Al Jubail.[12] Firm orders for four of Lockheed Martin's multi-mission surface combatant (MMSC) variants of its *Freedom* (LCS-1) class design now appear to be in place, with detailed design work and the construction of long lead items already underway. The design uses the same hull and propulsion system as the basic *Freedom* and shares the same basic combat system architecture. However, weapons and sensors – including an eight-cell Mk 41 vertical-launch system and surface-to-surface missiles – are upgraded at the expense of some loss of modularity. Saudi Arabia has also moved ahead with acquisition

of five Spanish Navantia 'Avante 2200' patrol corvettes. These are based on the design previously sold to Venezuela. However, they will have a more powerful armament with some similarities to the MMSCs they are intended to operate alongside. It appears that construction will take place in Navantia's Spanish yards, although the deal also involves the creation of a local industrial joint venture for systems integration and ongoing support and maintenance.

Beyond Saudi Arabia, **Qatar's** major naval contract with Fincantieri is moving ahead whilst the **United Arab Emirates** is reportedly in the final stages of negotiation for a pair of 'Gowind' corvettes similar to Egypt's ships. Meanwhile, **Iraq's** navy received an upgrade of a rather different kind at the end of June 2017 when two 'Assad' class corvettes were finally delivered from Italy after a 26-year delay. The corvettes were part of a class of six originally ordered in the 1980s but never delivered due to an UN-imposed arms embargo after Iraq's 1990 invasion of Kuwait. Four were subsequently sold to Malaysia. Although the embargo was lifted in 2003, it was not until 2014 that a revised deal to deliver the remaining pair was finally agreed. A planned modernisation was never carried out and the vessel were shipped from lay-up at La Spezia to Iraq on the heavy-lift vessel *Eide Trader* in close to their 1980s condition.

Much of the naval build-up in the Middle East has been driven by concerns over **Iran's** attempts to expand its influence in the region. The Islamic Republic of Iran Navy and the independent Iranian Revolutionary Guard Corps Naval Forces both continue to focus largely on A2/AD capabilities in the Persian Gulf, although reports of equipment deliveries are often contradictory. The navy is also active in the Caspian Sea, where its fleet suffered a major setback in January 2018. Here the second 'Moudge' class frigate *Damavand* hit the breakwater at Banadar-e-Anzali on 10 January and subsequently appears to have become a total loss.

Israel also continues with its naval modernisation efforts. Most significantly, signature of a memorandum of understanding for additional German submarines was confirmed in October 2017. The three new boats are expected to start to commission in the late 2020s, replacing the three oldest *Dolphin* class submarines. Meanwhile, construction of the last Dolphin Batch II trio – *Dakar* – continues at TKMS in Kiel. Work is also underway at Kiel on the lead 'Sa'ar 6' *Magen* class corvettes following a keel-laying ceremony in February 2018. The first of four vessels, she is expected to be operational by the end of the decade. The new ships will supplement the three 'Sa'ar 5' corvettes and eight 'Sa'ar 4.5' fast attack craft, which are all receiving major sensor upgrades.

Notes

1. See the press release dated 3 April 2018 'Remarks by the Secretary-General to the Pledging Conference on Yemen' (Geneva: The United Nations Office at Geneva, 2018).

2. See Jeremy Binnie's 'More attacks on naval vessels in Red Sea revealed', *Jane's Defence Weekly* – 30 May 2018 (Coulsdon: IHS Jane's, 2018), p.17.

3. The headline budget figure ignores spending on c. 2.5 million military pensions that adds around US$15bn to total military spending. Detailed analysis can be found in Laxman K Behara's annual budgetary review, this year entitled *Defence Budget 2018-19: The Imperative of Controlling Manpower Cost* (New Delhi: Institute for Defence Studies and Analyses, 2018), available by searching: idsa.in/

4. General Singh was quoted in Rahul Bedi's 'Briefing Indian defence procurement – Growing pains' *Jane's Defence Weekly* – 21 February 2018 (Coulsdon: IHS Jane's,

2018), pp.22–30. The article provides a comprehensive overview of current Indian procurement programmes and challenges.

5. See Jayanta Gupta's 'GRSE strives to achieve milestones despite major accident', *The Times of India* – 4 May 2018 (Mumbai: The Times Group, 2018).

6. *Arihant* was apparently flooded after the accidental opening of a hatch whilst she was in harbour allowed seawater to access part of the submarine. She returned to service in January 2018 after ten months of repairs. The leased nuclear-powered attack submarine *Chakra* was reportedly damaged when two panels were dislodged during a grounding. Repairs are not yet complete.

7. A good source of information on naval developments in Pakistan is the *Quwa Defence News & Analysis Group's* website at: quwa.org/

8. See Dean Wingrin's 'Navy looks backward for future acquisitions' posted to the *defenceWeb* site on 8 June

2018. The site at defenceweb.co.za/ remains an excellent source of information on ongoing developments with respect to African navies and the continent's wider militaries.

9. See the press release 'Pirate Attacks worsen in the Gulf of Guinea' posted to the *ICC* website: icc-ccs.org/ on 10 April 2018.

10. Some reports suggest the new corvette – named *Rais Hassen Barbiar* – is an enlarged 62m variant of the original 58m design with much greater use of Chinese weaponry than the earlier vessels.

11. More detail on Egypt's new naval infrastructure is contained in Jeremy Binnie's 'Egypt building three new naval bases', *Jane's Defence Weekly* – 1 November 2017 (Coulsdon: IHS Jane's, 2017), p.14.

12. Saudi Arabia's topography means it needs to split its naval forces between a Western Fleet in the Red Sea based at Jeddah and the Persian Gulf-based Eastern Fleet.

2.4 REGIONAL REVIEW

EUROPE AND RUSSIA

Author:
Conrad Waters

INTRODUCTION

One consequence of the shift in naval power from Europe towards the Asian economies has been an increasingly uncertain outlook for the Continent's once globally-dominant warship building sector. The impact of the Cold War's end resulted in a dramatic reduction in the size of most European navies and an associated decline in demand for new ships. Initially, this could be mitigated by leveraging the industry's technological strengths to switch surplus capacity to meet the needs of growing navies overseas. However, the resulting orders often came with a requirement for the transfer of technology and know-how to support local production. Ships – and equipment – that would once have been built in, say, Glasgow, Kiel or Lorient are now being assembled in Mumbai, Shanghai or Ulsan. A particularly vivid example of the new reality was the delivery of Indonesia's new Type 209/1400 submarine *Nagapasa* from South Korea's DSME in August 2017. The order was won in competition against the Type 209's original German designer and with only limited overseas technological assistance.

The last year has seen various European naval shipbuilding nations adopt new approaches in the face of this threat. In September 2017, the United Kingdom's government published its long-awaited *National Shipbuilding Strategy*.[1] Building on a previous report from respected industrialist Sir John Parker, it essentially aims to establish secure foundations for a competitive naval shipbuilding sector, including its supply chain. This includes develop-

ment of a long-term plan for warship procurement and designing ships with an emphasis on exports from the outset. Pragmatically, there appears to be a recognition that the sale of project management, design, equipment and sub-systems is likely to be at least as significant as the export of entire ships. The strategy places significant emphasis on the value of competition. It seemingly seeks to break BAE Systems' current monopoly in the construction of major warships and confirms that construction of 'non-warships' will be open to international bids. The planned programme for five Type 31e general purpose frigates is intended to be a pathfinder for the new approach. In the meantime, the strategy received a major boost in June 2018 with the selection of BAE Systems' Type 26 Global Combat Ship to meet Australia's Future Frigate requirement. The deal represents Britain's most significant involvement in an overseas navy programme for many decades.

Meanwhile France and Italy appear to have determined that strengthened collaboration is the best response to current challenges. Discussions are underway that would expand previous cooperation on programmes such as the 'Horizon' and FREMM classes of surface combatants. The aim is full merger of the Fincantieri and Naval Group yards building surface warships. The mooted deal follows Fincantieri's plan to assume effective control over STX's facility at St-Nazaire, France's major commercial shipyard. An announcement of the terms of the arrangement was anticipated by June 2018. However, this had been delayed by the emergence of a new

Italian government. There is also a need to establish how key equipment suppliers Leonardo and Thales will interface with the new venture. The prospect of establishing a Franco-Italian naval powerhouse has obvious attractions in terms of achieving synergies in areas such as development and procurement. It should also ensure a coordinated approach to future international competitions. However, the challenges involved in managing any future conflict between differing national defence and industrial priorities are likely to be significant.

An example of the potential pitfalls of overly-ambitious expansion are provided by Germany's ThyssenKrupp Marine Systems (TKMS). Its previous attempts to secure a commanding presence in the European naval sector through acquisitions in Greece and Sweden have long been reversed. However, it now seems that its remaining operations – the HDW submarine yard in Kiel and a design and project management capability – are in danger of being sold. In March 2018, it was revealed that the group's joint bid with Lürssen for the German Navy's next MKS180 surface combatant had been rejected. Local press reports suggest excessive cost and poor performance delivering the previous F125 *Baden-Württemberg* class frigates were largely to blame.[2] Whilst the new ships will ultimately still be built in Germany, they may well be designed elsewhere. The result could therefore be the end of a long track record of German success in warship development that can be traced back to the early modular MEKO designs of the late 1970s.

The United Kingdom's new National Shipbuilding Strategy – published in September 2017 – aims to inject greater competition into British warship acquisition. Babcock International's 'Arrowhead 120' light frigate was one of a number of concepts prepared in relation to the resulting Type 31e procurement competition. However, Babcock has subsequently substituted a larger 'Arrowhead 140' design based on the Danish *Iver Huitfeldt* hull form as the basis of its proposal. *(Babcock International)*

TABLE 2.4.1: FLEET STRENGTHS IN WESTERN EUROPE – LARGER NAVIES (MID 2018)

COUNTRY	FRANCE	GERMANY	GREECE	ITALY	NETHERLANDS	SPAIN	TURKEY	UK
Aircraft Carrier (CVN/CV)	1	–	–	1	–	–	–	1
Support/Helicopter Carrier (CVS/CVH)	–	–	–	1	–	–	–	–
Strategic Missile Submarine (SSBN)	4	–	–	–	–	–	–	4
Attack Submarine (SSN)	6	–	–	–	–	–	–	7
Patrol Submarine (SSK)	–	6	11[2]	8	4	3	12	–
Fleet Escort (DDG/FFG)	17	9	13	18[2]	6	11	16	19
Patrol Escort/Corvette (FFG/FSG/FS)	15	5	–	2	–	–	8	–
Missile Armed Attack Craft (PGG/PTG)	–	–	17	–	–	–	19	–
Mine Countermeasures Vessel (MCMV)	14	10[1]	4	10	6	6	11	13
Major Amphibious (LHD/LPD/LPH/LSD)	3	–	–	3	2[3]	3	–	5

Notes:

1 Two further units used as support vessels.

2 Headline figures overstate the actual position, as old ships will be withdrawn once new units are fully operational.

3 Also one joint support ship with amphibious capabilities.

MAJOR REGIONAL POWERS – FRANCE

The last year has seen France publish both a *Defence & National Security Review 2017* and a revised *Military Planning Law 2019/2025*.[3] The former is a policy document setting out the main challenges to French security and the military capabilities that are required to deal with them. It concludes that the risk and threats previously identified in the last, 2013, defence white paper have evolved more rapidly than expected. As such, the French military are faced with the prospect of more difficult conflicts and better-armed potential adversaries in an unstable strategic environment. It therefore sees a need to rebuild capacity to ensure a balanced, full-spectrum defence capability to ensure France's strategic autonomy and independence of action, albeit in strong partnership with the European Union and France's other traditional allies.

The *Military Planning Law* sets out the resources that are required to achieve these objectives. In order to end the past erosion of military capabilities, spending will increase by c. twenty-three percent in the period 2019–2023 compared with 2014–2018 and reach the NATO target of two percent of GDP by 2025. The additional resources will secure the completion of existing programmes and allow some

to be accelerated and expanded. They will also allow the start of the expensive process of renewing the airborne and underwater elements of France's strategic nuclear deterrent. This will cost around €25bn in the period 2019–2023, over twenty percent of the budget devoted to equipment.

The proposed development of the *Marine Nationale*'s force structure under the new law is contained in Table 2.4.2.[4] In spite of the substantial increase in spending, force levels are only projected to increase marginally. This possibly reflects the degree of underfunding contained in previous plans. Brief comments with respect to major warship categories follow:

Aircraft Carriers and Amphibious Ships: The aircraft carrier *Charles de Gaulle* is now entering the final stages of her nuclear-refuelling and modernisation at Toulon. She should return to operational service in 2019. Preliminary studies have already commenced into a next-generation aircraft carrier that will form her eventual replacement. Naval Group, STX and the TechnicAtome reactor manufacturer are all involved in the study, suggesting a nuclear-powered carrier is being sought. The final go-ahead for the project is not scheduled until the

latter half of the 2020s. At that stage a decision will be taken on whether to embark on a two-ship programme to ensure a continuous carrier strike capability.

The new planning law maintains the previously reduced three-strong amphibious assault ship force, as well as four B2M *bâtiment multi-mission* type vessels. The last of these, *Dumont D'Urville*, is currently being built by Piriou at Concarneau under its Kership alliance with Naval Group.

Submarines: Submarine construction is currently focused on the six new 'Barracuda' or *Suffren* class nuclear-powered attack submarines. Completion of the lead boat has slipped further to the right in the course of the past year and a definite date for launch had still to be published as at June 2018. However, it is envisaged that sea trials will commence in 2019 prior to delivery in 2020, some three years later than initially planned. A formal order for the fifth member of the class, which will now be named *Rubis*, was placed on 7 May 2018. The service life of the existing *Rubis* – now over thirty-five years old – has been extended until *Suffren* arrives.

Surface Combatants: Construction of FREMM

Table 2.4.2 FRENCH NAVY – FORCE STRUCTURE EVOLUTION

TYPE	2019	2025	FORCE GOAL	COMMENTS
Aircraft Carrier	1	1	1	Increase to 2 carriers to be considered at time of replacement
Strategic Submarines	4	4	4	Work on replacements to commence
Attack Submarines	6	6	6	4 *Suffren* + 2 *Rubis* by 2025
Amphibious Assault Ships	3	3	3	
Fleet Escorts	17	17[1]	15	2 'Horizon' + 8 FREMM +2 FTI + 5 *La Fayette* by 2025.
Patrol Escorts	6	6	Not stated	
Patrol Vessels	16	18	19[2]	11 new vessels + 7 legacy vessels by 2025
Replenishment Vessels	3	3	4[3]	2 new vessels + 1 *Durance* by 2025.
MCMVs	15	14	Not stated	5 'Tripartite' + 3 *Vulcain* + 2 mother ship +4 drones by 2025
Multi-Mission Ships (B2M)	3	4	Not stated	
Support Ships (BSAH)	2	4	Not stated	
Strike Fighters	41	42	40	All Rafale
Heavy/Medium Helicopters	36	27	27	All NFH90
Light Helicopters	45	45	49	
Maritime Patrol Aircraft	22	18	18	All modernised ATL2 aircraft by 2025
Surveillance Aircraft	13	11	Not stated	

Notes
1 Represents an increase of 2 on previous plans.
2 Represents an increase of 2 on previous plans.
3 Represents an increase of 1 on previous plans.

frigates is now entering its final phases, with fabrication of the eighth and final French unit, *Lorraine*, commencing at Lorient in June 2018. Steel cutting for the first of the planned *frégates de taille intermédiaire* (FTI) is then scheduled around the end of 2019. This will allow the first of class to be delivered in 2023. Subsequent ships will follow at an approximate annual drumbeat. Although previous plans restricting modernisation of the *La Fayette* class to just three of the five ships have been maintained, all will still be in service in 2025 to maintain a seventeen-strong fleet of front-line surface combatants. This is two more ships than previously envisaged. Meanwhile, the remaining FASM-70 frigates of the *Georges Leygues* class are being withdrawn from service as the FREMMs arrive. *Montcalm* was decommissioned in July 2017 and the remainder will follow at approximately annual intervals between now and 2021.

Patrol Vessels: The new planning law accelerated long-awaited plans to replace France's outdated force of offshore patrol vessels. Moreover, numbers will ultimately increase from the current sixteen to an eventual total of nineteen. This is two more than previously planned. However, there was a sting in the tale. The previous BATSIMAR (*bâtiments de surveillance et d'intervention maritime*) project will now be split into two. Smaller and cheaper *patouilleurs outre-mer* (POM) will be acquired to police the overseas territories, with higher specification *patouilleurs de haute mer de nouvelle génération* (PHM-NG) following at a somewhat slower pace. The two *La Confiance* or PLG light patrol vessels specifically designed for operations in the shallow waters off French Guiana will also be joined by a third unit ordered in December 2017 for service in the French Antilles. It seems likely, however, that there will be some short-term dip in numbers as existing vessels are decommissioned. Notably, 2018 should see the start of the withdrawal of the reclassified A-69 class *avisos*, with *l'Herminier* and *Lavallée* both scheduled for decommissioning before the end of the year.

The new polar patrol and logistic support ship *L'Astrolabe* was completed in the summer of 2017 and officially delivered on 11 September 2017 on arrival at her new operating base of La Réunion.

Auxiliaries and Other Ships: Another significant programme confirmed in the recent defence

The French A-69 class *aviso Commandant L'Herminier* pictured on the River Clyde in April 2018. The remaining French ships are now classified as patrol vessels and will start to be replaced by new ships during the 2019–25 procurement period. *(Michael Leek)*

The French polar patrol ship *L'Astrolabe* has now commenced her duties in the southern hemisphere. This picture shows her departing Concarneau in the course of trials during July 2017. *(Bruno Huriet)*

TABLE 2.4.3: FRENCH NAVY: PRINCIPAL UNITS AS AT MID 2018

TYPE	CLASS	NUMBER	TONNAGE	DIMENSIONS	PROPULSION	CREW	DATE
Aircraft Carriers							
Aircraft Carrier – CVN	CHARLES DE GAULLE	1	42,000 tons	262m x 33/64m x 9m	Nuclear, 27 knots	1,950	2001
Principal Surface Escorts							
Frigate – FFG	AQUITAINE (FREMM)	5	6,000 tons	142m x 20m x 5m	CODLOG, 27 knots	110	2012
Frigate – FFG	FORBIN ('Horizon')	2	7,100 tons	153m x 20m x 5m	CODOG, 29+ knots	195	2008
Frigate – FFG	CASSARD (FAA-70)	2	5,000 tons	139m x 15m x 5m	CODAD, 30 knots	250	1988
Frigate – FFG	GEORGES LEYGUES (FASM-70)	3	4,800 tons	139m x 15m x 5m	CODOG, 30 knots	240	1979
Frigate – FFG	LA FAYETTE	5	3,600 tons	125m x 15m x 5m	CODAD, 25 knots	150	1996
Frigate – FSG	FLORÉAL	6	3,000 tons	94m x 14m x 4m	CODAD, 20 knots	90	1992
Frigate – FS[1]	D'ESTIENNE D'ORVES (A-69)	9[1]	1,300 tons	80m x 10m x 3m	Diesel, 24 knots	90	1976
Submarines							
Submarine – SSBN	LE TRIOMPHANT	4	14,400 tons	138m x 13m x 11m	Nuclear, 25 knots	110	1997
Submarine – SSN	RUBIS	6	2,700 tons	74m x 8m x 6m	Nuclear, 25+ knots	70	1983
Major Amphibious Units							
Amph Assault Ship – LHD	MISTRAL	3	21,500 tons	199m x 32m x 6m	Diesel-electric, 19 knots	160	2006

Note:

1 Now officially reclassified as offshore patrol vessels. Two to be withdrawn before the end of 2018.

announcements is the FLOTLOG project to replace the remaining three *Durance* class replenishment oilers. The imminent completion of Fincantieri's acquisition of STX has solidified plans to use a variant of the Italian *Vulcano* design for the planned order, which has now been increased to four ships. Naval Group will take responsibility for combat system integration. Deliveries are scheduled for 2022, 2025, 2027 and 2029, when the planned force structure will be achieved.[5]

Plans for the mine countermeasures force envisage a measured transition towards autonomous vehicles, with two mother ships and four autonomous systems scheduled to be available for deployment by 2025. These are likely to be based on the results of the Anglo-French Maritime Mine Countermeasures (MMC) programme launched in 2016.

Table 2.4.3 provides further granularity with respect to current fleet composition.

MAJOR REGIONAL POWERS – ITALY

Details of the *Marina Militare*'s major vessels as of mid-2018 are set out in Table 2.4.4. As for France, the key driver of surface fleet modernisation in recent years has been the delivery of FREMM multi-mission frigates. These are continuing to be commissioned on an annual basis. The seventh of ten units – the general purpose variant *Federico Martinengo* – was the latest to enter service on 24

April 2018. Her arrival was balanced by the withdrawal of the 'Soldati' class frigate *Bersagliere* during the same month. This leaves just *Aviere* of the original quartet still in service and she is also likely to leave the fleet soon.

The imminent demise of the 'Soldati' class is reflective of a broader picture of block obsolescence that will significantly impact fleet strength over the next few years. Notably, inroads are also being made into the *Maestrale* class, with the unmodernised *Euro* and *Espero* likely to be decommissioned during the coming twelve months. The remaining four have benefitted from a major midlife upgrade and will probably remain active for a while yet. Other pending withdrawals include the last two *Minerva* class corvettes and more *Lerici* class mine countermeasures vessels.

Good progress is, however, being made with the large programme of new construction authorised to counterbalance the fleet's decline under the 2014 'Naval Law.' The initial two of seven firmly-ordered PPA (*Pattugliatore Polivalente d'Altura*) 'patrol vessels' are now under construction at Fincantieri's Riva Trigoso yard following a first steel cutting ceremony for the second member of the class on 3 October 2017. The first of the 6,000-ton, frigate-type vessels – which are being completed with various equipment fits on a common hull – remains on schedule for launch in early 2019 and delivery in

2021. Work is also moving forward on the new LHD-type amphibious assault ship ordered from Fincantieri under the same programme. The carrier-like vessel is being built at Castellammare di Stabia near Naples. The start of fabrication in July 2017 was followed by a formal keel laying ceremony on 20 February 2018. Current plans envisage her entering service by 2022 to replace the carrier *Giuseppe Garibaldi* and at least one of the *San Giorgio* class amphibious transport docks.

The construction programme approved in 2014 also includes the replenishment oiler *Vulcano*. She has been fabricated in three sections at Riva Trigoso and Castellammare di Stabia, which have then been integrated at Fincantieri's floating dock at Muggiano near La Spezia. Launch of the joined sections took place on 22 June 2018. The new ship displaces c. 27,000 tons and features a combined diesel-electric and diesel propulsion system that provides an endurance of 7,000 nautical miles at 16 knots. Officially designated as a logistic support ship, she is equipped with a hangar for two helicopters and a CH-53-capable flight deck. A NATO role 2 hospital and extensive maintenance facilities complement the liquid and solid stores replenishment equipment fitted for her core role. She is able to accommodate around 250 personnel, including a crew of 167.

The final element of the new surface ship

The Italian Navy is continuing to take delivery of FREMM class frigates on an annual basis. *Federico Martinengo* was the latest member of the class to be commissioned on 24 April 2018. *(OCCAR)*

construction programme is two UNPAV (*unità navale polifunzionale ad altissima velocità*) high-speed interceptors. Propelled by diesel-powered waterjets, the 44m craft displace around 190 tons and have a speed 'in excess of 30 knots'. The two new vessels are reportedly intended to support Special Forces operations and incorporate a launch and recovery system for a rigid inflatable boat. The lead unit – named *Angelo Cabrini* – was launched from Intermarine's Messina yard on 26 May 2018.[6] She will be delivered in 2020.

Underneath the waves, the Italian Navy has a requirement to replace the remaining quartet of *Sauro* class submarines that are all currently scheduled to retire within the next five years. In March 2017, a memorandum of collaboration was signed with Germany on future underwater collaboration, paving the way for participation in the evolved Type 212 series that HDW is developing in conjunction with Norway. It was originally thought that two additional submarines would be acquired to supplement Italy's existing quartet of Type 212A *Todaro* class boats, meeting a minimum six submarine force

Table 2.4.4: ITALIAN NAVY: PRINCIPAL UNITS AS AT MID 2018

TYPE	CLASS	NUMBER	TONNAGE	DIMENSIONS	PROPULSION	CREW	DATE
Aircraft Carriers							
Aircraft Carrier – CV	CAVOUR	1	27,100 tons	244m x 30/39m x 9m	COGAG, 29 knots	800	2008
Aircraft Carrier – CVS	GIUSEPPE GARIBALDI[1]	1	13,900 tons	180m x 23/31m x 7m	COGAG, 30 knots	825	1985
Principal Surface Escorts							
Frigate – FFG	CARLO BERGAMINI (FREMM)[2]	7	6,700 tons	144m x 20m x 5m	CODLOG, 27 knots	145	2013
Frigate – FFG	ANDREA DORIA ('Horizon')	2	7,100 tons	153m x 20m x 5m	CODOG, 29+ knots	190	2007
Destroyer – DDG	DE LA PENNE	2	5,400 tons	148m x 16m x 5m	CODOG, 31 knots	375	1993
Frigate – FFG	MAESTRALE	6	3,100 tons	123m x 13m x 4m	CODOG, 30+ knots	225	1982
Frigate – FFG	ARTIGLIERE	1	2,500 tons	114m x 12m x 4m	CODOG, 35 knots	185	1994
Frigate – FS	MINERVA	2	1,300 tons	87m x 11m x 3m	Diesel, 25 knots	120	1987
Submarines							
Submarine – SSK	TODARO (Type 212A)	4	1,800 tons	56m x 7m x 6m	AIP, 20+ knots	30	2006
Submarine – SSK	PELOSI	4	1,700 tons	64m x 7m x 6m	Diesel-electric, 20 knots	50	1988
Major Amphibious Units							
Landing Platform Dock – LPD	SAN GIORGIO	3	8,000 tons	133m x 21m x 5m	Diesel, 20 knots	165	1987

Note:

1 Now operates largely as a LPH.

2 Class includes BERGAMINI (GP) and FASAN (ASW) variants.

The new Spanish F110 class frigate design is now largely completed and orders for five vessels are expected shortly. (*Navantia*)

Audaz is the lead ship of a pair of additional Spanish 'BAM' type oceanic patrol vessels authorised in 2014. This picture shows her on sea trials in May 2018. (*Navantia*)

structure requirement. However, subsequent reports suggest four new submarines will be acquired to replace the remaining *Sauros* on a one-for-one basis.[7]

MAJOR REGIONAL POWERS – SPAIN

The fleet structure set out for the *Armada Española* listed in Table 2.4.5 continues to show no change for a fifth consecutive year. It appears that the Spanish Navy is now ready to launch new acquisition programmes after the lengthy pause in activity that followed the Eurozone crisis.[8] Moreover, 2018 has seen a significant increase in defence funding to help launch the long-delayed procurement cycle. However, the recent change in government had delayed implantation of these plans, with no firm contracts awarded as of mid-2018.

Once procurement does get underway, the key priority will be confirmation of an order for five new general-purpose F-110 type frigates to replace the six obsolescent *Santa María* (FFG-7) class ships. Platform design on the new vessels has been underway since 2015, with images released to date suggesting they will essentially be an evolution of the existing, successful F-100 *Álvaro de Bazán* class. It has already been confirmed that the new frigates will be equipped with the US Aegis weapons system found in the previous ships. This will be linked to the indigenous SCOMBA combat-management system that is widely used throughout the Spanish fleet. Other features include a distinctive integrated mast and a multi-mission bay. The frigates will also have a greater orientation towards anti-submarine warfare than the air defence-focused F-100 design. This will probably be reflected in the availability of electric propulsion option and an improved sonar outfit.

Current construction is focused on the long-delayed S-80 submarines and two BAM-type *Meteoro* class offshore patrol vessels. The cost of the

Table 2.4.5: SPANISH NAVY: PRINCIPAL UNITS AS AT MID 2018

TYPE	CLASS	NUMBER	TONNAGE	DIMENSIONS	PROPULSION	CREW	DATE
Principal Surface Escorts							
Frigate – FFG	ÁLVARO DE BAZÁN (F-100)	5	6,300 tons	147m x 19m x 5m	CODOG, 28 knots	200	2002
Frigate – FFG	SANTA MARIA (FFG-7)	6	4,100 tons	138m x 14m x 5m	COGAG, 30 knots	225	1986
Submarines							
Submarine – SSK	GALERNA (S-70/AGOSTA)	3	1,800 tons	68m x 7m x 6m	Diesel-electric, 21 knots	60	1983
Major Amphibious Units							
Amph Assault Ship – LHD	JUAN CARLOS I	1	27,100 tons	231m x 32m x 7m	IEP, 21 knots	245	2010
Landing Platform Dock – LPD	GALICIA	2	13,000 tons	160m x 25m x 6m	Diesel, 20 knots	185	1998

four-boat submarine programme is now anticipated to amount to c. €3.7bn (US$4.4bn) but assembly of the first of the lengthened and renamed S-81 Plus class appears to be progressing in line with revised plans. This envisages the lead boat being launched during 2020 for delivery by 2022. Meanwhile, the first of the new BAMs – *Audaz* – completed trials in June 2018 to meet a planned July commissioning date. Her sister, *Furor*, is also expected to join the fleet before the year's end and an additional ship may be acquired in a submarine support configuration. The imminent delivery of the new vessels is allowing further withdrawals of the *Descubierta* class corvettes previously converted into offshore patrol ships. *Cazadora* was the latest of the class to decommission in April 2018, leaving just two out of an original six ships in service.

MAJOR REGIONAL POWERS – UNITED KINGDOM

The last year has been a busy one for the British Royal Navy. The dominant highlight was inevitably the commissioning of the new aircraft carrier *Queen Elizabeth* in December 2017. However, the past twelve months have also seen the delivery of the two lead units of other warship and auxiliary classes, as well as significant progress with three new procurement programmes.

Current fleet strength is set out in Table 2.4.6. The arrival of *Queen Elizabeth* was balanced by the withdrawal of the helicopter carrier *Ocean*. She was decommissioned on 27 March 2018 and has subsequently been transferred to Brazil. Also departing the fleet following a decommissioning ceremony on 17 July 2017 was the attack submarine *Torbay*, leaving just three *Trafalgar* class boats in service. Her replacement, the *Astute* class submarine *Audacious*, is expected to be delivered in the second half of 2018. In spite of rumours that the *Astute* class programme may be truncated to just six submarines, an order for the seventh and final boat was placed in May 2018. In a change of plan, she is to be named *Agincourt*. The announcement of the contract for her construction was combined with the release of nearly £1bn (US$1.3bn) of additional funding for the next generation *Dreadnought* class strategic submarines.

There have also been significant changes to the second-line fleet. The lead Batch 2 'River' class offshore patrol vessel, *Forth*, arrived at Portsmouth Naval Base for the first time on 26 February 2018 and subsequently commissioned on Friday 13 April

Royal Navy attack submarine numbers temporarily dipped to just six boats after the decommissioning of *Torbay* on 17 July 2017. Her replacement, *Audacious*, is expected to join the fleet in the second half of 2018. This picture shows *Torbay*'s final entry into Devonport on 24 June 2017. *(Crown Copyright 2017)*

The first 'River Batch II' offshore patrol vessel *Forth* is the lead ship of one of three classes of new warships and auxiliaries delivered to the Royal Navy over the past year. This picture shows her maiden arrival in Portsmouth in February 2018. *(Derek Fox)*

Table 2.4.6: BRITISH ROYAL NAVY: PRINCIPAL UNITS AS AT MID 2018

TYPE	CLASS	NUMBER	TONNAGE	DIMENSIONS	PROPULSION	CREW	DATE
Aircraft Carriers							
Aircraft Carrier – CV	QUEEN ELIZABETH	1	65,000 tons	284m x 73m x 11m	IEP, 26 knots+	1,600	2017
Principal Surface Escorts[1]							
Destroyer – DDG	**DARING** (Type 45)	6	7,500 tons	152m x 21m x 5m	IEP, 30 knots	190	2008
Frigate – FFG	**NORFOLK** (Type 23)	13	4,900 tons	133m x 16m x 5m	CODLAG, 30 knots	185	1990
Submarines							
Submarine – SSBN	**VANGUARD**	4	16,000 tons	150m x 13m x 12m	Nuclear, 25+ knots	135	1993
Submarine – SSN	**ASTUTE**	4	7,800 tons	93m x 11m x 10m	Nuclear, 30+ knots	100	2010
Submarine – SSN	**TRAFALGAR**	3	5,200 tons	85m x 10m x 10m	Nuclear, 30+ knots	130	1983
Major Amphibious Units							
Landing Platform Dock – LPD	**ALBION**	2[2]	18,500 tons	176m x 29m x 7m	IEP, 18 knots	325	2003
Landing Ship Dock – LSD (A)	**LARGS BAY**	3	16,200 tons	176m x 26m x 6m	Diesel-electric, 18 knots	60	2006

Notes:

1. One or two at extended readiness as harbour training ships pending refit.

2. One at extended readiness.

2018. The date may have been inauspicious as a number of defects subsequently emerged that have delayed her entry into operational service. Two additional vessels – *Medway* and *Trent* – of the planned five-ship class have also been launched over the past year. The older Batch I 'River' class vessels *Tyne* and *Severn* have been retired to provide crews for the new ships but remain in reserve in case additional maritime patrol capabilities are required after Brexit.

There have also been revisions to the mine countermeasures flotilla. The 'Hunt' class vessels *Atherstone* and *Quorn* were both decommissioned on 14 December 2017 after a decision was taken to cancel their planned refits to fund increased investment in autonomous systems. Another vessel departing the fleet was the survey launch *Gleaner*, which had completed nearly thirty-five years of service when she decommissioned at Devonport in February 2018. Her replacement is the catamaran *Magpie*, which was built by Safehaven Marine in Cork to their Wildcat 60 design. She is reportedly the first warship built in Ireland for the Royal Navy since Irish Independence. She forms part of a wider £48m contract for up to thirty-eight workboats ranging from 11m to 18m in size that will support a range of diving, passenger transfer, survey and training requirements.

The Royal Fleet Auxiliary (RFA) marked the arrival of the lead vessel of its own new class with a dedication ceremony for *Tidespring*, the first of four new, 39,000-tonne 'Tide' class tankers, on 27 November 2017. Constructed by DSME in South Korea, she entered service after the installation of communications and other military equipment at A&P Falmouth. Two other members of the class have now arrived in the UK for similar outfitting

Orders for the first three Type 26 Global Combat Ships were placed at the start of July 2017 after years of delays. The programme is now gaining momentum and the design has also been selected as the basis for Australia's new *Hunter* class. *(BAE Systems)*

and trials. The programme will be completed with delivery of the fourth vessel, *Tideforce*, which is expected to enter service in 2019.

Turning to future procurement, 2 July 2017 saw the long-delayed announcement of a £3.7bn (c. US$5bn) contract to build the first three Type 26 Global Combat Ships. With a length of 149m and a displacement of 6,900 tons, the new frigates will approach the previous Type 45 *Daring* class destroyers in overall size. They are intended to be multi-mission warships capable of operating in a range of intensive warfare scenarios. However, their main Royal Navy tasking will be as high-end anti-submarine escorts to protect the strategic submarine force and support carrier task groups. Delivery of the first three – *Glasgow*, *Cardiff* and *Belfast* – is not expected to commence until the mid-2020s and it will not be until a decade later that the planned eight-ship class will be complete. The design is being pitched in a number of export campaigns and was selected for Australia's Future Frigate programme at the end of June 2018. It is also considered a leading contender for the Canadian Surface Combatant design competition, which will reach a decision by the year's end.[9]

The 2015 Strategic Defence & Security Review (SDSR) determined that the original plan for thirteen Type 26 frigates would be reduced to eight, with five cheaper light frigates balancing the reduction. Further details of the new programme have emerged over the past year. The Type 31e (for export) programme forms a key part of the new National Shipbuilding Strategy (NSS). It is being procured competitively to a flexible specification that is intended to attract export orders. A challenging procurement schedule anticipates the first ship entering service in 2023 whilst a £1.25bn (c. US$1.7bn) budget for all five ships – approximately the same as one Type 26 – has resulted in challenging questions being asked as to the level of capability the class will bring. In spite of this, the programme has resulted in credible proposals being made by consortia led by Cammell Laird (Team Leander) and Babcock Team 31. The former are working on a proposal based on a stretched version of the 'Khareef' class corvettes built by BAE Systems for Oman whilst Babcock is promoting a much larger ship evolved from Denmark's *Iver Huitfeldt* design.[10] A decision on the way forward is anticipated by the first quarter of 2019.

The other major procurement programme being conducted under NSS principles is for new JSS joint solid support ships. They will replace the existing 'Fort' classes and are intended to replenish carrier and other task groups with non-liquid supplies. As they are 'non-warships', the programme is subject to international bids, a prospect that had drawn some political and trade union ire. However, injection of competition into the process will avoid the huge costs the Royal Canadian Navy has faced for pre-assigned local construction of similar ships and could well result in a cost-effective British proposal. The requirement is for two ships with an option for a third; a potential reduction of the SDSR 2015's firm requirement for three vessels.

The potential reduction in the JSS order is indicative of wider pressures on UK defence spending that have resulted from overly-ambitious expectations of efficiency savings and the impact of Britain's planned withdrawal from the European Union on the cost of imported defence equipment. A report by the UK's National Audit Office in January 2018 indicated that the £180bn ten-year equipment plan was between £5bn and £21bn over budget.[11] A mini-defence review – the Modernising Defence Programme – is currently underway amid reports that significant force reductions could prove necessary if additional funding is not provided. The review was due to report in July 2018 but could well be delayed amongst reports the British premier, Teresa May, is no longer prepared to support the UK's status as a 'tier one' military power.[12]

The debate comes at a time when the Royal Navy – doubtless influenced by a political agenda to build new defence and trading partnerships in a post Brexit world – is attempting to step up its international presence. The end of 2018 will have seen three Royal Navy warships deploy to the Far East during the course of the year – the first such missions for five years – to provide an almost continuous presence in the region. A new UK Naval Support Facility – HMS *Jufair* – also opened in Bahrain in April 2018 and it has been announced a Type 23 frigate will be permanently based in the Persian Gulf to join the mine countermeasures vessels that are already forward-deployed there. The new strategy will expand the practice of rotational crewing used, for example, with the patrol vessel *Clyde* in the Falkland Islands and allow a stretched fleet to maintain more vessels on station. Further

developments are likely as the fleet transitions from single-ship deployments towards a greater emphasis on carrier group operations.

MID-SIZED REGIONAL FLEETS

Germany: The last twelve months have seen the *Deutsche Marine* face a number of challenges. In line with the rest of the German Armed Forces, operational readiness has become a major problem putting pressure on the force's ability to meet NATO and European Union commitments. A *Report on the Operational Readiness of the Bundeswehr's Primary Weapons Systems 2017* suggested that there were times when none of the navy's six submarines and as few as four of its frigates were fully operational. Lack of readiness also extended to other warships and auxiliaries, whilst there were two months when just one P-3C Orion maritime patrol aircraft was available. A major problem seems to have been reduction in procurement of spares as an economy measure in the post-Cold War era, meaning that maintenance periods have had to be extended whilst missing parts have been procured.[13]

Fleet availability has been exacerbated by difficulties with the F125 *Baden-Württemberg* class stabilisation frigate programme that have meant that none of the four new ships in the class have been accepted to date.[14] The ships had already been delayed by a number of problems that arose during the manufacturing phase and it has been reported the lead ship is significantly overweight. However, the main challenge appears to be integrating the new Atlas Naval Combat System (ANCS), which is critical to the ship's lean manning concept. Accordingly, *Baden-Württemberg* has been returned to the builders for the problems to be fixed. There is also likely to be a consequent knock-on impact on delivery of the remaining ships. This could result in a further temporary dip from the current front-line fleet strength of nine frigates unless the service lives of the two remaining F122 *Bremen* class frigates are extended.

The decision to reject the TKMS-led bid for the follow-on MKS180/F126 programme due to the F125 debacle is likely to have further adverse consequences. The programme calls for a total of six multi-purpose combatants, with consortia headed by German Naval Yards (GNY) and the Dutch Damen group now remaining in the competition. As neither has recent expertise in large warship design, project delivery could well slip further back-

Lübeck – seen here in April 2018 – is one of two German F122 class frigates remaining in service. The frigate force is currently under pressure due to production problems with the F125 class of stabilisation frigates. *(Michael Leek)*

wards. However, some respite will be provided by the decision to order a further batch of five K130 corvettes, doubling class numbers to ten. The contract was formally signed in September 2017, with work to be split between an ARGE K130 consortium comprising GNY, Lürssen and TKMS. The first unit will be delivered in 2022 and all should be operational by 2025.

Looking forward, an apparent increasing willingness by German politicians to step up defence spending should see some improvements to a difficult situation. Remedying the readiness problems previously discussed will probably have first call on any additional funding but there should be sufficient money to advance other pending procurement projects. These include up to twenty-eight new sea control helicopters to replace the existing twenty-two Lynx rotorcraft deployed from the navy's frigates and the acquisition of evolved Type 212 submarines in a joint programme with Norway.

Greece: The Hellenic Navy has largely stagnated since the Eurozone crisis erupted, although delivery of Type 214 submarines ordered before the country's financial problems began has produced a large submarine flotilla with a core of modern boats. The only procurement programme currently active is the completion of the two remaining *Roussen* class fast attack craft at the Elefsis shipyard. However, reports on actual progress are sparse.

The fleet's current major weakness is its core surface flotilla, which comprises increasingly elderly and obsolescent ships with particularly weak anti-air warfare capabilities. The Hellenic Navy has long been exploring the possibility of acquiring new French-built frigates to remedy this deficiency and recent tensions with Turkey – including a collision between coast guard vessels and the accidental loss of a Greek fighter jet after a mock dogfight with Turkish aircraft – has resulted in renewed interest in a possible deal. Reports suggest an outline agreement has been reached that involves the lease of two French FREMM units pending the delivery of new 'Belh@rra' export variants of the FTI type.[15]

The Netherlands and Belgium: The Royal Netherlands Navy's future direction has been clarified by the March 2018 *Defence White Paper*. This sets out a number of longer term operational objectives for the country's naval forces. They include a major deployment of a five-strong maritime task force for a limited period of time or, alternatively, more enduring deployments of two surface ships and single submarines and minehunters supplemented by shorter marine battalion and maritime logistics support operations.

The white paper has earmarked substantial funds for a major process of fleet renewal to achieve these objectives. Much of this activity will be carried out in conjunction with the Belgian Naval Component in line with the terms of a joint naval procurement agreement. The two fleets have become increasingly integrated at the operational level in recent years and also utilise a significant amount of common equipment.

Two shared Belgo-Dutch procurement programmes are now underway. One will replace the two pairs of 'M' or *Karel Doorman* class frigates operated by the respective fleets on a like-for-like basis. The c. €2bn (US$2.4bn) programme is being carried out under Dutch leadership, with their Defence Materiel Organisation taking responsibility for developing the new ships' basic design that will then be refined in conjunction with the Damen group. Actual construction is likely to be shared between Damen's yards at Vlissingen in the Netherlands and Galati in Romania, with deliveries expected to commence around 2024. The new ships will be multi-mission combatants with a particular emphasis on anti-submarine warfare. The use of extensive automation is intended to reduce crewing requirements to around 110 personnel. Armament will include a sixteen-cell Mk 41 vertical launch system, new surface-to-surface missiles and a hangar for a helicopter and UAVs.

The other joint procurement will see the two navies each acquire six new mine countermeasures vessels to replace existing 'Tripartite' class ships. Belgium is leading this exercise which is being carried out by means of an international tender. The new vessels are intended to stand-off the area requiring clearance and deploy a range of robotic vehicles to search for and then dispose of any mines discovered. The programme is also expected to cost around €2bn and should see deliveries commence from around 2023.

Two national procurement programmes are also

well advanced. Notably, it has been determined that four manned submarines will replace the existing *Walrus* class from 2027 onwards. A number of shipbuilders have proposed designs for the programme but a variant of the Swedish A26 design being offered by a consortium of Damen and Saab looks to be in the strongest position. The white paper also approved acquisition of a new replenishment ship to supplement the JSS joint support ship *Karel Doorman* in what was the only actual increase in fleet numbers. Reports suggest that the new ship will be a smaller version of the existing JSS without its military sealift and sea basing capabilities. Major acquisitions are supported by provision for investment in a wide range of new equipment, including replacements for the Goalkeeper close-in-weapons systems, 127mm guns and Harpoon surface-to-surface missiles. Provision is also made to start planning work for the replacement of a range of other warships and auxiliaries over the course of the next decade.[16]

Turkey: The last twelve months have seen the Turkish Navy focus on the delivery of existing procurement projects rather than the launch of new acquisitions. The third indigenous 'Milgem' corvette/light frigate *Burgazada* commenced sea trials in March 2018 prior to delivery scheduled for September 2018. Construction of the fourth and final member of the 'Ada' variant, *Kinaliada*, is running around a year behind that of her sister following her launch on 3 July 2017. Attention is already starting to transfer to *Istanbul*, the lead ship of four larger evolved 'I' class vessels. Fabrication started in January 2017 and her keel was formally laid at Istanbul Naval Shipyard on the same day as *Kinaliada*'s launch. The 'Milgem' design is also attracting considerable overseas interest and a deal to sell four of the class to Pakistan is expected to be concluded shortly.

Renewal of the amphibious force saw delivery of the second *Bayraktar* class tank landing ship, *Sancaktar*, in April 2018. Looking forward, construction of the LHD-type amphibious assault ship *Anadolu* is probably the navy's most important current project and the laying of the ship's first keel block at Sedef Shipbuilding in February 2018 marked a major step forward towards the new ship's completion. The ship is a diesel-powered variant of Navantia's *Juan Carlos I* design and is able to operate STOVL jet fighters. The Turkish Navy has shown

An interesting aerial view of Istanbul Naval Shipyard in mid-2018 showing three 'Milgem' class light frigates in the course of construction. The nearly-complete *Burgazada* is in the foreground to the right whilst her sister *Kinaliada* can be seen fitting out to her left. The initial blocks of the first 'I' class variant, *Istanbul*, are being assembled on the slipway behind the two launched vessels. *(Editor's Collection)*

The Turkish Navy took delivery of its second new *Bayraktar* class tank landing ship, *Sancaktar*, in April 2018. The much larger amphibious assault ship *Anadolu* is currently under construction. *(Devrim Yaylali)*

considerable interest in acquiring F-35B STOVL variants of the Lockheed Martin Lightning II to embark in the ship. However, this may be hindered by American resistance to the Erdogan regime's growing links with Russia.

Modernisation of the submarine flotilla is focused on licensed production of the German Type 214 AIP-equipped design at Gölcük Naval Shipyard. Three submarines out of a six-boat programme are now under construction following as keel laying ceremony for *Murat Reis* in February 2018. The submarines are reportedly slightly longer and heavier than those delivered to other navies and incorporate some improvements to their AIP system. Turkey's twelve-strong submarine flotilla makes it the largest submarine operator in Europe but some of the remaining quartet of Type 209/1200 boats are now rather long in the tooth and numbers are therefore likely to decline before the new class starts to commission. Turkey has ambitious plans to commission a 'Milden' national submarine by 2030. Whilst it is developing the technological capabilities to make this a realistic possibility, the experience of past projects suggests the timescale is unlikely to be met. Meanwhile, delivery of the submarine rescues vessel *Alemdar* in January 2017 has been followed by the arrival of the towage and rescue vessels *Akın* and *Işın*.[17]

OTHER REGIONAL FLEETS

Black Sea and Mediterranean: Longstanding ambitions held by a number of Black Sea navies to modernise their fleets in the face of Russian expansionary ambitions have made some progress in the past year. Notably, **Romania's** previously delayed plans to acquire new corvettes are now back on the agenda, with a formal procurement process launched in February 2018. The Dutch Damen group has a strong industrial presence in the country. Accordingly, a variant of the company's 'Sigma' design looks a likely winner for the c. €1.5bn contract for four ships in spite of competition from Naval Group's 'Gowind'. Romania also has plans to undertake an extensive modernisation programme for its pair of Type 22 frigates and is reportedly considering longer terms to establish an operational underwater flotilla comprising three submarines.

Bulgaria's stop/start acquisition of two similar multifunction 'patrol vessels' has also been resurrected with a June 2018 statement that the budget for the programme will be increased. The previous sole bidder for the c. €500m contract – local yard MTG Dolphin – had previously dropped its bid following changes to the tax regime relating to defence procurement.[18] Meanwhile **Ukraine's** navy continues to struggle to adapt to the vastly changed circumstances it finds itself in following Russia's annexation of the Crimea. A heated internal debate has resulted in a decision to focus short-term efforts on creation of a 'mosquito navy' of small littoral combatants to secure Ukraine's coastal waters. Typical of these vessels are the small Project 58150/5 armoured gunboats that started joining the fleet towards the end of 2016. The class should eventually extend to some twenty vessels. Larger ships such as the new Project 58250 corvettes, which have now seen construction suspended for a number of years, will ultimately be delivered over a longer timescale.[19]

There have been no significant procurement developments amongst southern Europe's other minor navies in the Mediterranean and Adriatic over the last year. The main backdrop to naval operations remains the flow of migrants across the inland sea, which continues to extract a significant toll in lives in spite of overall refugee numbers falling dramatically since their 2015 peak. The United Nations have estimated more than 16,000 people have died or are missing from 2014 to date. A crackdown on private rescue operations by Italy's new government against the backdrop of the European Union's failure to agree equitable handling arrangements is reportedly pushing up casualties. However, an equal factor in this complex and seemingly intractable human crisis is the effective closing off of easier transit routes in the Eastern Mediterranean, resulting in migrants attempting more hazardous crossings elsewhere.

Atlantic: Turning to the Atlantic, **Portugal** is now making good progress with a programme of fleet renewal focused on updating its constabulary forces. This essentially has two main strands. The old 'colonial corvettes' of the *João Coutinho* and *Baptista de Andrade* classes – only three of which now remain in service – are being replaced with the new *Viana do Castello* offshore patrol vessels. *Sines*, the lead ship of a second pair ordered in 2015, carried out successful sea trials in May 2018 and will be delivered shortly. Her sister, *Setúbal*, was launched from the West Sea Viana Shipyard in September 2017 and will enter service in 2019. Original plans called for the construction of up to ten of the class to replace the legacy corvettes on a like-for-like basis but these collapsed against a backdrop of industrial problems and the Eurozone crisis. The successful resurrection of the programme under the Viana yard's new owners might therefore see additional ships being ordered.

The other element of the constabulary renewal

Current Ukrainian Navy plans place emphasis on creating a 'mosquito navy' of small littoral combatants to rebuild its fleet. These plans include construction of around twenty Project 58150/5 armoured gunboats armed with twin KAU-30M integrated weapons stations. The 24m-long vessels displace around 25 tons and have a maximum speed in the region of 25 knots. *(Ministry of Defence of Ukraine)*

programme has been achieved by acquisition of surplus Danish *Flyvefisken* (StanFlex 300) hulls that are being converted to coastal patrol vessels at the Portuguese Navy's naval dockyard in Lisbon. Three vessels have now entered service with the commissioning of *Mondego* on 12 June 2018 and two more are still to be modernised. This includes an additional fifth hull that was originally acquired as a source of spares. They are replacing the remaining *Cacine* class colonial patrol vessels. Only two of these remain in service with the withdrawal of *Cacine* herself in July 2017.

The Portuguese fleet's combatant force is focused on two relatively new Type 214 submarines and five frigates. The latter are being subject to a programme of mid-life upgrades that commenced with the arrival of the former Dutch 'M' class frigate *Bartolomeu Dias* at Den Helder in May 2018. The navy also requires a new replenishment ship to replace the veteran fleet tanker *Bérrio*, which first entered service as the British RFA's *Blue Rover* in 1970. Project studies are already underway and a new ship is likely to be delivered in the early 2020s.

Elsewhere in the Atlantic, **Ireland's** Naval Service is looking forward to taking delivery of its fourth and final *Samuel Beckett* class offshore patrol vessel, *George Bernard Shaw*, which was floated out on 3 March 2018. The next procurement programme will be for a new multi-purpose vessel to replace the fleet flagship *Eithne* under plans set out in the white paper on defence published in 2015.

The Baltic and Scandinavia: The Scandinavian and Baltic region has become focused on a process of force modernisation and expansion following the re-emergence of tensions with Russia. It is probably **Sweden** that has experienced the most profound reversal of the previous trend towards regional demilitarisation. This is particularly demonstrated by the reintroduction of conscription in January 2018. Work is also underway to re-establish the Cold War 'total defence' concept that involves the preparation of all elements of civic infrastructure to resist a potential aggressor.[20] Final decisions on the extent of this revised civil defence structure will probably be taken in 2020, when the country's next defence review is due.

The review will also allow decisions to be taken on the Swedish Navy's future structure. This is currently built around a force of seven operational surface combatants of the *Visby* and *Gävle* classes

The Irish Naval Service's third *Samuel Beckett* class offshore patrol vessel *William Butler Yeats* pictured in July 2017. The final member of the class, *George Bernard Shaw*, will be delivered in the second half of 2018. *(Irish Defence Forces)*

and the five *Götland* and *Södermanland* class submarines. Life extensions of the two active *Gävle* class vessels have already been agreed but the review will probably lay out plans for their eventual replacement. In the meantime, two new A26 class submarines are on order to replace the *Södermanland* class and at least two of the *Götlands* are being modernised under a major upgrade programme. In June 2018 *Götland* was relaunched after completion of her package of work. It included insertion of a new 2m hull section, updated Stirling AIP modules, sensor enhancements and a modern optronic mast. Many technologies used will be inserted in the new A26 class.[21]

Neighbouring **Norway** also has a requirement for new submarines and has entered into a partnership with Germany to acquire a derivative of the Type 212A class. Four units will replace its existing six *Ula* class submarines. The other major current procurement project for the front-line navy is that for the logistic support ship *Maud*, a half-sister of the RFA's 'Tide' class. She undertook delayed preliminary sea trials from DSME in South Korea at the end of 2017 but machinery problems mean that delivery is not now scheduled until the autumn of 2018. The Norwegian Coast Guard is also due to receive new ships and a NOK5.2bn (c. US$650m)

order for three 136m ice-strengthened patrol vessels confirmed in June 2018. The three ships will be completed locally by Vard Langsten from hulls fabricated by Vard Tulcea in Romania and delivered between 2022 and 2024.

Denmark's political parties signed a new Defence Agreement for the period 2018–2023 in January 2018 that will result in additional spending of DKK4.8bn (c. US$750m) annually by 2023.[22] In a possible reflection of previously inadequate spending, the new money allocated to the navy is directed at making good deficiencies with existing equipment rather than any force expansion. This includes acquisition of area air defence missiles for the three *Iver Huitfeldt* class frigates, investment in new sonar and torpedo defence equipment and the provision of anti-submarine torpedoes for the recently acquired MH-60R helicopters.

Finland's navy continues to focus on delivery of the 'Squadron 2020' programme for four new corvettes. The new c. 105m long ships are expected to displace up to 3,000 tons and will be the largest warships operated by the *Merivoimet* since the two *Väinämöinen* class coastal defence ships of the interwar period. Work is expected to commence at Rauma Marine in the course of 2019 to allow sea trials of the lead unit to commence in 2027. All four

The Swedish submarine *Götland* has been relaunched after a major upgrade programme that has seen insertion of a new 2m hull section. Much of the new equipment incorporated into the upgrade will also be used in the new A26 class submarine design. *(Saab AB)*

ships will be delivered by 2027. They will operate alongside the existing quartet of 250-ton *Hamina* class fast attack craft. These are currently being upgraded to ensure a degree of commonality with the new corvettes.

Poland also has ambitions plans for new naval acquisitions but a stop-start procurement process means that little tangible progress is being achieved. The most significant requirement is for three new submarines but launch of the programme is slipping steadily backwards. In the interim, the existing submarine flotilla has declined to just three old boats following the decommissioning of the Type 207 class *Kondor* in December 2017 and *Sokól* in June 2018. The only significant boost to the fleet has been delivery of the lead 'Kormoran II' minehunter *Kormoran* by Renontowa Shipbuilding in November 2017. She is reportedly the first new vessel delivered to the Polish Navy for over twenty years. A c. US$350m contract for two follow-on vessels was signed the following month and a new submarine salvage and rescue ship has also been ordered. However, plans for new coastal defence and patrol vessels appear to be in abeyance. This has necessitated extending the lives of the two existing FFG-7 class frigates to maintain a semblance of a surface combatant force.

RUSSIA

As noted in the Introduction, available information on Russia's latest State Armaments Programme for 2018–2027 (GPV2027) suggests a reduced emphasis on naval capabilities compared with previous plans. This is particularly the case with respect to the 'blue water' surface fleet. There are a number of potential explanations for the change of focus. Lower commodity prices and the impact of Western sanctions certainly mean that there is less money for the Russian military than previously expected. This may have resulted in a clearer focus on achieving land-based continental domination over distant maritime power projection. The experience of recent interventions, such as that in Syria, has also demonstrated the value of the fleet's submarines and missile-armed littoral corvettes. In particular, the successful integration of the 'Kalibr' cruise missile with smaller vessels to provide a cost-effective strategic strike capability may have resulted in questions over the added value offered by larger warships. Another factor may have been the run-down shipbuilding sector's apparent difficulties putting new designs of larger and more complex ships into operational service. There may simply have been a pragmatic decision to give the maritime sector more time to put its house in order before considering the construction of sophisticated major combatants.

Whatever the underlying reasoning, the outcome of GPV2027 suggests the Russian Navy's basic structure will remain largely similar to the current picture set out in Table 2.4.7. The ocean-going fleet is likely to remain focused on a disparate group of modernised but increasingly elderly Soviet-era ships supplemented by a handful of modern frigates. The bulk of naval investment will be channelled into an increasingly modern force of littoral warfare corvettes and – particularly – the submarine flotilla. The latter will retain its traditional priority in the navy's strategic thinking in terms of providing both conventional and nuclear deterrence.

Comments on major current procurement programmes follow:

Submarine Construction: The modernisation of the strategic submarine force remains the Russian Navy's top priority. Work is currently focused on the Project 955A 'Borey II' programme at Sevmash's Severodvinsk plant. This has seen five of the class laid down between 2012 and 2016 to supplement the three earlier Project 955 boats that were commissioned in 2013 and 2014. The lead 'Borey II', *Knyaz Vladimir*, was floated out on 17 November 2017 and is likely to enter service before the end of the decade. Whilst there have previously been reports that subsequent production would transition to an improved type, it appears that construction of a further six Project 955As is envisaged under GPV2027.[23] These will presumably replace the six Project 667BDRM 'Delta IV' boats currently serving in the Northern Fleet.

The latest Russian State Armaments programme prioritises the construction of smaller littoral combatants over larger surface warships. Ships like the Project 2163.1 'Buyan M' corvettes pack a powerful punch for only modest cost. However, as demonstrated by this 2016 picture of *Zelenyy Dol* next to a navy tug during transit to the Mediterranean, they are not best-suited for longer distance deployments. *(Crown Copyright 2016)*

Progress with the series production of improved Project 855M 'Yasen' class attack submarines is somewhat slower than for the strategic boats. The first, *Kazan*, was launched in March 2017. However, she is not currently expected to join the prototype, *Severodvinsk*, in the fleet until 2019. A further five of these large, c. 13,500-ton boats are now under construction following commencement of work on *Ulyanovsk* in July 2017. Production is then likely to transition to a new type, possibly the modular, 'multi-role' fifth-generation 'Husky' type currently under development by the Malakhit Design Bureau. However, it seems questionable whether actual assembly will commence during the life of GPV2027.

The extent to which the design problems associated with the Project 677 diesel-electric submarine design have now been fully resolved is currently unclear. Although *Sankt Peterburg* remains the only unit that has been completed to date, reports suggest the other two members of the class will be delivered during 2019. There have also been suggestions of plans for further orders. In the meantime, production remains focused on the Project 636.6 'Kilo' class variants ordered for the Eastern Fleet. The first pair of a further batch of six – *Petropavlovsk-Kamchatsky* and *Volkhov* – were laid down by the Admiralty Shipyard in Saint Petersburg in July 2017.

Surface Combatant Construction: Russian construc-

tion of surface combatants continues to be typified by an almost bewildering variety of programmes supported by various shipyards and design bureaus.

Another enduring factor – sometimes shared with counterparts in the West – is the seeming difficultly shipyards find in delivering operational ships in a timely and efficient manner. Notably, the lead Project 2235.0 *Admiral Gorshkov* class frigate was still in the course of completing trials in mid-2018, nearly four years after her initial voyage in November 2014.

Construction of Project 2235.0 frigates is currently the main surface combatant programme. Three ships in addition to *Gorshkov* are currently in various stages of assembly at Severnaya Verf in Saint Petersburg. Of these, *Admiral Kasatonov* is likely to commence sea trials before the end of 2018 and *Admiral Golovko* should be launched soon. Work on

The lead Project 1171.1 landing ship *Ivan Gren* was commissioned on 20 June 2018. An additional ship has been launched but plans for further vessels have been cancelled. *(Yantar)*

Admiral Isakov is somewhat less advanced. Future production may then well transition to an improved and enlarged Project 2235.0M class design. Meanwhile, delivery of the third Project 1135.6 *Admiral Grigorovich* class frigate, *Admiral Marakov*, has marked an end to current construction of the type at the Yantar yard in Kaliningrad due to lack of Ukrainian-supplied gas turbines. The facility will soon start to build more units of the class for India but it is unclear whether these will use any of the suspended hulls originally intended for Russia.

There are currently no less than five classes of corvette under construction. The most established are Project 2038.0/2038.1 *Steregushchy* class light frigates. These first entered service in 2008. The ships are being built at Severnaya Verf and at the Amur Shipyard in the Far East. Five of the class are currently in service following the delivery of the first Amur-built unit, *Sovershennyy*, in July 2017. A further five are under construction. The original plan was to transition to a new Project 2038.5

design with German-supplied diesels but Western sanctions resulted in the class being truncated at just two units. The lead ship, *Gremyashchy*, was launched on 30 June 2017. Instead, work has started on a third, Project 2038.6 variant featuring significant use of stealth technology. *Derzkiy*, the first of an extended series, was laid down in October 2018.

The other two classes are smaller coastal units that owe something to similar Soviet-era vessels such as the Project 1241 'Tarantul' type. Nine out of a series of 15 diminutive Project 2163.0 'Buyan' and Project 2163.1 'Buyan M' class ships have now been delivered following the commissioning of the Zelenodolsk-built *Vyshniy Volochyok* on 1 June 2018. They will soon be supplemented by the new Project 2280.0 'Karakurt' design, which is of similar concept but has a more seaworthy hull. The class is being built in considerable numbers by a range of shipyards. The first, *Uragan*, was undertaking sea trials as of mid-2018, by which time two further

units had been launched. It seems at least eighteen will eventually be completed.

The front-line corvettes are supplemented by yet further patrol vessels, which are relatively heavily armed compared with their constabulary-focused Western counterparts. *Vasily Bykov*, the lead ship of a class of at least six new Project 2216.0 offshore patrol ships, was another new design commencing sea trials during the course of the year. A class of larger Project 2335.0 Arctic patrol ships is also under construction.

Other Programmes: The long-delayed modernisation of the carrier *Admiral Kuznetsov* looks set to get underway in earnest in 2018 after signature of contracts for an upgrade package. There have been conflicting reports on the scope of the work. However, most agree that refurbishment or replacement of the ship's unreliable propulsion system and improved aircraft operating facilities will be the key priorities. The work is expected to be completed by

TABLE 2.4.7: RUSSIAN NAVY: SELECTED PRINCIPAL UNITS AS AT MID 2018

TYPE	CLASS	NUMBER[1]	TONNAGE	DIMENSIONS	PROPULSION	CREW	DATE
Aircraft carriers							
Aircraft Carrier – CV	Project 1143.5 **KUZNETSOV**	1	60,000 tons	306m x 35/73m x 10m	Steam, 32 knots	2,600	1991
Principal Surface Escorts							
Battlecruiser – BCGN	Project 1144.2 **KIROV**	1 (1)	25,000 tons	252m x 29m x 9m	CONAS, 32 knots	740	1980
Cruiser – CG	Project 1164 **MOSKVA** ('Slava')	3	12,500 tons	186m x 21m x 8m	COGAG, 32 knots	530	1982
Destroyer – DDG	Project 956/956A **SOVREMENNY**	c.5	8,000 tons	156m x 17m x 6m	Steam, 32 knots	300	1980
Destroyer – DDG	Project 1155.1 **CHABANENKO** ('Udaloy II')	1	9,000 tons	163m x 19m x 6m	COGAG, 29 knots	250	1999
Destroyer – DDG	Project 1155 **UDALOY**	c.8	8.500 tons	163m x 19m x 6m	COGAG, 30 knots	300	1980
Frigate – FFG	Project 1136.6M **GRIGOROVICH**	3	4,000 tons	125m x 15m x 4m	COGAG, 30 knots	200	2016
Frigate – FFG	Project 1154 **NEUSTRASHIMY**	2	4,400 tons	139m x 16m x 6m	COGAG, 30 knots	210	1993
Frigate – FFG	Project 1135 **BDITELNNY** ('Krivak I/II')	c.2	3,700 tons	123m x 14m x 5m	COGAG, 32 knots	180	1970
Frigate – FFG	Project 2038.0 **STEREGUSHCHY**	5	2,200 tons	105m x 11m x 4m	CODAD, 27 knots	100	2008
Frigate – FFG	Project 1161.1 **TATARSTAN** ('Gepard')	2	2,000 tons	102m x 13m x 4m	CODOG, 27 knots	100	2002
Submarines							
Submarine – SSBN	Project 955 **YURY DOLGORUKY** ('Borey')	3	17,000+ tons	170m x 13m x 10m	Nuclear, 25+ knots	110	2010
Submarine – SSBN	Project 941 **DONSKOY** ('Typhoon')	1	33,000 tons	173m x 23m x 12m	Nuclear, 26 knots	150	1981
Submarine – SSBN	Project 677BDRM **VERKHOTURYE** ('Delta IV')	6	18,000 tons	167m x 12m x 9m	Nuclear, 24 knots	130	1985
Submarine – SSBN	Project 677BDR **ZVEZDA** ('Delta III')	1	12,000 tons	160m x 12m x 9m	Nuclear, 24 knots	130	1976
Submarine – SSGN	Project 855 **SEVERODVINSK** ('Yasen')	1	13,500 tons+	120m x 14m x 9m	Nuclear, 30+ knots	90	2013
Submarine – SSGN	Project 949A ('Oscar II')	c.5	17,500 tons	154m x 8m x 9m	Nuclear, 30+ knots	100	1986
Submarine – SSN	Project 971 ('Akula I/II')	c.10	9,500 tons	110m x 14m x 10m	Nuclear, 30+ knots	60	1986
Submarine – SSK	Project 677 **ST PETERSBURG** ('Lada')	1	2,700 tons	72m x 7m x 7m	Diesel-electric, 21 knots	40	2010
Submarine – SSK	Project 877/636 ('Kilo')	c.20	3,000 tons	73m x 10m x 7m	Diesel-electric, 20 knots	55	1981

Notes:

1 Table only includes main types and focuses on operational units: bracketed figures are ships being refurbished or in maintained reserve.

2021 but this looks optimistic given the long delays to other Russian naval programmes.

The amphibious forces have been boosted by the delivery of the new Project 1171.1 landing ship *Ivan Gren*, which was commissioned on 20 June 2018 after two years of trials. A second ship, *Pyotr Morgunov*, was launched on 25 May 2018 but plans for further ships of the class have been cancelled. The navy appears to be more interested in amphibious assault ship and amphibious transport dock concepts with greater aviation capabilities. Given such ships are relatively cost-effective to acquire, it is possible procurement will be launched during the lifespan of GPV2027. The major procurement programmes are being supplemented by a wide range of other construction. For example, the second and third Project 1270.0 minehunters were launched in the past year and another pair of a contracted total of eight are under assembly. A particularly interesting arrival into the fleet was the second Project 1828.0 intelligence gathering ship, *Ivan Khurs*. It is ultimately intended to assign one ship of the class to each of the four fleets to perform communications reconnaissance and other electronic warfare operations.

The postponed construction of major combatants will inevitably result in a focus on modernisation to keep elements of the Soviet fleet operational for a little while longer. This will be challenging. For example the battlecruiser *Admiral Nakhimov*'s overhaul has now been extended into the 2020s, making refurbishment of the two other members of the class less and less likely. With most of the Project 956 *Sovremenny* class destroyers now also decommissioned, there will be heavy reliance on maintaining the Project 1164 *Slava* class cruisers and Project 1155 *Udaloy* class destroyers – and their Ukrainian gas turbines – in operational condition if an oceanic presence is to be maintained.

Notes

1. *National Shipbuilding Strategy: The Future of Naval Shipbuilding in the UK* (London: Ministry of Defence, 2017).

2. See, for example, Martin Murphy & Donata Riedel 'ThyssenKrupp blocked from warship tender' posted to the *Handelsblatt Global* site on 2 March 2018, currently available at: global.handelsblatt.com/companies/thyssenkrupp-blocked-warship-tender-893609. In late 2017 it emerged that *Baden-Württemberg* had been returned to the builder for defect rectification, reportedly the first time this had happened after a German warship delivery.

3. See *Revue Stratégique de Défense et de Sécurité Nationale* 2017 (Paris: République Française, 2017) and *Projet de Loi de Programnation Militaire 2019/2025* (Paris: Ministère des Armées, 2018). English language summaries of both documents have also been published.

4. Data is taken from *Projet de Loi de Programnation Militaire 2019/2025 – Dossier de presse* (Paris: Ministère des Armées, 2018), pp.69–70, supplemented by other official documents released on publication of the new law.

5. See Michel Cabirol's 'Pétrolier ravitailleur: la France monte à bord du programme italien Vulcano', *La Tribune* – 15 June 2018 (Paris: La Tribune Nouvelle, 2018).

6. Angelo Cabrini (1917–87) was the pilot of the explosive motor boat responsible for the destruction of the cruiser *HMS York* in Suda Bay, Crete in 1941.

7. For further details see Lee Willett's 'Briefing Italy's submarine fleet – Defending from the deep', *Jane's Defence Weekly* – 9 May 2018 (Coulsdon: IHS Jane's, 2018) pp.28–32.

8. See Esteban Villarejo's 'Spain Ready to Launch a New Investment Cycle in Defence', *European Security & Defence* – 2/2018 (Bonn: Mittler Report Verlag GmbH, 2018), pp.55–8.

9. For further detail see the editor's 'Type 26 Global Combat Ship: Status Report', *European Security & Defence* – 6/2017 (Bonn: Mittler Report Verlag GmbH, 2017), pp.68–73.

10. There have been unconfirmed reports a third proposal – possibly based on TKMS' MEKO technology – may also have been submitted.

11. See *The Equipment Plan 2017-2027* (London: National Audit Office, 2018).

12. See George Parker and David Bond, 'May casts doubt on UK status as "tier one" military power', *The Financial Times* – 20 June 2018 (London: Nikkei Inc., 2018).

13. The German-language report is entitled *Bericht zur materiellen Einsatzbereitschaft der Hauptwaffensysteme der Bundeswehr 2017* (Berlin: Federal Ministry of Defence, 2018). A number of summaries of its main conclusions have appeared in the English-language press.

14. For a more detailed overview of the F125 programme see the editor's '*Baden-Württemberg* Class: Germany's F125 type stabilisation frigates', *Seaforth World Naval Review 2018* (Barnsley: Seaforth Publishing, 2017), pp.116–31. The article was written before the latest problems with the class's construction became apparent.

15. See Kostas Tigkos, 'Greece moves closer to leasing FREMM frigates from France', *Jane's Defence Weekly* – 25 April 2018 (Coulsdon: IHS Jane's, 2018), p.6.

16. For further detail see Jaime Karremann's 'The Royal Netherlands Navy', *European Security & Defence* – 4/2018 (Bonn: Mittler Report Verlag GmbH, 2018), pp.48–53. Mr Karreman is editor-in-chief of the Dutch naval website marineschepen.nl, an excellent source of information on current Dutch naval developments.

17. Devrim Yaylali's *Bosphorus Naval News* blog at: turkishnavy.net/ remains the premier English language source for Turkish Navy developments.

18. The report of the increased budget was reported in 'Bulgaria proposes updated naval patrol vessel project' carried on 27 June 2018 by *The Sofia Globe* (Sofia: Sofia Globe Media, 2018).

19. For a detailed review of the Ukrainian Navy's current status and future prospects see Eugene Kogan's 'Status Report: The Ukrainian Navy', *European Security & Defence* – 3/2018 (Bonn: Mittler Report Verlag GmbH, 2018), pp.37–9.

20. For more detail see Aaron Mehta's article 'Fortress Sweden: Inside the plan to mobilize Swedish society against Russia' posted to the *Defense News* site on 14 March 2018 at: defensenews.com/global/europe/2018/03/14/fortress-sweden-inside-the-plan-to-mobilize-swedish-society-against-russia/

21. Saab currently maintains an interest microsite on the *Götland* class modernisation at: submarineevolution.creo.se/saab2018

22. An English language copy of the *Defence Agreement 2018-2023* can be found by searching the Forsvarsministeriet website at: fmn.dk/eng/Pages/frontpage.aspx#

23. See 'Russia to build 6 more Borei-A strategic nuclear-powered submarines – source', posted to the *TASS Russian News Agency* site on 21 May 2018 at: tass.com/defense/1005356

3.1 SIGNIFICANT SHIPS

FORD (CVN-78) CLASS AIRCRAFT CARRIERS

A 'Ford' in the Fleet

Author:
Scott Truver

'American steel and American hands have constructed this 100,000-ton message to the world,' President Donald P. Trump said of the USS *Gerald R. Ford* (CVN-78) at the warship's commissioning on 22 July 2017.[1] The president praised the bravery and spirit of US Service members and underscored his earlier call for a defence build-up after years of draconian budget cuts and sequestration – as well as an increase to a fleet of twelve aircraft carriers, one more than in service in 2018.

'American might is second to none and we're getting bigger and better and stronger every day of my administration …' the president trumpeted. 'Wherever this vessel cuts through the horizon, our allies will rest easy and our enemies will shake with fear because everyone will know that America is coming, and America is coming strong,' Trump crowed. He likened the c. US$13bn warship to '… an incredible work of art …' and boasted about the American labour that went into building a vessel that will house thousands of sailors.[2]

However, it has been a difficult transit from the initial concepts for a next-generation CVNX/ CVN-21 in the immediate post-Cold War world of the mid-1990s to the heat and humidity at Naval Station Norfolk, where the *Ford* 'came to life'.[3] Built by Huntington Ingalls Industries' Newport News Shipbuilding (HII/NNS), with suppliers from virtually every state in the Union, *Ford* is the lead ship of the US Navy's first new carrier class in forty-two years. The first of the last class, *Nimitz* (CVN-68) was commissioned in 1975. Under design, engineering development and construction for more than fifteen years, the *Ford* brings a host of new capabilities, reserve capacity for future enhancements, and new technologies and systems to the fleet. These include a new nuclear reactor design, an advanced power-distribution system, the Electromagnetic Aircraft Launching System

Two views of *Gerald R. Ford* (CVN-78) taken during preliminary sea trials in April 2017. Commissioned on 22 July 2017, *Ford* is the lead ship of the US Navy's first new carrier class for over forty years. *(US Navy)*

(EMALS), Advanced Arresting Gear (AAG), a new Dual-Band Radar (DBR) and Advanced Weapons Elevators (AWE). 'In all,' Rear Admiral Bruce Lindsey, USN, wrote, '23 new or modified systems distinguish *Gerald R. Ford* from aircraft carriers of the *Nimitz* class, bringing increased safety, effectiveness and efficiency to the ship's crew members, flight deck, propulsion system, electric plant, machinery control and integrated warfare systems.'[4]

Integrating and managing this extensive list of new systems and upgrades into a new-design carrier hull has not come without cost and technological 'birthing' pains. Not all of the technologies, especially the EMALS and AAG, matured in synch with the ship's construction schedule. The US Navy applied additional engineering and oversight to the newest systems presenting the most risk to the programme. Testing of new systems for the first time after installation on the ship identified issues that required further engineering and analysis to correct. Funding fluctuations from year to year also proved hard to control, and the programme had to be managed within a a cost cap – currently US$12.9bn – set by the US Congress. The navy was forced to limit further engineering efforts to those essential to deliver within this cap. One invaluable lesson learned from this experience is to avoid the risk of incorporating so many new technologies and systems into one hull in the future.

'As we look forward to designing and building ships of the future, particularly given how quickly technology is advancing, maybe we take smaller steps,' Chief of Naval Operations (CNO) Admiral John Richardson told USNI News at *Ford*'s commissioning.[5] 'Instead of something that will deliver in 15 or 20 years, we do something that will deliver in five years … we sort of take smaller steps to arrive at the technology and capability curve and deliver with more confidence and on budget, on schedule.'

Ford's sister carriers, *John F. Kennedy* (CVN-79) and *Enterprise* (CVN-80), are also under construction as of mid-2018, with *Kennedy* expected to enter the fleet in 2022 and *Enterprise* later in the decade. The US Navy is seeking Congressional approval to procure CVN-80 and the yet-to-be-named CVN-81 using a combined block-buy strategy, a process the service maintains will save upwards of US$2bn. There is a precedent. In 1982 and 1988 the US Navy and Congress agreed on two back-to-back two-carrier programmes, CVN-72/73 and CVN-74/75. The Congressional Research Service's Specialist in Naval Affairs, Ronald O'Rourke notes that when the first two-carrier buy was proposed, the US Navy estimated that the block buy would reduce

A F/A-18F Super Hornet assigned to Air Test and Evaluation Squadron 23 piloted by Lt. Cmdr. Jamie Struck performed the *Ford*'s first arrested landing and catapult launch on 28 July 2017. This was also the first time the carrier's new AAG arrestor and EMALS launch technology had been used at sea. *(US Navy)*

Gerald R. Ford (CVN-78): Major Milestones	
14 November 2009:	Keel laid.
9 November 2013:	Christening.
17 November 2013:	Floated out.
8 April 2017:	Underway under own power for builder's trials, completed 14 April 2017.
24 May 2017:	Underway for US Navy acceptance trials, completed 26 May 2017.
31 May 2017:	Delivered.
22 July 2017:	Commissioned.

the combined cost of CVN-72 and CVN-73 by 5.6 percent in real terms.[6] As Vice Admiral Thomas Moore, Commander, US Naval Sea Systems Command, explained in a March 2018 interview, 'The facts are pretty clear: when we've had a chance to do two-ship buys on the carrier side, with CVN-72 and 73 and then again with 74 and 75, in terms of the total cost performance of the ships and the number of man-hours it took to build those ships, within the *Nimitz* class, those four ships were built for the fewest man-hours and the lowest cost.'[7]

Following its commissioning, *Ford* immediately entered a vigorous testing and evaluation phase, during which the ship was underway for much of the year, wringing out the performance from the host of new capabilities. *Ford* had already been performing a graduated series of independent steaming exercises that extended the operational envelope and progressively expanded the complexity of the testing and evaluation regime. Then, only a week after *Ford's* commissioning – on 28 July 2017 – Lt. Cmdr. Jamie Struck of Air Test and Evaluation Squadron 23 (VX-23) performed the carrier's first arrested landing and catapult launch in an F/A-18F Super Hornet, underway off the Virginia USA coast. This not only marked the ship's first successful aircraft launch and recovery but also the first at-sea demonstration of both the AAG and the EMALS.

With service lives projected at fifty years, the navy expects the (potential) ten-strong *Ford* class will be part of the fleet some ninety years. Thus means that the class will have, over time, to accept new technologies and systems that can be only dimly perceived as of 2018.

FORD CLASS PROVENANCE

The provenance of the *Ford* programme harkens to the mid-1990s, when naval aviation leaders first began to think about a follow-on to the *Nimitz* class aircraft carriers.[8] First commissioned in May 1975,

Nimitz incorporated late-1960s and early-1970s technologies and systems. Subsequent *Nimitz* class carriers were a series of 'modified repeats' of the previously-acquired ships, sometimes incorporating only minor changes but often integrating significant modifications and upgrades to address evolving threats and requirements. A 2005 RAND report concluded, '… the biggest problems facing the *Nimitz* class are the limited electrical power generation capability and the upgrade-driven increase in ship weight and erosion of the center-of-gravity margin needed to maintain ship stability'.[9]

With leaders increasingly convinced that two decades of modifications and upgrades had wrung out most of the warfighting, weight and volume growth margins of the baseline *Nimitz* class hull, the US Navy assessed seventy-five conceptual designs over a three-year period from 1996, including a variety of sizes, alternative propulsion concepts, and design concepts.[10] 'It was clear,' retired *Ford* programme manager Captain Tal Manvel and Dr. David Perin commented in 2014,

… a next-generation ship entailed major research, development, testing, and design efforts – including a new electrical-distribution architecture, a new reactor, a new electrical-generation plant, a new flight-deck layout and composite island structure, a new combat system, and electromagnetic systems to replace existing steam catapults, hydraulic arresting gear and elevators, and other steam-driven auxiliary systems. Research-and-development costs were estimated to add at least $5 billion to the cost for the ship herself. Two basic

The veteran aircraft carrier *Nimitz* (CVN-68) being manoeuvred into dry dock at Puget Sound Naval Shipyard, Bremerton in March 2018 to begin a ten-month overall. First commissioned in May 1975, she incorporates many late 1960s and early 1970s technologies and systems. Whilst later members of the ten-ship class incorporate many improvements, by the 1990s the US Navy appreciated the design had reached its limits. *(US Navy)*

approaches were considered: a clean-sheet design that made all of the changes in one ship, and an evolutionary approach that phased in changes over several ships.

Non-nuclear designs were assessed but ultimately nuclear-power warfighting benefits prevailed, and the resulting CVNX was dubbed CVN-21 – the 'CVN for the 21st Century' – to help 'brand' the next-gen carriers.

In 1998 the renamed Future Carrier Program estimated the costs of a one-step 'clean-sheet' design for a large, nuclear-powered aircraft carrier in fiscal year (FY) 2006 at US$6.4bn, with the R&D investments

for its non-recurring design and technology development coming in at an additional US$7.1bn, for a total of US$13.5bn (as of FY2006) for the first-of-class CVNX. However, Congress under-funded the programme, cutting US$100m from design in the spring 1998. This led one navy official to lament, 'We just cannot afford the investment needed to achieve the hoped for long term savings.'[11]

The Department of Defense (DoD) instead approved a three-ship evolutionary acquisition approach for the last *Nimitz* class carrier (CVN-77) and the next two carriers, CVNX-1 (CVN-78) and CVNX-2 (CVN-79). These ships were to be acquired over a sixteen-year programme, from CVN-

77 starting in 2002 to the commissioning of CVN-79 in 2018. The US Navy clearly recognised the risk of concurrently developing and integrating new technologies and systems into a single, lead-ship design – common practice in shipbuilding – in spite of pressures to deliver a much-needed capability whilst advancing technology and outpacing obsolescence. Instead, an incremental, evolutionary 'build-a-little learn-a-lot' approach was borrowed from the Aegis guided-missile cruiser and destroyer programmes. As Ronald O'Rourke of the Congressional Research Service reported in February 2002:

The Navy plans to gradually evolve the design

Pictured here in December 2016, *George H. W. Bush* (CVN-77) was the tenth and final member of the *Nimitz* class, commissioning on 10 January 2009. CVN-77 was originally intended to be the first in a three-ship series of transitional carriers that would steadily evolve the legacy *Nimitz* design to accommodate a wide range of next-generation systems and technologies. A subsequent change in plan meant that she was built as a repeat *Nimitz*, based largely on her immediate predecessor *Ronald Reagan* (CVN-76). *(US Navy)*

of its aircraft carriers by introducing new technologies into CVN-77 (an aircraft carrier procured in FY2001), CVNX-1, and CVNX-2 (a carrier planned for procurement around FY2011). The Navy estimates that CVNX-1 will cost $2.54 billion to develop and $7.48 billion to procure, bringing its total acquisition (development plus procurement) cost to $10.02 billion. The Navy estimates that CVNX-2 will cost $1.29 billion to design and $7.49 billion to procure, for a total acquisition cost of $8.78 billion [all constant-year dollars].

The modified-repeat CVN-77 would use the existing *Nimitz* class hull, mechanical and electrical (HM&E) architecture. However, it would combine advanced information network technology with new multifunction, dual-band radars borrowed from the then-proposed 32-ship *Zumwalt* (DDG-1000) land-attack destroyer programme to transform the carrier's combat systems and the air wing's mission planning system into an integrated warfare system.[12] O'Rourke noted CVN-77 was to incorporate a variety of new technologies, including several that would reduce the annual operating and support cost of the ship compared to other *Nimitz* class ships and would require about 550 fewer sailors to operate. Where feasible, some of these new technologies might be retrofitted into the other nine in-service *Nimitz* CVNs. O'Rourke explained:

… the Navy originally wanted CVNX-1 to be a completely new, next-generation aircraft carrier (hence the program name CVNX-1, rather than CVN-78). In May 1998, however, the Navy decided that it could not afford to develop an all-new hull and design for that ship and instead decided to continue to modify the *Nimitz* class design with the existing *Nimitz* class hull with each new carrier that it procured. Under this strategy, CVN-77 and CVNX-1 [were] to be, technologically, the first and second ships in a series of transitional aircraft carrier designs.

A view of the distinctive island used on *Gerald R. Ford* (CVN-78), including the fixed arrays of the DBR dual-band radar incorporated into its superstructure. It was originally intended to incorporate DBR into CVN-77 but delays putting the new radar system into production meant that *Ford* was the first – and only – ship to receive the full system. (*US Navy*)

The design focus for the evolutionary CVNX-1 was a new HM&E architecture within the legacy CVN 77 hull, which included a new reactor plant design, increased electrical generating capacity, new zonal electrical distribution, and new electrical systems to replace steam auxiliaries. The flight deck would employ a new electromagnetic aircraft launch system. The navy also defined goals for reduced/optimal manning and improved maintainability. For example, CVNX-1 would require at least 350 fewer sailors to operate compared with CVN-77.

The CVNX-2 was to 'open the aperture' for new technologies and systems, such as the advanced arresting gear and advanced weapons elevators that would be ready in time for the third ship in the series. A new flight deck design would be the most visible aspect of CVNX-2 but there were also to be internal improvements to the hull to improve survivability. There would be further reductions in crewing and maintenance costs. The intent was to apply the lessons learned from the design and construction of the first two ships to the third carrier. Under 2002 US Navy long-range plans, CVNX-2 would be procured in FY2011 and enter service in 2018 as the

replacement for the oil-fired *John F. Kennedy* (CV-67), which would then be fifty years old.

By the end of 2002 the DoD estimated that a three-ship programme would have a total acquisition cost of about US$36.1bn in constant dollars – US$4.33bn for development and US$31.75bn for procurement – or an average of about US$12bn per ship.[13] Remember that 'about US$12bn' figure!

TRANSFORMING CARRIERS AND PROGRAMMES

With the inauguration of President George W. Bush in January 2001 came the demand for the 'transformation' of virtually everything military. Taking his cue from a decade of thinking about what the Soviet Union called the 'revolution in military affairs', Secretary of Defense Donald H. Rumsfeld wrote, '… a revolution in military affairs is about more than building new high-tech weapons – although that is certainly part of it. It's also about new ways of thinking and new ways of fighting.'[14]

'Transformation' for US Naval Aviation meant a completely revamped approach for acquiring aircraft carriers. In 2002, Rumsfeld's DoD team threw out

the navy's incremental three-ship strategy and instead directed a single transformational 'leap-ahead' from CVN-77 to CVN-78. Under the revised strategy, CVN-77 was a modified, repeat *Nimitz* (based on CVN-76, *Ronald Reagan*) but without the advanced integrated warfare system and dual band radar to minimise risk, integration work and construction costs. Subsequently, the 2004 revised operational requirements document defined a new baseline, with CVN-78 as the lead ship. Originally scheduled for a FY2006 start, budget constraints now delayed commencement of the programme to FY2007.

'This required "pulling forward" all the technologies identified in 1998 that were not ready to go on the CVNX1 by 2006 but were now somehow ready to go on it by 2007 with four less years of development,' Manvel and Perin explained. They added, 'The DoD gave the Navy 18 months to transform the plan to a single ship with a complete redesign to accommodate the new technologies … the undertaking was renamed the CVN-21 Program, and CVNX-1 (CVN-78) became CVN-21 lead ship; CVNX-2 (CVN-79) became CVN-22, follow ship; and CVN-80 (the next *Enterprise*) was also authorized as the third ship in low-rate initial-production planning. After further adjustments, with a start in 2008, the CVN-78 procurement in 2005 was estimated at $10.5 billion, with $2.3 billion in R&D. But notice the R&D bill. It was estimated in 1998 at $7.1 billion for a 2006 start. Then in 2005 it was $4.8 billion less at $2.3 billion for a 2008 start.'[15]

As noted by Manvel and Perin, formal launch of the CVN-78 programme was delayed by another year to FY2008, again largely because of budget constraints. However, the shift to a transformational acquisition approach – implementing all the planned changes in a single ship – was confirmed. As a result, the traditional serial evolution of technology development, ship concept design, detail design, and construction – including the twenty-three developmental systems incorporating new technologies originally planned across three carriers – was compressed into the single CVN-78. This was inevitably to have significant consequences with respect to both timely delivery and overall cost.

On 10 September 2008, the US Navy signed a US$5.1bn contract with Northrop Grumman Shipbuilding to design and construct the new carrier. Northrop had already begun advanced construction work on the carrier under a US$2.7bn

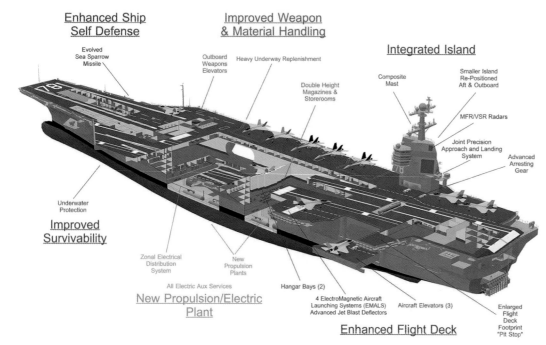

Enhanced Ship Self Defense

Evolved Sea Sparrow Missile

Improved Weapon & Material Handling

Outboard Weapons Elevators

Heavy Underway Replenishment

Double Height Magazines & Storerooms

Integrated Island

Composite Mast

Smaller Island Re-Positioned Aft & Outboard

MFR/VSR Radars

Joint Precision Approach and Landing System

Advanced Arresting Gear

Underwater Protection

Improved Survivability

Zonal Electrical Distribution System

New Propulsion Plants

All Electric Aux Services

Hangar Bays (2)

New Propulsion/Electric Plant

4 ElectroMagnetic Aircraft Launching Systems (EMALS) Advanced Jet Blast Deflectors

Aircraft Elevators (3)

Enlarged Flight Deck Footprint "Pit Stop"

Enhanced Flight Deck

A schematic showing the new technologies incorporated into the CVN-78 *Ford* class design. Under the original, evolutionary approach to carrier procurement these changes would have been slowly introduced over a series of three ships. A changed approach to procurement led by then Secretary of State for Defense Donald H Rumsfeld saw all the improvements being incorporated into a single ship, with all the challenges that entailed. *(US Navy)*

contract awarded in 2005. *Ford* was constructed at Northrop Grumman's (subsequently HII's) Newport News Shipbuilding facilities in Newport News, Virginia.[16] The ship was originally scheduled for launch in July 2013 and delivery in 2015. Production delays meant that the launch had ultimately to be postponed until November 2013, with delivery on 31 May 2017.

BIRTHING PAINS

Every first-of-class warship endures 'birthing pains'. The daunting challenge is to control costs and schedules while delivering required capabilities.[17] Only in exceptional cases will the US Navy design and build a prototype warship, therefore much is learned – often at the expense of projected budgets and sharpened oversight – from the construction of the lead ship. The compressed development schedule and transformational expectations associated with CVN-78 made this challenge all the greater. The programme became an easy target for critics when the almost inevitable construction delays and cost increases ultimately occurred. Much of this criticism has been exaggerated or unfounded. Notably, whilst programme costs have indeed risen, the facts suggest that the *Ford* class is faring rather better than many other shipbuilding projects in spite of the programme's huge complexities.

The RAND National Defense Research Institute 2006 study *Why has the Cost of Navy Ships Risen?* provides a useful starting point. This found a 7–11 percent annual cost escalation for military shipbuilding for the period from 1950 to 2000.[18] Dr. Eric Labs of the Congressional Budget Office estimated that the cost-growth in CVN-78 was 23 percent. This compared favourably to an average of 45 percent for the lead ships of various programmes, including surface warships, small combatants, amphibious warfare ships, submarines, and combat logistics and support vessels.[19]

The navy generated the cost estimate for CVN-78 a decade ago when the design was immature. When Congress authorised the procurement of CVN-78 in FY2008, the navy estimated the total cost for this first-of-class ship at US$10.5bn (then-year dollars) in addition to one off programme R&D expense. At the time, the navy reported that its confidence in the estimate was less than 40 percent, meaning there was more than a 60 percent chance that the estimates would be exceeded. Indeed, the combination of cost increases in government-furnished equipment, first-

A picture of *Gerald R. Ford* (CVN-78) during her christening at Huntington Ingalls Industries' Newport News Shipbuilding facility on 9 November 2013. The ceremony was conducted by Susan Ford Bales, daughter of the ship's namesake president. At this time, construction was running a few months behind schedule but delays with many of the new systems intended for the ship meant that delivery was subject to significantly greater delay. *(Huntington Ingalls Industries)*

Gerald R Ford (CVN-78) pictured during the commencement of the floating-out process at Newport News Shipbuilding. This took place on 17 November 2013, just over a week after her christening ceremony. *(US Navy)*

of-class design and production issues, and inflation associated with the delayed start of ship construction meant there was an increase in the final estimated cost to nearly US$13bn. This figure includes approximately US$3.3bn of non-recurring engineering (NRE) activities associated with CVN-78 as lead ship of the class. Therefore, the overall out-turn – even when taking R&D into account – does not compare unfavourably with the US$12bn average per-carrier cost of the 2002 incremental three-ship strategy.

The navy and industry have taken substantial steps to control cost growth despite continuing to deal with first-of-class issues. However, there were no viable recovery plans that could undo the cost growth identified earlier in the construction of the lead ship – the increases were truly 'sunk costs'. One of several efforts to help control *Ford* costs called for the shipbuilder to focus on activities most critical to CVN-78 going to sea. Completion of nearly 370 non-critical compartments – e.g., air wing berthing, bathroom facilities, and offices – were deferred to the carrier's post-shakedown availability. Importantly, however, work deferred to post-delivery will still be accomplished within the cost cap established by Congress. In May 2018, however, the USN acknowledged issues arising during tests would require a further US$120m to

How Much Do Carriers Really Cost? It Depends

One of the challenges of getting the facts right about the costs of the US Navy's aircraft carrier programmes is understanding the difference between 'then-year' and 'constant-year' dollars. Many observers quote dollar amounts and often do not indicate which is being referenced, or use them both without clarification. 'Then-year' dollars are the actual cash amounts paid in the year(s) of purchase. 'Constant-year' dollars are indexed to a certain, usually baseline, programme year to account for annual variations in the dollar's buying power. This is typically done by applying inflation rates to then-year dollars and revising these to a specific 'constant' year.

For example, US Navy data show that the *Nimitz* (CVN-68) cost US$0.7bn in then-year (1974) dollars; using navy methodology to escalate US$0.7bn to constant-year 2013 dollars, the baseline *Nimitz* would cost about US$7.5 bn. A more recent example, *George H. W. Bush* (CVN-77) was delivered in 2009 for US$6.2bn (then-year) dollars, but the FY 2013 constant-year dollars cost was US$9.0bn. *Gerald R. Ford* (CVN-78) costs US$13 billion in then-year dollars, and that includes the US$3.3bn of first-in-class NRE costs. So, when accounting for historical inflation, *Nimitz* class carriers were not significantly cheaper than the *Ford*. Moreover, navy officials are quick to explain that not only are they not significantly more expensive in inflation-adjusted dollars, they will provide significantly more capability at reduced total ownership costs compared to the *Nimitz*.

Figure 1 shows the planning and production hours to build each *Nimitz* class and *Ford* class carrier. Key takeaways include:

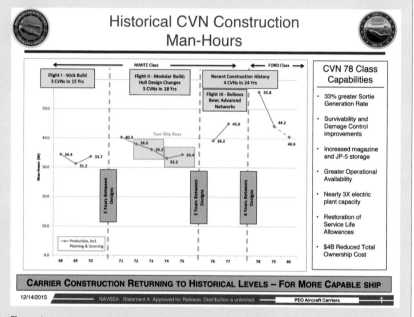

Figure 1

- Nimitz class production hours were lowest when the time between builds was less and, particularly, when Congress authorised two-carrier buys.
- Major changes in design (CVN-71, CVN-76 and CVN-78) always result in step increases in labour-hours for the first ship of the new design.
- Increasing the intervals between carriers increases workload learning curves and drives up hours; in 2009 the Secretary of Defense stipulated five-year intervals between new-starts.
- CVN-79 labour-hours will be about 18 percent less than CVN-78 which is less than expended on the construction of the last of the *Nimitz* class, with another 10 percent labour-hours reduction projected in CVN-80, which restores the construction hours to near historical *Nimitz*-class levels for a ship that is much more complex to build
- While the Navy is on a course through CVN-80 and the follow-on *Ford* class carriers to return to near-historical construction-hour levels, it will also deliver significantly improved operational capabilities with a projected US$4bn reduction in total ownership cost during the lifetime of each ship.

Lessons learned from the 42-year *Nimitz*-class programme directly informed *Ford*-class programme acquisition decisions.[1] Optimised intervals between construction starts, efficient construction durations, design refinements to improve affordability, economic order quantity purchases of equipment and materials, careful control of costly design changes through block buys, and investments in more efficient facilities are decisions that will contribute to more affordable and combat-effective multi-mission warships for the next fifty years and more.

Note:
1. Department of the Navy, Director Air Warfare (N98) and PEO Carriers' *Report to Congress – Aircraft Carrier Construction John F. Kennedy (CVN-79)* – March 2013 reproduced in Ronald O'Rourke *Navy Ford (CVN-78) Aircraft Carrier Program RS20643*, issued 17 April 2018, pp. 66-82.

fix, thus slightly exceeding the cap.

Since 2014, both cost and schedule performance for CVN-78 have been steady, and the *Ford* programme is capitalising on investments to deliver future ships at best cost and on schedule. In other words, the navy is ready to proceed to the process of serial construction that has previously proven successful in driving down cost. As O'Rourke summarised in 2018:

■ While the estimated cost of CVN-78 grew considerably between the FY2008 budget (the budget in which CVN-78 was procured) and the FY2014 budget, since the FY2014 budget, it has grown by only a small amount (about 1 percent)

■ While the estimated cost of CVN-79 grew considerably between the FY2008 budget and the FY2013 budget (in part because the procurement date for the ship was deferred by one year in the FY2010 budget), since the FY2013 budget it has declined by a small amount (less than 1 percent)

■ While the estimated cost of CVN-79 grew considerably between the FY2008 budget and the FY2013 budget (in part because the procurement date for the ship was deferred by two years in the FY2010 budget), since the FY2013 budget it has declined by about 7 percent.

A series of images showing the second *Ford* class carrier, *John F. Kennedy* (CVN-79), slowly taking shape in one of Newport News Shipbuilding's dry docks in the two years between April 2016 and April 2018. Like *Ford*, *Kennedy* is being built using modular construction, a process where smaller sections of the ship are welded together to form larger structural units or 'superlifts'. Equipment is then installed and the superlifts lifted into the dry dock using a 1,050-ton gantry crane. Lessons learned from the sometimes difficult construction of *Ford* – and from that of the previous *Nimitz* class – are being applied to the process; for example, *Kennedy* is expected to be completed with 445 lifts; 51 less than *Ford* and 149 less than *George H. W. Bush* (CVN-77). *(Huntington Ingalls Industries)*

CVN-78 construction began in parallel with detailed design to minimise the length of time the navy would operate with only ten aircraft carriers rather than the Congressionally-mandated force of eleven CVNs.[20] However, it also meant concurrent design, engineering and new technology development during construction caused delays in material procurement, manufacturing and assembly. This drove up costs and caused missed schedules.[21] The navy took early and significant steps to mitigate perceived risks in EMALS component manufacturing, installation and testing. Issues with the AAG and DBR surfaced later and also had to be addressed. During the test phase of construction, additional issues were identified related to the ship's electric plant; the navy's plan for reduced manning; and with electromagnetic interference between systems on the ship. These further extended the need for engineering services. The DBR radar was four and a half years late, the AAG some two and a half years late, and the EMALS nearly three years late. Manvel and Perin noted that these three systems accounting for more than US$800m in cost growth.

Incorporating all the many developmental systems at various levels of technical maturity significantly compounded the inherent challenges associ-

Table 3.2.1.

GERALD R. FORD (CVN-78) PRINCIPAL PARTICULARS

Building Information:

Keel Laid:	14 November 2009[1]
Floated Out:	17 November 2013[2]
Commissioned:	22 July 2017
Builders:	Huntington Ingalls Industries' Newport News Shipbuilding facility at Newport News, VA.

Dimensions:

Displacement:	c. 100,000 tons full load displacement.
Overall Dimensions:	333m x 78m x 12m. Waterline dimensions are 317m x 41m.

Equipment:

Aircraft:	Typical air group of up to 75 fast jets and helicopters. 4 x EMALS catapults. 3 x deck-edge aircraft elevators
Guns:	2 x octuple Mk 29 launchers for RIM-62 ESSM; 2 x 21-cell Mk 49 RAM launchers for RIM-116 surface-to-air missiles; 3 x Mk 15 Phalanx 20mm CIWS.
Countermeasures:	Includes SLQ-32(V) 4 jammer and SLQ-25A 'Nixie' torpedo defence system.
Principal Sensors:	Dual Band Radar (DBR) system comprising AN/SPY-3 multifunction radar and AN/SPY-4 volume-search radar, AN/SPN-41 series ICLS, TACAN homing beacon, navigation radar.
Combat System:	Integrated Warfare System encompassing Ship Self Defense System (SSDS) Mk 2 Mod 6 and CEC. Communications systems include Links 11, Link 16 and 22.

Propulsion System:

Machinery:	Nuclear. 2 x A1B pressurised water reactors and 4 x steam turbines generate a total of c. 280,000SHP through four shafts.
Speed:	Designed maximum speed is over 30 knots. Endurance is limited only by a nuclear core life of c. 25 years.

Other Details:

Complement:	A typical crew comprises c. 2,800 personnel plus c. 1,800 additional crew in the embarked air wing.[3]
Class:	*Gerald R. Ford* (CVN-78) commissioned, with *John F. Kennedy* (CVN-79) and *Enterprise* (CVN-80) in various stages of construction as of mid-2018. Up to ten vessels ultimately planned.

Notes:

1. Advance construction began on 11 August 2005.

2 Christening took place on 9 November 2013

3. Complement and total accommodation numbers vary significantly, even in official sources.

ated with delivering the first new aircraft carrier design in more than forty years. The impact of this high degree of concurrency significantly exceeded the risk attributed to any single new system or risk issue and ultimately manifested itself in terms of delay and cost growth in each element of programme execution – development, engineering, material procurement and construction. Additionally, the US Navy's decision to shift the

integrated warfare system and DBR development and associated costs entirely to CVN-78, rather than sharing with the DDG-1000 destroyer programme, added an enormous burden to the new carrier's design and construction.

The navy continues to address the ripple effect of compression and concurrency, as well as changes to assumptions made to overall programme planning more than a decade ago.

KEY CHARACTERISTICS

Table 3.1.1 lists *Gerald R. Ford's* key design characteristics.

Looking in from the outside, the most obvious difference between CVN-78 and the *Nimitz* class is that *Ford's* island is shorter in length and 20ft (6m) taller than that in the previous class; it is also set 140ft (42.6m) further aft and 3ft (1m) closer to the edge of the ship. Flat panels on the island are a

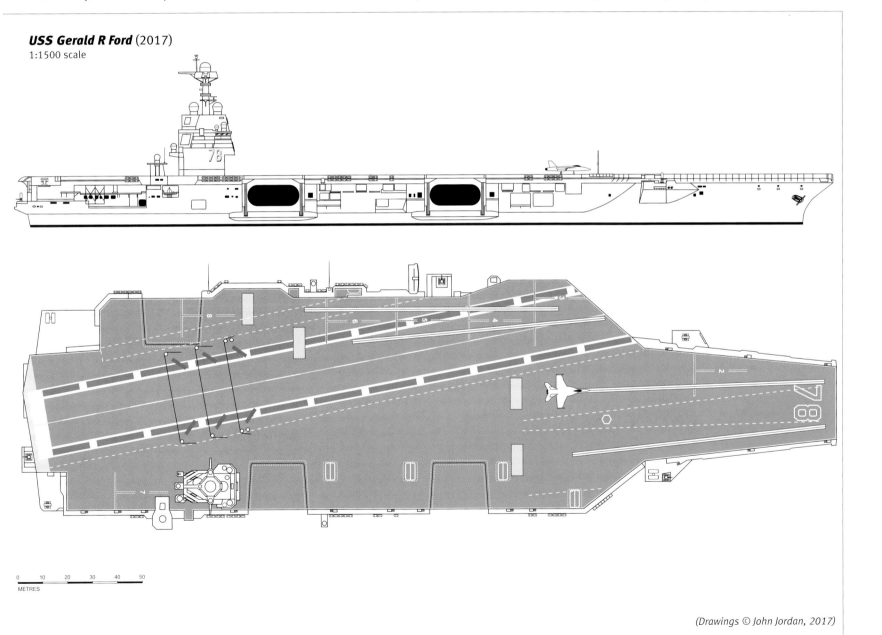

USS Gerald R Ford (2017)
1:1500 scale

0 10 20 30 40 50
METRES

(Drawings © John Jordan, 2017)

Gerald R Ford (CVN-78) taken off Norfolk, Virginia on 8 April 2017, the day she commenced builder's sea trials. Her island – of new design – is located significantly further aft and slightly closer to the ship's starboard side than that in the previous *Nimitz* class design. This has created additional deck space and helped to secure an improved sortie generation rate. Her basic hull form is largely identical to that used in later members of the *Nimitz* class. *(US Navy)*

A major emphasis in *Ford*'s design has been an effort to simplify and improve aircraft and munitions flows through a series of improvements to the flight-deck layout and weapons-handling arrangements. The number of aircraft lifts from hangar to flight deck level has been reduced from four to three, freeing up valuable deck space. Shifting the island aft has created further deck space for a centralised rearming and refuelling location. The visual impact of these changes is evident in this July 2017 view. *(US Navy)*

visible reminder that the *Ford* is equipped with AN/SPY-3 and AN/SPY-4 active electronically scanned, multifunction dual-band radars. And – although much less obvious – changes to the flight deck improve aircraft handling, storage and flow, weapons and material handling, all to increase sortie rate. Some of the most important of these changes are dealt with in more detail below.

AIRCRAFT AND MUNITIONS HANDLING

A major emphasis in *Ford*'s design has been an effort to simplify and improve aircraft and munitions flows through a series of improvements to the flight-deck layout and weapons-handling arrangements compared with the previous *Nimitz* class. For example, catapult Number 4 on the *Nimitz* class cannot launch fully-loaded aircraft because of a wing clearance constraint along the flight deck edge. By contrast, *Ford* has no catapult-specific restrictions on launching aircraft, whilst retaining four (two bow and two waist) catapults. The number of aircraft elevators from hangar deck to flight deck level has, however, been reduced from four to three, freeing up valuable deck space. Shifting the island aft has created further deck space for a centralised rearming and refuelling location, reducing the number of times that an aircraft will have to be moved after landing before it can be re-launched.

Movement of weapons from storage and assembly to the aircraft on the flight deck has been streamlined and accelerated. Ordnance is moved to the centralised rearming location via re-located, higher-capacity advanced weapon elevators that use linear motors. The new path that ordnance follows does not cross any areas of aircraft movement, thereby reducing traffic problems in the hangar and on the flight deck. Fewer aircraft movements require, in turn, fewer deck hands to accomplish them, reducing the size of the ship's crew and increasing sortie rate. Coupled with EMALS and AAG, these flight deck changes support the requirements for 160 sorties per day for 30 days' operations, with surges to 270 per day. In comparison, *Nimitz* class sortie rates are on the order of 120 per day (up to 240 for a surge), but with significantly more crew members than the *Ford* class.

The navy has used modern equipment and extensive automation to reduce *Ford*'s crew – about 600 fewer than the *Nimitz* class – and, therefore, the total cost of future aircraft carriers. With many ship-wide efficiencies in place, it estimates it will save some US$4bn in each carrier's operating costs throughout a fifty-year service life.

POWER GENERATION

Nowhere is the focus on efficiency more apparent than in the ship's power-generation plant. As noted by Manvel and Perin, the first nuclear-powered aircraft carrier, *Enterprise* (CVN-65) had eight reactors, thirty-two steam generators, sixteen electrical generators and more than 5,000 main steam valves for her four main engines and her catapults. The *Nimitz* design reduced the number of reactors to two and reduced steam generators and electrical generators to eight, while cutting the number of main steam valves to far fewer than 1,500; more than a 3-to-1 reduction. The new *Ford* class design takes further steps to continue this evolutionary process of simplification and improvement.

Whilst *Ford* retains two nuclear reactors, these are of a new, advanced type with a higher core density developed by Bechtel Corporation. These two A1B reactors are believed to generate twenty-five percent more power output than the two A4W reactors found in the *Nimitz* class.[22] Moreover, the *Ford's* plant has cut the steam and electrical generators in half to four each from the previous class, whilst reducing the number of main steam valves to fewer than 300 – in large part because of the change from steam to electromagnetic catapults. These improvements have led to simpler construction, reduced maintenance requirements, and only a third of the manpower/watch-standing burden in a more compact system that requires less ship volume. Another significant, although largely unseen improvement, has been the redesign of electrical distribution to a zonal system that is lighter and more survivable than the radial arrangement found in older ships.

As *Ford* is primarily an 'all-electric' carrier, electrical capacity of the ship's generators was increased 2.5 times that of *Nimitz*. Systems such as heating, galleys and laundries – previously largely operated by steam – are now powered by electricity. However, the most significant requirement for power results from the new aircraft launching and arresting systems used in the ship.

EMALS AND AAG

Replacing the *Nimitz* class's steam catapults, the EMALS electromagnetic aircraft launching system

Ford at sea during the course of preliminary builder's sea trials in April 2017. The navy has used modern equipment and extensive automation to reduce *Ford*'s crew by about 600 compared with the previous *Nimitz* class. *(US Navy)*

The *Ford* class carriers are equipped with a new design of A1B nuclear reactor that is lighter and more efficient than the legacy A4W design used in the previous *Nimitz* series of carriers. The two reactors' greater capacity for power generation feeds new launch and recovery equipment whilst allowing the class to maintain a speed comfortably in excess of 30 knots. Here *Ford* is seen at speed during initial work up in August 2017. *(US Navy)*

uses an electrically-generated moving magnetic field to propel the catapult and launch the aircraft, which places less physical stress on aircraft compared to steam-piston catapult launchers. Developed by General Atomics, this innovation eliminates the traditional requirement to generate and store steam, freeing up considerable volume below deck. Its primary operational advantage is that it accelerates aircraft more smoothly, putting less stress on their airframes. Compared to steam catapults, the EMALS also weighs less, is expected to cost less in upkeep and require less maintenance, and can launch both heavier and lighter aircraft than a steam piston-driven system. It also reduces a carrier's requirement for fresh water, thus reducing the demand for energy-intensive desalination. The EMALS uses a linear induction motor (LIM), which uses electric currents to generate magnetic fields that propel a carriage along a track to launch the aircraft. The LIM consists of a row of stator coils with the same function as the circular stator coils in a conventional induction motor. When energised, the motor accelerates the carriage along the track. Only the section of the coils surrounding the carriage is energized at any given time, thereby minimising reactive losses. The EMALS' 300ft (91m) LIM can accelerate a 100,000lb (4,536kg) aircraft to 130 knots.

Electromagnets are also used in the AAG advanced arresting gear system, another system built by General Atomics. The traditional *Nimitz* arresting system uses hydraulics connected to an arresting gear cable to slow and stop a landing aircraft. While this hydraulic technology is effective – as demonstrated by more than fifty years of operations – AAG offers several improvements. For example, the legacy system is unable to capture UAVs without damaging them due to extreme stresses on the airframe. UAVs do not typically have sufficient mass to drive the large hydraulic piston used to trap heavier manned aircraft. By contrast, electromagnetics – controlled by a turbo-electric engine – makes the trap smoother and reduce shock on airframes. Rotary engines that use simple energy-absorbing water turbines (or 'twisters') coupled to a large induction motor provide finer control of the arresting forces. While the system looks the same from the flight deck as its predecessor, it will ultimately prove to be more flexible, safe and reliable, and will require less maintenance and manning compared to the hydraulic system.

ACCOMMODATION

But it is not all about hardware. 'Other design changes provide for the comfort and well-being of the sailors in the crew, air wing and embarked staffs in *Gerald R. Ford*,' Rear Admiral Lindsey explained.[23]

Gerald R. Ford (CVN-78) pulls alongside the dry cargo and ammunition ship *William McLean* (T-AKE-12) during a practice underway replenishment exercise in August 2017. The new electromagnetic EMALS catapults and AAG arrestors are not noticeably different than their predecessors but are more susceptible to adjustment to operate a wide range of aircraft, including unmanned aerial vehicles. *(US Navy)*

Crewmembers will find more privacy in redesigned sleeping areas with fewer racks per room and easier access to restroom and shower facilities. Separate spaces hold crew recreation and television viewing areas, providing consistent quiet for sleeping crewmembers. Wider passageways make travel through the ship more efficient in both peace and combat. Well-equipped gyms enable a variety of exercise routines. Increased air conditioning capacity adds to crew comfort and reduces maintenance caused by high heat and humidity. Even the lighting is better; 44,000 high-efficiency fluorescent T-8 light bulbs produces more light and last nearly twice as long as lighting on a *Nimitz* class carrier.

SENSORS AND WEAPONS

The *Ford*'s DBR dual-band radar integrates (i) the AN/SPY-3 X Band (NATO I/J Band) multifunction radar for horizon search, surface search and navigation, and missile guidance with (ii) the AN/SPY-4 S (NATO E/F) Band volume-search radar for long-range, above-horizon, surveillance and air-traffic control capabilities. The system was originally developed by Raytheon for the *Zumwalt* programme. However, in 2010, the navy decided to omit the DBR from the *Zumwalt* class as a cost-saving measure but to continue to use the system in *Ford*.

The basic dual-band operating concept is for the SPY-4 to hand off a detected target to the SPY-3 for close in tracking and engagement. The radars are fully automatic and are controlled by a common processor suite requiring no human intervention. The only human interaction is for maintenance and repair. This new system has no moving parts, minimising maintenance and manning requirements for operation. The AN/SPY-3 consists of three active, fixed arrays with the receiver/exciter cabinets above decks and the signal and data processor subsystem below-decks. The SPY-4 volume-search radar has a similar architecture, with the beamforming and narrowband down-conversion functionality occurring in two additional cabinets per array. A central controller (the resource manager) resides in the data processor. The DBR is the first radar system that uses a central controller and two active-array radars operating at different frequencies.

In spite of the dual-band radar's technological innovation and undoubted capabilities, the navy had decided that it offers a degree of sophistication that

A F/A-18F Super Hornet is caught *by Gerald R. Ford*'s (CVN-78) AAG advanced arrestor gear. While the system looks the same from the flight deck as its hydraulic predecessor, it will ultimately prove to be more flexible, safe, and reliable, and will require less maintenance and manning. *(US Navy)*

An internal schematic of the new AAG introduced on *Ford*. Rotary engines using energy-absorbing water turbines (or twisters) coupled to a large induction motor provide better control of the arresting forces. *(NAVAIR)*

is unaffordable in future ships. Follow-on members of the class will therefore be equipped with the cheaper Raytheon Enterprise Air Surveillance Radar (EASR). This leverages the design of the AN/SPY-6 Air Defence and Missile Radar (ADMR) equipping the latest US Navy destroyers.

In addition to the around seventy-five aircraft that form her air wing, *Ford* is armed with a layered combination of Raytheon's Evolved Sea Sparrow Missile (ESSM), the Raytheon/Ramsys Rolling Airframe Missile (RAM) and the Raytheon Phalanx CIWS found in previous US Navy carriers. Weapons control functions are largely performed by the latest iteration of the Ship Self Defense System (SSDS) found in other large US Navy surface vessels not equipped with Aegis. SSDS forms part of the wider Integrated Warfare System designed for the ship.

THE WAY AHEAD – CVN-79/80/81 ...

The lessons learned from *Ford's* construction are being applied to follow-on ships *John F. Kennedy*, *Enterprise* and the still-unnamed CVN-81. At present, efforts are inevitably being focused on *Kennedy*, on which work commenced in 2011 and which was formally laid down on 22 August 2015. In addition to economies associated with system changes – notably substation of the DBR with the EASR – costs are also being controlled by turning down opportunities to add features to the ship that would have made the ship more capable than *Ford* but would also have increased cost. The navy instead is using a build strategy for the ship that incorporates improvements compared to the build strategy that was used for CVN-78. These build-strategy improvements include:

- Achieving a higher percentage of outfitting of ship modules before modules are stacked together to form the ship
- Achieving 'learning inside the ship,' which means producing similar-looking ship modules in an assembly line-like series, so as to achieve

A detailed view of the two forward-facing panels of the DBR dual-band radar system that is only installed in *Gerald R. Ford* (CVN-78). The system integrates an AN/SPY-4 S Band volume search radar with an AN/SPY-3 X Band multi-function array, the latter used largely for air-traffic and weapons control functions. Each system has three fixed panels, considerably easing the significant space demands of the various rotating arrays found on earlier carriers. *(US Navy)*

The differing island designs of the Nimitz class *Dwight D. Eisenhower* (CVN-69) and *Gerald R. Ford* (CVN-78) are captured in this May 2017 photograph. The innovative multifunction DBR dual-band radar used in the *Ford* class has permitted use of a much more compact island structure. *(US Navy)*

improved production learning curve benefits in the fabrication of these modules; and

▥ More economical ordering of parts and materials including greater use of batch ordering of parts and materials, as opposed to ordering parts and materials on an individual basis as each is needed.

Another interesting cost-saving measure is a two-phase delivery strategy, under which *Kennedy* will initially be delivered to a Phase 1 standard but not be fully complete until Phase 2 systems have been installed. This process will be completed before she is scheduled to make her first deployment as the numerical relief for *Nimitz*. Phase 1 comprises basic ship HM&E construction and the core systems for ship propulsion and navigation, as well as for aircraft launch and recovery. While all communication and navigation systems required for a safe-to-sail capability will be installed during Phase 1, the ship's combat systems, tactical data links and intelligence systems are planned for a Phase 2 install. Aviation systems installed during Phase 2 include those needed for a precision landing capability and to enable onboard mission planning. In addition to saving costs, this strategy also gives the navy and shipbuilder the flexibility to procure and install – at the latest date possible – shipboard electronic systems that otherwise would be obsolete by *Kennedy*'s first deployment. In this way, the navy will avoid the cost of significant technology 'refresh.' However, the strategy does mean that it will take longer for *Kennedy* to achieve full operational capability and the plan may still founder on Congressional opposition.

Looking further to the future, US Navy officials have also expressed interest in combining the

The *Ford* incorporates a layered self-defence system that includes ESSM medium-range surface-to-air missile launchers, RAM short-range missile launchers and the Phalanx CIWS, the latter pictured here. These are supplemented by electronic warfare jammers and decoys. Weapons control functions are largely performed by the latest iteration of the Ship Self Defense System (SSDS), also found in other large US Navy surface vessels not equipped with Aegis. *(US Navy)*

Integrated Digital Shipbuilding (iDS) technology is being used to drive productivity improvements as construction of *Ford* class carriers continues. This picture shows a demonstration of the Rapid Operational Virtual Reality tool – that helps construction teams collaborate, consider improvements and trouble-shoot – during a visit to the Newport News Shipyard by Republican Senator Mike Conaway. *(Huntington Ingalls Industries)*

procurement of CVN-80 with CVN-81 to reduce carrier procurement costs further. On 19 March 2018, the navy released a request for proposal to HII/NNS for a two-ship buy. 'In keeping with the National Defense Strategy, the Navy developed an acquisition strategy to combine the CVN-80 and CVN-81 procurements to better achieve the Department's objectives of building a more lethal force with greater performance and affordability,' said James F. Geurts, Assistant Secretary of the Navy, Research Development and Acquisition. 'This opportunity for a two-ship contract is dependent on significant savings that the shipbuilding industry and government must demonstrate. The navy is requesting a proposal from HII/NNS in order to evaluate whether we can achieve significant savings.'[24]

The two-ship buy is a contracting strategy the US Navy effectively used in the 1980s to procure four *Nimitz* class aircraft carriers and achieve significant acquisition cost savings compared to contracting for the ships individually. While the CVN-80/81 two-ship buy negotiations continue, the navy is, however, pursuing the contracting actions necessary to continue CVN-80 fabrication in FY2018 and preserve the current schedule. However, the navy plans to award the CVN-80 construction contract in FY2019 as a two-ship buy subject to the necessary congressional approval.

Another significant transformation is underway at HII/NNS. Integrated Digital Shipbuilding (iDS) is enhancing performance and empowering the work-force by providing easier access to secure informa-tion through efforts that include 3-D work instruc-tions, augmented reality, modelling and simulation, laser scanning, and more. For example, Huntington Ingalls is experimenting with augmented reality goggles that would superimpose digital plans on the wearer's view of the real world, letting

Gerald R Ford (CVN-78) pictured heading for sea on 8 April 2017, her first day underway under her own power. In the words of US President Donald P. Trump she is a '100,000-ton' message to the world. *(US Navy)*

workers see exactly where the next part should go.

'What I would say on these big mega-projects is you're starting to see the era of digital,' Assistant Secretary Geurts remarked in February 2018. 'We're starting to see on the second carrier, the second *Ford* [class] carrier, huge savings, and I think that's just going to continue … We had folks, workers that had been working on ships forever, starting to see this new technology and very creative on how to do things differently.'[25]

Thus contributing to President Trump's '100,000-ton message to the world'.

Notes

1. President Trump was quoted by Darlene Superville of the Associated Press in 'Trump: USS Ford is "100,000-ton Message to the World"', *Navy Times* – 22 July 2017 (Tysons VA: Sightline Media Group, 2017) currently available at: navytimes.com/news/2017/07/23/trump-uss-ford-is-100000-ton-message-to-the-world/

2. This review of the US Navy's programme for the *Gerald R. Ford* (CVN-78) and perhaps as many as nine follow-on *Ford* class carriers relies heavily on the numerous reports produced by Ronald O'Rourke of the US Congressional Research Service since at least 2002. Amongst the earliest is *Navy CVNX Aircraft Carrier Program: Background and Issues for Congress RS20643* (Washington DC: Congressional Research Service, 2002), with the most recent as of mid-2018 being, *Navy Ford (CVN-78) Aircraft Carrier Program: Background and Issues for Congress RS20643* (Washington DC: Congressional Research Service, 2018). Where these series of reports are specifically referenced in this text, the date of the report is provided. Another valuable source is Norman Polmar's *The Naval Institute Guide to the Ships and Aircraft of the U.S. Fleet* – 19th edition. (Annapolis, MD: Naval Institute Press, 2013) pp.110–15. The author of this *Ford* essay provided strategy and policy support to the Navy's Air Warfare Division (N88/N98) during the early phase of the programme.

3. For further background see Robert H. Holzer's and Scott C. Truver's 'The US Navy in Review' in *USNI Proceedings* – May 2018 (Annapolis MD: US Naval Institute, 2018) pp.72–9.

4. See Rear Admiral Bruce Lindsey, 'USS Gerald R. Ford Ushers in New Age of Technology and Innovation,' in *Navy Live: The Official Blog of the U.S. Navy* – 21 July 2017, currently available at: navylive.dodlive.mil/2017/07/21/uss-gerald-r-ford-ushers-in-new-age-of-technology-and-innovation/. At the time of writing the admiral was Commander, Naval Air Force Atlantic.

5. See Megan Eckstein's 'Newly Commissioned Carrier Ford's Leap-Ahead Technology Approach May Be a Thing of the Past' carried on the *USNI News* website on 24 July 2017, currently available at: news.usni.org/2017/07/24/newly-commissioned-carrier-fords-leap-ahead-technology-approach-may-be-a-thing-of-the-past

6. See, *Request to Fully Fund Two Nuclear Aircraft Carriers in Fiscal Year 1983 MASAD-82-87 (B-206847)* (Washington DC: General Accounting Office, 1982). The figure of 5.6 percent was derived by dividing US$450m in non-inflation cost avoidance by the combined estimated cost of the two ships (absent a block buy) of US$8.024bn.

7. See Megan Eckstein's 'Navy, Newport News Taking Steps Towards Two-Carrier Buy' on the *USNI News* website on 19 March 2018, currently available at: news.usni.org/2018/03/19/navy-newport-news-taking-steps-towards-two-carrier-buy

8. *Navy's Aircraft Carrier Program: Investment Strategy Options GAO/NSIAD-95-17* (Washington DC: General Accounting Office, National Security and International Affairs Division, 1995). See: gao.gov/assets/230/220466.pdf.

9. John Schank, et al, *Modernizing the U.S. Aircraft Carrier Fleet: Accelerating CVN-21 Production Versus Mid-Life Refueling* (Santa Monica CA: RAND Corporation, 2005), p.76.

10. Captain J. Talbot Manvel Jr., U.S. Navy (Retired) and David Perin, 'Christened by Champaign, Challenged by Cost,' *USNI Proceedings* – May 2014 (Annapolis MD: US Naval Institute, 2018) currently available at: usni.org/magazines/proceedings/2014-05/christened-champagne-challenged-cost

11. Norman Polmar, op cit, p. 113, quoting 'Navy takes new look at CVX plan, cost,' *Navy News and Undersea Technology* – 1 June 1998, p.1.

12. See Edward Feege and Scott C. Truver. 'Zumwalt (DDG-1000) Past and Future Tense', *Seaforth World Naval Review 2017* (Barnsley: Seaforth Publishing, 2016), pp.136–55.

13. Ronald O'Rourke, *Navy CVN-21 Aircraft Carrier Program RS20643*, issued 25 May 2005.

14. Donald H. Rumsfeld, 'Transforming the Military,' *Foreign Affairs* – May/June 2002 (New York City, NY: Council on Foreign Affairs, 2002).

15. Captain J. Talbot Manvel Jr., U.S. Navy (Retired) and David Perin, op cit.

16. Northrop Grumman Shipbuilding was subsequently spun off from its parent in 2011 to become Huntington Ingalls Industries. Newport News Shipbuilding is now one of the new company's major divisions.

17. See *Navy Shipbuilding: Past Performance Provides Valuable Lessons for Future Investments GAO-18-238SP* (Washington DC: US Government Accountability Office, 2018). The *Ford* class 'case study' is at p.17.

18. Mark V. Arena *et al*, *Why has the Cost of Navy Ships Risen?* (Santa Monica CA: RAND Corporation, 2006).

19. Eric J. Labs, *An Analysis of the Navy's Fiscal Year 2016 Shipbuilding Plan* (Washington DC: CBO, October 2015).

20. The inactivation of the *Enterprise* (CVN-65) on 1 December 2012, several years before commissioning of the *Ford* in 2017, created a gap in required carrier force levels. This required congressional action to agree to a force of only ten CVNs for a temporary period.

21. The problems associated with the development of the *Ford* class's technology have been attested to in many contemporary US Department of Defense and press reports.

22. US Navy nomenclature for reactors is based on the platform; the design generation of the nuclear core; and the associated contractor. Thus the A4W reactor in the *Nimitz* class is intended for use on aircraft carriers (A), and is the fourth-generation of that type of platform core (4) designed by the associated contractor, Westinghouse (W). Similarly the A1B reactor is an aircraft carrier core and is the first of its generation of Bechtel reactors. Both types of reactor have been designed and built at the same government-owned but contractor-operated facilities so there is more continuity than the designations suggest.

23. Rear Admiral Bruce Lindsey, op cit.

24. See the press release entitled 'Navy Seeks Savings, Releases Two-Carrier RFP' issued by the Naval Sea Systems Command Public Affairs on 20 March 2018.

25. Assistant Secretary Geurts was quoted by Sydney J. Freedberg Jr in an article entitled 'Let's Get Digital: Hondo Geurts Wants Ships for Less $$,' on the *Breaking Defense website* – 8 February 2018, available at: breakingdefense.com/2018/02/lets-get-digital-hondo-geurts-wants-ships-for-less/.

3.2 SIGNIFICANT SHIPS

QUEEN ELIZABETH CLASS AIRCRAFT CARRIERS

The Royal Navy's New Monarchs of the Seas

Author:
Conrad Waters

In the early afternoon of Monday 26 June 2017, the Royal Navy's new aircraft carrier *Queen Elizabeth* slowly edged away from the quayside at her building yard at Rosyth prior to passing under the Forth bridges and commencing an initial series of sea trials. Her departure marked a major step towards the re-establishment of a British carrier strike capability that had been, perhaps, the most important outcome of the 1998 Strategic Defence Review (SDR) published nearly twenty years previously.

The intervening years have been marked by the need to overcome a series of often conflicting political, financial, design and construction challenges that many believed would ultimately result in the programme's demise. The success of the broadly-based project team that has overcome these hurdles and brought the programme close to its fruition is

The lead *Queen Elizabeth* class aircraft carrier pictured at speed whilst undertaking replenishment at sea trials with the fleet tanker *Tidespring* in June 2018. Her delivery is an important step towards realising a strike carrier programme first embarked upon some twenty years previously. *(Crown Copyright 2018)*

therefore a significant – and timely – accomplishment. From a military perspective, *Queen Elizabeth*'s arrival provides a major enhancement to the United Kingdom's military capabilities against the backdrop of an international environment that is becoming far more dangerous and unpredictable. Equally, the technical achievement represented by *Queen Elizabeth* and her forthcoming sister, *Prince of Wales*, provides a material boost to the maritime sector at a time when manufacturing capabilities have assumed renewed importance in Brexit Britain.

This chapter aims to provide an overview of the design and construction process that has resulted in the *Queen Elizabeth* class aircraft carriers. It also describes the main elements of the carrier design and some of the steps that still need to be completed before the programme's aims are fully realised.

PROJECT ORIGINS

The two *Queen Elizabeth* class carriers trace their origins to preliminary concept studies to replace the three small *Invincible* class support carriers conducted by the then Directorate of Future Projects (Naval) from the first half of the 1990s

onwards. These studies examined a number of new-build catapult assisted take-off but arrested recovery (CATOBAR), short take-off and vertical landing (STOVL), and short take-off but arrested recovery (STOBAR) designs carrying between fifteen and forty aircraft. Service life extensions to the existing *Invincible*s, as well as merchant ship conversions, were also considered.[1] The broad conclusion reached was that new construction was the most cost-effective way forward. Moreover, the resultant ships should be bigger and deploy larger air groups than the existing support carriers. These findings were endorsed in the SDR produced by the incoming Labour government in July 1998, reflecting the growing focus on expeditionary stabilisation operations in the post-Cold War era. The review committed the government to replacing the three existing carriers with two larger ships in the second decade of the new millennium. It was suggested the new ships might displace from 30,000 to 40,000 tons and be able to carry up to fifty aircraft.

The political decision to proceed with the new ships was followed by approval for launch of a design assessment phase ('initial gate') towards the end of

1998.[2] Invitations for competitive industry design studies were issued the following year. Two industry consortia led by what are now BAE Systems (then British Aerospace) and Thales (Thomson-CSF) were awarded contracts to carry out the work under what was by then known as the future aircraft carrier or CVF project. Their work was informed by a single statement of mission need, viz. that the ships were to be a 'joint defence asset with the primary purpose of providing the UK with an expeditionary offensive air capability which has the flexibility to operate the largest possible range of aircraft in the widest possible range of roles'. This broad statement was further refined into nine key user requirements (KURs) outlined in the text box, in turn impacting more specific design aspects such as sortie generation rate, minimum deck alert profile, aircraft stowage and ship range and endurance. It was anticipated that the assessment phase would end with award of a construction contract around the end of 2003. This would permit an 'in service date' of the first ship of August 2012.

Initially, the consortia were tasked with examining a range of CATOBAR, STOVL and STOBAR options with smaller and larger air groups. This partly reflected the fact that operating characteristics of the new jet aircraft to be operated from the ships – the future carrier-borne aircraft (FCBA) – had not been determined. As time progressed, decisions initially to select the US Joint Strike Fighter (JSF) for the FCBA requirement and then to adopt the F-35B STOVL variant of this aircraft helped solidify the carrier design requirement. The latter decision, announced in September 2002, was accompanied by a request to the two consortia to focus on an 'adaptable' design based on their CATOBAR design concepts. This was to be initially laid out for STOVL operation but have sufficient flexibility to be reconfigured as a CATOBAR carrier with catapults and arrestor gear should it be necessary to operate conventional aircraft later in the class's life.

In January 2003 it was announced that the design submitted by the Thales-led team – reportedly largely a product of the BMT design consultancy

that formed part of the Thales consortium – had been selected over BAE Systems' competing proposal for further development. However, political and industrial considerations meant that a compromise solution was devised. This resulted in Thales and BAE agreeing to form a joint aircraft carrier teaming arrangement to take the programme forward. Under this arrangement, BAE Systems was appointed as prime contractor with Thales acting as a key supplier providing the actual class design and the MOD acting as a risk partner in the project. Although much criticised at the time as a political 'fudge', this decision played to the particular strengths of the two consortia leaders, forming the basis of the successful partnership structure that was eventually to play a vital role in the delivery of the programme. The aim at this stage was to complete the design assessment phase and award a build contract in April 2004. This would allow the two ships to enter service in line with previous plans in 2012 and 2015.

DESIGN ITERATIONS

The competition-winning submission – subsequently known as Design Alpha – incorporated characteristics developed from an initial assessment of previous ships that was carried out to develop a full appreciation of the fundamental drivers of aircraft carrier design. These included the concepts produced under the preliminary 1990s studies, as well as the abortive 1960s' CVA-01 fleet carrier and the US Navy's *Nimitz* (CVN-68) class.[3] This resulted in the Thales' team focusing on four key design factors, viz. (i) the arrangement and size of the flight deck; (ii) the interaction between flight and hangar decks; (iii) the balance between seakeeping and stability; and (iv) the arrangement of major spaces such as magazines and machinery rooms in relation to the flight deck and hangar. Other considerations included survivability; ease of maintenance; ease of construction; future growth margins; and achieving optimum manning levels.

The key characteristics of the resulting design are summarised in Table 3.2.1. A notable outcome of the Thales design team's assessments was a much larger ship than initially envisaged. This seems to have been driven largely by the need to ensure efficient air operations and an associated high sortie generation rate (SGR). More specifically, the flight deck had to be large enough to allow a safe and effective aircraft flow and the hangar had to be arranged

---

QUEEN ELIZABETH CLASS: KEY USER REQUIREMENTS

- ■ **Interoperability:** The class shall be able to operate with joint/combined forces to deliver a medium scale offensive air effort for power projection, focused intervention and peace enforcement operations.
- ■ **Integration:** The class shall be able to integrate with all elements of joint/combined forces necessary to conduct strike operations and support agile mission groups.
- ■ **Availability:** The class shall provide, using one platform, at high readiness for its principal role of carrier strike (CS) at medium scale and also at very high readiness for CS small scale focused intervention at all times.
- ■ **Deployability:** The class shall be able to deploy for operations in the core regions as defined in Defence Strategic Guidance 05.
- ■ **Sustainability:** The class shall be able to conduct deployments away from port facilities for operations lasting 9 months continuously and support air operations for up to seventy days with afloat support.
- ■ **Aircraft Operations:** The class shall be able to deploy the full medium scale offensive air effort.

- ■ **Survivability:** The class shall achieve a high probability of protection, survivability and recoverability against both natural incidents and those threats identified by the Defence Intelligence Scale Threat Statement (October 2004).
- ■ **Flexibility:** The class shall be able to operate and support the full range of defined aircraft and be adaptable such that it could operate air vehicles which require assisted launch/recovery.
- ■ **Versatility:** The class shall be able to deploy agile mission groups.

Note:

The key user requirements for the *Queen Elizabeth* class seem to have been first made public in the National Audit Office's *The Major Projects Report 2009* (London: NAO, 2009) and reflect the requirements as of final Main Gate Approval in 2007. These will inevitably have varied somewhat from the initial user requirement document produced as part of the initial assessment phase in 1998 but it appears that they encompassed the same core elements. See S T D Knight's 'The Design of HMS *Queen Elizabeth* and HMS *Prince of Wales*' in the *Journal of Naval Engineering* Volume 45, Book 1 (London: RINA, 2009), p.76.

to enable the designated air group to be easily maintained. This impacted more than just the space allocated to these specific areas. For example, deck edge lifts were preferred because of their reduced impact on flight deck and hangar operations compared with the internal lifts found in, e.g., the *Invincible* class but these would be vulnerable to damage from heavy seas in a smaller ship.

Another key design outcome – the unusual twin-island superstructure – was also influenced by the need to maximise flight deck area. It allowed navigation and flying-control functions to be placed in optimum locations and key sensors placed sufficiently far apart to avoid mutual interference whilst minimising overall superstructure footprint. Additionally, the separated arrangement aided survivability by facilitating the separation of uptakes from the integrated electric propulsion system's generators, thereby making it easier to disperse the generators themselves. The use of integrated electric propulsion allowed the prime movers to be located remotely from the propulsors themselves, with two of the proposed four gas turbines located in sponsons under the islands. Podded propulsors were proposed to free up volume within the hull.

It is clear that the Alpha design was a very capable ship that, moreover, was provided with armour and other protection that ensured a very high level of survivability. Unfortunately, it quite quickly

The 1998 SDR decided to replace the three small *Invincible* class carriers with two bigger strike carriers. This picture – which shows the second *Invincible* class carrier, *Illustrious*, alongside *Queen Elizabeth* shortly before the latter's naming ceremony in July 2014 – clearly demonstrates the size of the winning Thales design, which – driven by the needs of efficient air operations – was a much larger ship than initially envisaged. *(Crown Copyright 2014)*

Table 3.2.1: *QUEEN ELIZABETH* CLASS AIRCRAFT CARRIERS – DESIGN ITERATIONS

DESIGN[1]	ALPHA	BRAVO	CHARLIE	DELTA[4]
Displacement	73,000 tons	55,000 tons	55,000 tons	65,000 tons
Length Overall	290m	265m	265m	280m
Hull Decks[2]	10 (+hold)	9 (+hold)	9 (+hold)	9 (+hold)
Watertight Sub-division	19 sections	14 sections	20 sections	19 sections
Damage Control Zones	5 citadels + hangar	5 citadels + hangar	5 citadels + hangar	5 citadels + hangar
Air Group	40 (50 surge)	34 (40 surge)	34 (40 surge)	34 (40 surge)
Hangar Capacity (F-35)	26	20	20	c. 20+
Sortie Generation Rate (Max)	150 per day	110 per day	110 per day	110 per day
Magazine Complexes	3, fully automated	2, semi-automated	2, semi-automated	2, semi-automated
Propulsion[3]	IEP	IEP	IEP	IEP
	4 x MT-30 gas turbines	2 x MT-30 gas turbines	2 x MT-30 gas turbines	2 x MT-30 gas turbines
		2 x diesel generators	2 x diesel generators	4 x diesel generators
	140MW total output	95MW total output	95MW total output	110MW total output
	4 x propulsion pods	2 x shaftlines	2 x shaftlines	2 x shaftlines
	Bow thrusters	No bow thrusters	No bow thrusters	No bow thrusters
Deck Crane	Yes	No	No	No
Vehicle Ramp	Yes	No	No	No
Accommodation	c. 1,600	c. 1,450	c. 1,450	c. 1,600

Notes:
1. Data has been drawn from a range of contemporary sources, some of which conflict, and should be regarded as indicative only. Many figures are rounded.
2. Including the hangar deck. Descriptions of deck numbers vary, some counting decks below the hangar.
3. Propulsive outputs relate to power provided by the relevant alternators; the theoretical generating capacity of the various turbines and diesels is somewhat higher.
4. The Delta design was essentially the design used for the *Queen Elizabeth* class. Some sources also reference production of an Echo design, which applied new damage-control deck code guidance to the original Alpha concept.

Two images depicting the evolution of the Thales-led team's original design for the future aircraft carrier (CVF) project. The image on the left was one of a series that were issued by the new alliance arrangement of BAE Systems and Thales around May 2003, a few months after the winning design announcement. This iteration was subsequently known as Design Alpha. It was somewhat larger than the *Queen Elizabeth* class as built and was provided with two STOVL launch positions, as well as what appears to be BAE Systems' Sampson radar. Cost considerations resulted in a number of smaller variants of this design being developed. By early 2004, a Design Delta (right-hand image) had emerged as the agreed basis from which to take forward future carrier construction. This image was released during 2005 and largely represents the *Queen Elizabeth* class as built. However, the sharp-eyed reader will note a number of detailed variations, notably changes to the design of the islands and deletion of the jet blast deflector. *(Aircraft Carrier Alliance)*

emerged that the overall growth from the original 30,000–40,000-ton design expectation had resulted in a rise in estimated cost that was considered unaffordable. The result was a decision to scale down the Alpha concept to produce what was considered the lowest technically-viable design in order to produce a cheaper ship. The resultant Bravo design was smaller, with one less deck and a smaller aircraft-carrying capacity. Other changes included a reversion to conventional shaftlines – partly because of concerns over the technical maturity and resilience of such a solution – and a reduction in watertight sub-division and other survivability features. It appears that it was quickly realised that the latter process had gone too far. Accordingly, a revised Charlie design was produced. This essentially involved the incorporation of five additional transverse bulkheads into the hull to improve stability in the event of damage.

The final major design iteration was Design Delta. This was produced to resolve remaining concerns over power generation capability and deck area capacity in the smaller design. Key changes included a growth in length much closer to the original Alpha concept and an increase in generating capacity. Although much detailed design work remained to be done, the Delta design essentially reflected the *Queen Elizabeth* class as built in its essential elements.

CONSTRUCTION AND DELIVERY

Whilst the *Queen Elizabeth* class's basic design had largely been finalised by 2004, several years were still to elapse before construction began. This reflected both financial and industrial considerations. In spite of design economies, it was still apparent that the new ships could not be built within the budget allocated to them. This had apparently been estimated at around £2bn (US$2.7bn) for the pair when the programme was launched and had risen to c. £2.8bn (US$3.8bn) by the time the original Thales' Alpha design was selected. However, this was still much lower than industry estimates of the true cost of the ships. The result was several years of acrimonious debate until a price could be agreed. When final (so-called main gate) approval for construction was finally given in July 2007, the budgeted figure for the demonstration and manufacture element programme amounted to £3.5bn (US$4.8bn) with an estimated range of between £3.2bn and £3.8bn. The design assessment phase had cost an additional £0.3bn. In the event, the actual cost of completing the programme was to significantly exceed budget. Delivery timescales had also slipped, with the lead ship scheduled for delivery in 2015 when the main gate decision was taken.

It also took time to iron-out arrangements for the industrial structure needed to build the ships. Considerable negotiation was inevitably needed to finalise the innovative alliance structure used to manage the project. This was further complicated by a process of consolidation within the British maritime sector that was ultimately to see BAE Systems acquire the then VT Group's shipbuilding interests. For a time, there was also French interest in joining the project to meet its *deuxième porte-avions* (PA2) requirement. This would have seen completion of a CATOBAR variant of the carrier in French yards for the *Marine Nationale* under an arrange-

A major feature of the adaptable CVF designs was the ability to switch the initial STOVL configuration for CTOL operation. France's *Marine Nationale* seriously considered building their own variant of the design for CTOL operations and *Prince of Wales* was earmarked for completion as a CTOL carrier with US Navy magnetic catapults and advanced arrestor gear as a result of the 2010 defence review. The plan was reversed when the time and cost associated with the switch proved prohibitive. *(Aircraft Carrier Alliance)*

A key factor in the *Queen Elizabeth* class carrier build strategy was the assembly of the ship from blocks built in yards around the UK. The left-hand image shows *Queen Elizabeth*'s Lower Block 03 departing the Clyde on completion of fabrication in August 2011. The assembly encompassed the central area of the ship from the hangar sides downwards. The image above depicts the ship's forward island under construction at what was then BAE System's shipbuilding hall at Portsmouth in May 2012. It was installed on the ship in March 2013. *(BAE Systems)*

The *Queen Elizabeth* class aircraft carriers' constituent blocks were assembled at Babcock's huge industrial complex at Rosyth Dockyard on the north bank of the River Forth (right). Improvements to the site to facilitate carrier construction included enlarging the entry to its No. 1 dock and installing a giant Goliath crane to ease the handling of upper blocks. Integration was carried out in three phases or cycles. Those for *Queen Elizabeth* commenced with the arrival her Lower Block 03 in August 2011 and ended with installation of sponson SPN-41 in June 2014. The picture above shows the crane being used to lower the forward section of *Queen Elizabeth*'s flight deck into position on 8 February 2013. *(Aircraft Carrier Alliance)*

ment that would probably have seen some work-sharing between British and French industry. However, France ultimately abandoned its tentative involvement in the programme.

Although main gate approval for the project was announced on 25 July 2007, the construction contract for the two ships was only placed twelve months later. The 3 July 2008 announcement confirmed that the work would be overseen by a revamped Aircraft Carrier Alliance comprising Babcock International, BAE Systems, Thales UK and the MOD.[4] A noteworthy feature of the build

strategy was the fabrication of the ships' constituent blocks at shipyards around the UK. Yards ultimately involved in the programme included BAE Systems' facilities at Govan and Portsmouth, Cammell Laird in Birkenhead, A&P Group on the Tyne and Babcock's Appledore yard. Final assembly was allocated to Babcock's dockyard at Rosyth, near Edinburgh. The Babcock yard – one of the largest industrial facilities in Scotland hosting operations ranging from the fabrication of civil nuclear assemblies to ship refit – received substantial investment to fulfil its part in the project. This included work to

widen the entrance to Rosyth's No. 1 dock where both ships were built; the installation of a 1,000-tonne capacity Goliath crane to facilitate assembly of carrier sub-blocks and other components; and enhancements to the tidal basin where outfitting activity has been concentrated.

Formal construction commenced on 7 July 2009 when a first steel-cutting ceremony for *Queen Elizabeth* was held at BAE Systems' yard at Govan on the River Clyde. However, actual fabrication had started several months earlier on 15 December 2008 when Babcock's Appledore facility began work on the first sub-sections of lower block 1.[5] Physical assembly of *Queen Elizabeth*'s constituent blocks commenced at Rosyth in the second half of 2011, being carried out in three integration stages or 'cycles'. Assembly of the various blocks was completed in early June 2014 prior to a high profile naming ceremony conducted by HM Queen Elizabeth II on 4 July 2014. The ship was subsequently floated out of her building berth some two weeks later on 17 July 2014, clearing the way for assembly of *Prince of Wales* to begin.

Although structurally complete by this stage, considerable fitting-out had still to be completed before the lengthy process of setting *Queen Elizabeth*'s equipment to work could commence. One complicating factor was the use of the sole building dock for *Prince of Wales*' assembly. As a result, some significant work had to be carried out underwater, not least installation of the ship's two propellers. These were fitted by divers after completion of initial tests of the propulsion system, which were conducted whilst the carrier was still berthed at Rosyth. Other strands of work included bringing to life the various platform management and mission systems and the associated fibre-optic cable network needed to ensure the carrier's effective operation. Completed compartments were handed over on a phased basis from February 2016 onwards but it was not until the end of May 2017 that the ship was ready for her crew to move onboard. The successful completion of a simulated cruise shortly afterwards allowed sea trials to commence on 26 June 2017.

Local topography meant that the carrier's departure from Rosyth involved a complicated series of manoeuvres that had to be carried out within a given tidal window and in suitable weather conditions. Notably, exit from the basin at Rosyth had to be conducted at high tide and with only inches to spare on either side of the basin's entrance. This evolution

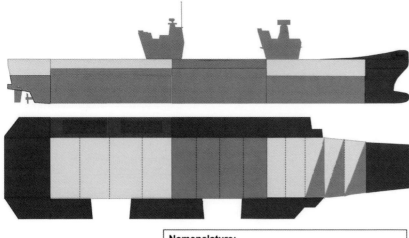

aircraft carrier
ALLIANCE
Delivering the Nation's Flagships

Nomenclature:

UB - Upper Block (the 'Islands')
CB - Centre Blocks (aka 'Central Upper Blocks')
SP - Sponsons
LB - Lower Block (main hull blocks)

Queen Elizabeth Class Aircraft Carriers – Supporting UK Shipyards

For HMS Queen Elizabeth only

aircraft carrier
ALLIANCE
Delivering the Nation's Flagships

A schematic illustrating the distributed block fabrication strategy adopted for *Queen Elizabeth* class carrier construction under which constituent parts for the two ships were built at yards around the country and then transported to Rosyth for final assembly. This graphic shows intended block allocation around the time construction began. There were subsequent changes, particularly with respect to *Prince of Wales* following closure of BAE System's shipbuilding operations in Portsmouth. *(Aircraft Carrier Alliance)*

was completed in the afternoon of 26 June. Subsequently, the ship anchored in the River Forth until the tide fell sufficiently for her to squeeze under the Forth Railway Bridge, the lowest of the three bridges linking Edinburgh with northern Scotland. Transit of the bridges took place shortly before midnight with less than 6ft of clearance from *Queen Elizabeth*'s highest point and with a shallower depth of water under her keel. Thereafter, trials progressed largely smoothly; inevitable teething troubles associated with testing a large and complex lead ship excepted. The ship made her maiden entry into her designated home port of Portsmouth on 16 August 2017. Following a second series of sea trials in November, she was formally commissioned into the Royal Navy on 7 December 2017.[6]

Work on *Prince of Wales* started with a formal steel cutting ceremony on 26 May 2011. Physical integration commenced in early September 2014 and she was floated out shortly before Christmas 2017 after being named on 8 September. Float-out was therefore somewhat later in her build cycle than *Queen Elizabeth* and this allowed more work to be done in dock, reflected in the fact that she was c. 3,000 tons heavier at this stage. Lessons learned from *Queen Elizabeth*'s construction have been fully incorporated in her build process, helped by the creation of four delivery integrated project teams that have brought an enhanced level of collaborative working. One advantage has been that areas are far more complete when handed over for the commissioning of specialist equipment, reducing associated time and cost.[7] Another benefit has been the development of more effective teamworking between industry and the ship's future complement, with builders and sailors using their combined skills most efficiently to speed the setting-to-work process. Current plans envisage *Prince of Wales* commencing her own sea trials in 2019 and being delivered before the end of that year.

The period marking the ships' construction has not been without further policy changes. Economies in 2009 caused delivery dates to be further delayed. More significantly, the 2010 Strategic Security & Defence Review (SDSR) initiated by the UK's new coalition government considered cancelling the project outright as part of spending cuts. It ultimately decided to complete *Prince of Wales* in CATOBAR configuration and to 'mothball' or sell *Queen Elizabeth* once she had completed ship platform trials.[8] However, the complexity and cost of this conversion proved to be much greater than

Queen Elizabeth pictured alongside *Illustrious* on 4 July 2014, the day of her naming ceremony. *(Conrad Waters)*

Queen Elizabeth pictured being floated out of her building berth on 17 July 2014, just under two weeks after her formal naming ceremony. The berth had to be cleared before assembly of the constituent blocks of her sister, *Prince of Wales*, could commence. *(Aircraft Carrier Alliance)*

In the early afternoon of 26 June 2017 *Queen Elizabeth* commenced a complicated series of manoeuvres that would see her clear the narrow entrance to Rosyth's non-tidal basin and then transit under the Forth bridges on the way to the open sea. Whilst exit into the River Forth had to be carried out at high tide, limited air draught under the bridges meant that she had to anchor until the tide dropped to allow sufficient clearance. One interesting point of note is the position of the pole mast on the aft island. This is fitted with a hydraulic mechanism that allows it to be lowered to an angle of 77° to provide sufficient clearance to pass under the bridges. *(Crown Copyright 2017/Conrad Waters)*

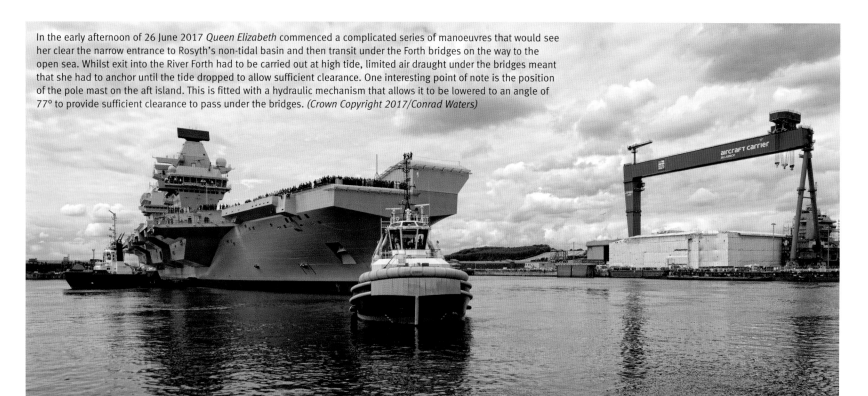

envisaged. The adaptable design had been based on the assumption that traditional steam catapults and Mk 7 arrestor gear would be used for any CATOBAR conversion but the selection of the latest electromagnetic EMALS launch system and AAG adopted by the US Navy in their *Gerald R. Ford* (CVN-78) significantly increased the extent of the work involved. In 2012, the decision was reversed, leaving both ships to be completed as STOVL carriers. In September 2014 – in another change of plan – it was announced both ships would be brought into operational service after all. This decision was confirmed in the subsequent 2015 SDSR.

DESIGN DESCRIPTION
OVERALL LAYOUT
The two *Queen Elizabeth* class aircraft carriers have an empty displacement in the region of 65,000 tons. This makes them the largest vessels ever to serve with the Royal Navy by some margin. With the exception of the Japanese Second World War *Yamato* class, they are also the largest warships to be completed anywhere in the world outside of the United States. Waterline length is 263m and beam 39m, increasing to 280m and 70m respectively at the level of the flight deck. The significant increase in beam is effected by the use of large hull sponsons.

Table 3.2.2.

QUEEN ELIZABETH (R08) PRINCIPAL PARTICULARS

Building Information:

Fabrication Commenced:	15 December 2008[1]
Floated Out:	17 July 2014
Commissioned:	7 December 2017
Builders:	Aircraft Carrier Alliance. Assembled at Babcock International Group's Rosyth shipyard from blocks manufactured around the UK

Dimensions:

Displacement:	c. 65,000 tons.
Overall Dimensions:	284m x 73m x 11m. Waterline dimensions are 263m x 39m.

Equipment:

Aircraft:	Typical air group of up to 40 fast jets and helicopters. Flight deck equipped with 12.5° ski jump and 6 helicopter operating spots.
Guns:	3 x Phalanx 20mm CIWS. 4 x DS30M 30mm Automated Small Calibre Guns (not yet fitted as of June 2018). Light machine guns.
Countermeasures:	Likely to include Outfit UAT RESM; launchers for Outfit DLF and Outfit DLH decoys and Surface Ship Torpedo Defence System.
Principal Sensors:	Type 1046 S1850 (Thales SMART-L derivative) long-range search radar; Type 997 Artisan medium-range radar, AN/SPN-41 series ICLS, TACAN homing beacon, navigation radar.
Combat System:	BAE Systems CMS combat management system. Thales integrated communications system includes Links 11 and 16 and provision for Link 22.

Propulsion System:

Machinery:	IEP. 2 x Rolls Royce MT-30 gas turbines generators generating 70MW; 2 x Wärtsilä 16V38 diesels generating 23MW; and 2 x Wärtsilä 12V38 diesels generating 17MW provide a total of c. 110MW to an 11kV high voltage distribution network. 4 x GE Power Conversion advanced induction motors each rated at a maximum of 20MW provide c. 100,000SHP through two shafts.
Speed:	Designed maximum speed is over 25 knots, with over 29 knots reported on trials. Endurance is c. 10,000 nautical miles at 15 knots.

Other Details:

Complement:	A typical crew comprises c. 670 core complement plus personnel from a wide potential range of embarked air groups and/or embarked military forces. Accommodation is provided for c. 1,600 personnel.
Class:	*Queen Elizabeth* (R08) and *Prince of Wales* (R09), the latter scheduled for delivery in 2019.

Notes:

1. A formal first steel-cutting ceremony was held on 7 July 2009.

Draught is 11m, whilst height from the bottom of the keel to the masthead is 56m. Key characteristics are summarised in Table 3.2.2.[9]

Each carrier is comprised of seventeen decks and a little over 3,000 compartments. Seven of these decks are located above the level of the flight deck in the twin island superstructures. The forward island is largely used for ship control purposes and houses the main, navigation bridge. The aft island serves as

the flying-control position, a role equivalent to an airport control tower. Both islands are able to assume the key functions of the other in an emergency, providing a degree of redundancy that is a useful aid to survivability. The islands also house the exhaust outlets for the ship's diesel and gas turbine generators and serve as platforms for radar and communications systems.

The remaining ten decks form part of the hull

proper. Deck 1 corresponds to the level of the flight deck, with lower decks being assigned progressively higher numbers. Deck 2, therefore, is one level below the flight deck and extends to a similar area. It is principally occupied by office and other spaces used to support air operations. Deck 3 is dominated by the upper area of the hangar, which extends a full two decks in height along the centreline of the carrier for around two-thirds of the ship's length at

HMS *Queen Elizabeth* (2017)
1:1250 scale

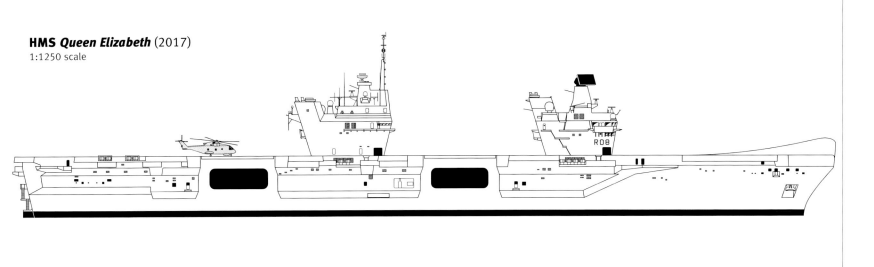

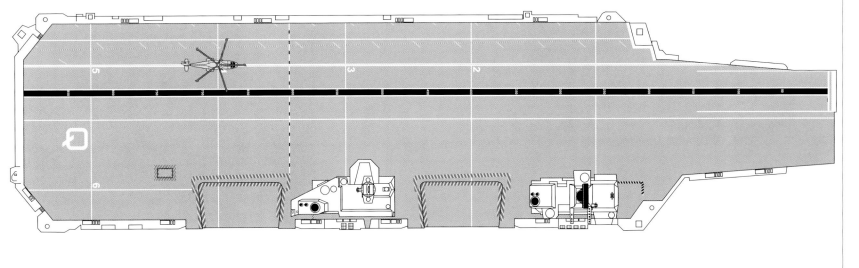

0 10 20 30 40 50
METRES

(Drawings © John Jordan, 2017)

this point. Hangar galleries, located to port and starboard, house facilities to support embarked air squadrons. Some space is also taken up with the uptakes from the gas turbines, which are located in sponsons on Deck 4. This deck is largely occupied by the base of the hangar.

Deck 5 is the carrier's control deck – the equivalent to Deck 2 in a typical Royal Navy frigate. It is the lowest deck level not completely sub-divided transversely by continuous bulkheads and principal compartments can be accessed by passageways running to port and starboard for much of the ship's length. It includes the main mess decks for personnel not forming part of the embarked air squadrons. Key compartments include the operations room (mission systems complex); the junior ratings' mess and galley; the medical complex; the machinery control room (ship control centre or SCC); the senior ratings' mess; galley facilities for senior ratings and officers; wardroom facilities; and cabins for the ship's senior officers. Accommodation includes provision for embarkation of a flag officer and his staff. Deck 6 – just above the waterline – is,

however, the principal accommodation deck. It comprises modular cabins outfitted in a variety of configurations depending largely on the seniority of the personnel housed.

The lower decks – Deck 7 through to Deck 9 – encompass the main machinery spaces; compartments for electrical and other auxiliary equipment and the principal storage areas. The four main diesel generators are housed in separate compartments located in widely-spaced forward and aft engine rooms. This arrangement is possible because, as previously mentioned, the use of integrated electrical propulsion means that the diesels – as well as the gas turbines installed higher in the ship – do not necessarily need to be proximate to the two electrical motors used to power each of the ship's twin shafts. These shaft lines are of different lengths, allowing a staggered arrangement of the electric motors across three separate transversely-divided watertight sections. In addition, longitudinal subdivision means that no two electric motors are in the same compartment. The remaining deck – Deck 10 – corresponds with the ship's keel.

🇬🇧 **NAVY NEWS**

1	Aviation store
2	**F35 Lightning II**
3	Phalanx automated close-in weapons system
4	**Forward island bridge**
5	Navigation radar
6	**Long range radar**
7	Forward engine and gas turbine uptakes
8	**Forward aircraft lift**
9	Merlin helicopter
10	**After island emergency conning bridge**
11	Mainmast
12	**Medium range radar**
13	Communication outfit
14	**After engine room and gas turbine uptakes**
15	Flying control position
16	**After aircraft lift**
17	Chinook helicopter
18	**Automatic small calibre gun**
19	Inflatable life-raft stowage
20	**Forward mooring deck**
21	Junior rates' six-berth cabins
22	**Junior rates' showers and toilets**
23	Ship's office complex
24	**Pyrolysis compartment**
25	Forward gas turbine space
26	**Forward engine down-takes**
27	Fire protection system
28	**Hangar forward bay**
29	Forward hangar doors
30	**Air squadron complex**
31	Mass evacuation system
32	**RN police office and cells**
33	After engine downtakes
34	**After gas turbine space**
35	After hangar doors
36	**Air filtration units**
37	Hangar mid bay
38	**Hangar aft bay**
39	Aft mooring deck
40	**Starboard mooring deck**
41	Port mooring deck
42	**Anchor (port and starboard)**
43	Water ballast compartment
44	**Chain locker trunk**
45	Gym
46	**Junior rates' recreation space**
47	Mission systems office
48	**Mission systems complex**
49	Forward engine room uptakes
50	**Bakery**
51	Pipe passage
52	**Junior rates' galley**
53	Junior rates' dining hall
54	**NAAFI canteen spaces**
55	Low voltage distribution compartment
56	**After engine room uptakes**
57	Hospital area
58	**Ward area**
59	General medical area
60	**HQ1 and ship control centre**
61	Senior rates' dining hall
62	**Officers' and senior rates' galley**
63	Wardroom
64	**Wardroom annexe**
65	Head of department cabins
66	**Flag and commanding officers' galley**
67	Flag officer and commanding officers' dining room
68	**Commanding officer's suite**
69	Flag officer's suite
70	**Rudder (port and starboard)**
71	Bulbous bow
72	**Auxiliary machinery space**
73	Naval stores complex
74	**Avcat tank**
75	Forward engine room
76	**Fresh water tanks**
77	Stabiliser compartment (port and starboard)
78	**Stabiliser (port and starboard)**
79	Heel correction tank (port and starboard)
80	**Bilge keel**
81	Void
82	**After engine room**
83	Officers' baggage store
84	**Propeller (port and starboard)**

1 Deck

3 Deck

5 Deck

This August 2017 view of *Queen Elizabeth*'s starboard profile provides a good view of her overall external layout. The distinct twin-island structure and large deck-edge lifts maximise flight-deck area and limit intrusions into the hangar. The main gas turbines are housed in the sponsons under the islands. *(Crown Copyright 2017)*

aircraft carrier
alliance
Delivering the Nation's Flagships

8 Deck

side HMS QUEEN ELIZABETH

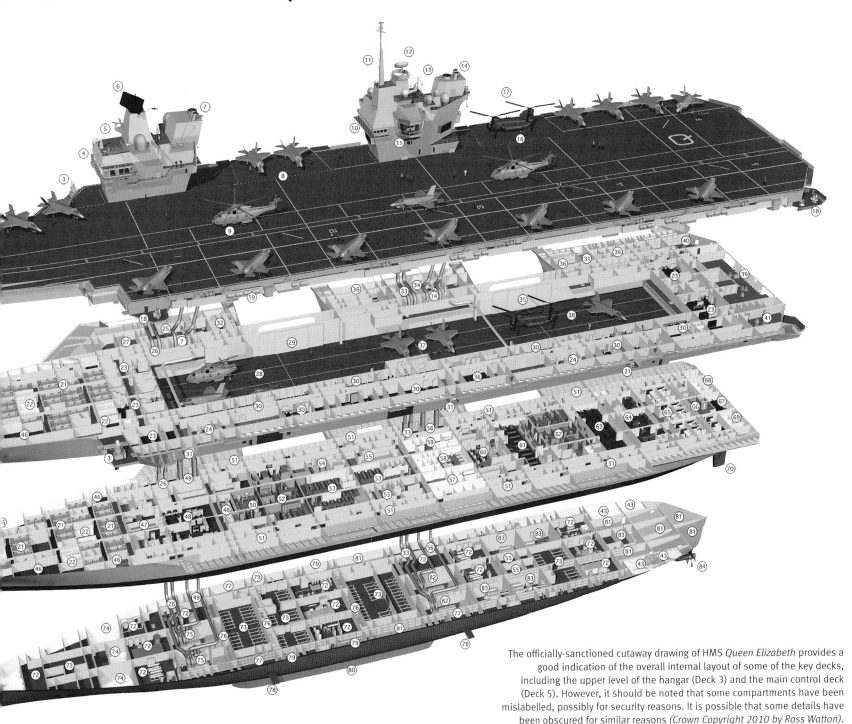

The officially-sanctioned cutaway drawing of HMS *Queen Elizabeth* provides a good indication of the overall internal layout of some of the key decks, including the upper level of the hangar (Deck 3) and the main control deck (Deck 5). However, it should be noted that some compartments have been mislabelled, possibly for security reasons. It is possible that some details have been obscured for similar reasons *(Crown Copyright 2010 by Ross Watton)*.

A composite view from a series of images of *Queen Elizabeth*'s starboard side taken on 26 June 2017, the day she departed Rosyth for trials. The c.280m long flight deck corresponds with Deck 1 level and incorporates a ski jump that is angled at 12.5º and has a length of some 200ft (61m), considerably longer than in the previous *Invincible* class. The optimum 'run up' starting position for launch varies according to factors such as take-off weight and wind over the flight deck. *(Conrad Waters)*

Longitudinally, each carrier is split into nineteen watertight sections running from 'A' to 'U' (there is no 'I' nor 'O' in RN nomenclature to avoid confusion with '1' and '0') by transverse bulkheads. The damage control organisation is run from the SCC (HQ1) and encompasses five main longitudinal zones, each with a section base and two fire and repair parties. The hangar is considered a separate, sixth damage-control zone, probably because it is outside of the gas-tight citadels used to provide nuclear, biological and chemical (NBC) protection. The overall aim is that incidents in each zone should be dealt with autonomously unless circumstances dictate otherwise, speeding response times whilst avoiding overload on the central HQ.

AVIATION FACILITIES

The *Queen Elizabeth* class aircraft carriers' aviation facilities have been designed around the primary carrier strike role. More specifically, contemporary reports at the time the design was under development suggest the aim is to sustain an operational tempo of seventy-two sorties per day from an embarked air group of thirty-six F-35B 'Lightning II' Joint Strike Fighters (i.e. two sorties per aircraft per day), rising to 108 sorties each day (three sorties per aircraft per day) for a limited period. Achieving this requirement has a significant impact not only on those design elements most clearly linked to air

operations – such as the flight deck, lifts and hangar – but also on less obvious characteristics, notably magazine and weapons-handling arrangements.

Aviation operations are inevitably focused on the 280m-long flight deck. This has a runway that is offset to the port side of the centreline and essentially runs the entire length of each ship. Following the 2012 decision to revert to STOVL configuration, fast jet launches will normally be carried with the aid of a ski-jump, a system first introduced with the previous *Invincible* class to help bolster the payload and range of their Sea Harrier 'jump jets'. The ski jump design used in the *Queen Elizabeth* class is angled at 12.5° and has a length of some 200ft (61m), considerably longer than those in the ships the new carriers replace. This should allow the larger and heavier F-35B to operate at close to its maximum potential. The optimum 'run up' starting position for launch varies according to factors such as take-off weight, wind over the flight deck and other environmental factors. The full 280m flight-deck length will therefore be required in certain circumstances.

Another design impact of F-35B operation has resulted from the heat generated by its large, powerful engine when undertaking vertical landings. This has necessitated the development of a new thermal coating that uses a combination of aluminium and titanium which is capable of

resisting temperatures of up to 1,500° Centigrade. This has been applied to three designated vertical landing zones occupying around 2,000m² of the total c. 14,000m² flight deck. In practice, it is anticipated that most F-35B landing evolutions will be carried out by Shipborne Rolling Vertical Landing (SRVL). This is a technique first adopted by the late Cold War era Soviet Navy when landing Yak-38 'Forger' aircraft on its *Kiev* class carriers. In its latest incarnation, it uses both vertical thrust from the F-35B's engine and lift from the aircraft's wings to achieve a more conventional landing trajectory. Advantages include the ability to land with a heavier weapons and fuel payload, as well as less wear and tear on the engine. A new visual landing aid system – the Bedford Array – will assist SRVL, particularly at night and in other low visibility conditions. This system has been installed in *Prince of Wales* from build and will be retrofitted to *Queen Elizabeth* during subsequent upgrades. Air operations will also be supported by the ubiquitous TACAN homing beacon on the mainmast and by installation of the US AN/SPN-41 Instrument Carrier Landing System (ICLS). The latter comprises two separate antennae transmitting azimuth and elevation information to provide flight path data to approaching aircraft.

The area of the flight deck to the starboard side of the runway is focused on aircraft fuelling and arming activities. These are concentrated on a number of 'pit stops' supposedly derived from Formula 1 practice. Aircraft ranged in these positions are supplied with aviation fuel by a number of fuelling points located in the catwalks and with munitions delivered by trolleys from transit points forward and aft of the two islands. There is also sufficient space for aircraft to refuel from the port side of ship and still leave the runway clear for operations.

Although the flight-deck layout is optimised to support F-35B flying activities, its large area is also invaluable for deploying the wide range of helicopters of up to Chinook size that will form part of the class's tailored air groups. The deck is marked out to allow the simultaneous deployment of six heavy helicopters when the runway is not being used for fast jet operations.

The flight deck is connected with the hangar on Deck 4 by two 70-ton capacity deck-edge aircraft lifts. Edinburgh-based manufacturer MacTaggart Scott claims that these are the largest in the world. One is located aft of each of the two island structures. They are each capable of simultaneously lifting two F-35Bs from the hangar to the flight deck in around sixty seconds. They can also handle a Chinook helicopter with its rotor blades extended. The c. 4,800m² hangar is approximately 163m long and can be divided into three separate bays by firetight curtains. It extends to at least 29m in width and 7m in height for most of its length, being equipped with three longitudinal gantries to assist with equipment removal and replacement. It is arranged so that more intensive maintenance work is carried out at its forward (e.g. repairs to composite materials used in items such as rotor blades) and aft (e.g. F-35B engine maintenance) ends, with day-today operational needs serviced from six maintenance spots in its central areas. As far as possible, spares and other equipment are housed in adjacent compartments, leaving the entirety of the hangar free for aircraft servicing. The hangar has capacity for twenty-two separate servicing bays for F-35B or equivalent aircraft.

A key factor in meeting the high sortie-generation rates expected is the design's Highly

Aviation operations on *Queen Elizabeth* are inevitably focused on the 14,000m² flight deck, which provides a take-off run of around 280m (900ft) for heavily-laden aircraft. The patches on the flight deck provide an indication where a heat resistant surface has been applied to prevent damage during F-35B vertical landings. *(Crown Copyright 2017)*

A view of *Queen Elizabeth*'s capacious hangar looking from forward aft. It can be split into three by fire curtains and is arranged so that heavy maintenance tasks are carried out at the ends, facilitating the flow of operational aircraft. *(Crown Copyright 2017)*

Queen Elizabeth pictured at speed whilst undertaking preliminary sea trials on 3 August 2017. An integrated electric propulsion system powers a total of four 20MW advanced induction motors arranged in tandem on each of the two shaftlines. They provide a maximum design speed in excess of 25 knots. *(Crown Copyright 2017)*

Mechanised Weapons Handling System (HMWHS). This is a remotely-operated munitions storage and transportation system developed by Babcock on the basis of commercial warehouse principles. It essentially involves the use of a network of tracks and lifts to enable a total of fifty-six remotely-controlled electric buggies ('moles') to transfer palletised bombs and missiles from the main magazines to where they are required. Two largely independent HMWHS networks serve the twin, two-storied magazine complexes located deep in the hull that house the bulk of munitions for embarked air groups. Weapons are typically taken onboard in the hangar and carried downwards by lifts. When required, munitions from these complexes are transported by the moles to the lifts and carried upwards to weapons preparation areas. Once prepared, weapons are transported by additional, upper stage lifts to the munitions transit points for onward transportation to aircraft by trolley. The whole transportation is provided with a considerable degree of interlocking and blast protection to aid survivability. The system normally requires around fifty personnel – although it can be operated by as few as twelve – and is both quicker and far less labour-intensive than historical weapons handling processes.

PROPULSION AND ELECTRICAL DISTRIBUTION

The *Queen Elizabeth* class carriers are equipped with an integrated electric propulsion system. Under this arrangement, each ship's gas turbines and diesels are used as generators to power electrical motors that drive the two shaft lines as opposed to having a direct mechanical connection with the shafts. The arrangement avoids the need to have separate generators to supply the electrical distribution network that supports 'hotel' services around the ship. It also provides considerable flexibility as to how the system is laid out.

The main generating plant on *Queen Elizabeth* and *Prince of Wales* comprises two Wärtsilä 16V38 diesel engines located in the aft engine room and two slightly smaller Wärtsilä 12V38 diesel engines in the forward engine room, supplemented by two Rolls-Royce MT-30 gas turbines in sponsons beneath the islands. All are equipped with GE Power Conversion (formerly Converteam) supplied alternators that convert their mechanical energy to AC electricity. The diesel engines provide a total elec-

Another impressive view of *Queen Elizabeth* at speed on 3 August 2017. Although some minor teething troubles with the propulsion system had to be resolved, the carrier is reported to have exceeded 29 knots in the course of her sea trials. *(Crown Copyright 2017)*

trical output of approximately 40MW, which is sufficient for most day-to-day operations. The higher-powered gas turbines – with a combined electrical output of around 70MW – are primarily used for higher-speed operation. The proportion of total output generated by the system's various generators is far more balanced than in the conceptually-similar system used in the Royal Navy's Type 45 destroyers,

thereby avoiding the vulnerability to power failure revealed in these ships.

The electrical power generated by the alternators is fed into an 11kV 60Hz high voltage distribution network controlled from two groups of twin high voltage switchboards. These are arranged so that two of the ship's four electrical motors are supplied from the forward switchboard group and the other two

from the aft switchboard group. This prevents total loss of propulsive power should one of the switchboard areas be damaged. The four 20MW GE Power Conversion advanced induction motors are arranged in tandem, with two located one behind each other on each of the twin shaftlines. They are almost identical to those used in a one unit per shaftline arrangement in the Type 45 class. One electric motor is sufficient to provide approximately seventy percent of the maximum output achievable from each shaft. Design speed is officially quoted as being a maximum of 'in excess of 25 knots', with over 29 knots reportedly being achieved in the course of sea trials.[10]

The high-voltage switchboards and associated distribution system also provide electrical energy to the series of low-voltage (LV) power distribution networks that supply electricity for ship equipment and other services. The most important of these is a

440V AC distribution system that is supplied from the HV system through a total of thirteen main LV switchboards that are located throughout the ship. As for the main propulsion system, it is normal practice to ensure a degree of redundancy in power

The two MT-30 gas turbines fitted to the *Queen Elizabeth* class can each provide around 35MW of energy and are largely intended to boost the primary diesel generators when higher speeds are required. Their location high in the ship in sponsons underneath the islands allows them to be easily swapped out for maintenance or repair. *(Rolls-Royce Group)*

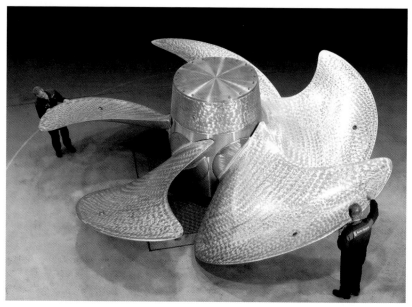

Each of the *Queen Elizabeth* class's two propellers weighs around 33 tons and has a diameter of 7m. They are made from nickel aluminium bronze and have five individual bolted blades. The most powerful propellers ever produced by Rolls-Royce, they are each capable of producing around 50,000 horsepower. *(Rolls-Royce Group)*

Queen Elizabeth's ship control centre also serves as the main damage control HQ (HQ1). It the hub of the platform management system that allows the automated control of the ship's mechanical and electrical systems. *(Crown Copyright 2017)*

One of the integrated platform management system consoles set up to show the aft area of Deck 5. Information can be customised through use of numerous display layers providing increasing levels of detail. *(Crown Copyright 2017)*

supply to key items of equipment such as the steering motors by providing power connections through two separate switchboards. In addition, the distribution system is sufficiently flexibly configured to allow supplies to be re-routed in the event of damage.

Shaftlines and propellers have both been supplied by Rolls-Royce's marine business. The shafts are of hollow-bored construction with bronze liners and have a total weight of c. 240 tons. The five-bladed adjustable bolted propellers are approximately 7m in diameter and weigh 33 tons each. Rolls-Royce was also responsible for manufacturing the steering gear and stabiliser systems. The former comprise twin compact RV-2600-3 three vane rotary systems with twisted blade design rudders to minimise cavitation effect. Both rudders are independent to maximise manoeuvrability. The stabiliser system is based on four Neptune retractable fins arranged in pairs forward and aft. An important aid to air operations, they are credited with achieving a near eighty percent reduction in roll at speeds of 18 knots.

SHIP AND DAMAGE-CONTROL FUNCTIONS

Ship system control is normally carried out from the SCC utilising an integrated platform management system (IPMS) devised by L3 as part of the Power & Propulsion Sub-Alliance that also includes Thales, Rolls-Royce and GE. The level of automation provided by the system has been key to achieving the objective of operating the class with broadly the same number of crew as the much smaller carriers they replaced.[11]

The IPMS integrates a number of sub-components crucial for effective ship operation. These include machinery control and surveillance; damage surveillance and monitoring; condition monitoring; and the electrical power control and management system (EPCAMS). The last-mentioned has been separately supplied by GE Power Conversion but is fully integrated into the wider system for ease of operation. The IPMS uses the ship's common data infrastructure – a network of fibre-optic cables in physically-protected conduits – to connect with its various elements and can be accessed from around sixty-five operator consoles. In addition to those in the SCC, these include consoles in an alternative, secondary machine control position and in the various damage control zones. These are supplemented by dedicated IPMS laptops that can be

The forward bridge is principally used for ship navigation and is located to provide optimum visibility. As in other areas of the ship, manning levels are minimised through extensive automation, notably by provision of Sperry Marine's integrated navigation bridge system. *(Crown Copyright 2017)*

plugged into a number of IPMS access points. As well as carrying out key machinery and damage control roles, the IPMS has interfaces with other core control functions such as the integrated bridge management system and the main mission/command system. Like most modern platform management systems, it also includes full training functionality.

The IPMS' crucial damage-control monitoring function is assisted by provision of large-screen displays incorporating touch-screen displays in both the SCC and the various damage control section bases. Information can be customised through use of numerous display layers of increasing levels of detail from incident board (overall general arrangement level) downwards, with a free draw function allowing additional data to be entered manually. So-called 'kill cards' provide predetermined checklists of action points to be implemented in the event of damage to a particular system or compartment. Active damage control systems interfacing with the IPMS includes an automated fire detection and protection system that can combat fires automati-

cally if the situation dictates. Fixed fire protection is based around a range of gas, water-mist and foam based technologies and includes pop-up firefighting points on the flight deck. Another important monitoring system is the network of some 220 CCTV cameras, providing visual imagery of key areas such as engine and machinery spaces, ship entrances and the access points to classified areas.

Another integrated system – Sperry Marine's integrated navigation bridge system – focused on the navigation bridge in the forward island superstructure facilitates the aim of performing day-to-day ship operations with a minimal crew. It includes navigation planning, electronic chart and radar display functions, supported by associated sensors and software. The forward location of the navigation bridge provides an excellent view of the ship's bow, with overall visibility further assisted by its two metre-high, floor to ceiling windows. Other compartments within the forward island include the chart room, observation deck, bridge mess and commanding officer's day cabin, as well as lift access to the below-decks operations room.

A bow view of *Queen Elizabeth* providing a clear view of the 12.5° ski-jump and the navigating bridge in the forward island, which is situated for optimum visibility. The S1850M volume-search radar on top of the island is principally used to provide long-range situational awareness. *(Crown Copyright 2017)*

COMBAT SYSTEMS, COMMUNICATIONS AND SENSORS

The *Queen Elizabeth* class's overall combat capabilities are coordinated from the mission system complex or operations room. This forms the brain of a sophisticated system that adds (i) communications and (ii) information provision to the (iii) more traditional air-management and ship-protection function. The focal point of the complex is a forward-facing command 'horseshoe' with a separate tactical information exchange located to port and clusters of air traffic control and weapons to its rear (i.e. further forward in the ship). Each of these areas is equipped with a series of multi-function consoles, all of which can be re-configured according to the particular needs of various users. The typically three-screen consoles operate off a variant of BAE Systems' Windows-based CMS software which is similar to that installed in the Type 45 destroyers. However, extra functionality is provided through an air traffic control bolt-on.

The mission system consoles are connected to relevant sensors and weapons by the common data infrastructure previously referenced when describing the IPMS. The two most important are probably the S1850M (RN designation Type 1046) long-range radar located on top of the forward island and the smaller Artisan (Type 997) medium-range system located on its aft counterpart. The former system is a long-range volume-search radar modified from the Thales Nederland SMART-L array working in the 1,000–2,000 MHz D (US Navy L) band frequency. It is equipped with integrated IFF (identification, friend or foe) technology. Capable of tracking up to 1,000 targets at ranges of up to 480km for air targets and 60km for surface targets, it is essentially used to produce a long-range air and surface picture for broad situational awareness. The BAE Systems

A view of *Queen Elizabeth*'s twin islands. The nearer, aft island is primarily intended as the flying control position and has excellent visibility over the flight deck. The location of key sensors such as the S1850M and Artisan radar on different islands helps to reduce mutual interference. *(Crown Copyright 2017)*

Queen Elizabeth pictured off Gibraltar during helicopter certification trials in February 2018. The distribution of key communications systems and sensors between the twin islands is an important design aspect of the two new aircraft carriers. *(Crown Copyright* 2018)

Artisan radar is a medium-range system working in the 2,000-4,000 MHz E/F bands (US Navy S band). This provides a sharper picture at ranges out to around 200km. Although capable of carrying out fire-control functions in conjunction with an active radar-homing missile such as MBDA's Common Anti-air Modular Missile (CAMM), Artisan's principal use in the *Queen Elizabeth* class is for air traffic control. The carriers are also equipped with three navigation arrays.

Other important equipment linked into the mission system will undoubtedly be a comprehensive range of electronic support measures (ESM) and other electronic warfare technologies. The Royal Navy is being tight-lipped about the carriers' precise equipment fit, some of which has yet to be fitted. However, Thales' digital Outfit UAT RESM radar

electronic support measures system that is being installed across the fleet will undoubtedly be an important component. Other countermeasures systems are likely to include launchers for Outfit DLH/Siren radiating and Outfit DLF passive decoys, as well as Ultra Electronics' S2170 Surface Ship Torpedo Defence (SSTD) system.

Thales has also been responsible for provision of the *Queen Elizabeth* class's complex communications system. This encompasses both internal and external elements. The former allows the ship's crew to communicate securely within the ship. It includes everything from the traditional phone and intercoms systems through to an innovative wireless communications network. The last-mentioned is a first on a Royal Navy vessels and allows key crew members to be readily contacted without recourse to

the main broadcast system. External communications encompass the usual radio and satellite links across a range of frequencies. NATO Link 11 and Link 16 tactical data transmission technology will be installed from completion. Provision is also made for the new Link 22.

One notable feature of the class's equipment outfit is the relatively modest provision for defensive weaponry. This is limited to systems primarily providing protection against asymmetric threats such as speedboats or used as a last-ditch defence against incoming missiles. Three Phalanx Block 1B CIWS close-in weapons systems will provide the only anti-missile defence, being arranged to provide 360° coverage. In practice, developments in missile technology mean they are more likely to be used against small surface targets, a role in which they will be supported by four 30mm DS30M Automated Small Calibre Guns and lighter machine guns. Although many of the post-war generation of Royal Navy carriers adopted a similar philosophy of placing complete reliance on supporting escorts for most defensive requirements, this approach has not been shared by other aircraft carrier operators.

OTHER SIGNIFICANT FEATURES

As previously indicated, a key focus area across the underlying *Queen Elizabeth* class design has been a desire to man the two ships with the lowest number of crew commensurate with safe and effective operation. The influence this requirement has had on factors such as weapons handling, machinery and damage control, and communications has already been touched upon. However, the emphasis on lean manning is much broader than this. It extends, for example, to the wide range of automated data provided by the information function within the mission system and even to the design of the six galleys found on each carrier. These are laid out to allow food to flow from storage through preparation and cooking to serving in the various messes as smoothly and quickly as possible. The aim is to be able to feed the ship's company within ninety minutes in normal conditions and in as little as forty-five minutes whilst at action stations.

The success of this overall approach is evidenced by the fact that the core crew is only a little over 670; split into the various branches summarised in Table 3.2.3. This compares very favourably both with personnel numbers required to operate previous Royal Navy aircraft carriers and with the complements of equivalent foreign vessels; for example, France's smaller *Charles de Gaulle* has a core crew of c. 1,250. Total accommodation provision in the *Queen Elizabeth* class is for c. 1,600. This would normally be largely taken up with the aircrew needed to operate a range of differently configured Tailored Air Groups. However, it could also house an embarked military force of up to 250 Royal Marines or refugees taken on board in response to a humanitarian crisis. The large amount of sheltered space on the hangar deck would presumably provide additional flexibility in this regard. Prefabricated cabin units are similar to those installed in other

A picture of one of *Queen Elizabeth*'s galleys taken during the course of fitting out. The ability to feed the ship's company quickly – in as little as forty-five minutes whilst at action stations – is a key aspect of ensuring optimum manning. The dispersal of the two main galleys in forward and aft locations is also another, subtle demonstration of the survivability considerations that have played a key part in the ship's design. *(Aircraft Carrier Alliance)*

A typical modular cabin on *Queen Elizabeth*. The cabins are large enough to house eight bunks but six is the normal maximum occupancy. *(Crown Copyright 2017)*

recent Royal Navy designs – and many other recent warships – and provide a similarly high level of accommodation.[12]

Each ship is equipped with a medical complex that encompasses treatment and consultation rooms, resuscitation and theatre areas, a dental facility and an isolation ward. A total of twelve bed spaces are provided. The usual medical team of eleven medical staff – supplemented by a further forty-two trained first aiders – is capable of providing Role 1 medical care. However, the facilities are sufficient to support a Role 2 capability – including performance of onboard operations and the provision of critical care – with the embarkation of a strengthened medical team.[13]

INTO SERVICE

Although *Queen Elizabeth* has now been commissioned into Royal Navy service and preparations for *Prince of Wales'* trials are well underway, much work still needs to be completed before an operational carrier capability is achieved. The process started in February 2018 when *Queen Elizabeth* departed Portsmouth for initial helicopter certification trials and training. During this period she undertook her first overseas port call when she docked in Gibraltar. The autumn of 2018 will see the commencement of trials with the F-35B Lightning II jets that will ultimately form the core of her strike capabilities. Further trials are scheduled for the following year. The current aim is to establish an initial operating capability with *Queen Elizabeth* in the strike carrier role by December 2020. This is effectively defined as the ability to deploy a single squadron of F-35B jets supplemented by Merlin helicopters carrying the new 'Crowsnest' early-warning radar and with supporting logistical services and infrastructure in place. Attention will then turn to the development of a broader-based carrier capability. This will be supported by *Prince of Wales'* delivery in 2019 and formation of a second squadron of F-35B aircraft in the early 2020s. The carriers' full potential will not be achieved until 2026 when the complete capability to operate in a variety of roles – known as Carrier Enabled Power Projection (CEPP) – will be established.[14]

The key element in CEPP is an aircraft carrier's inherent flexibility to operate a wide variety of different aircraft types so as to enable it to perform a broad spectrum of tasks. Current thinking envisages embarkation or a range of differently-configured

Table 3.2.3: *QUEEN ELIZABETH* CLASS: CORE COMPLEMENT

DEPARTMENT & RANK	NUMBER	SUB TOTAL//TOTAL	DEPARTMENT & RANK	NUMBER	SUB TOTAL//TOTAL
Warfare Department		245	**Logistics Department**		130
Captain	1		Commander	1	
Commander	3		Lieutenant Commander	1	
Lieutenant Commander	11		Lieutenant	4	
Lieutenant	29		Warrant Officer	3	
Sub Lieutenant	3		Chief Petty Officer	6	
Warrant Officer	6		Petty Officer	14	
Chief Petty Officer	14		Leading Hand	30	
Petty Officer	24		Able Rate	71	
Leading Hand	66				
Able Rate	88		**Medical Department**		11
			Commander	1	
Engineering Department		284	Lieutenant Commander	2	
Commander	3		Lieutenant	1	
Lieutenant Commander	4		Chief Petty Officer	1	
Lieutenant	9		Petty Officer	1	
Warrant Officer	8		Leading Hand	2	
Chief Petty Officer	14		Able Rate	3	
Petty Officer	54				
Leading Hand	70		**Welfare Department**		1
Able Rate	122		Warrant Officer	1	
			Chaplaincy Department		1
			Commander	1	
			Overall Total		672

Note:
Information provided as an answer to a House of Commons Parliamentary Question (reference HOC 210751) on 28 October 2014. Other sources suggest complement has been adjusted slightly subsequently.

Tailored Air Groups (TAGs) or carrier air wings in roles ranging from carrier strike to littoral manoeuvre (amphibious assault). The former tasking might, for example, involve deployment of an air group with a composition of two squadrons of twenty-four F-35Bs and supporting Merlin ASW and Crowsnest-configured helicopters. This would sustain an ongoing offensive air effort whilst providing strong surveillance and anti-submarine capabilities. In the amphibious role, some or all of the F-35Bs would be disembarked and replaced with Chinook and Merlin transport helicopters, as well as Apache and Wildcat attack helicopters. The transport rotorcraft would be used for airborne insertion of Royal Marine assault companies. It is also envisaged that the *Queen Elizabeth* class will often work in conjunction with allied aircraft, particularly the F-35Bs operated by the United States Marine Corps

(USMC). It is anticipated USMC jets will be embarked for *Queen Elizabeth's* maiden operational deployment in 2021.

CONCLUSION

The procurement of the *Queen Elizabeth* class aircraft carriers has undoubtedly been one of the Royal Navy's most complex, costly and controversial acquisition projects. Ongoing delays – largely associated with political and budgetary factors – have meant that the programme has taken far longer to achieve than first envisaged. Moreover, initial estimates of c. £2bn for medium-sized aircraft carriers proved to be naively over-optimistic, with the total cost of construction alone now expected to be in the order of £6.2bn. The National Audit Office has estimated that the total cost of delivering the initial carrier strike capability – adding in development

A view of *Queen Elizabeth*'s maiden arrival at her home port of Portsmouth on 16 August 2017. Although now accepted into naval service, much work remains outstanding before she achieves initial operating capability in the strike carrier role at the end of 2020. It will be even longer before complete capability to operate in a wider variety of roles – known as Carrier Enabled Power Projection (CEPP) – is established. (*Conrad Waters*)

Prince of Wales pictured at the time of her naming ceremony in September 2017. Appropriately her sponsor was Camilla, Duchess of Rothesay, wife of the current Prince of Wales. The carrier is expected to be delivered in the course of 2019, assisting the development of the CEPP capability that is at the heart of the *Queen Elizabeth* class aircraft carriers' intended operating concept. (*Crown Copyright 2017*)

Queen Elizabeth pictured manoeuvring at Portsmouth Naval Base in October 2017, shortly before she was accepted into service. *(BAE Systems)*

Helicopters ranged on the deck of *Queen Elizabeth*. The slow build-up of the F-35B jet force intended to operate from the new carriers has been one of the main criticisms of the wider programme. *(Crown Copyright 2017)*

costs, F-35B procurement through to March 2021 and acquisition of the 'Crowsnest' radar system – will approach £13bn.[15] This level of expenditure has inevitably been difficult to accommodate in a defence budget that has experienced a considerable squeeze during the age of austerity.

The austere budgetary backdrop has also been reflected in the capabilities the programme will deliver. In spite of the project's cost, it is evident that hard choices have had to be taken throughout the project to ensure its affordability. These include the revisions made to the original Alpha design, the limitations on defensive armament and – more broadly – the slow build-up of F-35B squadron numbers. Another key area of economy appears to be supporting infrastructure. Considerable work – including dredging of a new channel to facilitate access to the harbour and completion of upgraded berthing facilities (the Princess Royal Jetty) – has, indeed, been completed at Portsmouth to accommodate the class. However, the lack of a dock sufficiently large to accommodate the ships at their home base and current uncertainty over where such a facility will be provided in future carry obvious risks. It is difficult to avoid the conclusion that the MOD's resources have been stretched to their limits in re-establishing a carrier strike capacity.

In spite of these observations, it is difficult not to be impressed with the scale of the achievement the Royal Navy and its partners in the ACA have attained in bringing the *Queen Elizabeth* class aircraft carriers into service. Militarily, the combination of the two carriers and their embarked F-35B strike fighters will provide the United Kingdom with a naval aviation capability arguably second only to the United States during the 2020s and a significant means of global power projection. Much has been written about the vulnerability of such ships to modern missiles and torpedoes, *Queen Elizabeth* herself being '… a large, convenient naval target …' according to the Russian Defence Ministry. However, the fact that no aircraft carrier has sustained material damage from enemy action in the more than seventy years that have passed since the end of the Second World War does

Queen Elizabeth pictured off the Scottish coast on 30 June 2017, the day when her flight deck saw its first helicopter landings and take-offs. The construction of *Queen Elizabeth* and her sister *Prince of Wales* represent a significant national achievement that reflects considerable credit on all those involved in their design and construction. *(Crown Copyright 2017)*

not support this contention. Indeed, few countries outside a handful of major powers possess sufficient numbers of anti-shipping weapons to penetrate the layered defences of a carrier task group with a good prospect of success. Just as importantly, many air forces would struggle to counter the air group that a *Queen Elizabeth* class carrier could embark. The arrival of the new aircraft carriers therefore provides the United Kingdom with an invaluable boost to its defences in a dangerous world.

Equally, the *Queen Elizabeth* class has had a major industrial significance, helping to rejuvenate a maritime sector that had suffered from decades of under-investment and contraction. The two ships represent a major triumph for ACA commercial members BAE Systems, Babcock and Thales, demonstrating their technical capabilities across a wide range of technologies and helping to bolster their credentials for future orders. This effect has also filtered down to the myriad of suppliers of varying sizes involved in the programme. Notably, the new UK National Shipbuilding Strategy published in September 2017 seeks to capitalise on the investment made in the aircraft carriers to ensure the continued revitalisation of the sector through a longer-term plan for warship procurement with exports and competition at its heart. More broadly, it seems likely that the *Queen Elizabeth* class's key focus on design elements such as flight deck efficiency and overall automation will have an impact on future carrier designs the world over. The new Italian amphibious assault ship *Trieste* has already adopted the *Queen Elizabeth*'s twin-island arrangement and uses similar Rolls-Royce MT-30 gas turbines, albeit the latter will operate in a more conventional combined diesel electric or gas (CODLOG) configuration.

In conclusion, the construction of *Queen Elizabeth* and her sister *Prince of Wales* represent a significant national achievement that reflects considerable credit on all those involved in their design and construction. They will provide good service in the decades ahead.

Notes

1. An overview of the 1990s concept studies is provided in 'Appendix 6: The Future Aircraft Carrier' in D K Brown and George Moore's *Rebuilding the Royal Navy* (London: Chatham Publishing, 2003), pp.197–8.

2. An excellent, largely contemporary source of the convoluted process that resulted in the eventual orders for the *Queen Elizabeth* class was provided by Richard Beedall's *Navy Matters* website. Although this site is now defunct, many of the relevant articles can still be found using the Wayback Machine internet archive.

3. A review of the considerations influencing Thales' CVF design and its subsequent iterations is provided by S T D Knight's 'The Design of HMS *Queen Elizabeth* and HMS *Prince of Wales*' in the *Journal of Naval Engineering* Volume 45, Book 1 (London: RINA, 2009), pp.74–93. Simon Knight can be considered as the father of the *Queen Elizabeth* class design, leading the ship design studies for the Thales consortium during the competitive assessment phase and subsequently acting as Platform Design Director for the ACA.

4. At the time the contract was awarded, the then VT Group and BAE Systems had merged their surface shipbuilding yards into a joint venture, BVT Surface Fleet. Both BAE and BVT were originally part of the construction alliance. BAE subsequently acquired full ownership of BVT Surface Fleet and merged it into its own operations.

5. The *Pymes 75* website provides a detailed record of the fabrication and assembly dates of the two ships' constituent blocks. This is currently available at: pymes75.plus.com/military/cvf.htm

6. *Queen Elizabeth*'s sea trials are well documented through extensive media coverage, not least in the BBC Two documentary *Britain*'s *Biggest Warship*.

7. It is understood that costs associated with the physical assembly of *Prince of Wales* could be c. 10–20 percent lower than for *Queen Elizabeth* as a result of the efficiencies achieved. (ACA Programme Director Neil Holm in interview with the author; 24 April 2018)

8. For a full description of the impact of SDSR 2010 on the Royal Navy generally and the carrier programme in particular see Richard Beedall's 'United Kingdom: Defence Review Shapes the Royal Navy' in *Seaforth World Naval Review 2012* (Barnsley: Seaforth Publishing, 2011), pp.97–107.

9. When catwalks and other hull extensions are taken into account, overall dimensions increase to 284m x 73m. Stated accounts of the ship's total height vary considerably; this is probably because different points of measurement are used.

10. Information on the class's high-voltage power and propulsion system is partly drawn from a GE Power Conversion case study entitled *Queen Elizabeth Class (QEC) Aircraft Carrier* first published in 2012 and currently available at: gepowerconversion.com/sites/gepc/files/ MARINE_GEA20337%20-%20Queen%20Elizabeth%20-%20Case%20Study.pdf The considerable amount of Rolls-Royce Group equipment installed in the design is described in a paper, *Powering the Queen Elizabeth Class Aircraft Carriers*, available at: rolls-royce.com/~/media/ Files/R/Rolls-Royce /documents/ news/6-page-qe-booklet-tcm92-58802.pdf

11. A much more detailed description of the *Queen Elizabeth* class carrier's IPMS is provided by Jim Davies and Stuart Jewell in a paper entitled *Controlling the Royal Navy*'s *Queen Elizabeth Class Aircraft Carriers* currently available on the L3 MAPPS website at: mapps.l3t.com/ whitepapers.html

12. For further information on modern naval accommodation standards see Bruno Huriet's 'Modern Warship Accommodation: Some Considerations' in *Seaforth World Naval Review 2018* (Barnsley: Seaforth Publishing, 2017), pp.183–91.

13. Under standard NATO terminology, there are four tiers ('Roles') of medical support, defined on the basis of capabilities and resources. Role 4 is the most extensive tier of medical support and Role 1 the least. Role 1 encompasses basic first aid, lifesaving resuscitation and triage, whilst Role 2 extends to non-specialist surgical capabilities.

14. A detailed overview of the planned schedule for delivering both carrier strike and the wider CEPP concept of operations was provided in a National Audit Office Report entitled *Delivering Carrier Strike* (London: NAO, 2017).

15. *Delivering Carrier Strike*, ibid.

16. The author acknowledges with gratitude the support of the following industrial and Royal Navy personnel in facilitating this chapter's production, not least through a comprehensive series of briefings and tour of *Prince of Wales* in build at Babcock International's Rosyth facility on 24 April 2018:

- Captain Ian Groom, RN: Senior Naval Officer, HMS *Prince of Wales*.
- Neil Holm: Programme Director, Aircraft Carrier Alliance.
- Graeme Mair: External Communications Manager, Babcock International Group.
- William Watson: Operations Director, Energy & Marine Services, Babcock International Group.
- Lt Commander Chris Wood, RN: HMS *Prince of Wales*.

Author:
David Hobbs

4.1 TECHNOLOGICAL REVIEW

WORLD NAVAL AVIATION

An Overview of Recent Developments

Carrier-led strike groups continue to form the heart of the US Navy's power but it seems that it will be a struggle to achieve the desired twelve-strong carrier force. The November 2017 pictures above and opposite show three *Nimitz* class vessels – *Theodore Roosevelt* (CVN-71), *Ronald Reagan* (CVN-76) and *Nimitz* (CVN-68) herself – undertaking a rare combined carrier force exercise in the Western Pacific as part of a series of exercises held in the region to counter Chinese naval expansionism. *(US Navy)*

The tenth edition of *World Naval Review* is an appropriate point to look back at how naval aviation has evolved since 2010. Accordingly – whilst following its usual format – this annual overview of world naval aviation will also look back over the past decade and comment on a range of developments. During this period, nothing has changed the fundamental importance of sea power or the importance of aircraft as part of the naval forces that implement it. What has changed, is the ongoing digital revolution that has transformed ships, aircraft, weapons and even fighting vehicles moving ashore from amphibious warships into a network-centric system of computers. Their connectivity is what counts in today's battlespace.

US NAVY AIRCRAFT CARRIERS AND THEIR AIRCRAFT

President Trump's 2016 election campaign included an ambition to expand the US Navy from the present fleet of just over 280 warships to 350, a figure broadly in line with the December 2016 Force Structure Assessment (FSA) objective of 355 vessels. However, as noted in a March 2018 Congressional Budget Office (CBO) report, current shipbuilding funding levels of c. US$22bn p.a. are barely adequate to maintain the status quo in the longer term. It estimated more than US$26bn p.a. would be required to hit the 'sweet spot' of building the 12–13 new ships needed every year to reach 355 ships by 2037. Even the US Navy's own FY2019

long-range construction plan estimates the 2016 FSA objective will not be achieved until the 2050s. Within this total, the targeted force of twelve aircraft carriers can be reached briefly in FY2022 but will drop back to eleven when *Nimitz* (CVN-68) reaches the end of her fifty-year life in 2025.[1]

New aircraft carrier construction is focused on the nuclear-powered *Gerald R. Ford* (CVN-78) class; a prime example of former Secretary of Defense Donald Rumsfeld's transformational procurement policy of the new millennium's early years, which sought to procure new weapons systems at the limit

of technical possibility. In 2010, the USN intended she would enter service in the middle of the decade. However, delays emerged due to unexpectedly difficult development challenges associated with the range of new technologies incorporated into the design, notably her Dual-Band Radar (DBR), Electromagnetic Aircraft Launch System (EMALS) and Advanced Arrester Gear (AAG). She was eventually handed over in 2017 but is not due to enter the deployment cycle until an extensive trials and work-up period has been concluded. She has also proved to be more expensive than initially projected.

The next two ships of the class – *John F. Kennedy* (CVN-79) and *Enterprise* (CVN-80) – will not have the DBR but will instead have the more affordable Enterprise Air Surveillance Radar (EASR). This is based on Raytheon's scalable S Band (NATO E/F Band) SPY-6 Air and Missile Defence Radar (AMDR) fitted in the Flight III *Arleigh Burke* class destroyers. It has a production run spread over the new aircraft carriers, amphibious assault ships and destroyers, giving economy of scale to drive down cost. However, EMALS and AAG offer significant improvements over the earlier systems installed in

Table 4.1.1: US NAVY PLANNED AIRCRAFT PROCUREMENT: FY2018-FY2023

TYPE	MISSION	FY2018 Requested[1]	FY2018 Authorised[1]	FY2019 Requested	FY2020 Planned	FY2021 Planned	FY2022 Planned	FY2023 Planned
Fixed Wing (Carrier Based)								
F-35B Lightning II JSF	Strike Fighter (STOVL)	20	24	20	20	20	20	21
F-35C Lightning II JSF	Strike Fighter (CV)	4	10	9	16	24	24	24
FA-18E/F Super Hornet	Strike Fighter (CV)	14	24	24	24	24	21	17
E-2D Advanced Hawkeye	Surveillance/Control	5	5	4	4	4	5	7
Fixed Wing (Land Based)								
P-8A Poseidon	Maritime Patrol	7	10	10	9	0	0	0
C-40A Clipper	Transport	0	2	2	0	0	0	0
KC-130J Hercules	Tanker	2	6	2	2	5	6	8
T-44 Replacement[2]	Training	0	0	0	0	0	0	10
Rotary Wing								
AH-1Z/UH-1Y Viper/Venom	Attack/Utility	22	29	25	0	0	0	0
VH-92A	Presidential Transport	0	0	6	6	5	0	0
CH-53K Super Stallion	Heavy-Lift	4	6	8	9	14	19	19
C/MV-22B 22 Osprey	Transport	6	14	7	10	9	11	15
MH-60R Seahawk	Sea Control	0	8	0	0	0	0	0
TH-57 Replacement[3]	Training	0	0	0	25	25	25	10
Unmanned Aerial Vehicles								
MQ-8C Fire Scout	Reconnaissance	0	6	0	0	0	0	0
MQ-25A Stingray	Refuelling	0	0	0	0	0	0	4
MQ-4C Triton	Maritime Patrol	3	3	3	3	3	3	5
RQ-21A Blackjack	Tactical reconnaissance	4	4	0	0	0	0	0
Totals:		91	151	120	128	133	134	140

Notes

1. FY2018 requested figures reflect aircraft numbers set out in the Trump Administration's Presidential Budget Request of 23 May 2017; the authorised numbers reflect numbers actually funded in the Consolidated Appropriations Act signed into law on 23 March 2018. As is frequently the case, the US Congress added significant numbers of aircraft over the original request.
2. Refers to replacement of the T-44 Pegasus (Beechcraft King Air series) twin-engine turboprop trainer.
3. Refers to replacement of the TH-57 Sea Ranger (Bell 206 series) training helicopter.

the ten ships of the *Nimitz* class and will be fitted in all new CVNs.

Future procurement costs could be substantially reduced by placing orders for two carriers together. This previously occurred with some of the *Nimitz* class during the later stages of the Cold War and is being seriously considered for CVN-80 and CVN-81. It would be accompanied by reducing the gaps or 'centers' between assembling the two ships. Currently, the hull of CVN-79 is well advanced and work has started on steel work for CVN-80 but they have programmed delivery dates five years apart. This causes a 'labour valley' as work force levels drop when the first ship is completed and the second is not sufficiently advanced for them to transfer. By

accelerating CVN-81 this problem could be avoided for the third and fourth ships and the same drawings, technical products and build plan could be used for both. Larger equipment orders would also make significant savings. Assuming CVN-80 and CVN-81 were centred three and a half to four years apart, savings could amount to US$1.6bn according to a statement made by Newport News Shipbuilding President Jennifer Boykin at the Navy League's 2018 Sea/Air/Space Exposition. US Navy acquisition chief James Geurts also told reporters after a Senate hearing in April 2018 that the navy is looking into similar economies of scale with contractors supplying government-furnished equipment for the two ships. When combined with the shipyard's

US$1.6bn, the total savings could be as much as US$2.5bn or around a sixth of CVN-81's projected US$15.1bn cost.[2]

Another possible source of savings is to take another look at future carrier design. Notably, Senator John McCain, a former naval pilot, presidential candidate and now chairman of the Senate Armed Services Committee (SASC), has for years been an advocate of procuring light aircraft carriers (CVLs) to create a high/low force mix with CVNs. Many believe that this would be a useful development, resulting in an ability to spread the USN's airborne network more widely and providing an alternative to big, nuclear-powered carriers in low-key operations. The cheapest option would probably be an adaptation of the US Marine Corps' 'Lightning Carrier' concept; an *America* (LHA-6) class amphibious assault ship modified to operate about twenty F-35B STOVL strike fighters and a small number of MV-22B Ospreys acting as air-to-air tankers. Cost would be a little over US$3bn per unit and additional orders might even drive down the unit price significantly. The big 'but' is *America*'s lack of catapults and arrester wires, making it unable to operate conventional aircraft such as the EA-18G Growler, F/A-18E/F Super Hornet and E-2D Advanced Hawkeye, thereby severely limiting the capability of its networked air wing in comparison with a CVN. Arguably, an airborne early warning (AEW) version of the MV-22 could be developed to fill the gap but its cost would have to be set against supposed economy of the light carrier. The CVL would also have to find space to embark MH-60 Seahawk series helicopters to defend its battle group against submarine attack, reducing the number of F-35Bs that could be embarked.

More capability could be delivered by a redesigned *America* with an angled deck, catapults and arrester wires, able to operate any type of aircraft that a CVN could but in smaller numbers. Again there is an expensive 'but' since adding complexity also adds cost. If two light carriers cost more than a single CVN but, even combined, operate fewer aircraft, they represent poor value for money. Also, the basic *America* class are amphibious ships with relatively low-powered gas-turbine machinery giving a maximum speed below 25 knots. The basic design would almost certainly lack sufficient electrical generation capacity for EMALS and some way would have to be found for providing that power or of installing steam catapults like those in the *Nimitz* class. Is the US Navy likely to find light carriers attractive? To date proposed funding increases have come nowhere near funding an enlarged navy. However, if a viable CVL design could be procured without detriment to other programmes, they would arguably fit in the 'nice to have' category – although not if other programmes had to be curtailed to fund them. Shipyard capacity for them is also a question. In any event, light carriers are likely to remain on the agenda as long as Senator McCain is in office.

Turning to aircraft procurement, the FY2019 Presidential Budget Request saw a significant rebound in planned orders from the temporary dip seen in the FY2018 proposal and looks to see further modest growth in the remaining years of the Future

Years Defense Program. Details are provided in Table 4.1.1.[3] Funding is also requested to accelerate the MQ-25A development programme and refurbish F/A-18s to combat the growing fighter shortage. A notable feature is a continuation of orders for Boeing F-18E/F Super Hornets alongside Lockheed Martin F-35 Lightning II variants for the foreseeable future, with Super Hornet production now set to continue until at least 2023.

Development of the F-35 Lightning II Joint Strike Fighter (JSF) is a theme that has run through all ten editions of *World Naval Review*. The last flight of the System Development and Demonstration (SDD) phase took place on 11 April 2018 when an F-35C flown by British pilot Peter Wilson flew from NAS Patuxent River, Maryland. The F-35 Programme Executive Officer, Vice Admiral Mat Winter, told the Navy League's 2018 Sea-Air-Space Exposition that a total of over 9,200 sorties had been achieved during the SDD phase and more than 65,000 test points had been accumulated. However, a mass of data still needs to be correlated to verify that the three variants meet their specifications by the end of 2018. The next phase is Initial Operational Test and Evaluation (IOT&E), due to

start in late 2018. A decision on the start of full-rate F-35 production is planned for the last quarter of 2019 but the programme will not begin to deliver the numbers the US Navy needs for some time after that. All aircraft coming off the production lines in the USA, Italy and Japan now have Block 3F software and the first iteration of Block 4 is to fly in June 2018 for evaluation. Unit cost has always been an issue and Winter informed the Exposition that Lot 10 aircraft delivered in 2018 cost US$94.3 million for the 'A' variant, US$122.4 million for the 'B' variant and US$121.2 million for the 'C'. However, he pledged that all three would drop below $100 million from Lot 14 onwards.

Rear Admiral Scott Conn, Director of Air Warfare in the Chief of Naval Operations' (CNO) Office, testified before a sub-committee of the SASC on 6 March 2018 that the first front-line navy F-35C unit, Strike Fighter Squadron (VFA) 147, the 'Argonauts', is expected to reach Initial Operational Capability (IOC) in late 2018 but stressed that the navy regards IOC as being capability-, not calendar-based. The Argonauts' aircraft must have Block 3F software with weapons and sensors able to perform in a threat-representative environment to the stan-

The lead *America* (LHA-6) class amphibious assault ship passing the nuclear-powered aircraft carrier *Carl Vinson* (CVN-70) on 20 January 2018. There is an ongoing debate as to whether a light carrier-type variant of the *America* design should be built to operate alongside the large carriers as part of a shift to a high-end/low-end carrier force mix. *(US Navy)*

The US Navy is currently focused on achieving initial operational capability (IOC) for its F-35C variant Lightning II strike fighters, which is currently planned for late 2018. This photograph shows a F-35C of VFA-125, the 'Rough Raiders' undertaking a night-time launch from *Abraham Lincoln* (CVN-72) during fleet replacement (training) squadron carrier qualifications on the type in December 2017. *(US Navy)*

dards identified in the operational requirements document. VFA-147's IOT&E is expected to commence in September 2018 and complete in early 2019. Meanwhile, in August 2018 the USS *Abraham Lincoln* (CVN-72) is due to embark a detachment of F-35Cs from VX-9, the 'Vampires', based at Edwards Air Force Base, California, for an embarked period of IOT&E alongside carrier Air Wing 7 (CVW-7) to clear the type for future operational embarkations. VFA-147 is due to carry out carrier qualification in October 2018 and its first operational deployment is to be on the USS *Carl Vinson* (CVN-70) in 2021.

Two other F-35C Squadrons, VFA-101, the 'Grim Reapers', and VFA-125, the 'Rough Raiders', are based at Eglin Air Force Base (East Coast) and Naval Air Station (NAS) Lemoore (West Coast) in the fleet replacement (training) role. They are tasked with converting front-line squadrons from other types onto the F-35C. Fleet replacement squadron carrier qualifications for the first aviators from these

squadrons were completed alongside VX-9 on *Abraham Lincoln* in December 2017.

As of March 2018, twenty-eight F-35Cs had been delivered, twenty-one to the US Navy and seven to the USMC, out of a planned total of 273 for the USN and sixty-seven for the USMC. By 2024 the Navy plans to have F-35C squadrons in four carrier air wings and by 2030 it intends to operate standardised air wings, each comprising four VFA squadrons; two with twelve F/A-18E/F each and two with ten F-35C each. The remainder of the air wing will comprise squadrons of EA-18Gs, E-2Ds, MQ-25A Stingray unmanned tankers and MH-60R/S helicopters, a total of about eighty aircraft. Beyond 2040 the USN is expecting to replace the capabilities of the Super Hornet and is beginning to look into ways in which this can be achieved avoiding massive, transformational development costs like the F-35. It is favouring an incremental approach which may take the form of continued F-35 production to a hypothetical Block 4 or even later standard or a

new platform tentatively referred to as F/A-XX. Both approaches could have manned and unmanned options and directed energy weapons but whichever path is adopted the critical factor is open-architecture computing power and network connectivity. The US Navy sees the Naval Integrated Fire Control-Counter Air (NIFC-CA) system of systems as the key to its ability to fight in the twenty-first century battlespace.[4]

The delayed introduction of the F-35C and intense operational use of Hornets and Super Hornets during continuous combat operations in the Middle East have used up flying hours much faster than predicted. At the end of 2017 the then Commander Naval Air Forces, Vice Admiral Troy Shoemaker, briefed the House of Representatives Armed Services Committee that only half the navy's total of 542 F/A-18E/F airframes were flyable in the short term and only 170, or thirty-one percent, were fully mission-capable and ready for combat. With four carrier air wings deployed to support combat operations during 2018, some aircraft from non-deployed squadrons have been 'cannibalised' to provide deployed units with what they need. The 6,000-hour airframe life for both the legacy Hornets and newer Super Hornets was originally considered acceptable on the basis of the original delivery schedule for the F-35C and a less demanding operational tempo but things are now very different. Strategies in place to get through the strike fighter shortage include the extended production of F/A-18E/F airframes already referenced. Further relief will be gained when the MQ-25A Stingray enters service as an unmanned tanker to take over the role from F/A-18s which spend thirty percent of their airborne time in this secondary role. However, these steps are unlikely to be sufficient on their own and attention has therefore turned to a Super Hornet life-extension programme to bridge the gap.

The so-called Super Hornet Service Life Modification (SLM) commenced under an initial US$73m contract awarded to Boeing on 1 March 2018. The first four airframes entered the programme in April 2018, with the ultimate aim being to extend airframe life to at least 9,000 hours. Work will be done at Boeing facilities at St Louis, Missouri, and San Antonio, Texas, although the US Navy has the right to offload some or all of the work to naval depots in future. Since Boeing builds the Super Hornet and has delivered most of them early and under budget, it seems reasonable to suppose that they will bring the same efficiency to bear on the SLM lines. Lessons have been learned from a previous Service Life Extension Programme (SLEP) for legacy Hornets at naval aviation repair depots, which proved less than successful.[5] Two early F/A-18s, an 'E' and an 'F', had previously been delivered to St Louis where they were 'torn down' to see what state they were in under a Service Life Assessment Program (SLAP). Encouragingly, they proved to be in better shape than expected. The gradual build-up of airframe numbers requiring SLM – around 7–10 in 2019 and c. 18 in 2020 – will also help to establish the refurbishment lines efficiently.

From 2020, aircraft going through SLM will also be upgraded to Block III standard. The navy plans to receive up to fifty Block III SLM aircraft each year once the programme gets into full swing, supplementing the 110 new aircraft in the FY2019–2023 FYDP that will also be built to this standard. The F/A-18E/F Block III specification is the result of analysis of future carrier air wing capability require-

A US Navy F/A-18F Super Hornet assigned to the 'Fighting Redcocks' of VFA-22 pictured breaking the Sound Barrier whilst operating from the carrier *Theodore Roosevelt* (CVN-71). A Super Hornet Service Life Modification (SLM) is underway to extend the service lives of these aircraft, which have had far more intensive operational lives than first predicted. *(US Navy)*

US Navy ambitions to field an unmanned carrier-based aircraft are now focused on the MQ-25A Stingray, an air-to-air refuelling 'tanker' with some reconnaissance functions. This photograph shows Boeing's entrant for the competition – General Atomics and Lockheed Martin are proposing rival designs. *(Boeing)*

ments and is intended to enhance the Super Hornet's ability to operate as part of NIFC-CA and in a complementary way with other carrier aircraft. Work includes structural modifications to give the required 9,000-hour airframe life and other improvements, the most significant being conformal fuel tanks. A US$219 million contract to develop and integrate these onto both the F/A-18 and EA-18 upper fuselages was awarded to Boeing in February 2018. They add 3,200lbs (1,455kg) of fuel in a low-drag configuration that will increase range by up to 120 nautical miles and improve mission flexibility. Another upgrade introduces Elbit large, flat-panel cockpit displays featuring a new user interface. Block III interoperability will be improved by installation of the Distributed Target Processor Network (DTPN) and Tactical Targeting Network Technology (TTNT), both already fitted in the EA-18. The former provides increased computing power with multiple layers of security that allows new applications to be integrated into the aircraft quickly in order to adapt to new threats. The latter is a secure high-capacity network – known as a pipe – that plugs the Super Hornet into voice radio, video and other data shared with the EA-18 and E-2D, adding the ability to move a bandwidth of data back and forth

between platforms. Another important Block III addition is the integration of the Lockheed Martin ASG-34 infrared search and track sensor that will add passive long-range counter-air, counter-stealth and targeting to give the Super Hornet the ability to track targets without giving its own position away. A limited application of stealth coatings and treatments could also be applied to reduce the aircraft's radar signature, although it is not intended to try to match the F-35's characteristics in this regard.

The US Navy's ambition to include unmanned aircraft in carrier air wings is another theme that has run through *World Naval Review*'s first decade. In July 2013 an X-47B unmanned air vehicle (UAV), call-sign Salty-Dog 502, achieved successful autonomous catapult launches and arrested landings on *George H. W. Bush* (CVN-77). Later, it demonstrated air-to-air refuelling capability both as a tanker and a receiver and the USN studied the concept of a developed UAV as the airborne element of an unmanned carrier-launched strike and surveillance system (UCLASS). As the complexity of such a development became clear, however, the navy's plan evolved from a sophisticated, low-observable, tail-less strike platform into a simpler 'flying refuelling station' with a modest reconnaissance capability that could be developed

quickly using existing technology; it was designated the MQ-25A Stingray. A request for proposals was issued to industry in October 2017. The turn of events was not to the liking of Northrop Grumman, which had developed the X-47B. The company quickly withdrew from the competition, presumably because it lacked the cutting-edge technology the firm was interested in. Following its departure, three firms are competing for the work: Lockheed Martin, Boeing and General Atomic. The winner is to be selected in late 2018, with US$719m for research and development and four production airframes included in the FY2019 budget submission.

Urgency might play into the hands of Boeing. Both General Atomics and Lockheed Martin have 'paper projects' but Boeing has already built a company-funded prototype evolved from its original UCLASS design and built around a Rolls-Royce AE 3007 engine. It is a fuel-efficient design which had already carried out engine runs by the end of 2017 and the company claims that it could carry out deck handling demonstrations before the end of 2018. The navy has designated just two key performance parameters for the MQ-25A; the tanking mission and carrier suitability. Stingray is to be capable of delivering about 15,000lbs (6,818kg) of fuel up to 500 miles (800km) from the carrier. The Boeing design still looks stealthy, unsurprisingly given its origins, and photographs show the arrester hook enclosed behind a door when retracted, a stealth feature. However, there are no saw-tooth edges on undercarriage doors or access panels which would have been necessary in a design optimised for stealth. There are three air-data sensors on the nose, all non-stealthy probes, indicating triplex fly-by-wire flight control and there is a camera in the nose, presumably to enable a human operator to taxi the aircraft on deck. Whichever firm wins the contract, its design will have to undergo a deck-handling demonstration before final acceptance. The MQ-25A contract is for the air vehicle, with the navy responsible for developing the data links and ground control station as well as acting as the lead systems integrator. Much of that work has already been done as part of the X-47B launch and recovery demonstration in 2013–14. The breakthrough with MQ-25A will not be the air vehicle's ability to operate from a carrier deck; that has already been demonstrated. The learning opportunity is going to be the integration of manned and unmanned aircraft in the deck operating cycle of a CVN.

An undated photograph of two V-22 Osprey series tilt-rotors in flight. The Osprey has become an established part of US Marine Corps and Special Forces operations over the last decade and will enter service as a carrier onboard delivery aircraft in its CMV-22 variant from 2020 onwards. *(Boeing)*

Another new type on carrier decks from the 2020s is the CMV-22B Osprey which is to replace the long-serving C-2A Greyhound in the carrier-on-board (COD) delivery role. Twenty-six C-2As are to be replaced with thirty-eight CMV-22Bs and the first aircrew and maintainers are being trained by the USMC MV-22 training squadron, VMMT-204 'Raptors' at MCAS New River, North Carolina. CMV-22Bs are to operate from NAS North Island, California and NAS Norfolk, Virginia but the USN has not yet decided where it will base the fleet replacement squadron that will ultimately train all navy Osprey pilots and maintenance personnel. The CMV-22B is due to achieve IOC in 2020 with the last C-2As going out of service in 2026. Full operational capability with the new type is planned for 2024 with the last aircraft to be delivered in 2028. The naval COD variant differs from the Marines' MV-22 in having greater fuel capacity to give longer range and a public address system to allow the crew to brief passengers in flight. It will be more versatile in the COD role because it can land like a helicopter at any time day or night with the minimum manpower requirement on carrier decks. As important, it can land on big-deck amphibious assault ships or smaller vessels with suitable decks. C-2As have to land on carriers to unload stores which then have to be loaded onto helicopters to be taken around the task force, evolutions that require time, manpower and flying hours.

Two other aircraft show the benefit of the navy's carefully-considered procurement policy. The fleet electronic attack squadrons are now fully equipped with EA-18G Growlers and the type has proved very successful. A series of upgrades are planned to keep the aircraft effective in the rapidly-changing world of electronic warfare. Conversion of the fleet airborne early warning squadrons to the E-2D Advanced Hawkeye will be nearly complete by the end of 2019 and the navy sees the type as the cornerstone of NIFC-CA. Much has been made of the emergence of anti-access and area-denial weapons and the hypothetical threat posed to aircraft carriers by some nations equipped with them but the press seems not to have fully grasped the power of networked

Northrop Grumman's E-2D Advanced Hawkeye airborne early warning (AEW) aircraft is steadily taking over the carrier-based AEW role from older variants of the type and will be a cornerstone of the US Navy's future cooperative engagement capability. This image was released in late 2016 to mark the installation of aerial refuelling capability in the first aircraft to receive this equipment; series installation is scheduled to begin in 2018. *(Northrop Grumman)*

computers across the platform spectrum that the USN is able to deploy using E-2Ds as the hub. We are reaching the point where only those navies that have networked capability or can operate under the shield of the USN as a close ally, can realistically consider facing sophisticated opposition at sea

OTHER AIRCRAFT CARRIER OPERATORS

UNITED KINGDOM

The United Kingdom government has found to its cost that strike carrier operating skills are complicated and highly demanding for a navy to acquire in the first place, easy to lose and difficult to regain. The British Royal Navy has undoubtedly suffered more than most from political ineptitude but, with *Queen Elizabeth* at sea for her aircraft trials programme and *Prince of Wales* afloat fitting out in Rosyth there are some grounds for optimism. *Queen Elizabeth* was commissioned into the Royal Navy (RN) by Her Majesty Queen Elizabeth II on

7 December 2017.[6] In 2018 she embarked Merlin HM2 helicopters of 820 Naval Air Squadron (NAS) and a variety of other helicopter types – including RAF Chinooks – for helicopter trials in the Mediterranean. By May 2018 more than 1,000 rotary-wing deck landings had been logged. Periods at sea are interspersed with time alongside in Portsmouth known as capability insertion periods (CIP) in which new systems are installed. These include the Automated Logistic Information System (ALIS) that supports every aspect of F-35B operations ready for fixed-wing trials off the eastern coast of the USA in the second half of 2018 with 'orange-wired' test F-35Bs of 17 Squadron embarked. Another vital system installed in 2018 is the US-developed AN/APS-41/41A Instrument Carrier Landing System (ICLS) that transmits flight path data to aircraft approaching the deck that can be seen by pilots in their helmet-mounted displays. Two more CIPs are to follow before the ship becomes operational.

The F-35B trial in the autumn of 2018 is intended to clear the ship as safe to operate the type in every way from lashing on deck, moving, launching and recovery to every kind of emergency including a simulated crash on deck. It will provide a first opportunity to test rolling vertical landings which are unique to British plans for deck landing the F-35B. Further fixed-wing trials with a larger number of aircraft embarked take place in 2019 and 2020, with IOC for carrier strike anticipated in December 2020. With the withdrawal from service of *Ocean* in 2018 the new carrier will enter a hybrid phase with a limited capability as a helicopter carrier but needing continuing fixed-wing trials before an operational strike capability is declared.

The first British F-35B unit intended for operational use, 617 Squadron, started to arrive at RAF Marham from MCAS Beaufort on 6 June 2018 and is expected to reach shore-based IOC before the end of the year. Beyond that, the build-up of the Joint Lightning Force appears slow with a training unit, 207 Squadron, forming at Marham in 2019 and assuming that task from 2020. 809 Naval Air Squadron (NAS), announced with such pride by the then First Sea Lord in September 2013, is not even due to begin forming until 2021 for IOC in 2023, a decade later. The decision to operate the British F-35Bs as a joint force is arguably the weakest link in the re-creation of a strike carrier capability because units will be expected to operate from both land and sea, like Joint Force Harrier (JFH) prior to 2010. Land operations dominated that force's activities, causing embarkations of limited duration and making carrier operating skills hard to maintain. No other nation has gambled its security on carriers that lack dedicated air wings; if the idea had any merit they would surely have done so. It is worth mentioning words by Sir Thomas Inskip the Minister for Defence Coordination who directed, in 1937, that carrier-borne aircraft should in future always be an integral part of the RN. He said that such aircraft '… not only co-operate with the fleet, they are an integral part of it' and that 'The air unit in a carrier or a capital ship is a great deal more than a passenger in a convenient vehicle. It forms part of the organisation of the ship … and is its raison d'être'. A joint squadron based ashore on operations for any length of time, therefore, may have important duties to fulfil but it cannot remain part of the organisation of a strike carrier and nor can that ship's company train effectively for its primary role.

British and US Marine Corps F-35B Lightning II strike fighters engage in aerial manoeuvres over the east coast of England in July 2016; the type's first visit to the UK. The first aircraft from the Royal Air Force's 617 Squadron arrived at RAF Marham in June 2018 to establish a permanent British presence of the type. Trials of instrumented test aircraft onboard the new carrier *Queen Elizabeth* were also expected to commence off the United States' eastern seaboard in the second half of the year. *(Crown Copyright 2016)*

Another embryonic element of *Queen Elizabeth*'s air wing is 849 NAS's 'Crowsnest' airborne surveillance and control system (ASaC); a podded version of the Cerberus mission system that can replace anti-submarine warfare equipment in Merlin HM2s. The last of 849 NAS' Sea King ASaC7s will be withdrawn from service before the end of 2018. By then the first of the Merlins modified to 'Crowsnest' standard will be flying and aircrew training on the new type commenced. Reportedly six Merlins are to be fitted with 'Crowsnest' at any one time, allowing 849 NAS to run training courses for ASaC observers at Culdrose and deploy a front-line detachment to the operational carrier. Further sets in storage could convert more Merlins but even six Merlins in the ASaC role would leave only twenty-four in the anti-submarine role split between the training squadron, 824 NAS, and two front-line units, 820 and 814 NAS. The former is committed to *Queen Elizabeth* and has been embarked during 2018; the latter covers all other Merlin tasks including, since the disbandment of 829 NAS in early 2018, the deployment of flights to auxiliaries and frigates.

A French *Marine Nationale* Rafale M from Flotilla 17F seen embarked on the US Navy aircraft carrier *Abraham Lincoln* (CVN-72) on 10 May 2018. French Rafale and Hawkeye aircraft conducted training exercises on the US warship in the spring of 2018 to prepare for the return of their sole carrier – *Charles de Gaulle* – to operational service after a midlife refit. The deployment also served to improve interoperability between the two air arms. *(US Navy)*

FRANCE

The French CVN *Charles de Gaulle* will complete a major maintenance period and nuclear refuelling around the end of 2018. In the interim, her air wing of Rafale M omni-role fighters and E-2C Hawkeye airborne early warning aircraft embarked in the USS *George H. W. Bush* (CVN-77) in May 2018 as part of its work-up. Captain Jean-Emmanuel Roux-de-Luze told a press conference in Washington that the French navy wants more than carrier qualification from the deployment; it wants to demonstrate the ability to operate seamlessly with the USN in high intensity carrier operations. Roux-de-Luze added that joint operations build trust among navies and the French Navy is proud of the fact that it is ninety-five percent interoperable with the USN.

In February 2018 the French Government announced a modernisation programme for its armed forces. The total number of *Armée de l'Air* and *Marine Nationale* Rafales is to be increased from 143 to 171 by the end of 2025, although the number of navy jets will remain broadly unchanged at forty-two (compared with forty-one currently). Significantly, a fifth tranche of Rafales to be ordered in 2023 for delivery from 2030, will be built to an enhanced F4 standard to which older airframes will be upgraded. Procurement is also to be initiated for

an eventual E-2C replacement and studies will commence on a replacement carrier programme. These will also look at the possibility of returning to continuous carrier availability through constriction of a second ship. Despite having only one aircraft carrier which has been in refit since 2017, the *Aeronavale* remains an impressive, respected and well-equipped force.

INDIA

India's current sole carrier, *Vikramaditya* (the former Russian *Admiral Gorshkov*), is the key element of the surface navy and recent exercises including her have reflected a shift in Indian policy towards blue water operations in the wider ocean areas of the Asia Pacific region. The IN plans to establish two carrier task forces with the second based on the 40,000-ton indigenous *Vikrant II* which is expected to become operational in the 2020s. *Vikramaditya* is able to operate about twenty-four Mig-29K strike fighters but *Vikrant II*, built to a later and more efficient design, possibly up to thirty. Both ships have 'ski-jumps' and use the short take-off but arrested recovery (STOBAR) operating technique.

The Indian navy hopes to bring into service a second indigenous aircraft carrier, IAC-II – provi-

sionally named *Vishal* – by the late 2020s. It envisages a c. 65,000-ton ship capable of operating over 50 jets and fitted with catapults and arrester gear. Previous plans to procure the lightweight Indian Tejas fighter have been scrapped in favour of purchasing a foreign-sourced, twin-engined multi-role carrier-borne fighter that will better suit the potential capability offered by IAC-II. Both the Boeing F/A-18E/F and the Dassault Rafale M are said to be amongst the types under consideration. However, the protracted design and construction of *Vikrant II* has shown how difficult such projects can be and India is therefore seeking a strategic industrial partner to help with *Vishal*. Information about technology transfer has been requested from several international firms and a government-to-government agreement has been signed with the United States to share research and technology for an aircraft carrier to meet Indian requirements. It has reportedly already offered to make EMALS available and, as the world leader in nuclear power plants for aircraft carriers, might also offer this technology to enhance relations with India. However, recent reports cast doubt on whether *Vishal* will adopt nuclear propulsion, with IEP also under serious consideration. Whatever the outcome and with or without US technical assistance, making *Vishal* a reality will cost billions of dollars spread over at least a decade.

CHINA

The development of Chinese naval aviation has been another key theme of *World Naval Review*'s first ten years. Even a year ago, defence analysts were commenting that the Chinese People's Liberation Army Navy (PLAN) would need time to learn how best to co-ordinate carrier-borne aircraft within an effective task force. However, in early 2018 *Liaoning* deployed to the disputed South China Sea at the heart of a task force comprising about fifty warships and auxiliaries. Her notional air wing reportedly comprises twenty-four J-15 strike fighters, six Z-18F anti-submarine helicopters and four Z-18J AEW helicopters as well as a SAR flight of Z-9 helicopters, although it seems unlikely from published imagery that a full complement of aircraft was embarked on this occasion. The Z-18s are versions of the French SA-321 Super Frelon built under licence and the Z-9 is a licence-built version of the AS365 Dauphin. The point the analysts missed was determination; the PLAN is determined to develop efficient carrier task forces; setting targets and then working to achieve them at sea is a good way of making progress.

The PLAN launched its second carrier in 2017, an improved version of *Liaoning* designated as Type 001A. She subsequently departed China Shipbuilding Industry Corporation's Dalian yard on Sunday 13 May to commence preliminary sea trials. Reportedly named *Shandong* the new ship is reported to displace up to 70,000 tons and is also to be capable of operating twenty-four J-15 strike fighters using the STOBAR operating system. Modifications over the first vessel include installation of a Type 346 series multifunction radar similar to that used in the latest Type 052D destroyers and a significant re-arrangement of the ship's island structure to position the navigating bridge and flying control position in different decks.

Local reports suggest a third carrier was laid down in late 2017 at Shanghai Jiangnan Shipyard that is expected to differ significantly from the Type 001A. Designated the Type 002, it is said to have a displacement of about 80,000 tons, be conventionally powered and designed from the outset to have catapults and arrester wires so that it can launch a wider range of fighter, electronic warfare, AEW and tanker aircraft. Senior Chinese officers were initially

The People's Liberation Army Navy (PLAN) aircraft carrier *Liaoning* pictured in Hong Kong waters in July 2017. She has deployed more widely as the PLAN has become increasingly confident in carrier operations, conducting task group exercises with other PLAN vessels in the South China Sea in the early months of 2018. A half-sister – reportedly named *Shandong* – commenced initial trials in May 2018. *(Baycrest - Wikipedia user - CC-BY-SA-2.5)*

said to be concerned that the Type 002 was unable to generate sufficient electrical power for an indigenous EMALS without a nuclear power plant. However, according to an article in the South China Morning Post a team led by China's top naval engineer, Rear Admiral Ma Wei Ming, has developed a medium voltage, direct current (DC) transmission network to replace an earlier alternating current (AC) system which has solved the problem. Wang Ping, an expert in military technology at the Institute of Electrical Engineering in the Chinese Academy of Sciences in Beijing has reportedly said that the innovative design means that high energy consuming launch systems and weapons can now be used on a vessel driven by a conventional power plant. He added that this '… wasn't just a simple switch from AC to DC but a complete overhaul of the energy supply and distribution system – from steam boilers to the energy storage device'. A naval expert said to be close to the carrier project has confirmed that the as yet un-named Type 002 is being built with the new power option.[7]

Other reports suggest that, by 2030, the PLAN intends to have four aircraft carriers in service. Some defence analysts see this as a direct challenge to the United States. There is, however, an alternative way of looking at Chinese ambitions; China has always played the long game and may simply plan to inherit naval supremacy in the Pacific from the USN as its economy expands more quickly than that of its larger rival.

RUSSIA

Notwithstanding reports over the past few years that the Russian government is planning a replacement carrier programme, *Admiral Kuznetsov* remains the only Russian aircraft carrier. Its deployment to the Eastern Mediterranean in 2016 was not a success with two fighters, a Su-33 and a Mig-29K, lost due to poor operating techniques and arrester gear failures. Since her return to the Northern Fleet, *Admiral Kuznetsov*'s air wing has been disembarked to Khumeimim Air Base near Latakia to continue operations ashore. In late 2017 Sergei Vlasov, director general of the Nevsky PKB shipyard, told TASS news agency that the carrier's full modernisation will not now take place. Instead, the ship is to receive a more limited upgrade from 2018 onwards restricted to the replacement of four out of the ship's eight turbo-pressurised boilers, overhauling the other four and work to make the remaining machinery safe to operate. Even this relatively modest package is expected to take the shipyard two to three years to complete and there are reports that more extensive work has not been authorised because a deep modernisation might drag on for a decade

ITALY

Despite ongoing financial difficulties, the Italian navy still plans to receive fifteen F-35Bs out of the ninety 'A' and 'B' models that are to be assembled at the Italian final assembly and check out (FACO) facility. The first *Marina Militare* F-35B flew in STOVL mode on 18 January 2018 and then deployed across the Atlantic to NAS Patuxent River, Maryland for electromagnetic environmental certification before moving to MCAS Beaufort, South Carolina where it will be used to train Italian naval pilots and technicians alongside their USMC equivalents. After personnel training, Italian naval F-35Bs are to be based at NAS Grottaglie, near Taranto in south-eastern Italy where they are to work towards IOC as an AV-8B replacement. The navy plans to have *Cavour*, its only aircraft carrier, fully capable of operating up to twelve F-35Bs by 2023.[8]

BIG-DECK AMPHIBIOUS SHIPS AND THEIR AIRCRAFT

In the first *World Naval Review* the latent potential of big-deck amphibious ships with STOVL fighters embarked to operate as light aircraft carriers was mentioned. The USMC took this concept a step nearer reality on 5 March 2018 when six F-35Bs of Marine Fighter Attack Squadron (VMFA) 121, the 'Green Knights', embarked in *Wasp* (LHD-1) from MCAS Iwakuni in Japan for their first operational deployment. Later in 2018 VMFA-211, the 'Avengers', will embark in *Essex* from its base at MCAS Yuma, Arizona. VMFA-121 aircraft have Block 2 software but VMFA-211 has Block 3F. By the end of 2024 the USMC plans to have F-35B detachments deployed in eight amphibious assault ships.

Speaking in March 2018 at the National Defense Industrial Association's 2018 Expeditionary Warfare Division annual meeting, General Robert Neller, USMC Commandant said that the F-35B '… will prove invaluable as the service shifts away from ground-based conflicts in Iraq and land-locked Afghanistan back to its traditional role as a sea

The US Navy's amphibious assault ship *Wasp* (LHD-1) pictured refuelling the destroyer *Dewey* (DDG-105) on 12 April 2018. *Wasp* had embarked six F-35B Lightning II STOVL variants the previous month on their first operational deployment – five of these aircraft can be seen ranged on her flight deck aft of her island superstructure. Other aircraft present include MV-22 Osprey tilt-rotors and CH-53E Super Stallion heavy lift helicopters, as well as a single MH-60 series helicopter at No. 6 operating spot. *(US Navy)*

fighting force. The fighter's extended range and data collection capabilities can provide targeting information from far beyond the current range of amphibious warships and give Marines better eyes on the battlefield'. 'We have to be able to survive as part of sea denial … we are part of the fleet' he added. Speaking later off the cuff, Neller expressed the view that amphibious ships need upgraded command, control and networking systems to fully exploit the operational capabilities that the F-35 is beginning to demonstrate. Rear Admiral Ronald Boxall, Director of Navy Surface Warfare, agreed and said that the USN is looking at ways to carry out long-range intelligence, surveillance, reconnaissance and targeting to further the distributed lethality concept and absorbing amphibious forces into the network would go some way towards this.

US amphibious warfare seems to be in a strong place in 2018 with development of the CH-53K King Stallion heavy-lift helicopter progressing well. The first helicopter was delivered at Marine Corps Air Station New River on 16 May 2018. Sikorsky is expected to deliver twenty-four a year after full-rate production is authorised from 2020. Meanwhile, Cobham is starting to deliver V-22 aerial refuelling

system (VARS) kits from 2018, enabling MV-22s to operate from big-deck amphibious ships as air-to-air refuelling tankers to extend the radius of embarked F-35Bs. Measures have also begun to reduce over seventy distinct sub-variants of the MV-22 in service during 2018 to less than five in future through the Common Configuration-Readiness and Modernisation (CC-RAM) Programme. Improvements introduced into different production-line batches have now become problematical and even within a single squadron, aircraft might have different configurations, safety and mission capabilities and even differing spare part catalogues. Initially CC-RAM is to pass about 130 MV-22s through Boeing's Philadelphia production line for about eight months each. They are to be stripped down and refurbished to the latest production standard.

Another example of growing Franco-US cooperation occurred in December 2017, when about 1,000 sailors and marines from the USA and France took part in the annual Alligator Dagger exercise off the coast of Djibouti. This was the first time France had participated in this previously unilateral exercise. Personnel from the French amphibious assault ship *Tonnerre*, the USMC 5th Marine Expeditionary

Brigade and the new expeditionary sea base *Lewis B. Puller* (ESB-3) rehearsed amphibious operations and combat sustainment at sea and ashore. Brigadier General Francis Donovan who commands TF 51/5 described the exercise as a '… continuation of the professional development of our forces, allies and partner nations to further our efforts toward ensuring regional stability, freedom of navigation and the free flow of commerce within one of the most dynamic regions of the world'. He added that 'while naval integration is the foundation of TF 51/5's effectiveness and success, partnering with French land and maritime forces in Alligator Dagger represents an expansion of naval integration to include partners and allies'.

The Australian Defence Force (ADF) reached full operational capability with its *Canberra* class LHD type amphibious assault ships in 2018. The ADF decided early on that it was too small to create its own Marine Corps so a hybrid has been adopted that relies on some full-time experts and some rotating units. 2 Royal Australian Regiment (RAR) was selected to be the permanent force that conducts pre-landing activities and about 300 soldiers serve as the command and control element, small boat operators, reconnaissance and snipers that go ashore in small boats, a communications element and a logistics element. The actual ground combat unit that will be taken ashore for the fight is rotated each year and a series of exercises serve as training and certification events. Sea Explorer assesses command and control, Sea Horizon ensures that soldiers are proficient at embarking and debarking by surface craft and helicopters and Sea Raider is an overall demonstration of amphibious capability that certifies units as ready to deploy. Most embarked helicopters will be MRH-90 Taipans of the Army Air Corps but the RAN has its own MRH-90 unit, 808 NAS, which specialises in core amphibious skills.

Meanwhile, Japan has developed a new amphibious rapid deployment brigade. Like Australia, Japan has no marines. However, the Japan Ground Self Defence Force (GSDF) has built up the 2,100-man unit based at Camp Ainoura in Sasebo as part of a major re-organisation following tensions with China in the East China Sea. It comprises a main amphibious unit, a landing craft unit and plans to use V-22 Osprey tilt-rotors when they are delivered from the United States. Elements of the force and the V-22s when they enter service are to be capable of operating from the JMSDF's helicopter

The first CH-53K King Stallion heavy lift helicopter was delivered to the US Marine Corps on 16 May 2018. The new helicopter has much greater lifting capacity than current CH-53E Super Stallions. It is hoped to gain initial operational capability in the course of 2019. *(Lockheed Martin)*

carriers and the brigade's primary purpose is said to be the protection of Japan's remote southern islands against incursion.

France and Russia terminated their agreement on the construction and delivery of two *Mistral* class amphibious helicopter carriers in 2015 as a result of Russia's role in the Ukrainian conflict. The completed ships were sold to Egypt but technical details of the design had been given to Russia for the construction of two further *Mistral*s in Russian ship-yards. Press reports in 2017 claimed that Russia intends to make use of that data to assist with construction of helicopter carriers in the State Armament Programme for 2018–27 (GPV2027). More details emerged in 2018 with Zvezda, the military's official television network, mentioning two ships, known as the *Lavina* class. They will be able to operate up to twelve Ka-52 or anti-submarine helicopters, four Project 11770M or two Project 12061M landing craft from a stern dock with a landing force of up to 500 Marines, thirty main battle tanks and sixty light armoured vehicles. However, limited official reports on the final outcome of the GPV2027 have made no reference to the programme. Accordingly, as for the proposed Project 23000 'Shtorm' aircraft carrier and Project 23560 'Lider' destroyer, the *Lavina* class may remain a 'paper project' for the foreseeable future.

The Royal Navy's *Ocean* was formally de-commissioned in Portsmouth by Her Majesty Queen Elizabeth II on 27 March 2018. She entered service in 1998 with a design life of twenty years so her demise was not unexpected. However, it leaves the RN without a dedicated LPH-type helicopter carrier. She has been sold to Brazil for a reported price of £85m (US$115m) and will be delivered after a refit. Her role in the Brazilian Navy is not yet announced but she is capable of operating a range of assault, utility and anti-submarine helicopters. *Queen Elizabeth* and *Prince of Wales* will replace some of the lost amphibious capability, although they lack *Ocean*'s personnel landing craft. Their main amphibious role will be to operate Merlin HC4 helicopters of the RN's Commando Helicopter Force (CHF), with *Queen Elizabeth* set to achieve both naval and battlefield helicopter IOC in late 2018. CHF is part of the Joint Helicopter Command, which also includes Army Air Corps Wildcats and Apaches together with RAF Chinooks and all these types are expected to deploy operationally on the *Queen Elizabeth* class carriers in due course.

The Royal Australian Navy amphibious assault ship *Adelaide* pictured deploying a mobile hospital in one of her landing craft during a humanitarian assistance and disaster relief exercise off Timor Leste in September 2017. The two amphibious assault ships are now both fully operational. *(Australian Department of Defence)*

The British Royal Navy's veteran LPH-type helicopter carrier *Ocean* pictured at Portsmouth in February 2018. She was decommissioned on 27 March 2018 and has been sold to Brazil. *(Conrad Waters)*

Sea King HC4s operated by the CHF with success for many years were withdrawn from service in 2016, replaced by twenty-five former RAF Merlin HC3s which are being upgraded and made carrier-compatible as HC4s. The first aircraft modified to the new standard was delivered by Leonardo Helicopters in 2017 and the last is due to be delivered in 2020. Seven HC3s were modified to an interim HC3i standard to give some embarked capability until sufficient HC4s are available. The HC4 has a 'glass cockpit' similar to that of the HM2, a power-folding main rotor head and tail pylon together with improved communications and defensive aids. Unlike their predecessors they are painted grey like other naval helicopters and from 2020 845 NAS is to have ten deployable Merlins in up to three flights; 846 NAS is also to have ten with an operational conversion/training flight, a maritime counter-terrorism flight and a third flight capable of embarking to back up 845. The balance of five airframes are to be used to give flexibility for deep maintenance and as attrition reserves.

SEA CONTROL HELICOPTERS

The US Navy's WEST 2018 Conference in San Diego during February 2018 stimulated discussion about how to work unmanned aircraft into the sea control community. Panellist Commander Chris Richards believed that there were unlikely to be many new missions but that there would be a transformational evolution of existing data streams with faster processing capability and network distribution. Commander Aaron Taylor, requirements officer for the MH-60S, added that the surface community is pleased with the performance of the MQ-8B Fire Scout which delivers over-the-horizon targeting, threat detection, intelligence gathering and battle damage assessment in real time over significant distances. Both agreed that the MH-60 will need to be replaced one day and Taylor felt that the naval helicopter of the future will emerge as a chassis and propulsion system with different digital equipment fits for a variety of roles.

In April 2018 the USN declared the armed MQ-8B as being operational and ready for deployment to Littoral Combat Ships (LCS) but that these ships need their weapons-storage arrangements to be reconfigured to embark the unmanned helicopter's potential range of weapons. Captain Jeff Dodge, Fire Scout programme manager, briefed the Navy League 2018 Sea/Air/Space Exposition that the logistics problem was identified when a demonstration embarkation had been carried out. MQ-8B can carry the BAE Systems advanced precision kill weapon system (APKWS) and modified 70mm Hydra rockets fitted with a guidance system. The latter has to be assembled before use in an armoury and the LCS lacks suitable space, having only one magazine that is used to store all the ship's ammunition including any used by the embarked helicopters. Studies have looked at solutions but there is, as yet, no clear way forward. The problem will soon be exacerbated by the arrival in service of the larger MQ-8C with double the weapons capacity. The US Navy plans to have MQ-8s aboard all its LCS variants by the early 2020s with more on the FFG(X) future frigate and destroyers with upgraded air facilities. The MQ-8C is to be fitted with a Leonardo Osprey 30 active electronically-scanned array (AESA) radar and Link 16 datalink to distribute air-to-air and surface ship target engagement data to surface action groups. It is to be integrated with the Minotaur track management and mission control system that combines information from a variety sensors, including P-8A Poseidon patrol aircraft and MQ-4C Tritons, to create a unified, co-ordinated target picture for battle group commanders. Around thirty MQ-8Cs have been ordered to date to support the LCS fleet.

Norway decided in early 2018 that it could not use its NH-90 helicopters as originally intended. Fourteen were ordered in 2001, the last is due for delivery in 2019, and it was intended that they should achieve 5,400 flying hours per year between them split between SAR, fishery protection and coastguard border patrol duties based ashore and frigate-based anti-submarine tasks. However, further analysis suggests that only 2,100 hours can be achieved realistically and a report has concluded that re-assessment is needed. Admiral Haakon Bruun-

Two MQ-8C Fire Scout helicopters sit in the hangar bay of the *Independence* class Littoral Combat Ship *Montgomery* (LCS-8) during trials of the larger MQ-8 series unmanned aerial vehicle in April 2017. Its greater weapons-carrying capacity will exacerbate munitions-storage problems already discovered with the smaller MQ-8B type's deployment in Littoral Combat Ships. *(US Navy)*

Hanssen, Head of the Norwegian Armed Forces, has recommended they should be prioritised for frigate operations '...because the helicopter is a weapon platform that is crucial to the frigate's ability to detect and fight submarines'. While the anti-submarine mission cannot be performed by another platform, he noted, the coastguard requirements could be met by civilian helicopters or unmanned systems. The Norwegian Ministry of Defence is expected to consider the report's findings before making its final decision later in 2018 or 2019.[9]

Test firings of the Anglo-French MBDA Sea Venom anti-ship missile from a Dauphin test helicopter have been successful and the RN plans to equip its Wildcat HMA2 fleet with the new 110kg weapon from 2020 onwards. It is a 'fire and forget' weapon, relying on inertial navigation and terminal infrared guidance that give the target no early warning of its approach. The RN has been without a helicopter-launched anti-ship missile since the Lynx was retired and, surprisingly, the RN Wildcat still lacks a datalink system such as Link 16 and relies on voice radio to pass target information to other platforms.

A Norwegian NH90 helicopter pictured landing on the frigate *Thor Heyerdahl* during Exercise Flotex 2017 on 16 November 2017. The Norwegian Armed Forces have determined that it will not be practical to use the NH90 as intensively as first envisaged; accordingly frigate operations will be prioritised. (*Jakob Østheim/Norwegian Armed Forces*)

MARITIME PATROL AIRCRAFT

The P-8A Poseidon's development was a classic example of the US Navy's practical approach to aircraft procurement, using the tried and tested airframe and engines of the Boeing 737 to give an airframe that has the economy of scale but is fitted with the latest sensors, computers and networking systems. The design and development phase was completed on time, within budget in 2013 and the type has now re-equipped more than half the navy's patrol squadrons. The Indian Navy became the second P-8 operator – its P-8I having a slightly different equipment fit – and the Royal Australian Air Force was the third using P-8As identical to those of the USN and carrying American weapons including Mark 54 torpedoes.

Lieutenant Commander Karl Murray of VP-8 Squadron which deployed an aircraft to the 2018 Singapore Air Show described the P-8A as being more reliable than the P-3C Orion that it replaced, stating that its greater speed allows it to get on station faster. In turn this gives it longer on station and patrol time is to increase still further as air-to-air refuelling becomes routine.[10] All P-8As are delivered by Boeing equipped for aerial refuelling because the design incorporated features used in other military 737

applications and in February 2018 the USN cleared it to receive fuel from USAF KC-135 aerial tankers, allowing Poseidons to remain airborne for up to eighteen hours, the running limit of type's CFM-56 engine oil system. Other tanker aircraft are expected to be certified by the end of 2018 and both Australia and the UK are expected to certify their own P-8s for aerial refuelling. The RAAF also had a P-8 on static display at the Singapore Air Show and in March 2018 it announced that P-8As of its 11 Squadron had performed so well that they had achieved IOC five months ahead of the original schedule. The RAAF has ordered twelve Poseidons and has also committed to acquiring six unmanned MQ-4C Tritons to work alongside them from 2023 onwards under plans announced in June 2018.

The UK Ministry of Defence (MOD) announced in late 2017 that two RAF squadrons, 120 and 201, are to operate the P-8A, both based at RAF Lossiemouth in Scotland where a new hangar costing £132m (c. US$175m) is being built for them together with a tactical operations centre, squadron accommodation, training simulators and aircraft maintenance facilities. 120 Squadron began to form in April 2018 and is to be followed by 201 in 2021. Both will have aircrew trained by the USN and all nine aircraft have been ordered with the first

due in 2019. Like the RAAF, the RAF is to operate aircraft identical to the USN standard, allowing both to take advantage of US spiral improvements as they are developed. To hold down costs, both are to use US weapons, sonobuoys and other consumables and orders for initial quantities have been placed. The USA, UK and Norway – the fifth Poseidon customer – have agreed in principle to create a trilateral coalition built around P-8A operations in the North Atlantic. The deal apparently involves joint operations, information sharing and the possibility of sharing maintenance and training assets.

The second US Navy ocean surveillance platform is the unmanned MQ-4C Triton. VUP-19, the 'Big Red', began to form with the type in 2016 at NAS Jacksonville in Florida and in 2018 will achieve what the USN termed early operational capability (EOC) when a flight of two aircraft will be deployed to Andersen Air Force Base in Guam. Triton programme manager Captain Dan Mackin gave a briefing at the 2018 Navy League Sea/Air/Space Exposition in which he said that the MQ-4C is expected to reach IOC in 2021 when two more aircraft are added to the Guam flight. Four air vehicles are needed to make up one 24-hour, seven-day orbit; one on the way out, one on station, one on the way back and one in maintenance. The first air vehicles have electro-optical sensors and radar to track maritime targets from as high as 60,000 feet and compare them with automated identification systems. Information is relayed back to one of two main operating bases in the United States, one at Naval Station Mayport in Florida and the other at NAS Whidbey Island in Washington. Data can also be streamed to nearby P-8A aircraft and task forces. Part of the IOC process includes adding a top-secret 'multi-intelligence' function that will allow MQ-4Cs to eventually replace Navy EP-3E Aries II manned signals intelligence platforms. Congress has mandated that the Navy can only retire the EP-3E after a similar capability has demonstrated the ability to replace it. Eventually Tritons are to be capable of maintaining five four-aircraft orbits around the world. Their operators reside at Mayport and Whidbey Island but small parties will be forward-based with each flight to oversee the take-off and landing phases of flight and carry out maintenance. The forward bases have been named as Sigonella in Italy, Guam, Mayport, Point Mugu in California

and an as-yet unspecified location in the Middle East. A second squadron, VUP-11, is due to be formed to share the operating task with VUP-19.

CONCLUDING REMARKS

Naval aviation and its evolution over the past decade have been fascinating subjects to follow. The US Navy's pragmatic approach to aircraft development has been very successful with the F/A-18E/F, EA-18G, E-2D, MH-60R/S and P-8A standing out as prime examples of what can be achieved within budget and to a specified time scale when projects are carefully considered and taken forward one step at a time. On the other hand, more complex joint projects – exemplified by the F-35B variants – have taken far longer to develop than anyone imagined a decade ago. Such transformational aspirations also added to the build time and cost of the new *Ford* class carriers However, despite repeated calls for smaller, cheaper carriers to be evaluated, the US Navy continues to see the value of its CVN fleet and has undoubtedly maintained its world leadership in the technologies

that underpin it. More negatively, recent budget restrictions have dramatically reduced aircraft support infrastructure, especially the provision of spare parts, to levels where it has proved difficult to keep the majority of front-line fighters in a deployable state. Lack of spares and higher than anticipated operational usage rates have combined to inflict a fighter shortage on the US Navy and Marine Corps that is proving both difficult and expensive to resolve. This problem needs to be overcome before the US Navy begins President Trump's projected expansion.

The fortunes of naval aviation elsewhere have been more mixed. When the Royal Navy's Sea Harriers were prematurely retired in 2006 in one of the British government's less-well considered measures, it was assumed that F-35Bs would begin to replace them in about four years; under present plans an operational squadron will not embark until 2021 and then it will be a joint unit on a part-time basis. The total collapse of carrier aviation as a result of the 2010 defence review was certainly a major surprise and has resulted in a struggle to keep relevant experience alive on the basis of significant help from the US Navy. By contrast, the determined expansion of Chinese carrier aviation over the same time-frame has impressed analysts by the pace at which it is being carried forward. The French navy also stands out as a force that knows what it wants and is determined to achieve it without constant changes of direction; despite its relatively small size, it is probably closest to the USN in terms of capability. The Russian navy, however, seems unable to make progress and its sole carrier is of questionable value. If its planned refit is completed it must concentrate on training, maintenance and the perfection of technique to become a viable force capable of projecting power. India has made some progress but is finding the technology of carrier construction difficult to master.

For the author, the most striking change over the past decade has been the development of networked digital systems within the US Navy, of which NIFC-CA is a prime example. These are helping to build a cyber-domain in which a range of autonomous unmanned air vehicles such as the MQ-8B/C, MQ-4C and, in the near future, the MQ-25A tanker are expected to play a significant role. Like other 'tail-hookers', the author was fascinated to watch footage of the X-47B unmanned demonstrator landing on a carrier in 2013 and looks forward to seeing this technology used operationally at sea in the decade ahead. We are reaching the point where networked digital

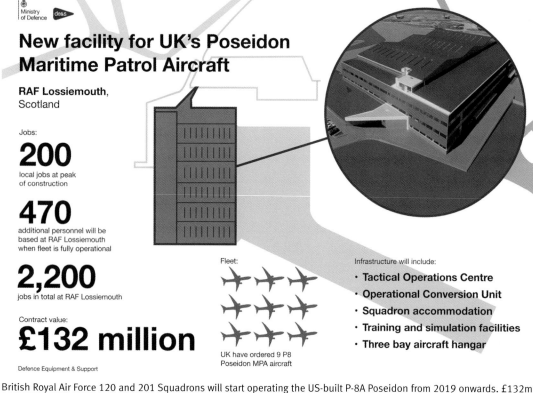

Ministry of Defence des

New facility for UK's Poseidon Maritime Patrol Aircraft

RAF Lossiemouth, Scotland

Jobs:

200
local jobs at peak of construction

470
additional personnel will be based at RAF Lossiemouth when fleet is fully operational

2,200
jobs in total at RAF Lossiemouth

Contract value:

£132 million

Defence Equipment & Support

Fleet:

UK have ordered 9 P8 Poseidon MPA aircraft

Infrastructure will include:
- **Tactical Operations Centre**
- **Operational Conversion Unit**
- **Squadron accommodation**
- **Training and simulation facilities**
- **Three bay aircraft hangar**

British Royal Air Force 120 and 201 Squadrons will start operating the US-built P-8A Poseidon from 2019 onwards. £132m has been invested in new infrastructure at Lossiemouth in Scotland to support the nine aircraft that are being acquired. *(Crown Copyright 2017)*

19. A MQ-4C Triton unmanned surveillance aircraft from Unmanned Patrol Squadron (VUP) 19 coming into land at Naval Base Ventura County, Point Mugu in November 2017. The UAV was officially welcomed into service at a ceremony held at the base on 31 May 2018. Aircraft from the squadron will achieve early operational capability in the course of 2018 when two MQ-4Cs are deployed to Guam. (US Navy)

systems really are changing the way war over, on and under the sea will be fought. Aircraft should no longer be thought of as platforms in their own right but as part of a system of inter-linked computers with combined access to sensors, weapons and an 'archive' of data about the enemy. Each will add information to the whole construct from different but interdependent parameters that benefit from variations in geographical position, altitude, speed and time to locate, track and guide the most suitable weapon from any platform onto a hostile target. As these systems mature, aircraft will become more concerned with connectivity than individual performance and the need for a man in the cockpit will become less and less important. The next decade is likely to be even more exciting than the last.

Notes

1. Further details of the US Navy's future shipbuilding programmes are contained in Chapter 2.1. The CBO report written by Eric J. Labbs was entitled *Comparing a 355-Ship Fleet With Smaller Naval Forces* (Washington DC: CBO, 2018) and can be found at: cbo.gov/publication/ 53637.

2. The ongoing discussions as to whether or not to adopt a two-ship acquisition for CVN-80 and CVN-81 have been covered in a series of articles by Megan Eckstein on the *USNI News* website. See: news.usni.org/tag/cvn-81

3. Although the original FY2018 Presidential Budget Request saw a significant drop in planned aircraft procurement, the US Congress added budgetary appropriations for no fewer than sixty additional aircraft, taking the total to 151. In practice, therefore, actual FY2018 aircraft procurement was broadly in line with that for recent years. Programmes to benefit included F-18E/F Super Hornet and F-35 Lightning II carrier aircraft, whilst production of MH-60R sea control and MQ-8C unmanned rotorcraft was extended.

4. Naval Integrated Fire Control-Counter Air (NIFC-CA) is a form of cooperative engagement capability (CEC) that seeks to combine aircraft and ship-based weapons and sensors into an integrated network to improve air defence capabilities. It was further described in last year's 'World Naval Aviation' overview.

5. When stripped down, many Hornets were found to be in a worse state than anticipated; no two required the same remedial work and each had to have an individual engineering management schedule. Until aircraft were opened up the number of broken parts could not be known and they could not be ordered until they were known because of budgetary restrictions. Depot capacity was also a factor as SLEP work displaced other important tasks, including work to bring early F-35s up to the latest standards. Accordingly, Captain David Kindley, F/A-18 and EA-18 Program Manager within Naval Air Systems Command, was reported as stating that the legacy Hornet SLEP 'is not in a state of production' as of mid-2018. In March 2018, a *Defense News* article by David B. Larter, available at: defensenews.com/naval/2018/03/06/ navy-to-scrap-scores-of-fighter-jets-from-its-inventory/, reported a total of 136 legacy Hornets would be scrapped over the next few years as their effective life was consumed.

6. See Chapter 3.2 for further information on the *Queen Elizabeth* class aircraft carriers' design and construction.

7. The report on the new carrier's innovative power system was written by Minnie Chan under the title 'New carrier to use breakthrough launch system' in the *South China Morning Post* – 1 November 2017 (Hong Kong: South China Morning Post Publishers Ltd, 2017). An online version is currently available at: scmp.com/news/china/ diplomacy-defence/article/2117947/breakthrough-power-most-advanced-jet-launch-system. Further reporting by Ms Chan on the third carrier includes an article entitled 'Work underway on third aircraft carrier, sources say' in the 4 January 2018 edition. See: scmp.com/news/china/ diplomacy-defence/article/2126883/china-has-started-building-its-third-aircraft-carrier.

8. The carrier *Giuseppe Garibaldi* also remains in service but is now primarily used for helicopter operations prior to being replaced by the new amphibious assault ship *Trieste* in the early 2020s.

9. Haakon Bruun-Hanssen was quoted in an article by Dominic Perry carried on the *FlightGlobal* website on 2 February 2018, currently available at: flightglobal.com/ news/articles/norway-runs-into-fresh-problem-with-nh90-helicopters-445470/

10. See Dzirhan Mahadzir's 'Navy P-8A Poseidon Expanding Operations in Asia' posted to the *USNI News* site on 14 February 2018 at: news.usni.org/2018/02/14/ navy-p-8a-poseidon-expanding-operations-asia

Author:
Norman Friedman

4.2 TECHNOLOGICAL REVIEW

MODERN NAVAL COMMUNICATIONS An Overview

If you look at a modern surface ship, it seems to sprout radomes – not for radars or for electronic countermeasures alone, but also for satellite dishes. They are the outward indication of a profound shift in naval warfare – at least in the West – towards operations beyond ships' horizons using information often collected centrally using what are now called national assets; things like reconnaissance satellites and big shore-based electronic intelligence collectors, in some cases even long-range over the horizon radars.[1]

Navies have always benefitted from centrally-collected intelligence, but in the past few decades the balance between what is collected at sea and what comes from a central headquarters seems to have changed dramatically. During the Second World War, for example, a US Navy carrier attacking a Japanese-held island relied mainly on her own photo aircraft for current intelligence, which was then processed on board in her intelligence centre. Other information might come from outside, for example concerning the island's defences. However, it was not easily brought aboard the carrier, and the ship's radios did not have the capacity to receive much of it. As late as the Vietnam War, the main development in carrier strike intelligence was computerisation to process what the carrier's big Vigilante reconnaissance aircraft could collect. The spectacular impact was that data on enemy radars collected in the morning could be used to redirect strike aircraft in the air a few hours later, because it could be processed and assessed much more rapidly.

Carriers still have their own ability to collect intelligence, particularly in the form of photographs, but a lot more of their strike planning is done using massive files downloaded from the United States or elsewhere. The difference between the 1960s and

The Japanese Maritime Self Defence Force's helicopter-carrying destroyer *Ise* pictured in company with the US Navy aircraft carrier *Nimitz* (CVN-68) on 12 November 2017. The plethora of radomes on both ships testify to the importance of centrally-collected intelligence to current maritime operations. *(US Navy)*

now is partly much more computer capacity aboard ship, but much more significantly a greater ability to pass information halfway around the world. For the future, the great question is whether that ability, which has changed naval warfare enormously, can be wrecked in a major war. Right now the information is carried by geo-synchronous satellites, hanging 23,000 miles or so above the major oceans. They are probably far too high to be destroyed by missiles, but there may still be other vulnerabilities. Moreover, their information is keyed to locations on the earth, which means that it is much less useful without the precision navigation (mainly via GPS) we now take for granted. The constellation of GPS satellites is a lot closer to the earth. How vulnerable are they?

HISTORICAL BACKGROUND

The current naval world is dramatically different from the past. Western naval tradition was shaped by the *lack* of easy communication. Now only submariners feel themselves cut off from easy contact, and even that is open to some question.[2] It can even be argued that a key reason naval officers think much more independently than their army brethren is that their culture harks back to a world without instant or even quick communication. In the age of sail a captain on a distant station could and did negotiate a treaty or fight a small war before the mail caught up with him, and long before his home government had much say in the matter. Once the home government was involved, it could decorate the captain or cashier him. If the government collected vital intelligence, it was always weeks or months late reaching the deployed captain.

Once radio made instant communication possible, the balance between the deployed commander and the headquarters at home changed. By 1914 the British Admiralty was an operational command centre, and the key question was how to balance what it knew against what a commander at sea understood. In both world wars, the Admiralty sprouted operational intelligence centres, and they

A US Navy RA-5C Vigilante reconnaissance aircraft pictured on the aircraft carrier *Kitty Hawk* (CV-63) during operations in the South China Sea in April 1966. Even as late as the 1960s, the use of computerisation to process data collected by the big RA-5C made a huge improvement to US Navy carrier strike intelligence at a time when there were limitations on the amount of centralised information that could be received. *(US Naval Heritage & History Command)*

The Royal Navy nuclear-powered attack submarine *Trenchant* presents a lonely image whilst surfaced in the Arctic's Beaufort Sea during an ICEX with the US Navy in March 2018. Western naval tradition was shaped by lack of easy communication with centralised command; this still applies to underwater operations to some extent but technological developments mean even this isolation is being eroded. *(Crown Copyright 2018)*

Missouri (BB-63) pictured towards the end of the Second World War. The move towards centralised communications made itself felt in both world wars and ship equipment changed in consequence. Whip aerials are scattered over the ship's superstructure, but despite their separation they are subject to mutual interference. The ship also communicates at lower frequencies, using the wires strung between her masts. Short dipoles, which are barely visible, are for ship-to-ship communication (TBS) and for ship-aircraft communication. Although communication systems are nearly invisible, they are pervasive – and expensive to change. During the 1950s the shift from VHF (as in the Second World War) to UHF for short-range purposes was agonising, yet it had to cover the whole NATO fleet. One reason navies abandoned their reserve fleets was the huge cost of bringing older ships up to modern communication standards, without which they literally could not participate in operations. *(US Navy)*

Communications works both ways: the reliable link which makes operations work smoothly may also enable an enemy to understand what is going on. *Renshaw* (DDE-449), converted into a fast anti-submarine escort, shows an example: an HF/DF mast aft. This photo was taken in July 1951. *(US Navy)*

are now commonplace. Even so, the capacity to communicate by radio, particularly by secure radio, was limited. So a choice had to be made as to how much of this capacity should be used to provide information that would be of value to a forward-based commander, and how much should be used to provide orders based on what the Admiralty might know. An effective way had to be found to meld local intelligence with information that came from the Admiralty's different resources, which in both World Wars included effective code-breaking, as well as interpretation of the data this obtained.

The world wars show both success and failure. In 1916 poor interpretation of what had been gained may have contributed to the failure to bring the Battle of Jutland to a decisive conclusion. In 1941, during the *Bismarck* chase, raw signals intelligence in the form of radio bearings was sent. However, for a time the deployed fleet commander was frustrated by poor interpretation at his end: *Bismarck* almost got away. The following year, Convoy PQ 17 was destroyed because the First Sea Lord, acting as an operational commander, misinterpreted his intelligence. Worse, it seems clear that the local commander would have seen matters rather differently.

SATELLITE COMMUNICATIONS

The satellite domes so evident now are part of an attempt to do much better. Until the space age, the best long-haul communication system – the one which had to be used at great distances at sea – was high-frequency (HF) radio.[3] It exploited the fact that at some frequencies radio waves bounce off the

COMMUNICATIONS SYSTEMS INTERFERENCE: PROBLEMS & SOLUTIONS

A particular problem with the widespread deployment of communications systems was the problem of interference. This was a particular challenge when the US Navy commissioned the task force flagship *Northampton* (CLC-1), shown here in June 1962. She needed a lot more communication channels than other ships. The attempted solution was to use fewer antennas modified to handle a broader range of frequencies. Hence the use of the metal base for the two dipoles visible forward. By the time this photo was taken, *Northampton* was a national command post. The radar dish on her mast, visible forward of her bridge, was actually part of a communications system which bounced signals off the troposphere, reaching out about 200 miles. *(US Navy)*

Ships are such complicated shapes that it is difficult to analyse radio interference on board them. Once they are completed, it is too late. The US Navy, and probably others, used brass models for the purpose. Here a model is being completed for the Naval Electronics Laboratory in San Diego, in 1972; it is probably of a *Perry* (FFG-7) class frigate. *(US Navy)*

ionosphere, and thus can carry remarkable distances. Because the ionosphere varies, and because it can move up and down, communication is not entirely reliable, and operators must choose different frequencies at different times. Most importantly, the bouncing radio signals can take different paths, and signals sent along those paths can interfere. The classic method of overcoming such interference is to use relatively long pulses – before the computer age high frequency meant 75 pulses per second.[4] Several thousand times as fast has been considered a rather slow Internet rate for years.

The dishes are there because satellites offered something far better. The ionosphere offers windows through which much higher-frequency (radar frequency and above) signals can pass.[5] Much higher frequency meant much more information capacity per unit time. A communications satellite

typically simply repeats what it receives in its relatively narrow (as shaped by the dish) up-link and resends it, generally at a different frequency, in a wide-beam down-link.

Navies initially found satellite communication extremely attractive as much for the security it seemed to offer as for its capacity. Conventional radio could often be detected at great distances and intercepted signals could be used to locate moving ships. The Royal Navy located the fleeing German battleship *Bismarck* that way, though only after the misinterpretation referenced above nearly aborted the hunt. Similarly, high-frequency direction finding (HF/DF) became an invaluable Allied tool in the Battle of the Atlantic, because German U-boat strategy required so much communication. In the 1960s, the US Navy found that the Soviets were using HF/DF to locate its carrier strike groups.[6] It

and the Royal Navy learned to operate in relative radio silence.

It must have seemed that pointing a relatively narrow beam directly up towards a satellite would solve the interception problem. Unless an enemy was listing in just the right place, between ship and satellite, it would not even hear the signal, much less find whoever had sent it. It turned out that there was a rub. Although communications satellites are generally described as geo-stationary, i.e., as hanging in the sky in a static position, in fact they move slightly during the day, describing a figure-eight in the sky. This movement slightly shifts the frequency of the up-linked signal *as the satellite receives it*. How much the frequency is shifted depends on where the ship sending up the signal is. Because the satellite takes what it receives and sends it back at a different frequency, it imposes the frequency shift on what it sends. Frequency can be measured very precisely, so attention to the frequency shift reveals the approximate location of the sending ship. Radio direction-finding made its way into the space age in a different form.

Among those who discovered this rather useful property of satellite down-links were academics advising the Argentine Navy in 1982. Their efforts were crowned with success when an Argentine Boeing 707 airliner, operating as a reconnaissance aircraft, found the British fleet *en route* to the Falklands. The subsequent air attack failed, but it demonstrated a naval vulnerability not previously understood. The rather subtle new means of finding ships at sea despite their use of satellites seems to have taken some years to gain prominence. In 1987, for example, a British advocate demonstrated it by using it to track a US amphibious group across the Atlantic. It appears that the Russians used it to track the build-up before the first Iraq War in 1990–1.

The US government did appreciate the problem, and it invested in a new-generation military communication satellite system, Milstar. Unlike earlier communications satellites, it was fully digital. Instead of processing the up-link as an analogue signal (and thus preserving the frequency shift in it), Milstar handled it as a string of digits, which it re-encoded and down-linked. That eliminated the loca-

tion information in the up-link. Digital operation limited the capacity of the satellite, so it was reserved for the most essential traffic. Digital processing has certainly fallen dramatically in cost since Milstar was conceived in the 1980s, but space-certified chips (which have to withstand cosmic radiation) are not common, and their production fell off sharply at the end of the Cold War. Current satellites are not generally described as analogue or digital, so it is not clear how vulnerable navies are to down-link

tracking. There is probably a considerable gap between something like Milstar, which incorporates expensive anti-jam characteristics, and the commercial satellites many navies use.

Satellite communications became available on a growing scale as the balance between intelligence collected centrally and what was known on board a deployed ship changed. Beginning in the 1960s, at least in the United States and the Soviet Union, intelligence satellites collected a growing mass of

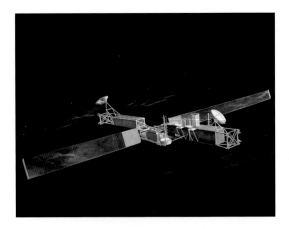

The realisation that it was possible for a potential adversary to locate ships communicating with analogue-based satellites resulted in the United States developing the Milstar series of digital satellites that eliminated the leakage of location information. This image shows a graphical representation of the first satellite in the series, which was launched by a Titan IV rocket in February 1994. Many navies still rely on commercial satellites that may be much less secure than the Milstar series. *(US Air Force)*

NATO DATA LINKS

NATO navies use and have used a variety of standardised data links, the content of which is generally computer-to-computer instructions with data attached. The instructions create the tactical pictures on the basis of which ships and aircraft fight. For a force to fight in a coordinated way, particularly against air and missile attack, it has to share a common tactical picture. That made data links a prerequisite for tactical coordination. When the US Navy adopted Link 11 in major units, it was extremely expensive because it required a powerful computer (by the standards of the 1960s) to turn the multi-frequency Link 11 messages into usable computer code. Navies which did not adopt Link 11 wholesale, like the British Royal Navy, employed gateway ships, such as the destroyer *Bristol*, which could join a Link 11 net and could translate their data into the less elaborate link (in this case, Link X) used by lesser ships. Link 11 became more and more widespread as computer power increased. For example, when they were built in the 1960s the US Navy *Charles F. Adams* (DDG-2) class destroyers were deemed too small to accommodate Link 11 and a computer combat direction system. Within a few years, however, the German version of the same ship had Link 11 and an associated combat system, and a decade later the austere *Perry* (FFG-7) class frigates had Link 11 and a combat direction system.[1]

After the Cold War Link 11 was adopted by NATO navies which had found it too expensive during the Cold War, because afterwards it was a prerequisite for effective cooperation in places like the Persian Gulf. This level of cooperation should be distinguished from the Internet -style communication that is now common.

Link systems incorporate a message structure (in

effect a vocabulary) which may or may not be sufficient. For example, as introduced in the 1960s, Link 11 characterised objects as either friendly, enemy, or unknown, presumed hostile. Many non-US NATO navies later added a neutral category. These categories were visible in the pictures created by the links on ships' computers. Link design also sets the number of ships or aircraft in the net, and the way in which they interact. The number generally depends on the cycle rate, the time it takes for a subscriber to come back up to send a new message. The tolerable rate depends on how much target motion the system can tolerate between refreshes. The faster an incoming target, the more rapidly the system as a whole has to update its position. Much depends on how well the positions of all the ships and aircraft in the net are coordinated (a problem called gridlock). A report from a subscriber whose position is not what it is supposed to be can add a spurious target to the tactical picture created by the net and thus waste effort. Gridlock was a terrible problem in early Link 11 nets, solved only in the late 1980s with the advent of more powerful computers. A prerequisite for Link 11 was precision navigation, which for many years meant the Ships Inertial Navigation System (SINS). In a Link 11 net, one ship acts as net controller, calling the roll to interrogate the other ships (if it is put out of action, another ship or aircraft can take over). Note that Internet-style communication is probably not an effective substitute for near-real time data links. The links in turn can be used to pass not only target data but also orders. When various NATO navies adopted the Link 11 used by the US Navy, they generally modified their version so that a US force commander could not issue orders which

data, including not only photographs but also electronic data showing where enemy forces might be. By the mid-1970s that included ships at sea. The Soviets led in deploying long-range anti-ship missiles, which would be useless without centrally-collected data beamed to the firing ships. After the Cold War, the United States often found itself firing long-range Tomahawk missiles. They would have been useless without current intelligence. Much the same is true of GPS-guided bombs, which are often dropped on targets pilots cannot see. It is difficult to imagine how a deployed naval strike group can attack land targets without exploiting reconnaissance information collected by a distant national headquarters, and provided via satellite links.

DATA LINKS AND CO-ORDINATION

This is aside from the question of how to co-ordinate seaborne forces, both those of one navy or of allied navies and those of ad hoc coalitions. When computers first came into general service in the 1960s, the US Navy and then other NATO navies used them for two connected purposes. One was to assemble a ship's tactical picture as a basis for action – to overcome the kind of saturation first experienced in 1945 when the Japanese adopted Kamikaze tactics. It took computers to assimilate the masses of data produced by radars observing masses of fast aircraft, not to mention air-launched missiles. The other purpose was to assimilate data from other

would automatically be executed by their ships' combat systems.

Many of the naval link designations incorporate what amount to numerical puns. The first naval link was the British digital plot transmission (DPT) link, which connected ships using the analogue Combat Direction System (CDS); on carriers it was associated with the big Type 984 radar. When NATO navies discussed tactical links, the DPT link was naturally designated Link I. It was limited to the Royal Navy. The multi-national link intended to connect digital computer systems naturally became Link II. When NATO switched to a wider variety of links designated by Arabic numerals (most of them non-naval), Link II became Link 11. Link II was also called TIDE (Tactical Information Distribution Equipment) – but the acronym actually came first. It was the name of a popular US laundry detergent, the idea being that the TIDE link (and the associated computer system) cleaned up plots. Equally naturally, when the Royal Navy bought a simpler and less expensive link, it was called Link X (later, Link 10) – because in the detergent commercials of the time, TIDE or its competitors were always being compared with 'Brand X'. In effect the Royal Navy was saying that Brand X was good enough. Compared to Link 11, Link X used a much simpler serial transmission system and thus was limited to 75 bits/sec; it was limited to reporting target positions without further elaboration. Designed to work with 24-bit computers, Link X used 24-bit messages (Link 11 used 30-bit messages). The messages were a subset of those used by Link 11 (two messages together offered enough bits). This link is now extinct, the Royal Navy having adopted Link 11. Signaal (now Thales Naval Nederland) produced a commercial version, Link Y, which was widely exported. Both Link 11 and Link 10 used HF radio, which offered coverage beyond the horizon (they relied on the surface wave, which reaches out to about 150nm to 180nm). Beyond-the-horizon performance was vital because naval forces had to spread out to limit their vulnerability to nuclear attack.

Link 11 is widely used but current US plans call for its elimination about 2025; its encryption systems are no longer in production, at least in the United States.

By the 1980s computers could compensate for the vagaries of HF transmission. Signaal introduced a Link Y Mk 2 which achieved at least the data rate of Link 11, with similar performance. It was widely sold.

France produced an unlicensed version of Link 11 called Link W (after its first application, Project SaWari for the Royal Saudi Navy), which is associated with various ships using French command and control systems. The standard Chinese People Liberation's Army Navy HN-900 data link may have been derived from Link W, the Chinese having bought the French TAVITAC combat data system in the 1980s. The Chinese are currently also credited with a Link 16-like link.

Three Arabic-numbered NATO links were or are used by NATO navies: Link 4, Link 16, and Link 22. Link 4A (TADIL-C) is an interceptor air-control link used by at least France and the United States, but presumably being superseded by Link 16. In the US Navy it was also a means of automatically landing aircraft on carriers. At one time many NATO fighters had two-way Link 4A. Link 16 (JTIDS, the Joint Tactical Information Distribution System) was intended as a replacement, but some countries presumably still use Link 4A. JTIDS uses a clock system which makes it possible to create a picture of the positions of all objects (ships and aircraft) in the Link 16 net. JTIDS operates in a line-of-sight radar frequency band (L-band); members of the net are assigned timed transmission slots. The lag between the start of the slot and the time when the message is received is a measure of the distance from the transmitter. Compared to Link 11, Link 16 offers much greater precision. It has sufficient capacity to carry voice, text, and images as well as the usual computer-to-computer data. Link 22 (meaning twice as good as Link 11) uses Link 16 messages carried by Link 11-type HF radio, hence extending beyond the horizon; it is called NATO Improved Link Eleven (NILE). There is also a satellite version of Link 16, which offers beyond-the-horizon capability.

There are numerous links not standardised by NATO. Important US ones (some of which have been adopted by allies) include Hawklink (for data from an MH-60 helicopter) and CEC (Cooperative Engagement Capability). The latter was conceived as a very precise link between Aegis ships, with a link providing the CEC picture to non-Aegis ships. CEC can also be fed by airborne assets such as the later version of the E-2 Hawkeye. Many countries have national links.

Notes
1. In the past, there was also Link 14, a receive-only system which enabled non-computer ships to receive elements of the Link 11 tactical picture. Typically the receiver ship used a teleprinter, whose output had to be manually plotted (automatic plotters were tried but not produced in any quantity, except in Japan). Once stand-alone Link 11 systems became inexpensive, Link 14 died. Few if any systems remain.

MODERN NAVAL COMMUNICATIONS: SPECIMEN WARSHIP COMMUNICATIONS OUTFIT ILLUSTRATIONS

US Navy carriers *George Washington* (CVN-73) and *Carl Vinson* (CVN-70) show their electronic arrays during Exercise Valiant Shield in the Pacific in this image taken on 20 September 2014. The big masthead radome is for the DCSC SHF satellite. Size is not only to work with this wavelength, it is also to increase gain and hence information capacity. Alongside the big dish are a pair of OE-82 'washbasins' which work with UHF satellites. The pairs of radomes atop the bridge are for higher-frequency links. The short topmast abaft the big radome carries a TACAN at its top, with the 'lampshade' of the CEC system below it. Not so visible is the collar associated with Link 16. Also less readily apparent are the antennas the carrier uses to communicate with her aircraft. One of them is visible just below the dish on which the ship's Mk 91 NATO Sea Sparrow point defence missile control radar sits, at the after end of the island (this antenna looks like two angled elements pointed up and down at each other). The dish protects the antenna from the radar's radiation. The ship also has a pair of HF whips between her mast and the two satellite dishes abaft the mast. Also visible is her rigging, which is mainly for lower-frequency radio traffic. Cramming so many antennas into a very small space creates serious problems of mutual interference. The distribution of communications equipment between two island structures – an approach adopted in the British Royal Navy's *Queen Elizabeth* class and the Italian Navy's new amphibious assault ship – is one potential solution. *(US Navy)*

In the Sulu Sea in August 2015, the Littoral Combat Ship *Fort Worth* (LCS-3) shows what must seem an extensive array of satellite dishes (atop her bridge) for a relatively minor unit. They are much the same ones as on board a destroyer. The LCS was conceived as a communications node in a larger net, processing data collected by its unmanned system and providing it to a battle group. Note the TACAN air navigation beacon at her masthead. Note that she has the collar of a Link 16 antenna, despite her limited size and status. Note, too, the whips of different lengths, the lengths corresponding to different wavelengths. *(US Navy)*

Photographed during the RIMPAC exercises in 2014, the Japanese missile destroyer *Kirishima* displays the whip antennas which have replaced most of the wire antennas of the past. Their lengths indicate their frequencies: longer means a lower frequency. She also has the Link 16 'collar' on her upper mast. The foremast dome is the Japanese equivalent to the US Hawk Link for a multi-purpose helicopter which shares its sensor data with a ship. Note the small spherical satellite antenna on the fore face of her bridge. *(US Navy)*

ships and from aircraft. The early tactical computer systems could also carry tactical instructions, for example to order one or another ship to fire at an incoming target. To make such systems work, NATO navies adopted formatted data links, which communicate on a computer to computer basis. Numerous different links now exist, and a major issue is how to connect them.[7]

Full co-ordination requires a lot more, particularly if it is done among navies which do not share detailed tactical practices. Coalition operations in places like the Gulf, after 2001, probably would not have been possible without what amounts to a naval Internet, carried by high-capacity systems such as satellites and satellite dishes used for line-of-sight links. An Australian officer who commanded a mixed task group said later that he had relied heavily on a chat room, which made it possible for him to explain his intent and to answer questions. Chat rooms are an Internet phenomenon, possible because the Internet operates at very high data rates. It came to do so because it used wires, although many current Internet users rely instead on what amounts to cell phones, meaning short-range radio.

There is so much communications capacity currently available that warships in many navies now frequently provide their crews with Internet access home, a capacity often described in the US Navy as Quality of Life (QOL) maintenance. QOL generally means using non-military satellites such as the ubiquitous INMARSAT designed for merchant ships. Presumably the QOL links would be shut down in a major war – or would they?

The rise of naval satellite communication affects even submarines, historically the least linked to the outside world. When the US Navy placed Tomahawk missiles on board its submarines, it had to provide targeting data. Initially that was simple: the submarines carried both strategic and anti-ship versions of the missile. Strategic targets could be pre-loaded before the submarine set out. An anti-ship attack required only knowledge of about where the enemy ship was. That was time-sensitive, so it had to be sent by satellite, but it did not require much message capacity, and the submarine did not have to spend much time receiving it. Reception did expose the submarine somewhat, but that was acceptable. Now, however, Tomahawk is used tactically, often against fleeting targets, and attacks involve a lot more information. The solution, at least in the US Navy, was the submarine version of an EHF satellite

A Tomahawk cruise missile being lowered from the tender *Frank Cable* (AS-40) onto the nuclear-powered attack submarine *Oklahoma City* (SSN-723) at Guam in 2012. One of the weapons of choice in various post-Cold War interventions, use of the Tomahawk has relied heavily on the exploitation of information provided by satellite link. However, receipt of this information means that a submarine has to come to close to the surface, leaving it potentially vulnerable. *(US Navy)*

dish. EHF (extremely high frequency) offers a high information rate, so the submarine exposing itself by using the dish risks relatively little – though against an alert enemy even that might not be good enough.

KEY NAVAL COMMUNICATIONS CONSIDERATIONS

All of this raises important questions. The most obvious is how vulnerable satellite links are to physical attack. Almost as important is the question of whether there are other ways of exploiting satellite communication to track ships at sea. For many centuries the most important fact of naval warfare was the tracklessness of the sea. Much of naval strategy and tactics arises from the need simply to find the enemy before engaging him. Reconnaissance satellites clearly affect naval stealth, though it is not at all obvious that they wreck it altogether. Is some new form of satellite communication exploitation coming, or already here? If so, will submarines be the only stealthy warships left?

The key question, however, is whether Western navies have come to rely so heavily on external information, relayed largely by satellite, that they would be relatively ineffective in its absence? Similar questions apply to tactical information relayed over the horizon within dispersed naval forces. To some extent they may be able to rely on long-endurance drones as 'poor men's satellites', but it does not seem likely that anything but a satellite can reach out half-way across the world. Much depends on means of attacking our communications satellites, and on our ability – if any – to replace them rapidly in an emergency.

As for the domes, they certainly seem to break up the otherwise stealthy shape of modern surface warships. When the US Navy ordered the *Zumwalt* class, one hope was that the domes could be replaced by broad-band electronically-scanned arrays, looking upward from that pyramid-shaped structure. Broadband was needed to handle the sheer variety of satellites the ship used. Electronic scanning would replace the earlier dishes, just as electronically-scanned radar

An artist's impression of the nuclear-powered guided missile submarine conversion that transformed the four oldest *Ohio* (SSBN-726) strategic submarines into Tomahawk cruise missile carriers. The tactical use of Tomahawk cruise missiles in the post-Cold War environment has meant that the safe and secure provision of targeting information to submarines has become a necessity; a need satisfied by the development of extremely high frequency (EHF) satellite links. These have very high information transfer rates, limiting the time the submarine has to expose itself close to the surface. An open question is whether limiting the period of vulnerability is, of itself, sufficient against an alert and sophisticated enemy. *(US Navy)*

arrays work without moving reflector antennas. Neither hope was realised; the ship's profile shows conventional antennas.

The satellite communications story is part of a much larger one concerning how ships fight. In the past it was easy to distinguish real-time combat systems, using tactical data links such as Link 11, from information systems which provided a ship with data on which strikes could be based. That made sense on board a carrier, as long as the long-range information was used to plan air strikes. However, with the rise of long-range anti-ship missiles, information on ships beyond the range of the carrier group's sensors was suddenly very relevant, as was information about long-range air attackers. How could the two kinds of information be merged? In the 1990s the US Navy found that problem very difficult, in part because the long-range information – the fruit of communications systems – was generally considered much more sensitive than radar and similar information intended to support combat. To what extent was the information received over the long-range links intelligence and to what extent should it be handled as sensor data? If some kinds of intelligence were now, in effect, sensor outputs, how could they be sanitised fast enough to be used? Could they be provided to allies? In some of its ships the German navy solved the problem by using a single space to handle both types of data and to merge them. The US Navy

The clean lines of the second *Zumwalt* (DDG-1000) class destroyer *Michael Monsoor* (DDG-1001) reflects a focus on stealth that was to include reliance on broad-band electronically-scanned arrays, looking upward from the pyramid-shaped superstructure. In practice, it seems that many conventional radomes will appear on her superstructure when full fitting-out has been completed. *(GD Bath Iron Works)*

The second German F124 *Sachsen* class air defence frigate *Hamburg* pictured approaching Portsmouth Harbour in March 2016. By the 1990s, there was a growing problem in determining how best to utilise and, as necessary, combine information gathered by (i) sensors associated with tactical combat systems and that obtained by (ii) long-range intelligence gathering systems. The German Navy attempted to solve this problem in some of its ships by creating a single area to handle both types of information and, as appropriate, merge the two. *(Conrad Waters)*

found itself developing computer systems specifically to sanitise some of the sensitive material coming over its communications systems.

This brief survey has been limited to above-water radio communication. Much more is happening. Submarine acoustic communication now offers the sort of capacity achieved in some dial-up Internet links, which means – amongst other things – that at some ranges submarines can transmit periscope video. Lasers offer interesting possibilities, including underwater ones.

Notes

1. All opinions expressed are the author's own, and do not necessarily reflect those of the US Navy or of other organisations with which he has been affiliated.

2. For submariners the key fact is that nearly all radio signals cannot penetrate very deep into the sea. The main exception is extremely low frequency (ELF), but its frequency drastically limits the signals it can carry. Navies generally rely on very low frequency (VLF) signals; submarines periodically listen. There are alternatives, such as towed HF receivers and, now, satellite receivers. The latter have to penetrate above the surface, and are therefore visible. They are viable now because Western submarines typically enjoy a sanctuary when they operate more than about fifty miles offshore. That would not be the case when operating against a major naval power, such as China. As late as 2001, the US Navy assumed that a submarine operating close inshore would have to rely on a satellite antenna offshore, linked to the submarine by a fibre-optic sea floor net with which the submarine could communicate using a blue-green laser (the vertical light path in the ocean was viable for short distances). That this idea (which was never translated into actual hardware) was soon abandoned shows just how transformational the EHF (extremely high frequency) satellite link described on page 182 has been.

3. This is somewhat simplified; for shorter distances, up to perhaps 2,500nm, medium and low frequencies are effective, and they were used during both world wars. HF

became widespread between the two world wars. US Navy reliance on it shows in the many whip antennas (short, because high-frequency wavelength is relatively short) on board US warships. They were not as efficient as long wire antennas strung between masts, but they had the advantage of not interfering with anti-aircraft fire. Using numerous whips operating at different frequencies raised problems of mutual interference, which required both centralised radio control and very careful analysis of complex interactions between antennas and a ship's metal structure. For years the US Naval Electronics Laboratory at San Diego built metal scale models of ships to test interference, because the mathematics involved was far too complex for computer simulation.

4. NATO Link 11 did better by transmitting simultaneously on fifteen frequencies and two polarisations, so it offered 2,250 bits/second. Note that a byte, the current computer standard, is 3 bits, so this is only 750 bytes/sec. Messages were transmitted in 30-bit frames, of which 24 bits were the message and 6 were intended to correct errors. The message standard was invented in the late 1950s by a joint American, British, and Canadian committee. Computers now make it possible to correct errors and to operate at much higher data rates.

5. Above HF, the ionosphere is fairly transparent up to 10 GHz (X-band radar). Other windows are at 30–40 GHz and 94, 150, and 240 GHz. Quite aside from communication, the windows mean that satellites designed for that purpose can easily detect virtually all radar emissions. On

the earth's surface, detection and direction-finding do not immediately yield target location; typically it takes cross-references from two stations to do that. A satellite is different, because it finds a line which passes through the surface of the earth where the emitter is. Satellite direction-finding is not a great threat to satellite communication because such communication is or ought to be very intermittent.

6. The first evidence was that 'Badger' reconnaissance bombers were flying directly out to the carrier groups without searching for them, as had previously been the case. That happened in the North Pacific. The Soviets were using large fixed circular HF/DF arrays (the system was called 'Krug') which were credited with ranges as great as 8,000nm.

7. Different links employ not only different computer languages (in effect they are instructions to the computers on board the ships which receive them) but also different data standards. For example, the old Link 11 describes targets with much less precision than the much newer Link 16. Even different versions of the same link may differ subtly in vocabulary. Presumably this is a particular problem for navies using systems from very different suppliers, including the Russians, whose electronics is probably utterly unlike that used in the West given that, among other things, it reflects a very different philosophy of command. That would seem to apply to both the Chinese and Indian navies, although the Chinese are standardising on their own systems.

Author:
Richard Scott

4.3 TECHNOLOGICAL REVIEW

AUTONOMOUS SYSTEMS

A New Horizon for Surface Fleets

Warship design and development is recognised as a generally conservative business. This reflects the desire of navies to ensure that the hard-won lessons of operations in both peacetime and war are not unwittingly cast overboard by the ill-founded adoption of untried technologies, techniques and concepts. Hence, advances in naval platforms and combat systems, and attendant operational concepts, are generally evolutionary and incremental in nature.

However, there is today a palpable sense that navies are on the cusp of a radical shift thanks to the rapid maturation of maritime autonomous systems technology. Already beginning to enter the 'mainstream' of mine countermeasures (MCM) and hydrographic operations, there is now a broad consensus that autonomous systems are going to play an increasingly important role in the surface fleets of the future.

This expectation reflects the fundamental change that autonomy is already bringing to other sectors of industry, commerce and society in sectors such as manufacturing, transportation and medicine. Similarly, there is a recognition that autonomy has many potential applications in defence, and will have a significant role in shaping the future operational environment, delivering efficiencies and maintaining competitive advantage.

The impact of this revolution is already being felt in militaries worldwide; according to Paul Scharre, author of the acclaimed study *Army of None*, at least thirty nations already possess autonomous weapon systems that operate under human supervision.[1] It is in the skies where the introduction of robotics has to date had the most transformative effect on military operations. Various types of unmanned air system (UAS) have proliferated over the past three decades to execute all manner of so-called 'dull, dirty and dangerous' missions. These include wide area surveillance, electronic eavesdropping, improvised explosive device (IED) detection and logistics resupply. Several 'weaponised' UASs have also entered service, adding a capability for the remote prosecution of ground targets using precision-guided weapons. The term 'drone strike' has now become part of the everyday lexicon.

The introduction of autonomy in the maritime battlespace, and particularly the surface domain, has been slower-paced and, for the time being, less pervasive. Yet the tide appears to be turning. For example, the US Navy has already incorporated an Optionally Unmanned Surface Combatant and an Unmanned Surface Combatant as an integral part of its long-term Surface Combatant Capability Evolution Plan.[2]

DEFINING AUTONOMY

It is important to understand what autonomy is, and what is so different about the technologies now coming to realisation in the surface-ship sphere. After all, radio-controlled craft operating under the direction of a remote operator have been employed

A REMUS 100 underwater autonomous vehicle being recovered by British Royal Navy personnel during a NATO exercise. Autonomous systems are already starting to enter the mainstream of underwater mine countermeasures and hydrographic operations but there is a growing consensus they will also play a significant role in the surface fleets of the future. *(Crown Copyright 2016)*

by navies for many years: examples include surface targets for force protection training and weapon trials, and minesweeping drones towing influence sweeping gear ahead of an MCM mother vessel.

Autonomy is different in that there is no longer a human operator 'in-the-loop' exercising some direct form of tele-control in real time. Instead, the vehicle or system embeds its own logic and reasoning so as to be able to build situational awareness, assess the situation in hand, and then take informed decisions as to a course (or courses) of action without human interaction/intervention within defined limits. This means that the system in question only requires to be given a mission or goal by the operator. The intention therefore is to put the human 'on-the-loop' in order to take an essentially supervisory role, and thus free to focus on safety-critical issues and overarching mission management.

While the terms 'autonomous' and 'unmanned' are often transposed, it should be remembered that not all unmanned vehicles are autonomous. Equally, some autonomous systems may have humans on board, or retain a reversionary manned mode. That

said, it is clear that the development of uninhabited robotic systems with advanced 'intelligent' autonomous behaviours is today the main focus of investment for navies and industry alike.

Unmanned vehicles offer many advantages over conventional manned platforms. Because there is no requirement to equip the platform with systems to sustain or safeguard a human operator or crew, such systems can be made smaller, lighter and more manoeuvrable. Also, they can remain on task well beyond the physiological limits of humans – in the case of an unmanned surface vessel (USV) this could be for weeks or even months at a time. Furthermore, robotic systems can be forward-deployed into high-risk areas in the full knowledge that damage or loss will not cost human lives.

Of course, the one major drawback of robotic vehicles is that there is no longer a highly trained and skilled operator able to exercise human intuition in complex scenarios. Early generations of unmanned systems have therefore been overwhelmingly remotely-controlled. However, this necessarily leaves them dependent on communications links

which may be degraded by environmental or geographic conditions, vulnerable to jamming, or potentially compromised by cyber-attack.

Embedding greater levels of autonomy is therefore increasingly seen as the means to unlock the full potential of unmanned systems. In *Army of None*, Scharre describes autonomy as the '... cognitive engine that powers robots' adding: 'Without autonomy, robots are only empty vessels, brainless husks that depend on human controllers for direction.'

Looking ahead, artificial intelligence and machine learning offer a route to potentially more advanced forms of autonomy. These powerful algorithmic techniques bring the capability to detect and characterise patterns and structures in data, and thereby adapt through progressive learning. One application of machine learning is in visual object recognition. This would allow an autonomous system to automatically classify different types of vessels and markers based on analysis of sensor feeds.

Yet while most naval planners accept that

A US Air Force MQ-9 Reaper unmanned aerial vehicle. It is in the skies where the introduction of robotics has to date had the most transformative effect on military operations to date but the future impact of autonomy on naval systems is likely to be just as pervasive. Note that – whilst the Reaper is capable of both remotely-piloted and fully autonomous operation – not all unmanned vehicles are autonomous. *(US Air Force)*

A spectrum of aerial, surface and underwater autonomous robotic systems. Autonomy is different from traditional remotely-operated vehicles in that there is no longer a human operator 'in-the-loop' exercising some direct form of tele-control in real time. Instead, the vehicle or system embeds its own logic and reasoning so as to be able to build situational awareness, assess the situation in hand, and then take informed decisions. *(Crown Copyright 2016)*

autonomy is coming, and that its long-term impact will be to re-shape both operational practice and force design, there are still many challenges and uncertainties to be resolved. For example, how do maritime autonomous systems integrate with each other, and/or with manned assets, or other? What impact will they have on concepts of operations? How does their introduction impact on the education, training and skills required of future sailors? And, with the expectation that these systems will carry weapons of their own, what are the legal and regulatory implications for tactical doctrines, notably with respect to Rules of Engagement?

For the time being at least, there is an acceptance that a human should have a final say on weapons release. But is it conceivable that one day an automaton will be delegated the authority to open fire in certain scenarios? That is no longer a question of technology, rather one of ethics.

Research, development and technology demonstration activities, drawing on the expertise available across defence science, industry and academia, are now attempting to tease out answers to these questions. The UK's 'Unmanned Warrior 2016' experiment, performed through October 2016, is perhaps the most high-profile example to date.[3]

There is also a 'cultural gap' to be bridged. Operational commanders must have confidence in the capabilities of autonomous systems, but at the same time they must understand their limitations. So as much as current research and development activities are about technology, they are also about building human trust in autonomous machines.

The Unmanned Warrior 2016 logo, emphasising the multi-domain nature of the exercise. The demonstration was intended to provide an opportunity for multiple robotic systems from different nations to exhibit their ability to achieve a spectrum of results in a 'real-world' environment. *(Crown Copyright 2016)*

TECHNOLOGY DEVELOPMENT

When examining developments in autonomous surface vessels, it is important not to view naval developments in isolation. The commercial shipping sector is also attracted to the idea of unmanned robotic ships, recognising the cost benefits that would accrue from reduced manpower requirements, optimised vessel design, increased fuel effi-

ciency and improved safety at sea. Such cost and efficiency advantages are similarly important to the naval community.

The technology enablers required to comply with safe navigation and collision avoidance rules – codified as the International Collision Regulations at Sea (COLREGS) – are also essentially common.[4] These include: sensor fusion to ensure the vessel, or its remote supervisor, is provided with an accurate picture of its local area at all times and in all conditions; control algorithms that allow the ship to react and re-plan so as to be compliant to COLREGS; and connectivity to enable mission supervision and system monitoring.

Of course, some requirements are unique to the military user, particularly with regard to operating profiles, the deployment of sensor and, potentially, weapon payloads, and operations as part of a wider integrated force. A large part of the challenge therefore is to understand the latent potential of maritime autonomous systems, and to understand the constraints and limitations of the technology.

Modelling and simulation using high-fidelity synthetic environments is one part of the answer. A simulation framework provides an environment in which algorithms can be tested and tuned in a controlled and repeatable manner. It also allows interfaces between multiple systems to be tested, and different scenarios rehearsed or 'gamed'. However, systems and algorithms that seem promising and successful in simulation in the laboratory may in fact prove to be less robust on the water. This challenge should not be underestimated.

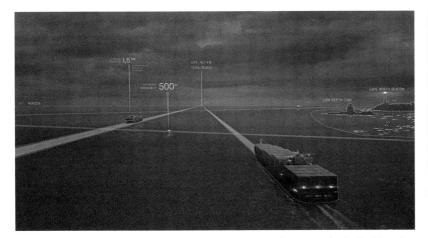
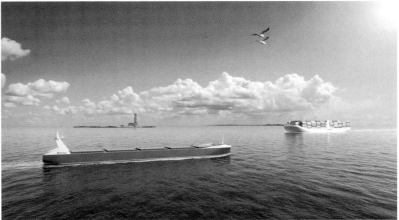

The commercial shipping sector is attracted to the concept of unmanned robotic ships. One company in the forefront of developing this approach is Rolls-Royce, which sees intelligent awareness systems fusing data from various sources as making ships safer, easier and more efficient to operate. Such technology has application to existing manned ships (left) but could also be used with respect to fully-autonomous ships (right). *(Rolls-Royce)*

Two views of the DARPA unmanned surface drone *Sea Hunter* on 7 April 2016, her commissioning day. Now managed by the ONR, Sea Hunter is being used to inform the future integration of autonomous systems in the US Navy fleet. *(DARPA)*

To give an example, consider a basic COLREG – 'overtaking vessel must keep clear'. This is an easy command for a human to understand, but for a machine it is necessary to define with absolute clarity when an overtaking manoeuvre begins and ends, precise angles, relative velocities and thresholds.

In theory this is manageable, but what now if the autonomous system finds itself on a threshold? What if there is error and jitter in both detection and control? What if the system drops then reacquires (an apparently different) vessel track midway through but needs to remember that it is overtaking? What are the processing latencies in the system and how is it possible to account for environmental effects and vessel dynamics? How do you ensure safety at all times?

Some of these issues can be explored in simulation. However, it is practically impossible to fully simulate the true level of real-world uncertainty, and myriad of special cases without practical experimentation. Reflecting this, prototype autonomous vessels have been developed on both sides of the Atlantic to de-risk and demonstrate autonomous technologies in realistic environments.

SEA HUNTER

The US Office of Naval Research (ONR) took charge of the *Sea Hunter* maritime autonomy testbed from the Defense Advanced Research Projects Agency (DARPA) in January 2018. Originally developed under DARPA's Anti-Submarine Warfare (ASW) Continuous Trail Unmanned Vessel (ACTUV) programme, *Sea Hunter* was designed as a semi-autonomous, ultra-long endurance surface drone to 'track and trail' quiet diesel-electric submarines. However, the demonstrator is now set to play a wider role with the ONR as the testbed for a new class of autonomous Medium Displacement Unmanned Surface Vehicle.

ACTUV was a DARPA initiative launched in 2010 with three principal goals in mind:

■ First, to investigate the performance potential of a surface platform conceived under the premise that a human should never step aboard at any point in the mission, so relaxing traditional naval architecture constraints with regard to layout, accessibility, crew support systems, and reserve buoyancy.

■ Second, to mature unmanned maritime system autonomy to enable independent deployment of systems capable of missions spanning thousands of kilometres of range and months of endurance under sparse remote supervisory control. This necessarily demands autonomous compliance with COLREGS, autonomous system management for operational reliability, and autonomous interactions with an intelligent adversary.

■ Third, to demonstrate the capability of the ACTUV system to employ non-conventional sensor technologies able to achieve robust and continuous tracking of quiet submarines at standoff ranges.

At the same time, DARPA recognised from the outset that the ACTUV programme would also demonstrate the utility of an affordable (less than US$20m unit production cost at volume quantities) and very long endurance (70–90 days) unmanned surface platform for a variety of naval missions.

Following an assessment of three concept design and risk-reduction studies, DARPA in August 2012 awarded an industry team led by SAIC (now Leidos) a US$58 million contract for the design and build of a prototype vessel based on a trimaran hull-form. The winning ACTUV team also included NASA's Jet Propulsion Laboratory (JPL) and Carnegie Mellon University National Robotics Engineering Center (NREC). The decision to bring JPL and NREC into the fold reflected their previous experience of developing autonomous capabilities: JPL developed the Control Architecture for Robotic Agent Command and Sensing (CARACaS) for the Mars Rover Project back in the 1990s; and NREC has previously developed an autonomy engine that gained first place in DARPA's 2007 Urban Challenge project.[5]

Constructed from composite (foam core with fiberglass skins), *Sea Hunter* is a 40m technology demonstrator displacing approximately 145 tons at full load. Adopting a trimaran hull-form with a main central hull and two slender outriggers, the vessel is powered by twin diesel engines, each driving separate shaftlines. This configuration delivers a maximum speed of 27 knots and a cruising range of 10,000nm at 12 knots.

The major challenge for Leidos was to develop an autonomy system able to sense its environment and the health of its own systems, make intelligent decisions to optimise machinery and sensor employment, avoid other ships and obstacles, and execute the intended mission. To achieve this the company developed what it describes as an Autonomy

Sea Hunter was originally conceived by DARPA as a semi-autonomous, ultra-long endurance surface drone to 'track and trail' quiet diesel-electric submarines. However, the demonstrator is now playing a wider role with the ONR as a testbed for a new class of autonomous Medium Displacement Unmanned Surface Vehicle. *(DARPA)*

Architecture with Remote Supervisory Control Station (RSCS). The autonomy suite contains decision algorithms embedded as software. The system architecture supports multiple decision engines, and incorporates 'arbitration logic' to choose the best decisions for future actions.

A High Level Mission Planner is provided with general instructions on where to go and what to do. A 'World Model' module in the autonomy architecture delivers situational awareness by maintaining data on capabilities and state/status (past, present, and future). This includes own-ship information (such as position, course and speed), environmental data, external entities (contacts), and data fusion. It also feeds any autonomy decision engine with the data required to determine needed platform manoeuvres and courses of action.

A second 'Intelligent Processing' module hosts the autonomy decision engines and autonomous behaviours that compute the best course of action according to mission parameters. It produces prioritised courses of action/routes by combining mission guidance (goals, rules, and objectives) from the High Level Mission Planner, 'World Model' content, and course of action/routes from autonomy decision engines/path planners (provided either by JPL or NREC).

Sea Hunter's autonomy architecture also incorporates built-in compatibility with a RSCS that can be located at sea or on shore. The RSCS provides the capability to remotely supervise *Sea Hunter*, communicate new mission instructions to the vessel (via the High Level Mission Planner) and, if necessary, exercise remote control.

Prior to taking *Sea Hunter* to sea, Leidos was required to demonstrate safe navigation and compliance with COLREGS. Over 26,000 simulation runs, modelling more than 750 different meeting, crossing and overtaking scenarios, were executed in the company's System Integration Laboratory (SIL) to demonstrate that the autonomy suite would direct actions in accordance with the COLREGS.

After satisfactory completion of SIL testing, the autonomy suite was installed on a workboat, R/V *Pathfinder*, which served as a surrogate for at-sea testing. *Pathfinder* enabled testing of all the autonomy software and sensor systems in parallel with ship construction. Just over 100 different scripted scenarios were executed at sea, during which the autonomy system directed course and speed changes of the surrogate to stay safely outside a 1,000m stand-off distance from interfering vessels. In addition to the structured test events, *Pathfinder* completed a 35nm voyage along the Gulf

Intracoastal Waterway, from Biloxi to Pascagoula, with only a navigational chart of the area loaded into its memory and inputs from its commercial off-the-shelf radars.

According to Leidos, the autonomy system '… functioned flawlessly, avoiding all obstacles, buoys, land, and interfering vessels … all without preplanned waypoints or human direction or intervention'. The voyage also demonstrated compliance to COLREGS during head-on situations with two tugs.

Sea Hunter is now operating from San Diego. The vessel has already tested a number of mission payloads, but its primary utility is as a demonstrator to inform concept of operations development and future force architecture. A second *Sea Hunter* Medium Displacement Unmanned Surface Vehicle was ordered in late 2017 to provide an additional asset in support of autonomous systems science and technology.

ADVANCED AUTONOMY

The UK's Defence Science and Technology Laboratory (Dstl) has also been exploring surface vessel autonomy as part of a wider portfolio of

autonomous systems research across all environments. As part of this activity, Dstl established an Advanced Capability USV Project which ASV Global was, in 2015, contracted to deliver. Established in 1998, ASV has accrued two decades of experience in the design, development, operation and support of USVs. In recent years the company has increasingly focused on maturing autonomous systems technologies and architectures that will transform 'dumb' remote-controlled platforms into highly-autonomous surface vehicles.

Dstl's Advanced Capability USV Project set out with the aim of developing a research testbed that could host a range of technologies appropriate to the development and test of tactics for future maritime autonomous systems. In particular, Dstl wanted to investigate the concept of an autonomous high-speed vessel able to safely navigate, in cluttered and crowded waterspace, into close proximity of other high-speed surface targets, and then execute manoeuvres against these moving targets. This demanded the provision of a highly advanced USV able to sense its environment, and detect and avoid obstacles.

To achieve this, ASV developed a prototype

control system for retrofit to a Dstl-owned Bladerunner high-speed hull. This became the Maritime Autonomy Surface Testbed (MAST). Built on the foundation of ASV's proprietary 'ASView' command and control architecture, the advanced USV system embodied in the MAST platform consists of a hierarchy of decision-making components sharing a common world model. These components comprise the route planner (generating routes over long distances taking account of water depth and potentially shipping lanes); the path planner (which considers the next few minutes, choosing paths that minimise collision risk in a COLREGs-compliant fashion with other vessels); the trajectory planner (managing the next few seconds to smoothly control and predict USV motion based on a dynamics model); and a 'last response' function to monitor the immediate vicinity and provide a 'failsafe' engine cut-out if an unexpected obstacle is detected.

Dstl's programme was predicated on a series of MAST demonstrations in the Solent/Isle of Wight sea areas to progressively de-risk development of advanced autonomous navigation. Beginning in late November 2015 with a demonstration of a basic path planner able to execute simple collision avoidance at low speed in open water, at-sea testing gradually increased in its complexity. By the time the fifth and final demonstration was conducted in March 2017, the MAST testbed was able to perform a representative end-to-end mission, operating autonomously on a long transit through shipping lanes and controlled waters around the Solent and around the east coast of the Isle of Wight.

In early 2018 ASV was awarded additional funding by Dstl to design and build a follow-on MAST testbed to replace the existing Bladerunner hull. According to the company, this custom built autonomous vessel will be used to support the expansion of advanced autonomous navigation capabilities, including COLREGS-compliant collision avoidance.

RISE OF THE MACHINES

Much as the experimental vessel *Turbinia* was instrumental in the development of steam turbine power at sea, so diminutive prototypes such as *Sea Hunter* and MAST can be seen as trailblazers for a new generation of autonomous surface combatants. Their trials are yielding valuable data that will pave the way for the autonomous systems and architec-

Dstl's MAST autonomous demonstrator seen here on the River Thames. The vessel, based on a Bladerunner high-speed hull-form, participated in the Unmanned Warrior 2016 exercises. *(Crown Copyright 2016)*

tures expected to come into naval service over the next decade.

The full impact that autonomous surface vessels will have on future surface force design is, for the time being at least, difficult to quantify. Certainly, there is no suggestion that manned warship will be replaced outright. Rather the focus is on the employment of smaller and cheaper autonomous surface systems as cost-effective 'force multipliers'.

This could bring with it new concepts of operations based around networked and distributed 'systems of systems'. Traditionally, sensors, weapons and command and control facilities have all been hosted on a single high-value platform. Unmanned autonomous systems provide an opportunity to break that tyranny, with sensors and effectors split physically from the command, but still connected via a network. This could enable a significant increase in the tempo of warfighting, but it will inevitably bring its own complexities and dependencies. Fascinating times lie ahead.

Notes

1. See Paul Scharre, *Army of None: Autonomous Weapons and the Future of War* (New York: W W Norton & Co, 2018).

2. The Surface Combatant Capability Evolution Plan was the subject of a briefing by Rear Admiral Ron Boxall, Director, Surface Warfare (N96), at the Surface Navy Association annual symposium, January 2018.

3. Unmanned Warrior 2016 – held as an adjunct to the UK-hosted Joint Warrior series of tri-service, multinational exercises – was intended to provide an opportunity for multiple robotic systems from different nations to exhibit their ability to achieve a spectrum of results in a 'real-world' environment. Trials were carried out across five distinct specialities or themes, although there was frequently a degree of cross-over. They encompassed (i) Hydrographic & Geospatial Intelligence (GEOINT); (ii) Anti-Submarine Warfare (ASW); (iii) Mine Counter-Measures (MCM); (iv) Intelligence Surveillance Targeting Acquisition and Reconnaissance (ISTAR); and (v) Command & Control (C2).

4. The International Maritime Organization-sponsored Convention on the International Regulations for Preventing Collisions at Sea was adopted in 1972 and came into effect in July 1977. Details can be found at: www.imo.org/en/About/Conventions/ListOfConventions/Pages/COLREG.aspx

5. The 2007 Urban Challenge was one of a series of DARPA-sponsored Grand Challenge prize competitions to spur the development of American autonomous ground vehicles.

Experimentation with the MAST testbed culminated in a representative mission operating autonomously on a long transit through shipping lanes and controlled waters around the Solent and the Isle of Wight. *(ASV Global)*

Saab Kockums has outlined a vision of a future fleet based on a distributed, networked force mixing a larger manned corvette design with a family of scaled autonomous/optionally manned surface craft configured for different missions. Such networked and distributed 'systems of systems' could well represent the future of naval warfare. *(Copyright Saab AB)*

Contributors

Norman Friedman: Norman Friedman is one of the best-known naval analysts and historians in the US and the author of over forty books. He has written on broad issues of modern military interest, including an award-winning history of the Cold War, whilst in the field of warship development his greatest sustained achievement is probably an eight-volume series on the design of different US warship types. A specialist in the intersection of technology and national strategy, his acclaimed *Network-Centric Warfare* was published in 2009 by the US Naval Institute Press. The holder of a PhD in theoretical physics from Columbia, Dr Friedman is a regular guest commentator on television and lectures widely on professional defence issues. He is a resident of New York.

David Hobbs: David Hobbs is an author and naval historian with an international reputation. He has written twenty books, the latest of which is *The Royal Navy's Air Service in the Great War*, and has contributed to many more. He has written for several journals and magazines and in 2005 won the award for the Aerospace Journalist of the Year, Best Defence Submission, in Paris. He also won the essay prize awarded by the Navy League of Australia in 2008. He has lectured on naval subjects worldwide including on cruise ships and has been on radio and TV in several countries. He served in the Royal Navy for thirty-three years and retired with the rank of Commander. He is qualified as both a fixed and rotary wing pilot and his log book contains 2,300 hours with over 800 carrier deck landings, 150 of which were at night. For eight years he was the Curator of the Fleet Air Arm Museum at Yeovilton.

Theodore Hughes-Riley: Dr Theodore Hughes-Riley is an academic living in Nottingham, England. He obtained his bachelor's degree in physics from Lancaster University in 2009, and proceeded to graduate with his PhD from the University of Nottingham in 2014. His writing experience has focussed on scientific articles relating to his research activities. He has a long-running interest in military matters, with a particular focus on maritime issues enthused by visits to Portsmouth and Chatham as a child. As an adult he has become well-read in these matters and has visited a large number of naval museum ships in Europe, as well as some further afield.

Mrityunjoy Mazumdar: Mr Mazumdar, who studied applied physics & mechanical engineering, has been a regular contributor to *Seaforth World Naval Review* since its inception. His interests are the sea services of South and Southeast Asian countries, as well as the lesser known naval and air forces around the world. His words, pictures, and research have appeared in many naval and military aircraft publications including *Jane's Navy International*, IOPC's *Defence Industry Bulletin*, *Shephard Media*, *Ships of the World*, *Warship Technology*, *Air Forces Monthly* as well as the standard naval reference books. Having grown up in India and Nigeria, Mr Mazumdar lives in the 'wine country' north of San Francisco with his wife.

Richard Scott: Richard Scott is a UK-based analyst and commentator who has specialised in coverage of naval operations and technology for over twenty-five years, with particular interests in the fields of naval aviation, guided weapons and electronic warfare. He has held a number of editorial position with Jane's, including the editorship of *Jane's Navy International* magazine, and is currently Group Consultant Editor - Naval. Mr Scott is also a regular contributor to several other periodicals including *Journal of Electronic Defense*, *Unmanned Vehicles*, *Defence Helicopter*, and *Warship World*.

Guy Toremans: Guy Toremans is a Belgian-based, maritime freelance correspondent and a member of the Association of Belgian & Foreign Journalists, an association accredited by NATO and the UN. His reports, ship profiles and interviews are published in the English language naval magazines *Jane's Navy International*, *Naval Forces* and *Warships IFR*, as well as in the French *Marines & Forces Navales* and the Japanese *J-Ships*. Since 1990, he has regularly embarked on NATO, Asian, South African and Pacific-based warships, including aircraft carriers, destroyers, frigates, mine-countermeasures vessels and support ships.

Scott Truver: Dr Scott C Truver is Director, Team Blue, at Gryphon Technologies LC, specialising in national and homeland security, and naval and maritime strategies, programmes and operations. He also serves the Center for Naval Analyses as Senior Advisor. Since 1972 Dr Truver has participated in numerous studies and assessments – supporting the Secretary of the Navy in articulating the *...From the Sea* white paper (1992) and the inter-agency task force drafting the US *National Strategy for Maritime Security* (2005) – and has written extensively for US and foreign publications. He has lectured at the US Naval Academy, Naval War College and Naval Postgraduate School, among others. His further qualifications include a PhD in marine policy studies and a MA in political science/ international relations from the University of Delaware.

Conrad Waters: A lawyer by training but banker by profession, Conrad Waters was educated at Liverpool University prior to being called to the bar at Gray's Inn in 1989. His interest in maritime affairs was stimulated by a family history of officers in the merchant navy and he has written on historical and current naval affairs for over thirty years. This included six years producing the 'World Navies in Review' chapter of the annual *Warship* before assuming responsibility for *Seaforth World Naval Review* as founding editor. He has also edited *Navies in the 21st Century* – shortlisted for the 2017 Mountbatten Maritime Award – whilst his latest book *Cruiser Birmingham: detailed in the original builders' plans* – was published in 2018. Conrad is married to Susan and has three children: Emma, Alexander and Imogen. He lives in Haslemere, Surrey.

Front cover – Front Cover – Top: *Queen Elizabeth*. *(Crown Copyright 2018)*; Bottom: *Gerald R. Ford*. *(US Navy)*
Back cover: NATO warships pictured off the Scottish coast during Exercise Joint Warrior in April 2018. *(Crown Copyright 2018)*